D0745281

# Arduino Robotics

John-David Warren
Josh Adams
Harald Molle

Apress®

HILLSBORO PUBLIC LIBRARIES
WITHDRAWN
Hillsboro, OR
Member of Washington County
COOPERATIVE LIBRARY SERVICES

**Arduino Robotics**

Copyright © 2011 by John-David Warren, Josh Adams, and Harald Molle

All rights reserved. No part of this work may be reproduced or transmitted in any form or by any means, electronic or mechanical, including photocopying, recording, or by any information storage or retrieval system, without the prior written permission of the copyright owner and the publisher.

ISBN-13 (pbk): 978-1-4302-3183-7

ISBN-13 (electronic): 978-1-4302-3184-4

Trademarked names, logos, and images may appear in this book. Rather than use a trademark symbol with every occurrence of a trademarked name, logo, or image we use the names, logos, and images only in an editorial fashion and to the benefit of the trademark owner, with no intention of infringement of the trademark.

The use in this publication of trade names, trademarks, service marks, and similar terms, even if they are not identified as such, is not to be taken as an expression of opinion as to whether or not they are subject to proprietary rights. 4731 2540 10/11

President and Publisher: Paul Manning
Lead Editor: Michelle Lowman and James Markham
Technical Reviewer: Guilherme Martins and Josh Adams
Editorial Board: Steve Anglin, Mark Beckner, Ewan Buckingham, Gary Cornell, Jonathan Gennick, Jonathan Hassell, Michelle Lowman, Matthew Moodie, Jeff Olson, Jeffrey Pepper, Frank Pohlmann, Douglas Pundick, Ben Renow-Clarke, Dominic Shakeshaft, Matt Wade, Tom Welsh
Coordinating Editor: Anita Castro
Copy Editor: Ginny Munroe and Mary Ann Fugate
Compositor: Bytheway Publishing Services
Indexer: BIM Indexing & Proofreading Services
Artist: April Milne
Cover Designer: Anna Ishchenko

Distributed to the book trade worldwide by Springer Science+Business Media, LLC., 233 Spring Street, 6th Floor, New York, NY 10013. Phone 1-800-SPRINGER, fax (201) 348-4505, e-mail orders-ny@springer-sbm.com, or visit www.springeronline.com.

For information on translations, please e-mail rights@apress.com, or visit www.apress.com.

Apress and friends of ED books may be purchased in bulk for academic, corporate, or promotional use. eBook versions and licenses are also available for most titles. For more information, reference our Special Bulk Sales–eBook Licensing web page at www.apress.com/info/bulksales.

The information in this book is distributed on an "as is" basis, without warranty. Although every precaution has been taken in the preparation of this work, neither the author(s) nor Apress shall have any liability to any person or entity with respect to any loss or damage caused or alleged to be caused directly or indirectly by the information contained in this work.

The source code for this book is available to readers at www.apress.com. You will need to answer questions pertaining to this book in order to successfully download the code.

WITHDRAWN

*To my dad, Poppy, and Papa Bert for showing me that even ordinary men can be extraordinary.*

*John-David Warren*

# Contents at a Glance

# Contents

# About the Authors

 J-D is an electronics hobbyist, builder, and relentless tinkerer. As a child, he took apart everything he owned to figure out how it worked. Since then he has built many different projects ranging from an electric fishing pole to a remote-controlled lawn mower, which was featured on the cover of *MAKE* magazine in April 2010. Having worked as a builder doing carpentry, plumbing, and electrical work for eight years, his knowledge is founded on real-world experience rather than text-book recitation.

In addition to building robots and remote-controlled toys, he enjoys automating everyday tasks, blinking LEDs, designing and etching PCBs, and lots of random things in between. Much of his time has been spent researching, building, and testing various motor-controllers to make his bots move. As a self-proclaimed "poor man's roboticist," he will always try to find the cheapest way to do something—usually by building it himself.

J-D graduated from the University of Alabama at Birmingham with a degree in business management. He currently lives in Birmingham, Alabama with his beautiful wife, Melissa, and their growing flock of animals.

 **Josh Adams** is a software developer with over ten years of professional experience building production-quality software and managing projects. He built a Tesla coil for a high-school science project that shot >27" bolts of lightning. Josh is Isotope Eleven's lead architect, and is responsible for overseeing architectural decisions and translating customer requirements into working software. Josh graduated from the University of Alabama at Birmingham (UAB) with Bachelor of Science degrees in both mathematics and philosophy. When he's not working, Josh enjoys spending time with his family.

■ **Harald Molle** has been a computer engineer since 1984. He started his career by becoming a researcher at a university in the southwest of Germany before cofounding an embedded systems company. Harald is also an expert scuba diver, a passion he is trying to combine with his work by developing a GPS-controlled robot to survey lakes. He is happily married to Jacqueline, who knows that an interest in robotics requires substantial amounts of time. And he owns a cat.

# About the Technical Reviewers

**Josh Adams** is a software developer with over ten years of professional experience building production-quality software and managing projects. He built a Tesla coil for a high-school science project that shot >27" bolts of lightning. Josh is Isotope Eleven's lead architect, and is responsible for overseeing architectural decisions and translating customer requirements into working software. Josh graduated from the University of Alabama at Birmingham (UAB) with Bachelor of Science degrees in both mathematics and philosophy. When he's not working, Josh enjoys spending time with his family.

**Guilherme Martins** was born in Lisbon in 1977. He has always been interested in many forms of art and started early to experiment with various mediums—photography, video, drawing, and painting. Guilherme has worked for several design studios and advertising agencies in Lisbon since 2000 and has been freelancing visual projects, usually related to motion graphics, visual effects, and web design. In 2007 he started to collaborate with the choreographer Rui Horta on visual content to be projected on stage during dance, theater, and opera performances.

As a tinkerer and inventor, he has a particular interest in experimenting with robotics and electronics in order to create innovative interactive experiences. Most of his research and professional work is online at http://guilhermemartins.net.

# Acknowledgments

Co-authors:
I would like to thank my friend and fellow hacker, Josh Adams, for his assistance in several of my projects as well as his constant support and ideas, and for introducing me to the Arduino in the first place. He also wrote a chapter in this book on alternate control (Chapter 13), using your PC with a game-pad and wireless serial link to control a large robot (Arduino + Processing). Josh makes my projects more awesome with his mad coding skills and by keeping up with all the latest hacks. Thanks for all of your help—you are a true friend.

I would also like to thank a fellow Arduino hacker, Harald Molle, for contributing his time and the details of his complex project, the GPS-guided RoboBoat (Chapter 9). Harald graciously took time out of his schedule to write a chapter that I was having issues with. I made three (unsuccessful) boat hulls before finding Harald's project on the Arduino forums and discovering that he had already been through the same pitfalls that I was encountering. He concocted a brilliant design for a catamaran-style boat that is easy to build and holds a straight line in the water. Upon realizing that he knew far more about this project than I could hope to learn, I was thrilled that he was willing to share his experience.

Tech editors:
A special thanks to Guilherme Martins and Josh Adams for their time reviewing the book—your suggestions and feedback were greatly appreciated.

Editors:
A big thanks to Michelle Lowman for giving me the opportunity to write this book, Anita Castro for being patient despite the extra time needed to complete the book, James Markham, Frank Pohlmann, and Dominic Shakeshaft for their help and guidance, and the rest of the Apress team that helped make this book happen—writing your first book is not easy.

Family:
I would like to thank my wife, Melissa, for being so understanding and helpful during this process. I could not have written this book without your support—I love you! Lastly, I would like to thank my family for their support and prayers during this project.

The Arduino community:
The Arduino community was the single largest source of inspiration for the various projects in this book. When I first started learning about the Arduino and physical computing (back in 2008), I had never touched a microcontroller or programmed a computer before, and I was welcomed with open arms. Random people gave me code examples, project advice, ideas for additional features, and, most of all, support. In a society where everyone is trying to make a buck, it is nice to be a part of something awesome that you know you can participate in without spending any money (other than the inexpensive Arduino board itself).

I would like to call out a few specific robotics enthusiasts, makers, and electronics gurus that have contributed to my learning and consequently this book: thanks to Massimo Banzi, Tom Igoe, and the rest of the Arduino development team, Limor Fried (Ladyada.net), Nathan Seidle (SparkFun.com), David Cood (Robotroom.com), and Jordi Munoz and Chris Anderson (DIYdrones.com) for their excellent Arduino tutorials, projects, and contributions to the open source community. There are a few people who were personally helpful with specific questions, projects, and parts: Larry Barello, John Dingley, Shane Colton, and Bob Blick.

Thanks to my common-thread friends that listened to my ranting ideas and nonsense, checked out my prototypes, offered suggestions, and even supplied me with parts to test when I could not afford my own: Josh Adams, Anthony DiGiovanni, and Laird Foret.

Though I took many photos for this book of various parts and procedures, there were some that did not turn out as well as I hoped, and for those I had help. The following photos originated from my various parts suppliers, and I would like to thank them for their help:

SparkFun.com: 1-10, 1-21, 1-30, 2-22, 2-24, 2-26, 2-27, 2-28, 2-29, 3-20

Digikey.com: 1-15, 1-16, 1-17

PartsForScooters.com: 10-4, 12-8, 12-18

DimensionEngineering.com: 10-20, 11-14

Adafruit.com: 2-16

Pololu.com: 10-22

Electronics-Tutorials.ws: 1-3

DannyG.com: 1-9

RobotMarketplace.com: 12-7

DFRobots.com: 5-11

HarborFreightTools.com: 10-3

John-David Warren

My wife, Kristen, who has been so patient with me fiddling with robots; my son, Matthew, who just wants to play with them; and my daughter, Gracie, who I'll meet in person real soon now.

Josh Adams

Thanks to Chris Anderson and Jordi Munoz, from DIYdrones.com, for their excellent pioneering work in building autopilots, Jean Margail from http://water.resist.free.fr for his plans of the catamaran hulls, Matthias Wolbert for making a 3D model out of these plans, and Robert Herrmann for his troubleshooting advice. Lastly, I dedicate this to my wife, Jacqueline—she knows why.

Harald Molle

# Introduction

This book was written for anyone interested in learning more about the Arduino and robotics in general. Though some projects are geared toward college students and adults, several early chapters cover robotics projects suitable for middle-school to high-school students. I will not, however, place an age restriction on the material in this book, since I have seen some absolutely awesome projects created by makers both young and old.

## Prerequisites

Ultimately, you will need to be able to use some basic power tools, hand tools, a voltage meter, and soldering iron. Do not worry if you are not yet experienced in these areas, as your first experience will get you well on your way (you have to start somewhere)! Just like riding a bike, you will get better at it the more you do it.

If you are an experienced robot builder, you will likely be able to improve upon some of my methods. If, however, you are a beginner, you might end up with a few extra holes drilled in the wrong spot, a wheel that is not mounted perfectly straight, or a downright ugly robot. Do not worry about trying to complete every step perfectly the first time; do your best the first time around and then go back and improve upon it later. It is better to have an imperfect robot that you can work on than no robot at all because you were too afraid to try!

In conclusion, this book is intended to provide fun projects for those interested in the Arduino. If you are working on one of these projects and you aren't having fun, you're doing it wrong. If you get stuck on a project, please ask for help—nobody wants you to be frustrated, but learning something new can sometimes make you want to drive your head through a wall...don't do that. Just keep with it, and you will *eventually* figure out your problem. I have created a Google web site to host the files for each project and provide a place to ask questions and get help:
https://sites.google.com/site/arduinorobotics/

If you would like to try some other Arduino projects, dealing with various types of sensors, LEDs, home automation, and various other projects, you might consider the following Arduino books from Apress:

*Practical Arduino* by Jonathan Oxer and Hugh Blemings (2009)

*Beginning Arduino* by Michael McRoberts (2010)

John-David Warren

# CHAPTER 1

# The Basics

The Arduino microcontroller (Figure 1-1) is like a little command center that is awaiting your orders. With a few lines of code, you can make your Arduino turn a light on or off, read a sensor value and display it on your computer screen, or even use it to build a homemade circuit to repair a broken kitchen appliance. Because of the versatility of the Arduino and the massive support available from the online community of Arduino users, it has attracted a new breed of electronics hobbyists who have never before touched a microcontroller, let alone programmed one.

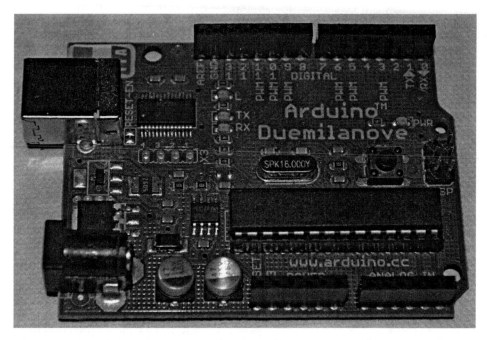

*Figure 1-1. An Arduino Duemilanove microcontroller*

The basic idea of the Arduino is to create an atmosphere where *anyone* who is interested can participate and contribute with little upfront cost. A basic Arduino board can be found online for around $20, and all of the software needed to program the Arduino is open-source (free to use and modify). You need only a computer and a standard USB cable. In addition to being inexpensive, the creators of

1

Arduino came up with an easy-to-learn programming language (derived from C++) that incorporates various complex programming functions into simple commands that are much easier for a beginner to learn.

This book integrates some basic robot-building techniques with the simplicity of the Arduino to create bots that you can modify and improve with a clear understanding of your work. This book is not intended to simply "show" you how to build a bot, but rather to educate the beginning robot builder and hopefully inspire creativity so that you can design, build, and modify your own robots.

One unavoidable obstacle that most people encounter when building a robot is cost. Obviously we can spend thousands of dollars adding top-of-the-line parts and expensive commercial products, but most hobby builders have neither the time nor the money to build such a robot. With that in mind, this book takes every opportunity to show you how to build a part from scratch—or as inexpensively as possible to get the job done. If any of these methods seem too involved, do not worry because there are substitute parts listed for you to purchase.

Please understand that each project in this book requires multiple tries before working—some of them even take weeks of "debugging." I can tell you from experience that when you are persistent, you will eventually solve your problem—and this will make the experience that much more rewarding. Figuring out why a robot is not working often requires a lot of troubleshooting. Troubleshooting requires understanding each step in the process from start to finish, and inspecting each step for errors. The more you tinker with something, the better you will understand it.

Lastly, do not be discouraged if some of the information in this book appears to be over your head. We try to assume that you are new to robotics and programming, and we focus on providing a *practical working knowledge* of the parts and code used in each project, rather than loading you down with electronics theory and complicated instructions. It is best to take a positive "I can do it" attitude before you start—this will be your greatest tool.

To better understand what is happening inside an Arduino, we should first discuss electricity and other basics in general (i.e., electronics and circuits). Although levels found in your Arduino (+5 DCV) are relatively harmless, if you don't know how electricity works you won't know at what point it becomes dangerous. As it turns out, the projects covered in this book do not use electrical levels high enough to conduct through your body, but electricity should still be handled with caution.

# Electricity

Electricity is nothing more than harnessed heat. This heat can be used to do a variety of different things like lighting up a lightbulb, spinning a motor, or simply heating a room. If electricity can transfer through an object easily, it is called a "conductor" (like copper wire). Every conductor has an internal resistance to the electricity that keeps it from transferring 100% of the power. Even a copper wire has some resistance that slows the flow of electricity, thereby generating heat. Conductors also have a maximum amount of power that they can transfer before "overheating" (if the conductor is a copper wire, that means melting). With regard to electricity, total power can also be referred to as total heat. This is why you might see a lightbulb or microwave that has its heat rating in watts. A watt is not only a measurement of heat, but of electrical power.

Some electrical devices (like the Arduino) consume little electricity therefore producing little heat, so no attention is given to heat dissipation. Other devices are made specifically to transfer large amounts of electricity (like a motor-controller) and must use metal heat-sinks or fans to aid in removing heat from the device. In either case, it is helpful to be able to determine the amount of heat that an electrical device produces so we know how to properly handle it.

# Electrical Analogy

Electricity is not usually seen (except maybe in a lightning storm), so it is difficult to understand what is happening inside of a wire when you turn on a lamp or kitchen appliance. For ease of illustration, consider an electrical system to be a tank of water with an outlet pipe at the bottom (see Figure 1-2).

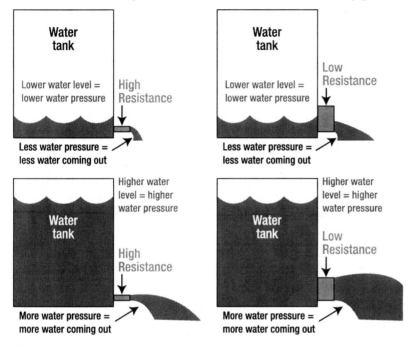

*Figure 1-2. An analogous electrical system*

The four images illustrate how resistance and pressure affect the water output from the tank. A higher resistance yields less water output, whereas a higher pressure yields more water output. You can also see that as the resistance is lowered, much more water is allowed to exit the tank, even with a lower pressure.

The more water that is in the tank, the faster (higher pressure) it pushes the water through the outlet pipe. If there were no outlet pipe, the tank of water would simply be a reservoir. The fact that there is an outlet pipe at the bottom of the tank enables water to exit, but only at a rate determined by the size of the pipe. The size of the outlet pipe determines the resistance to the water leaving the tank—so increasing or decreasing the size of the outlet pipe inversely increases or decreases the resistance to the water leaving the tank (i.e., smaller pipe = more resistance = less water exiting the tank).

Both the level (or pressure) of the water and the resistance (or size of the outlet pipe) can be measured, and using these measurements, you can calculate the amount of water exiting the tank at a given point in time. The difference in the water analogy and electricity flow is that the electricity must complete its path back to the source before it can be used.

# Electrical Basics

Notice that a higher water pressure yields a higher water output (keeping resistance the same). The same is true with the electrical equivalent of pressure, called "voltage" (V), which represents the potential energy that can be found in an electrical system. A higher system voltage has more energy to drive the components in the system. The amount of "resistance"(R) found in a system impedes (slow) the flow of electricity, just as the resistance caused by the outlet pipe slows the flow of water from the tank. This means that as the resistance increases, the voltage (pressure) must also increase to maintain the same amount of output power. The amount of electrical charge (in coulombs) that is passed through an electrical system each second is called the "amperage" (I) or "current," and can be calculated using the voltage, resistance, and Ohm's law. A "watt" (P) is a measure of electrical power that is calculated by multiplying the voltage times the amperage. In this chapter, we further discuss voltage, resistance, and amperage. First, let's look at the relationship among them, Ohm's law.

According to Wikipedia (*Source:* http://en.wikipedia.org/wiki/Ohm's_law), Ohm's law states that the current through a conductor between two points is directly proportional to the potential difference or voltage across the two points, and inversely proportional to the resistance between them.

There is a simple relationship among voltage, resistance, and amperage (current) that can be calculated mathematically. Given any two of the variables and Ohm's law, you can calculate the third. A watt is a measure of electrical power—it is related to Ohm's law because it can also be calculated using the same variables. See the formulas in Figure 1-3 where V = voltage, R = resistance, I = amperage, and P = watts.

---

■ **Note** The pie chart in Figure 3-1 is used courtesy of www.electronics-tutorials.ws. If you are interested in learning more about electronics, you should definitely visit this website —it has some helpful illustrations and descriptions.

---

The different views of Ohm's law include the following:

$V = I * R$

$I = V / R$

$R = V / I$

Use the following formulas to calculate total power:

$P = V * I$

$P = I^2 * R$

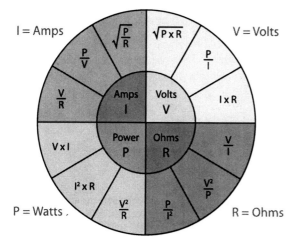

*Figure 1-3. Ohm's law to calculate power*

There are several other terms that you might come across when working on an electrical system; we discuss a few here. As you might know, an electrical system usually has a "power" wire and a "common" wire to complete the circuit. Depending on what you are reading, these two sides can be called different things. To help avoid the confusion that I experienced when I was learning, Table 1-1 provides a quick comparison of the various names for the positive and negative ends of an electrical system.

*Table 1-1. Common Names That Refer to the Positive and Negative Ends of an Electrical System*

| Voltage Bias | Polarized Terminal | Electrical Current Flow | Schematic Label | Common Name |
|---|---|---|---|---|
| Positive | Anode | Source | VCC | Power |
| Negative | Cathode | Sink | VSS | Ground (GND) |

We discussed Ohm's law and the common measurements that are used to describe the various properties of electrical current flow. Table 1-2 provides a list of standard electrical units and their symbols. These are used in every subsequent chapter of this book, so it is a good idea to get familiar with them.

*Table 1-2. Common Electrical Measurement Terms with Their Symbols*

| Measurement | Unit | Symbol |
|---|---|---|
| Voltage (energy) | Volt | V or E |
| Amperage (current) | Ampere (amp) | I or A |
| Resistance | Ohm | R or $\Omega$ |

| Measurement | Unit | Symbol |
|---|---|---|
| Power (electrical heat) | Watt | P or W |
| Capacitance | Farad | F |
| Frequency | Hertz | Hz |

Let's now talk more about the different parts of an electrical system.

# Circuits

The starting point of the electricity in a system is called the "source" and usually refers to the positive battery lead or power supply. The electricity flows from the source, through the system, and to the sink, which is usually the negative battery terminal or ground wire (GND). For electricity to flow, the circuit must be "closed," which means that the electrical current can get back to its starting point.

The term "ground" comes from the practice of connecting the return path of an AC circuit, directly into the ground outside using a copper rod. You might notice that most electrical meters also have a ground rod nearby that is clamped to a wire leading into the fuse-box. This ground wire gives the returning electrical current a path to exit the system. Even though the DC equivalent of GND is the negative battery terminal, we still call it GND.

---

**Note** the actual electron-flow of electrical current travels from negative to positive, but unless you are a physicist, that is not relevant here. For learning purposes, we assume the conventional electron-flow theory, which suggests that electrical current flows from Positive (+) ----> Negative (-) in a system.

---

An electrical system is called a "circuit," and can be simple like a string of Christmas lights plugged into a power outlet or very intricate like the motherboard in your PC. Now consider that in a circuit, the electricity flows only if something is there to complete the circuit, called a "load" (see Figure 1-6). In general, the load in a circuit is the device you intend to provide with electricity. This can be a lightbulb, electric motor, heater coil, loud speaker, computer CPU, or any other device that the circuit is intended to power.

There are three general types of circuits: open-circuit, closed-circuit, and short-circuit. Basically, an open-circuit is one that is turned off, a closed-circuit is one that is turned on, and a short-circuit is one that needs repair (unless you used a fuse). This is because a short-circuit implies that the electricity has found a path that bypasses the load and connects the positive battery terminal to the negative battery terminal. This is always bad and usually results in sparks and a cloud of smoke, with the occasional loud popping sound.

In Figure 1-4, the lightbulb is the load in this circuit and the switch on the left determines whether the circuit is open or closed. The image on the left shows an open-circuit with no electricity flowing through the load, whereas the image on the right shows a closed-circuit supplying power to the load.

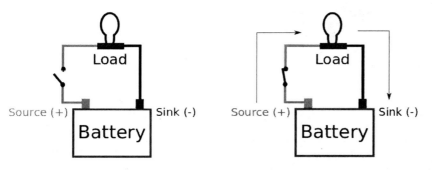

*Figure 1-4. Open- and closed-circuits*

## Measuring Electricity

Without a way to measure electrical signals, we would be flying blind—luckily, there is a device called a "multi-meter" that is inexpensive and can easily measure voltage, resistance, and small levels of current.

## Multi-Meters

There are different types of multi-meters that have varying features, but all we need is a basic meter that can measure voltage levels up to about 50DCV.

A typical multi-meter can measure the voltage level of a signal and the resistance of a component or load. Because you can calculate the amperage given the voltage and resistance, this is really all you need to do basic circuit testing. Although the full-featured digital multi-meter in Figure 1-5 (left) is priced around $50, you can usually find a simple analog multi-meter (right) that measures both voltage and resistance for under $10. Both meters will do basic testing and although the digital meter is nicer, I actually like to keep a cheap analog meter around to measure resistance, because you can see the intensity of the signal by how fast the needle moves to its value.

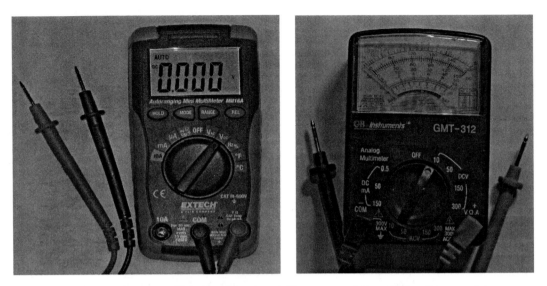

*Figure 1-5. The Extech MN16a digital multi-meter (left) measures AC and DC voltages, resistance, continuity, diode test, capacitance, frequency, temperature, and up to 10 amps of current. An inexpensive analog multi-meter purchased at my local hardware store (right) measures DC and AC voltages, resistance (1k ohm), and up to 150mA (0.15A) of current. Either work to diagnose an Arduino and most other circuits—but you definitely need one.*

The standard multi-meter has two insulated test-probes that plug into its base, and are used to contact the electrical device being tested. If you test the voltage of a circuit or battery, you should place the red probe (connected to the multi-meter "V, Ω, A" port) on the positive battery supply, and the black probe (connected to the multi-meter "COM" port) on the negative battery supply or GND.

## Measuring Voltage

Voltage is measured as either Alternating Current (AC), which is the type found in your home electrical outlets, or Direct Current (DC), which is found in batteries. Your multi-meter needs to be set accordingly to read the correct voltage type. Some multi-meters also have a range that you need to set before testing a voltage. The analog multi-meter in Figure 1-5 (right) is set to 10DCV, effectively setting the needle range from 0-10VDC.

Trying to read a voltage that is much higher than the selected range can result in a blown fuse, so you should always use a voltage range that is higher than the voltage you test. If you are unsure what voltage level you are testing, select the highest range setting (300VDC on this multi-meter) to get a better idea. The digital multi-meter in Figure 1-7 (left) has DC and AC voltage settings, but the range is automatically detected and the exact voltage number appears on the screen—just be sure not to exceed the maximum voltage ratings stated in the multi-meter owner's manual.

The voltage level of an electrical signal also determines whether or not it is capable of using your body as a conductor. The exact voltage level that passes through the human body is probably different depending on the size of the person (moisture levels, thickness of skin, etc.), but I can verify that accidentally touching a 120v AC wall outlet (phase wire) while standing on the ground produces quite a muscle convulsion, even if wearing rubber-soled shoes.

---

▓ **Caution** Voltage levels above 40v can be harmful to humans or pets. Always remember to disconnect the power source when working on your circuits and use insulated tools (with rubber grips) to test circuits. You don't want to end up in a hospital bed!

---

## Measuring Amperage

Most multi-meters have a feature to measure small amounts of amperage (250mA or less) of either AC or DC. The digital multi-meter in Figure 1-5 (left) can measure up to 10 amps of current for a few seconds at a time whereas the less featured meter can measure up to 150mA of current only. To measure large amounts of current (over 10A), you either need a current-sensor, ammeter, or voltage clamp, depending on the application.

This unit of measure depends on the operating voltage and resistance of the circuit. As the operating voltage decreases (batteries discharge) or the resistance fluctuates, the amperage draw also changes. On a large robot that is constantly moving, the amperage draw changes every time the robot drives over a rock or up a slight incline. This is because DC motors consume more amperage when presented with more resistance. An LED flashlight on the other hand, consumes a steady amount of current (about 20-100mA per LED) until the batteries run dead.

You might have noticed that batteries are rated in Amp/Hours (AH) to reflect the amount of electrical current they can supply and for how long. This loosely means that a battery rated for 6v and 12AH can supply a 6v lamp with 1 ampere of current for 12 hours or the same 6v lamp with 12 amperes for 1 hour. You might also notice that smaller batteries (like the common AA) are rated in milliamp/hours (mAH). Thus a 2200mAH battery has a rating equal to 2.2AH.

## Measuring Capacitance

Capacitance is the measure of electrical charge that can be stored in a device, measured in Farads—but 1 Farad is a huge amount of capacitance, so you will notice that most of the projects use capacitors with values in the microfarad (uF) range. A *capacitor* is an electrical device that can hold (store) electrical charge and supply it to other components in the circuit as needed. Though it might sound like a battery, a capacitor can be completely drained and recharged multiple times each second—the amount of capacitance determines how fast the capacitor can be drained and recharged.

Some multi-meters can measure the amount of capacitance that is present between two points in a circuit (or the value of a capacitor), like the Extech MN16a in Figure 1-5. Most multi-meters do not measure capacitance, because it is not usually of great importance in most circuits. Being able to test capacitance can be helpful when trying to achieve specific values or testing a capacitor, but generally you will not need this feature on your multi-meter.

■ **Caution** Larger capacitors can hold a significant charge for long periods of time, and touching the leads of a charged capacitor can cause electrical shock. Capacitors found in CRT computer monitors or televisions, motor-start capacitors, and even the small capacitors found in disposable cameras can provide a shock that leave your arm tingling for several minutes and even burn your skin. It is a good idea to "short" the leads of a capacitor together with an insulated screwdriver to discharge any stored current before attempting to handle it.

## Measuring Resistance

Resistance is measured in ohms and tells us how well a conductor transfers electricity. Current flow and resistance are inversely related. As resistance increases, current flow decreases. Thus, a conductor with lower resistance transfers more electricity than one with higher resistance. Every conductor has *some* resistance—some materials have such a high resistance to current flow, they are called "insulators" meaning that they will not transfer electricity. When electricity is resisted while passing through a conductor, it turns into heat; for this reason, we use conductors with the lowest resistance possible to avoid generating heat.

A *resistor* is an electrical device that has a known resistance value in ohms and is used to limit the amount of current that can flow through it (see Figure 1-6).

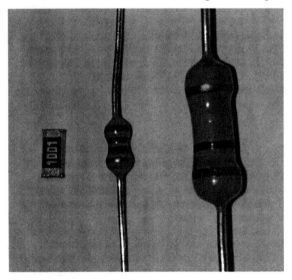

*Figure 1-6. Three resistors: 1/4 watt surface mount resistor (left), 1/8 watt through-hole resistor (center), and 1/4 watt through-hole resistor (right)*

Notice that the 1/4 watt surface mount resistor (left) is much smaller than the equivalent ¼ watt through-hole resistor (right), even though it dissipates the same amount of power. I typically use 1/8 watt through-hole resistors as they are small but still easy to work with.

You can use a resistor in-line with a component to limit the amount of electrical current delivered to the device, in order to ensure it stays within a safe operating range.

The number on the chip resistor designates its resistance value in ohms, while the color-coded stripes on the through-hole resistors designate their resistance value. If you want to manually check the resistance of a component, use your multi-meter on the Ohm (Ω) setting – polarity does not matter, unless you measure the resistance of a diode or transistor.

I use a neat web page that enables you to enter the colors of each band on a resistor, and it tells you the resistance value in ohms (see Figure 1-7). It is helpful for quick reference while prototyping or identifying a loose resistor's value. Visit http://www.dannyg.com/examples/res2/resistor.htm.

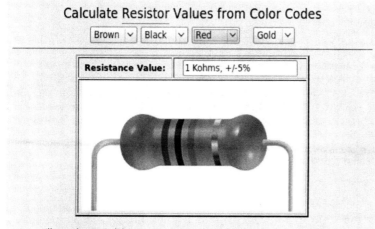

### Calculate Resistor Values from Color Codes

| Brown ∨ | Black ∨ | Red ∨ | Gold ∨ |

**Resistance Value:** 1 Kohms, +/-5%

Illustration Copyright 1996 Danny Goodman (AE9F). All Rights Reserved.

*Image used with permission from Danny Goodman.*

*Figure 1-7. This screen-shot shows the web application designed by Danny Goodman. I have this web page bookmarked in my web browser and use it often to check unfamiliar resistor color codes.*

## Calculating Resistor Power Using Ohm's Law

Remember that any time resistance is present in a circuit, heat will be generated, so it is always a good idea to calculate how much heat will be passed through a resistor (depending on the load) in order to select a resistor with a sufficient power rating. Resistors are not only rated in ohms, but also by how much power they can dissipate (get rid of) without failing. Common power ratings are 1/8 watt, ¼ watt, ½ watt, and so on, where larger watt values are typically larger resistors unless using surface mount components (see Figure 1-5).

To calculate the power dissipated in a resistor, you need to know the circuit voltage and the resistor value in ohms. First, we need to use Ohm's law to determine the current that will pass through the resistor. Then we can use the resistance and amperage to calculate the total heat that can be dissipated by the resistor in watts.

For example, if we have a 1000 ohm resistor (1kilo-Ohm) and a 12v power supply, how much amperage will be allowed to pass through the resistor? And what should the minimum power rating be for the resistor?

First we calculate the amperage through the resistor using Ohm's law:

$$V = I * R$$

$$I = V / R$$

$$I = 12v / 1000 \text{ ohm}$$

$$I = 0.012 \text{ amps or } 12 \text{ milliamps}$$

Now we use the amperage to calculate the total power (heat):

$$P = I^2 * R$$

$$P = (0.012 \text{ amps} * 0.012 \text{ amps}) * 1000 \text{ ohms}$$

$$P = 0.144 \text{ watts}$$

The total power is calculated as 0.144 watts, which means we should use a resistor with a power rating greater than .144w. Because common resistor values are usually 1/8w (0.125w), 1/4w (0.25w), 1/2w (0.5w), and so on, we should use a resistor with a power rating of at least 1/4w (a common size) and still safely dissipate 0.144w of power. Using a 1/2w resistor will not hurt anything if you can fit the larger size into the circuit–it will simply transfer heat more easily than a 1/4w resistor with the same resistance value.

Now you should be able to figure out if your resistors have an appropriate power rating for your application. Let's talk about the different types of load components.

# Oscilloscope

Although the multi-meter is great for measuring the voltage, resistance, and amperage, it is sometimes helpful to be able to see exactly what is going on in an electrical signal. There is another device that is designed to analyze electrical signals, called an "oscilloscope." The oscilloscope can detect repeated patterns or oscillations in an electrical signal, and display the wave-form of the signal on the screen of the device. It is effectively a microscope for electrical signals. These machines have been expensive ($500-$5000) until recently—some hobby grade oscilloscopes have entered the market for under $100.

The open-source DSO Nano (see Figure 1-8) digital oscilloscope built by Seeedstudio.com and also sold (in the United States) through Sparkfun.com (part #TOL-10244). I have had this oscilloscope for about a year and use it frequently because it is easy to use and about the size/weight of a cell-phone, all for about $89. It contains a rechargeable lithium battery and can be charged through a mini USB cable. It also has a memory card slot available for storing readings to view later on a PC.

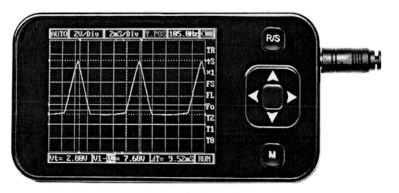

*Figure 1-8. The DSO Nano from SeeedStudio.com (and sold through Sparkfun.com) is an excellent choice for an inexpensive ($89), but full-featured, digital pocket oscilloscope.*

Although an oscilloscope is an invaluable tool to have when diagnosing electronic signals, it is not necessary to have for the projects in this book. You can get by with readings from a simple multi-meter. There are also other budget oscilloscope options available, including a DIY kit from Sparkfun.com for around $60 (part #KIT-09484).

# Loads

The "load" in a circuit refers to a device in the circuit that uses the electricity. There are many different examples of a load from a DC motor to an LED or a heater coil, and each will create a different reaction in the circuit. For instance, a heater coil (found in a hair dryer or space heater) is simply a coiled resistive wire made from a metal that can become glowing red when it is hot, but it does not melt. Whereas an electric motor uses electricity to energize an electro-magnetic field around a coil of wire, causing the motor shaft to physically move. There are two types of loads on which we focus: inductive and resistive.

## Inductive Loads

If you apply power to a device and it creates moving energy, it is likely an inductive load–this includes motors, relays, and solenoids. Inductive loads create an electro-magnetic field when energized and usually take some time to deenergize after the power is disconnected. When the power is disconnected using a switch, the magnetic field collapses and dumps the remaining current back to the power terminals. This phenomenon is called Back-EMF (Electro-Motive Force) and it can damage the switching components in a circuit if they are not protected by rectifying diodes.

## Resistive Loads

A resistive load uses electrical current to produce light or some other form of heat, rather than mechanical movement. This includes LEDs, heater elements, lightbulb filaments, welding machines, soldering irons, and many others. Resistive loads use a constant amount of electricity because their load is not affected by external influence.

# Electrical Connections

When building an electrical circuit, you should determine the desired operating voltage before selecting components with which to build the circuit. Although lowering AC voltage levels requires the use of a transformer, specific DC voltage levels can be achieved by using different wiring methods to connect several individual battery packs. There are two different types of electrical connections: series and parallel.

## Series Connections

To arrange a circuit in "series" means to place the devices in-line with or through one another. We often use a series connection with batteries to achieve a higher voltage. To demonstrate this circuit, we use two 6v 10-Ah batteries with the positive (+) terminal of the first battery connected to the negative (-) terminal of the second. The only open terminals now are the negative (-) terminal of the first and the positive (+) terminal of the second, which will produce a difference of 12v.

When two batteries are arranged in a series circuit (see Figure 1-9), the voltage is doubled but the Amp/Hour capacity stays the same. Thus the two 6v 10AH batteries work together to produce a single 12v 10AH battery pack. This technique can be helpful to reach specific voltage levels.

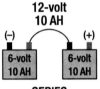

*Figure 1-9.* Two batteries arranged in a series circuit produce twice the voltage but the same Amp/Hour capacity.

## Parallel Connections

To arrange a circuit in "parallel" means to place all common terminals together. This means that all the positive terminals are connected together and all the negative terminals are connected together. If we place the two 6v 10AH batteries from the previous example into a parallel circuit (see Figure 1-10), the voltage will stay the same but the Amp/Hour capacity will double resulting in a single 6v 20AH battery pack.

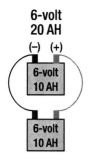

*Figure 1-10. Two batteries arranged in a parallel circuit produce the same voltage but with twice the Amp/Hour capacity.*

## Series and Parallel Connection

It is also perfectly acceptable to arrange several battery packs in both series and parallel at the same time, in order to achieve a specific voltage and Amp/Hour rating (see Figure 1-11). Notice that there are two sets of 6V, 10AH batteries arranged in series to produce 12V, and then the two series packs are arranged in parallel to produce the same voltage, but with 20AH capacity.

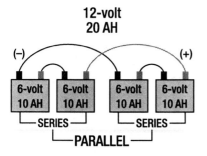

*Figure 1-11. By making two sets of series connections and placing them in parallel, you can create a 12v battery pack with 20AH of current capacity using four 6v 10AH battery packs.*

When building a battery pack, it is important to use batteries of the same voltage and AH capacity to build larger cells. This means that you should not pair a 12v battery with a 6v battery to achieve 18v. Instead use three 6v batteries with the same capacity to achieve 18v and avoid uneven charging/discharging.

## Electronics

The field of electronics deals with controlling the flow of electrical current through a circuit, specifically using the electronic switch. Prior to the invention of the electronic switch, electrical circuits were turned on and off using mechanical switches, which requires mechanical motion (i.e., your hand moving the switch up or down) to connect or disconnect the circuit. Although mechanical switches are perfectly acceptable and even preferred for some applications, they are limited to how fast they can be switched due to the physical motion that must occur during the switching process. Even an electro-mechanical switch (called a relay) does not qualify as an electronic device, because it uses electricity to generate a mechanical motion used to activate the switch.

The electronic switch forgoes the mechanical switching action by using an electrical reaction within the device, thus there are no moving parts. Without a physical movement, these devices can be switched extremely fast and with much greater reliability. The substances that these switches are made from conduct electricity only under certain circumstances—usually a specific voltage or current level must be present at the input and output of the device to open or close it. When the device is turned on, it conducts electricity with a specified amount of resistance. When the device is turned off, it does not conduct electricity and instead acts as an insulator. This type of electronic component is called a "semi-conductor" because it can become a conductor or insulator depending on the electrical conditions.

# Semi-Conductors

The use of semi-conductors in place of mechanical switches is what makes a circuit "electronic," because they enable electrical signals to be switched at extremely high speeds, which is not possible with mechanical circuits. There are many different semi-conductors, and we discuss a few important types that are used in most of our circuits.

- *Diode*: Like a one-way valve for electrical current, this device enables only electrical current to pass through it in one direction–extremely useful by itself, but also the basis for all solid state electronics.

- *Light Emitting Diode (LED)*: This type of diode emits a small amount of light when electrical current passes through it.

- *Light Dependent Resistor (LDR)*: This type of semi-conductor has a changing resistance, depending on the amount of light present.

- *Bipolar Junction Transistor (BJT*: This is a current-driven electronic switch used for its fast switching properties.

- *Metal-Oxide Semiconductor Field-Effect Transistor (moset)*: This is a voltage-driven electronic switch used for its fast switching properties, low resistance, and capability to be operated in a parallel circuit. These are the basis for most power amplifier circuits.

These devices all have multiple layers of positively and negatively charged silicon attached to a chip with conductive metal leads exposed for soldering into the circuit. Some transistors and mosfets have built-in diodes to protect them from reverse voltages and Back-EMF, so it is always a good idea to review the datasheet of the part you are using.

# Datasheets

Each device should have its own datasheet that can be obtained from the manufacturer–usually by downloading from its website. The datasheet has all of the important electrical information about the device. The upper limits, usually called "Absolute Maximum Ratings," show you at what point the device will fail (see Figure 1-12). The lower limits (if applicable) tell you at what level the device will no longer respond to inputs–these usually will not hurt the device, it just won't work.

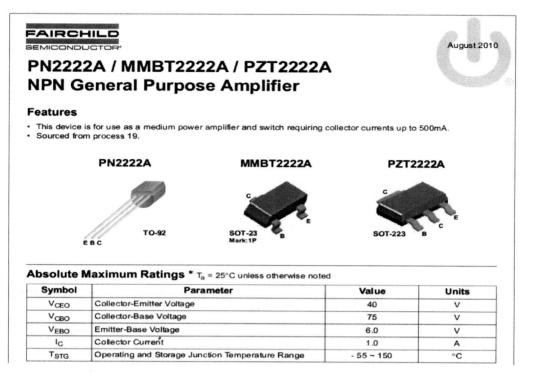

**Figure 1-12.** *Here you can see the first page of a sample datasheet from Fairchild Semiconductor for the popular 2n2222 NPN transistor switch. First it shows the available packages and pin-configurations, and then a brief listing of the absolute maximum ratings.*

There is also a section called "Electrical Characteristics" that tells you at what level the device operates properly. This usually shows the exact voltage or current level that will turn the device on or off. These ratings are helpful in determining what other component values (i.e., resistors and capacitors) should be selected or whether the device will work for the intended purpose.

The datasheet usually tells you far more than you know what to do with, ending with graphs and package dimensions. Some datasheets even have circuit layout recommendations and suggest ways to interface the component with a micro-controller. For popular or commonly used component parts, you can also check the manufacturer's website for additional documents that further describe how to use the component–these are called "application notes," and can be insightful.

## Integrated Circuits

Some semi-conductors include multiple components housed on the same chip, which are called Integrated Circuits (IC). An Integrated Circuit can contain thousands of transistors, diodes, resistors, and logic gates on a tiny chip (see Figure 1-13). These components are available in the larger "through-hole" packages and newer versions are being made on super-small "surface mount" chips.

*Figure 1-13. Here you can see an 8-pin Dual Inline Package (DIP) IC (left), and a 16-pin DIP IC (right). The Arduino's Atmega168/328 is a 28-pin DIP IC (14 pins on each side).*

## Packages

We use different types of semi-conductors in various packages. The component package refers to the physical shape, size, and pin-configuration in which it is available. Different packages allow for various heat dissipation depending on the semi-conductor. If you are going for high power, larger cases usually dissipate heat better. For low power circuits, it is usually desirable to be as compact as possible, so smaller package sizes might be of interest. The most common packages that we use are the TO-92 and the TO-220 (see Figure 1-14), which house anything from temperature sensors to transistors to diodes.

*Figure 1-14. The smaller TO-92 IC package (left) is used for low-power voltage regulators, signal transistors, and sensor ICs. The larger TO-220 package (right) is used for higher power voltage regulators, power Mosfet switches, and high-power diodes.*

The TO-92 is a smaller package that is usually used for low-power transistor switches and sensors. The TO-220 packaged is commonly used for high-powered applications and is the basis for most power Mosfet transistors, capable of handling close to 75 amperes before the metal leads on the chip will fail. The TO-220 package also has a built-in metal tab used to help dissipate more heat from the package, and allowing a heat sink to be attached if needed.

## Through-Hole Components

Throughout this book, we look for the easiest way to build and modify our projects. Usually that means using parts that can be replaced easily if needed and also using parts that are large enough for a beginner to feel comfortable soldering into place.

With respect to semi-conductor components, the term "through-hole" refers to any component whose leads are fed through holes drilled in the PCB and soldered to a copper "pad" on the bottom of the board. These parts are typically large enough to easily solder to a PCB, even for a beginner. Many through-hole components have pins that are much longer than needed, so it is recommended to solder the component in place and finish by snipping the excess from the bottom of each pin to avoid any short-circuits on the under-side of the PCB.

## IC Sockets

An "IC socket" is a plastic base that has metal contacts, which are intended to be soldered to the PCB (see Figure 1-15). The IC is then inserted into the socket after soldering is complete, alleviating the risk of overheating the IC during the soldering process. This is also helpful if something were to go wrong in the circuit, which causes the IC to fail. It is easily replaced without the need for additional soldering. We use IC sockets anytime we are able to for these reasons.

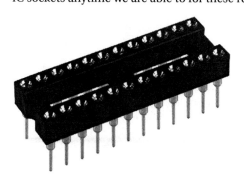

**Figure 1-15.** *An IC socket used to solder onto a PCB, in order to place the actual IC into once the circuit is built. These sockets are usually less than $1 each, so I try to use them whenever possible.*

## Surface-Mount Components (SMT or SMD)

With the technological leaps that manufacturers have made in recent years, smaller has become better. This has led to decreasing the size of components and ICs so that they can create smaller devices that do the same thing as their larger counterparts.

Although these devices are internally the same, their lead pins are much smaller and might be a bit frustrating for a beginner when trying to solder them to a PCB (see Figure 1-7 (left) for a surface-mount resistor). The main difference between these and through-hole components is that they are soldered to the top of the PCB and no holes need to be drilled in the PCB. They also typically sit close to the PCB and require little room to mount them, making them desirable for space-saving applications.

Some surface mount parts have exposed terminals that are able to be soldered by normal means, but, others have their terminals exposed only on the underside of the chip, which requires that they are soldered in an surface mount reflow oven. Although a make-shift reflow oven can be emulated using a toaster-oven, we attempt to stay away from surface mount parts in the circuits we build in this book to avoid the added difficulty present with SMD parts.

---

■ **Note** In Chapter 8, I could not find a through-hole part that was needed to complete the project, so I had to use a surface-mount chip. I looked for the biggest one available so it would be easy to solder, and it was easier than I expected.

---

With a few electronics terms and definitions out of the way, we should move on to some Arduino-specific topics.

# Arduino Primer

The Arduino is a programmable, AVR-based micro-controller with a robust set of features, 20 I/O pins, and it is inexpensive at around $30 for an assembled board. The basic Arduino connects to your computer using a standard USB cable, which provides both a serial connection to your PC and the 5v power supply needed to operate (no batteries required when using USB cable).

The Arduino team even developed a program to run on your computer (available for Windows, Mac, and Linux) that is used to compile your code and easily upload it to the Arduino board. The Arduino board has a USB adapter chip (FTDI) that enables your computer to recognize it as a serial device once plugged in. The most current drivers and software needed for programming can be downloaded at the www.arduino.cc website free of charge. Check out the "Getting Started" section of the Arduino home page to see step-by-step instructions for installing the Arduino software to your specific operating system:

http://arduino.cc/en/Guide/HomePage

The Arduino software is referred to as an Integrated Development Environment (IDE). This is the programming software that is used to upload code to the Arduino micro-controller. The IDE contains a text-editor and compiler that translates the simplified Arduino programming language (that we write) into a more complicated binary hex file that can be uploaded directly to the micro-controller.

The Arduino language is a variant of the C++ programming language, but uses built-in libraries to simplify complicated coding tasks to make it easier for beginners to pick up. If you have no prior programming experience, you will benefit greatly from the Arduino reference pages. These pages show each Arduino command and how to use it with an example snippet of code. You can either visit the Arduino website to view these pages, or check the Arduino IDE under "Help > Reference":

http://www.arduino.cc/en/Reference/HomePage

Because the Arduino language is an open source project, it is constantly being improved and updated. New versions of the Arduino IDE are released often, so it is best to update your system with the newest release available. Most of the projects in this book use the IDE 0019–0021, which can be downloaded at the Arduino homepage.

# Arduino Variants

The Arduino comes in many different shapes and sizes, but there are only two models that use completely different chips: the Standard and the Mega. The Standard is the basic Arduino and refers to the Atmega8/168/328 chip, whereas the Mega is a different Arduino board with more I/O pins and uses the beefier Atmega1280 chip. Because the Arduino design is open source, anyone can design a new version of the Arduino board and distribute it as he pleases. For this reason, several other manufacturers have created Arduino "clones" that operate as the standard Arduino, but are made by a third party or offered as a kit to build yourself.

There are also Arduino boards that do not have an onboard USB converter, so you must use a special USB (FTDI) programming cable to program them (see Figure 1-18—left). The FTDI programming cable is about $20 from Sparkfun.com (part #DEV-09718). The upside to using the FTDI chip on a separate programming cable instead of the Arduino board itself is that you can then easily make your own Arduino-type boards, using only an Atmega328 chip, 16mHz resonator, and a few other easy-to-find components. If you add a few header pins, you can even program your homemade Arduino boards in-circuit (see Figure 1-16).

After buying the FTDI programming cable from Sparkfun.com, I went on an unintended but inspired building spree and made about 15 different Arduino clones that had different pin configurations, screw-terminals, R/C headers, powered Servo plugs, and even a few stackable Arduino extension boards. Although none of my homemade boards had onboard USB functionality, several had a 6-pin FTDI programming header to enable in-circuit programming. This way, I had to purchase only $8 in parts to build each board. If you enjoy prototyping, this is the cost-effective way to go.

You might notice in Figure 1-16, that the homemade Arduino board has very few parts. This is because there are only three absolutely necessary parts to make a homemade Arduino board work: the Atmega168 chip, 16MHz resonator, and +5v voltage regulator. The capacitors, power LED, header pins, and reset button are not required, but recommended for reliability and easy integration into a project.

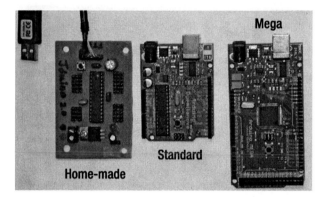

**Figure 1-16.** *Three different types of Arduino boards*

Note that a homemade variation on the left uses the same Atmega168 chip as the Standard Arduino but is programmed using an FTDI programming cable; the center board is a Standard Arduino Duemilanove; and the last board on the right is an Arduino Mega.

## Standard Arduino

The standard Arduino was originally based on the Atmel Atmega8 chip, a 28-pin microcontroller with 20 total available Inputs/Outputs (I/O). Of the 20 controllable pins, 6 are used as Analog inputs, 6 can be used as PWM outputs, and there are 2 external interrupts available for use. The standard Arduino runs at 16mHz and has three adjustable timers to allow for changing the PWM frequencies (discussed later in this chapter).

There are two other variations that are pin-compatible with this chip, the Atmgea168 and the Atmega328 each containing more onboard memory than the previous. The newer versions of the standard Arduino come with the newer Atmega328 chips instead of the older Atmega8/168 chips. If you have an older model Arduino and would like to upgrade to the newer chip with more memory, you can purchase a new Atmega328 chip for around $5.50 and simply plug it into your existing Arduino (these chips are pin-compatible and physically the same). This should be an issue only if you have a sketch that uses more memory than the Atmega8 has available–a problem for more advanced users and larger projects.

One of the key advantages to this chip is that it is available in a through-hole package IC that can be removed from the Arduino board and is easily mounted on a breadboard or soldered onto perforated prototyping board to make a standalone Arduino clone for permanent use in a project. The through-hole Atmega328 chip is perfect for prototyping, paired with a 28-DIP IC socket.

---

■ **Note** If you somehow destroy a pin on your Arduino, it can most likely be remedied by replacing the Atmega168/328 chip with a new one–they are about $5.50 each and you can buy them with the Arduino bootloader preinstalled from Sparkfun.com (part #DEV-09217). I have had this happen several times and am still using my first Arduino board!

---

## Arduino Mega

The Arduino Mega is the *other* model that uses a beefier Atmega1280 chip, which is like a standard Arduino on steroids, featuring 70 total I/O pins (see Figure 1-16—right). Of these there are 16 Analog inputs, 12PWM outputs, and 6 external interrupts available. The same software is used for all Arduino models and each command in the Arduino language works on each device.

This model is available only with the Atmega1280 surface mounted to the board and cannot be removed, thus limiting its versatility compared to the standard Arduino. The initial cost of this board was around $75 but several companies have introduced Arduino Mega clones that can be found for around $45. If you can afford an extra Arduino, it is nice to have around when more I/O pins are needed without changing any hardware.

## Clones

Although there are only two models that use different base processing chips, there is an endless number of Arduino clones circulating around the Internet for you to build or buy in many cases. An Arduino clone, is not an officially supported Arduino board, but instead each clone board might have its own specific pin setup, size, and intended purpose. All that is required to be compatible with the Arduino, is that it uses the Arduino IDE software to upload the Arduino code.

There are even clones that stray away from the standard hardware specifications, but are still supported by the Arduino IDE, like the Arduino Pro Mini that operates at 3.3v and 8MHz instead of 5v and 16MHz as the standard. You can use any of the Arduino clones with the Arduino IDE software, but you must select the correct board from the Tools menu.

In short, it does not matter what Arduino you buy to get started with this book–as long as it mentions Arduino, it should work just fine. We specifically use the standard Arduino for several projects, an Arduino mega for one project, an Ardupilot (GPS enabled Arduino) for one chapter, and several homemade Arduino clones. Now let's look at the Arduino IDE to get a better understanding of how it works.

# Arduino IDE

Assuming you have already followed the instruction to download and install the Arduino IDE, you now need to open the program. The first time you open the Arduino IDE on your computer, it might ask you where you would like to place your "sketchbook" (if using Windows or Linux). If using a Mac, your sketchbook should be automatically created at user/documents/Arduino. Your sketchbook is the folder that the IDE will store all of the sketches that you create within the IDE. After you select your sketchbook folder, all of its contents will appear in the File > Sketchbook menu.

Upon opening the IDE, you will notice a blank white screen ready for you to enter code, and a blue colored toolbar at the top of the screen that provides shortcut buttons to common commands within the IDE (see Figure 1-17). Table 1-3 provides a description of each one.

*Figure 1-17. The IDE has a toolbar at the top that contains shortcuts for common tasks. You can hover your mouse cursor over each button when using the IDE to see a description.*

*Table 1-3. Arduino IDE Toolbar Buttons*

 *Compile*: This button is used to check the "syntax" or correctness of your code. If you have anything labeled incorrectly or any variables that were not defined, you will see an error code in red letters at the bottom of the IDE screen. If, however, your code is correct, you will see the message "Done Compiling" along with the size of your sketch in kilo-bytes. This is the button you press to check your code for errors.

 *Stop*: If you are running a program that is communicating with your computer, pressing this button will stop the program.

 *New*: This button clears the screen and enables you to begin working on a blank page.

 *Open*: This button lets you open an existing sketch from file. You will use this when you need to open a file that you have downloaded or have previously worked on.

 *Save*: Select this button to save your current work.

*Upload*: This is the magic button, which enables you to upload your code to the Arduino. The IDE compiles your code before it tries to upload it to the board, but I always press the Compile button before uploading. You might get an error message if you have the wrong board selected from the Tools > Board menu.

 *Serial Monitor*: The serial monitor is a tool for debugging (figuring out what is wrong). The Arduino language includes a command to print values that are gathered from the Arduino during the loop function, and print them onto your computer screen so you can see them. This feature can be extremely helpful if you are not getting the result you anticipated, because it can show you exactly what is going on. We use this feature extensively to test the code before installing into a project.

## The Sketch

The sketch is nothing more than a set of instructions for the Arduino to carry out. Sketches created using the Arduino IDE are saved as .pde files. To create a sketch, you need to make the three main parts: Variable declaration, the Setup function, and the main Loop function.

### Variable Declaration

Variable declaration is a fancy term that means you need to type the names of each input or output that you want to use in your sketch. You can rename an Arduino input/output pin number with any name (i.e., led_pin, led, my_led, led2, pot_pin, motor_pin, etc.) and you can refer to the pin by that name throughout the sketch rather than the pin number. You can also declare a variable for a simple value (not attached to an I/O pin) and use that name to refer to the value of that variable. Thus, when you want to use the value of the variable later in the sketch, it is easy to recall. These variables can be declared as several different types, but the most common that we use is an integer (int). In the Arduino language, an integer variable can contain a value ranging from -32,768 to 32,767. Other variable types are used in later examples (i.e., float, long, unsigned int, char, byte, etc.) and are explained when used.

Following is an example variable declaration:

```
int my_led = 13;
```

Instead of sending commands to the pin number of the Arduino (i.e., 13), we rename pin 13 to be "my_led." Anytime we want to use pin 13, we call my_led instead. This is helpful when you have many references to my_led throughout the sketch. If you decide to change the pin number that my_led is attached to (i.e., to pin 4), you change this once in the variable declaration and then all references to my_led lead to pin 4—this is meant for easier coding.

### The Setup Function

This function runs once, each time the Arduino is powered on. This is usually where we determine which of the variables declared are inputs or outputs using the pinMode() command.

Example setup() function:

```
void setup() {
  pinMode(my_led, OUTPUT);
}
```

We just used the setup() function to declare my_led as an output (OUTPUT needs to be all CAPS in the code). You can do other things in the setup() function like turn on the Arduinos Serial port, but that is all for now.

## The Loop Function

This function is where the main code is placed and will run over and over again continuously until the Arduino is powered off. This is where we tell the Arduino what to do in the sketch. Each time the sketch reaches the end of the loop function, it will return the beginning of the loop.

In this example, the loop function simply blinks the LED on and off by using the delay(ms) function. Changing the first delay(1000) effects how long the LED stays on, whereas changing the second delay(1000) effects how long the LED stays off.

The following is an example loop() function:

```
void loop() {
                                    // beginning of loop, do the following things:
  digitalWrite(my_led, HIGH);       // turn LED On
  delay(1000);                      // wait 1 second
  digitalWrite(my_led, LOW);        // turn LED Off
  delay(1000);                      // wait 1 second
                                    // end loop, go back to beginning of loop
}
```

If you combine these sections of code together, you will have a complete sketch. Your Arduino should have an LED built in to digital pin 13, so this sketch renames that pin my_led. The LED will be turned on for 1,000 milliseconds (1 second) and then turned off for 1,000 milliseconds, indefinitely until you unplug it. I encourage you to change the delay() times in the Listing 1-1 and upload to see what you find.

*Listing 1-1. Blink example*

```
//Code 1.1 - Blink example
// Blink the LED on pin 13

int my_led = 13;            // declare the variable my_led

void setup() {
  pinMode(my_led, OUTPUT);  // use the pinMode() command to set my_led as an OUTPUT
}

void loop() {
  digitalWrite(my_led, HIGH);   // set my_led HIGH (turn it On)
  delay(1000);                  // do nothing for 1 second (1000mS)
  digitalWrite(my_led, LOW);    // set my_led LOW (turn it Off)
```

```
    delay(1000);                    // do nothing again for 1 second

}                                   // return to beginning of loop

// end code
```

You can copy this code example into your Arduino IDE screen and press the Compile button (see Figure 1-18). With your Arduino plugged in to the USB port, you should be able to press the Upload button to send the code to the Arduino. If you type the code manually, you do not have to add the comments because they will not be compiled into code. This code does not require any input after it is uploaded–but you can change the delay() time and reupload to see the difference.

---

■ **Note** You will notice that in many sketches, there are comments throughout that are denoted by adding two backslashes (//) and then some text. Any text added after the two backslashes will not be converted into code and will are for reference purposes only: // *This is a comment; it will not be processed as code.*

---

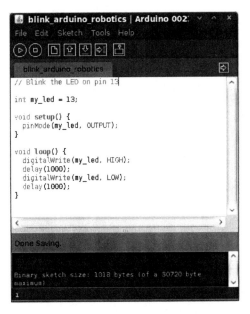

*Figure 1-18. Screen of the Arduino IDE program with the Blink example sketch in Listing 1-1*

# Signals

There are several types of signals that the Arduino can both read and write, but they can be distinguished into two main groups: digital and analog. A digital signal is either +5v or 0v but an analog signal can be any linear voltage between 0v and +5v. You can also read and write digital pulse signals and Serial commands using the Arduino and various included functions.

# Digital Signals

The Arduino Uno/Diecimila/Duemilanove has 14 digital input/output pins labeled D0-D13. Each digital pin on the Arduino can be configured as either an INPUT or an OUTPUT by using the pinMode() command in the setup() function. A digital signal on the Arduino can be only in two states: HIGH or LOW. This is true whether the digital signal is an input or an output. When a pin is at 5v it is considered HIGH, and when it is at 0v or GND, it is considered LOW.

## Digital Inputs

Digital inputs are useful if you want to determine when a button has been pressed (i.e., a bump sensor), whether a switch is on or off, or if you want to read a pulse from a sensor to determine its hidden value. To determine whether an input is HIGH or LOW, you use the digitalRead(pin) command. Sometimes a digital input signal might not always have a full 5v available, so the threshold to drive an input pin HIGH is around 3v, and anything below this threshold is considered to be LOW.

R/C receivers used for hobby airplanes/boats/cars output "servo signals," which are pulses of electricity that are driven HIGH for a short but specific length of time before going back to LOW. The duration of the pulse specifies the position of the R/C transmitter control sticks. If you try to check this type of signal with your voltage-meter, you won't see the needle move. That's because the pulse is too short to register on the meter, but any digital input on the Arduino can read a pulse length like a servo signal using the pulseIn() command.

We can read information from a digital input, not only by whether it is HIGH or LOW, but by *how long* it is HIGH or LOW. The Arduino is good at precisely measuring the length of short electrical pulses, down to about 10 microseconds! This means that quite a bit of information can be encoded into a digital input in the form of a pulse or Serial command.

## Digital Outputs

A digital output is equally simple, yet can be used to do complicated tasks. If you have an Arduino, you have seen the Hello World! sketch, which simply blinks the LED on pin D13 that is built in to the board—this is the most simple use of a digital output. Each pin on the Arduino is capable of supplying or sourcing about 40mA of current at 5v.

Often the current supplied by an Arduino pin is not sufficient to power anything more than an LED, so a level-shifter or amplifier can be used to increase the voltage and current that is switched ON and OFF by the Arduino to a more usable level for controlling motors, lights, or relays. Digital pins are also the basis for serial data transfer, which can send multiple commands through a single digital output (Listing 1-2).

*Listing 1-2. Setting up a digital input and output in the same sketch*

```
// Code Example: Input and Output
// This code will set up a digital input on Arduino pin 2 and a digital output on↩
 Arduino pin 13.
// If the input is HIGH the output LED will be LOW

int switch_pin = 2;    // this tells the Arduino that we want to name digital↩
```

```
 pin 2 "switch_pin"
int switch_value;        // we need a variable to store the value of switch_pin, so we make↵
 "switch_value"
int my_led = 13;         // tell Arduino to name digital pin 13 = "my_led"

void setup(){
    pinMode(switch_pin, INPUT);                // let Arduino know to use switch_pin↵
 (pin 2) as an Input
    pinMode(my_led, OUTPUT);                   // lct Arduino know to use my_led↵
 (pin 13) as an Output
}

void loop(){
    switch_value = digitalRead(switch_pin);    // read switch_pin and record the value↵
 to switch_value

    if (switch_value == HIGH){                 // if that value "is equal to (==)"↵
 HIGH...
        digitalWrite(my_led, LOW);             // ... then turn the LED off
    }
    else {                                     // otherwise...
        digitalWrite(my_led, HIGH);            // ...turn the LED on.
    }

}
// end code
```

This code example makes use of a simple if statement to test the value of the switch_pin. You can use a jumper wire connected to pin 2 of the Arduino (switch_pin)—connect the other end of the jumper wire to either GND or +5v to see the LED change values. If the input value is HIGH, the Arduino sets the my_led pin LOW (Off). If the input value is LOW, the Arduino sets the my_led pin HIGH (On). To learn more about if/else statements with examples, see the Arduino Reference pages at `http://arduino.cc/en/Reference/Else`.

## Special Case: External Interrupts

When using the digitalRead() command for an input pin on the Arduino, you receive only the value that is available at the exact moment when the command is called. However, the Arduino has the capability to determine when the state of a pin changes, without using the digitalRead() command. This is called an *interrupt*. An interrupt is an input method that notifies you when the state of particular pin changes, without you checking. The standard Arduino has two external interrupts on digital pins 2 and 3. Whereas the Arduino Mega has six external interrupts on digital pins 2, 3, 21, 20, 19, and 18.

The interrupt must be initiated once in the setup and must use a special function called an Interrupt Service Routine (ISR) that is run each time the interrupt is triggered (see Code 1.3). The interrupts can be set to trigger when a pin changes from LOW to HIGH (RISING), from HIGH to LOW (FALLING), or simply any time the pin CHANGES states in either direction.

To better illustrate this process, imagine that you are mowing the grass in your backyard before lunch. You know that lunch will be ready shortly and you don't want to miss it, but you also don't want to stop your lawn mower every 5 minutes to go inside and check the food. Instead, you ask the cook to come outside and tell you when lunch is ready. This way, you can continue mowing the grass without worrying about missing lunch.

You are *interrupted* when lunch is ready (the pin changes states), and after you are done *eating* (the Interrupt Service Routine), you can return to *mowing the grass* (the main loop).

This is helpful because regularly checking the state of a pin that does not regularly change states can slow down the other functions in the main loop. The interrupt will simply STOP the main loop for only as long as it takes to run through the ISR, and then immediately return to the exact place in the loop where it left off. You can use an interrupt pin to monitor a bump-sensor on a robot that needs to stop the motors as soon as it is pressed, or use an interrupt pin to capture pulses from an R/C receiver without pausing the rest of the program.

Listing 1-3 requires the use of a Hobby R/C radio system. The R/C receiver can be powered using the Arduinos +5v and GND, whereas the R/C signal should be connected to Arduino pin 2. If you do not yet have an R/C receiver, you can test this example later.

*Listing 1-3. Using an interrupt pin to capture an R/C pulse length*

```
// Code Example - Using an Interrupt pin to capture an R/C pulse length
// Connect signal from R/C receiver into Arduino digital pin 2
// Turn On R/C transmitter ed when using the Arduinos two external interrupts is that
// If valid signal is received, you should see the LED on pin 13 turn On.
// If no valid signal is received, you will see the LED turned Off.

int my_led = 13;

volatile long servo_startPulse;
volatile unsigned int pulse_val;
int servo_val;

void setup() {
  Serial.begin(9600);
  pinMode(servo_val, INPUT);

  attachInterrupt(0, rc_begin, RISING);      // initiate the interrupt for a rising signal
}

// set up the rising interrupt
void rc_begin() {
  servo_startPulse = micros();
  detachInterrupt(0);  // turn Off the rising interrupt
  attachInterrupt(0, rc_end, FALLING); // turn On the falling interrupt
}

// set up the falling interrupt
void rc_end() {
  pulse_val = micros() - servo_startPulse;
  detachInterrupt(0);  // turn Off the falling interrupt
  attachInterrupt(0, rc_begin, RISING); // turn On the rising interrupt
      }

void loop() {
  servo_val = pulse_val; // record the value that the Interrupt Service Routine calculated
```

```
if (servo_val > 600 && servo_val < 2400){
    digitalWrite(my_led, HIGH);    // if the value is within R/C range, turn the LED On
    Serial.println(servo_val);
}
else {
    digitalWrite(my_led, LOW);    // If the value is not within R/C range, turn the LED Off.
}
    }
```

This Arduino code looks for any valid R/C servo pulse signal from an R/C receiver plugged into Arduino digital pin 2, which is where the Arduino "external interrupt 0" is located. If a valid pulse is detected (must be between 600uS and 2400uS in length), the LED on digital pin 13 will turn on. If no pulse is detected, the LED will stay Off.

Because Listing 1-3 uses an interrupt, it captures only the R/C pulses when they are available instead of checking for a pulse each loop cycle (polling). Some projects require many different tasks to be carried out each loop cycle (reading sensors, commanding motors, sending serial data, etc.), and using interrupts can save valuable processing time by only interrupting the main loop when something changes at the interrupt pin.

The only problem I have encountered when using the Arduinos two external interrupts is that they are available only on digital pins 2 and 3 of the Arduino, which conflicts with the use of digital pin 3 as a PWM output.

## Analog Signals

We have established that a digital I/O signal must either be LOW (0v) or HIGH (5v). Analog voltages can be anywhere in between (2v, 3.4v, 4.6v, etc.) and the Arduino has six special inputs that can read the value of such voltages. These six 10-bit Analog inputs (with digital to analog converters) can determine the exact value of an analog voltage.

### Analog Inputs

The input is looking for a voltage level between 0-5vdc and will scale that voltage into a 10-bit value, or from 0-1023. This means that if you apply 0v to the input you will see an analog value of 0; apply 5v and you will see an analog value of 1023; and anything in-between will be proportional to the input.

To read an analog pin, you must use the analogRead() command with the analog pin (0-5) that you would like to read. One interesting note about Analog inputs on the Arduino is that they do not have to be declared as variables or as inputs in the setup. By using the analogRead() command, the Arduino automatically knows that you are trying to read one of the A0-A5 pins instead of a digital pin.

A potentiometer (variable resistor) acts as a voltage divider and can be useful for outputting a low-current analog voltage that can be read by the Arduino using an analog input (see Figure 1-19). Listing 1-4 provides an example of how to read a potentiometer value.

*Figure 1-19. This typical turn-style potentiometer has three terminals. The outer two terminals should be connected to GND and +5v respectively (orientation does not matter), whereas the center terminal should connect to an analog Input pin on the Arduino.*

*Listing 1-4. How to read an Analog input*

```
// Code Example - Analog Input
// Read potentiometer from analog pin 0
// And display 10-bit value (0-1023) on the serial monitor
// After uploading, open serial monitor from Arduino IDE at 9600bps.

int pot_val;    // use variable "pot_val" to store the value of the potentiometer

void setup(){
    Serial.begin(9600);  // start Arduino serial communication at 9600 bps
}

void loop(){
    pot_value = analogRead(0);  // use analogRead on analog pin 0
    Serial.println(pot_val);    // use the Serial.print() command to send the value to the↲
 monitor
}

// end code
```

Copy the previous code into the IDE and upload to your Arduino. This sketch enables the Serial port on the Arduino pins 0 and 1 using the Serial.begin() command–you will be able to open the Serial monitor from the IDE and view the converted analog values from the potentiometer as it is adjusted.

## Analog Outputs (PWM)

This is not technically an analog output, but it is the digital equivalent to an analog voltage available at an output pin. This feature is called Pulse Width Modulation and is an efficient way of delivering a voltage level that is somewhere between the Source and GND.

In electronics, you hear the term PWM used quite frequently because it is an important and usable feature in a micro-controller. The term stands for Pulse Width Modulation and is the digital equivalent to an Analog voltage you find with a potentiometer. The Arduino has six of these outputs on digital pins

3, 5, 6, 9, 10, and 11. The Arduino can easily change the duty-cycle or output at any time in the sketch, by using the analogWrite() command.

To use the analogWrite(PWM_pin, speed) command, you must write to a PWM pin (pins 3, 5, 6, 9, 10, 11). The PWM duty-cycle ranges from 0 to 255, so you do not want to write any value above or below that to the pin. I usually add a filter to make sure that no speed value above 255 or below 0 is written to a PWM pin, because this can cause erratic and unwanted behavior (see Listing 1-5).

*Listing 1-5. How to command a PWM output*

```
// Code Example - Analog Input - PWM Output
// Read potentiometer from analog pin 0
// PWM output on pin 3 will be proportional to potentiometer input (check with voltage meter).

int pot_val;      // use variable "pot_val" to store the value of the potentiometer
int pwm_pin = 3;  // name pin Arduino PWM 3 = "pwm_pin"

void setup(){
    pinMode(pwm_pin, OUTPUT);
}

void loop(){

    pot_value = analogRead(0);  // read potentiometer value on analog pin 0

    pwm_value = pot_value / 4;  // pot_value max = 1023 / 4 = 255

    if (pwm_value > 255){       // filter to make sure pwm_value does not exceed 255
        pwm_value = 255;
    }
    if (pwm_value < 0){         // filter to make sure pwm_value does not go below 0
        pwm_value = 0;
    }

    analogWrite(pwm_pin, pwm_value);  // write pwm_value to pwm_pin
}
// end code
```

This code reads the potentiometer as in Listing 1-4, but now it also commands a proportional PWM output signal to Arduino digital pin 3. You can check the output of pin 3 with a voltage meter–it should read from 0v-5v depending on the position of the potentiometer.

If you have a 330ohm resistor and an LED laying around, you can connect the resistor in series with either LED lead (just make sure the LED polarity is correct) to Arduino pin 3 and GND to see the LED fade from 0% to 100% brightness using a digital PWM signal. We cannot use the LED on pin 13 for this example, because it does not have PWM capability.

## Duty-Cycle

In a 1kHz PWM signal, there are 1,000 On/Off cycles each second that are 1 millisecond long each. During each of these 1mS cycles, the signal can be HIGH part of the time and LOW the rest of the time. A 0% duty cycle indicates that the signal is LOW the entire 1mS, whereas a 100% duty-cycle is HIGH the entire 1mS. A 70% duty-cycle is HIGH for 700 microseconds and LOW for the remaining 300 uS, for each of the 1,000 cycles per second–thus the overall effect of the signal is 70% of the total available.

The duty-cycle of a PWM output on the Arduino is determined using the analogWrite(pin, duty-cycle) command. The duty cycle can range from 0-255 and can be changed at any time during the program–it is important to keep the duty-cycle value from exceeding 255 or going below 0, because this will cause unwanted effects on the PWM pin.

Most motor speed controllers vary the duty cycle (keeping the frequency constant) of the PWM signal that controls the motor power switches in order to vary the speed of the motor. This is the preferred way to control the speed of a motor, because relatively no heat is wasted in the switching process.

## Frequency

Frequency is rated in Hertz (Hz), and reflects the number of (switching) cycles per second. A switching cycle is a short period of time when the output line goes from completely HIGH to completely LOW. PWM signals typically have a set frequency and varying duty-cycle, but you can change the Arduino PWM frequencies from 30Hz up to 62kHz (that's 62,000Hz) by adding a single line of code for each set of PWM pins.

At 30Hz, the output line is switched only from HIGH to LOW 30 times per second, which will have visible effects on a resistive load like an LED making it appear to pulse on and off. Using a 30Hz frequency works just fine for an inductive load like a DC motor that takes more time to deenergize than allowed between switching cycles, resulting in a seemingly smooth operation.

The higher the frequency, the less visible the switching effects are on the operation of the load, but too high a frequency and the switching devices start generating excess heat. This is because as the frequency increases, the length of the switching-cycle is decreased (see Table 1-4), and if the switching cycle is too short, the output does not have enough time to switch completely from HIGH to LOW before going back to HIGH. The switch instead stays somewhere in between on and off, in a cross-conduction state (also called "shoot-through") that will generate heat.

It is simple to determine the total length of each duty-cycle by dividing the time by the frequency. Because the frequency determines the number of duty-cycles during a 1-second interval, simply divide 1 second (or 1,000 milliseconds) by the PWM frequency to determine the length of each switching cycle.

For quick reference, here are some common time/speed conversions:

- 1000 milliseconds = 1 second

- 1000 microseconds (uS) = 1 millisecond (mS)

- 1,000,000 microseconds (uS) = 1 second

- 1000 hertz (Hz) = 1 kilohertz (1 kHz)

Table 1-4 shows all of the available frequencies for the Arduino PWM pins and which pins each frequency is available on.

*Table 1-4. PWM Frequency Versus Cycle-Time Chart*

| PWM Frequency in Hertz | Time per Switching Cycle | Arduino PWM Pins |
|---|---|---|
| 30Hz | 32 milliseconds | 9 & 10, 11 & 3 |

| PWM Frequency in Hertz | Time per Switching Cycle | Arduino PWM Pins |
|---|---|---|
| 61Hz | 16 milliseconds | 5 & 6 |
| 122Hz | 8 milliseconds | 9 & 10, 11 & 3 |
| 244Hz | 4 milliseconds | 5 & 6, 11 & 3, |
| 488Hz | 2 milliseconds | 9 & 10, 11 & 3 |
| 976Hz (1kHz) | 1 millisecond (1,000 uS) | 5 & 6, 11 & 3, |
| 3,906Hz (4kHz) | 256 microseconds | 9 & 10, 11 & 3 |
| 7,812Hz (8kHz) | 128 microseconds | 5 & 6 |
| 31,250Hz (32kHz) | 32 microseconds | 9 & 10, 11 & 3 |
| 62,500Hz (62kHz) | 16 microseconds | 5 & 6 |

For more information on changing the system timers to operate at different PWM frequencies, visit the Arduino playground website:

`http://www.arduino.cc/playground/Main/TimerPWMCheatsheet`

## Homemade PWM Example

To simulate frequency and duty-cycle using manual timing (for learning and experimenting purposes), combine the Listings 1-1 (Blink) and 1-4 (Potentiometer) to enable you to change the frequency and duty-cycle of a pseudo-PWM output on pin 13 (the built-in LED). All you need is a potentiometer connected to Analog pin 0 of your Arduino.

Using manual timing and the built-in LED on Arduino pin 13, we can simulate a PWM signal at different frequencies and with different duty-cycles from 0% to 100%, as shown in Listing 1-6.

*Listing 1-6. Pseudo-PWM example*

```
//Code Example - Pseudo-PWM example (home-made Pulse Width Modulation code)
// Blink the LED on pin 13 with varying duty-cycle
// Duty-cycle is determined by potentiometer value read from Analog pin 0
// Change frequency of PWM by lowering of variable "cycle_val" to the following↵
  millisecond values:
// 10 milliseconds = 100 Hz frequency (fast switching)
// 16 milliseconds = 60 Hz (normal lighting frequency)
// 33 milliseconds = 30 Hz  (medium switching)
// 100 milliseconds = 10 Hz  (slow switching)
// 1000 milliseconds = 1 Hz  (extremely slow switching) - unusable, but try it anyways.

int my_led = 13;   // declare the variable my_led
```

```
int pot_val;        // use variable "pot_val" to store the value of the potentiometer
int adj_val;        // use this variable to adjust the pot_val into a variable frequency value
int cycle_val = 33;  // Use this value to manually adjust the frequency of the pseudo-PWM↵
 signal

void setup() {
  pinMode(my_led, OUTPUT);     // use the pinMode() command to set my_led as an OUTPUT
}

void loop() {
  pot_val = analogRead(0); // read potentiometer value from A0 (returns a value from 0 - 1023)
  adj_val = map(pot_val, 0, 1023, 0, cycle_val); // map 0 - 1023 analog input from↵
0 - cycle_val

  digitalWrite(my_led, HIGH);     // set my_led HIGH (turn it On)
  delay(adj_val);                 // stay turned on for this amount of time
  digitalWrite(my_led, LOW);      // set my_led LOW (turn it Off)
  delay(cycle_val - adj_val);     // stay turned off for this amount of time

}

// end code
```

Listing 1-6 shows how to adjust the duty-cycle for an LED that is blinking at 60Hz (16 switching cycles each second). This example sketch is for educational purposes only. Because the value of cycle_val also dictates how many steps are in the LEDs fading range, you will lose duty-cycle resolution as you increase frequency. I chose 60Hz to demonstrate a frequency that is about the same as the lightbulbs in your home. At this switching speed, your human eye cannot easily detect the pulsing and the LED appears to be solidly emitting light proportional to the duty-cycle.

If you want to manually increase the frequency of the pseudo-PWM signal in the previous sketch, you can change the cycle_val variable to something a bit higher (lower frequency). – To change the frequency from 60Hz to 30Hz, you need to change the cycle time by changing the variable cycle_val from 16 milliseconds to 33 milliseconds. You can still operate the potentiometer to achieve the same duty-cycles, but the results will be noticeably less smooth. As the PWM frequency falls below 60Hz, you can see a pulsing sensation in the LED at any duty-cycle (except 100%).

Now that we have discussed several of the basic Arduino functions, let's discuss the basics of circuit building.

# Building Circuits

It is one thing to be able to program the Arduino and test an electrical circuit, but what happens if you can't find the exact circuit that you need? It might be easiest for you to build the circuit yourself. First you need to know how to read electrical blueprints, called schematics. An electrical schematic shows a universal symbol for each electronic component (along with a name and value) and a depiction of how it connects to the other components in the circuit.

## Circuit Design

Circuit designing can be done on a notepad or piece of paper, but replicating handmade circuits can be time-consuming and tedious. If you care to invest a small amount of time in your project, you can use an open-source or freeware program to create both a schematic and circuit-board design (PCB) for your circuit. I now prefer to do all of my circuit designing on the computer–even if I am not planning on etching a PCB from the design, I at least like to make a schematic for the circuit.

There are several good computer programs that can be used to design circuits. For beginners, I recommend the open-source program called Fritzing, which makes use of a nicely illustrated parts library to give the user a visual feel for how the circuit will look, as well as a proper schematic for each project. There is even an Arduino board available in the parts library for you to use in your schematics–I used this program to generate several of the smaller schematics and illustration examples.

Download Fritzing at: http://fritzing.org/

For the more serious user, Eagle CAD is an excellent circuit design program that can be used as freeware or paid versions, and has extensive parts libraries and professional design tools. This program is also used in several chapters to open and print PCB design files from your computer.

Download Eagle Cad at: http://www.cadsoft.de/

Eagle Cad enables you to create reliable, compact, and professional-looking PCBs that are tailored to fit your exact needs. You will spend a bit more time on the preparation of the circuit, but you will then be able to reproduce as many copies as you like easily–a tedious task using the simpler point-to-point wiring method. Don't be afraid of all the buttons available in the program. If you scan the mouse over a button, it will tell you what it does. Think of Eagle as a really geeky paint program.

This program is a printed circuit board (PCB) editor and has a freeware version available for hobby use (with board size restrictions). It enables you to open, edit, and print both Schematics and PC Board files with up to two layers and a 3.2"x4.0" silkscreen area. Don't be fooled by the restricted size; it is more than large enough to build any of the circuits used in this book and plenty of others. If you did, however, want to build your own PC motherboard or something similar, you might need to buy the professional license for an unlimited PC board size.

We further discuss using design software to create circuits in Chapter 6. For now we focus on some different types of components and their function. Although there are many component parts available, there are only a handful of parts that are used in the projects throughout this book. Let's look at some pictures, electrical symbols, and descriptions of each.

## Schematics

A schematic is a graphical representation of a circuit that uses a standard symbol for each electrical device with a number to represent its value. It can be helpful to ensure proper polarity and orientation of each device as it is placed into the circuit for soldering. A schematic can also stay the same, even if the values or packages of the devices used in the circuit change. See Table 1-5 for some common electrical components and symbols found in a schematic.

*Table 1-5. Common Component Symbols That You Might Encounter When Reading a Schematic*

| Component | Schematic Symbol | Description |
|---|---|---|
| | VCC1 | *VCC:* The common symbol for a battery power supply. A battery is a portable type of power supply that uses cells to store electrical charge. Cells can be arranged in different orders to produce specific voltage levels. Here is a 9v battery, typically used in a remote control or smoke detector. |
| | S1 | *Switch:* A simple switch used to open or close a circuit. This type of switch, called a "momentary button switch" closes the circuit when the button is pushed. Upon releasing the button, the circuit will be opened again. These buttons are commonly used in electronic circuits for low-power applications. |
| | D1 | *Diode:* The symbol for a diode, the back side of the triangle (left side) is called the "anode" or positive end, and the striped end (right side) is called the "cathode" or negative end. The diode acts as a one-way valve – there are many different types of diodes, and they also used to construct logic-gates, transistors, and nearly every other type of semi-conductor made. Get used to this symbol, as you see it often. |
| | LED1 | *Light Emitting Diode (LED):* LEDs are commonly used in electronics circuits as indicator lights because they are inexpensive, consume little current, last a long time, and are very bright for their size. I have a bag of various colored LEDs on my workbench, because it is inevitable that I will use at least one in each project. |
| | R1 | *Resistor:* A resistor is a wire component with a specific resistance, used to resist the flow of current through a circuit or to a device in the circuit. Resistors are not polarized, meaning that current can flow in either direction and it does not matter what orientation they are installed. |

| Component | Schematic Symbol | Description |
|---|---|---|
| | R2 | *Variable resistor (potentiometer)*: This is what you typically think of as a volume knob. A variable resistor uses a wiper mechanism to slide a contactor across a plane of linear variable resistance.<br><br>Typically, there are three pins on a potentiometer and the outer two are connected to +5v and GND (in either order), whereas the center tab is the variable analog voltage output of the potentiometer–the center tab should be connected to the input of the Arduino, or other control circuitry. |
| | Q-N | *Transistor switch NPN*: A transistor is the simplest type of digital switch. There are several different variations of transistors, but we use only BJT and Mosfet types. Pictured is a 2n3904 NPN bipolar junction transistor commonly used in electronic circuits as a switch for current levels up to about 200mA.<br><br>The BJT is commonly used as a high-frequency, low-power electronic switch that is easily controlled using an Arduino. The N-type transistor is considered a low-side switch that is often used in conjunction with P-type transistors. |
| | Q-P | *Transistor switch PNP*: The PNP transistor is similar to the NPN type, but it can be used only as a high-side switch. Pictured is the 2n3906 PNP transistor, which is also capable of switching loads up to 200mA and designed to complement the 2n3904 NPN type.<br><br>By combining PNP and NPN transistors together, you can create an amplifying circuit or signal buffer (see Chapter 3 for more information). |
| | C1 | *Capacitor*: A capacitor is a device that can hold a specific amount of electrical charge, used to supply current to the rest of the circuit or absorb voltage spikes for signal smoothing. This electroclytic capacitor is rated at 100uF and 25v. You should always select a capacitor with a voltage rating that is at least 10v higher than the system operating voltage. Exceeding the voltage limit results in an exploding capacitor!<br><br>Some capacitors are polarized and have a designated GND terminal (denoted by a stripe or shorter lead pin), whereas others are non-polarized and can be placed in either direction. |
| | 16MHz | *Ceramic resonator*: This ceramic resonator takes the place of a crystal and two capacitors, because it has two capacitors built-in. You simply connect the center pin to GND and the outer pins to the Xtal1 and Xtal2 pins of the Atmega168 chip (in either order). This device provides a base for all of the timing functions on the Arduino—think of it as a digital metronome. |

| Component | Schematic Symbol | Description |
|---|---|---|
| | M1 <br> (M) | *Motor.* This symbol usually indicates a standard two-wire DC motor. This DC motor with gear-box attached is a small hobby type motor that can be used in a robotic project. There are typically two wires used to operate this type of motor, where reversing the polarity to the wires will reverse the direction of the motor output shaft. |
| | 5V | *Voltage regulator.* The LM7805 linear voltage regulator chip is useful to convert any DC voltage input from 6v–25v into a regulated output supply of +5v. It can supply only around 1 ampere of current, so you don't want to use this to power DC motors on a robot—but it works extremely well for prototyping on a breadboard or to power the Atmega168 in a homemade Arduino circuit. |
| | | *GROUND (GND):* This symbol universally signifies the GND signal in a circuit. Every circuit has a GND signal, because it is the return path that completes the circuit–all of the GND signals in a circuit should be connected together, and lead back to the negative terminal of the power supply. |

In Figure 1-20, we use some of the symbols from Table 1-5 for a simple circuit schematic with a battery (VCC1), switch (S1), current limiting resistor (R1), and an LED light (LED1). In the schematic you can see the symbols for each component connected with black lines, denoting an electrical connection. To see what the schematic looks like when connected, see Figure 1-21.

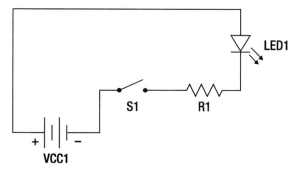

*Figure 1-20. This schematic shows the circuit symbols for four different components in a simple circuit.*

The previous schematic is intended to show the electrical connections of the hardware components shown in Figure 1-21. If everything is connected as shown in the schematic, the circuit will work as intended. This enables users to assemble circuits without regard for their physical size or appearance.

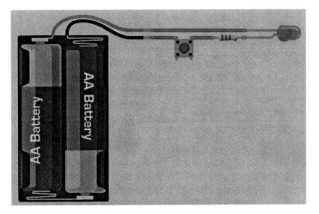

*Figure 1-21. This image shows an illustration of the circuit from the schematic in Figure 1-22. You can see the battery pack (VCC1), the switch (S1), the current limiting resistor (R1), and the red LED light (LED1). Upon pushing the button, the circuit is closed and the LED turns on. Releasing the button turns the LED off.*

# Prototyping

Prototyping describes the art of building a design or concept in a raw form that is not intended to be perfect, but rather to test the feasibility of an idea. Even if you are comfortable enough with your math calculations to be able to determine the approximate weight and speed of your bot, you won't actually know how it works until you build it and try it out. This is where the prototype comes in handy.

You can build a temporary frame with whatever you feel comfortable building with (wood, PVC, metal, etc.). As long as it is sturdy enough to temporarily mount the motors and batteries to, you should be able to get a good idea of the actual speed and handling of the bot, and adjust the drive gearing, battery capacity, or system voltage accordingly.

Prototyping not only refers to installing motors and gears, but also to designing, building, and testing electronic circuits as well. We also discuss some handy tools available that make testing and building circuits much easier.

## Breadboard

A breadboard is a plastic experiment board that can be purchased at most electronics supply shops for under $20 (see Figure 1-22). It is a valuable tool to the electronics experimenter because you can add or remove components for testing by simply placing them into the plastic grid with no soldering required. Breadboards cannot carry large amounts of current so they should not be used for high-powered projects, but I recommend using a breadboard to test any circuit you build before creating a permanent model.

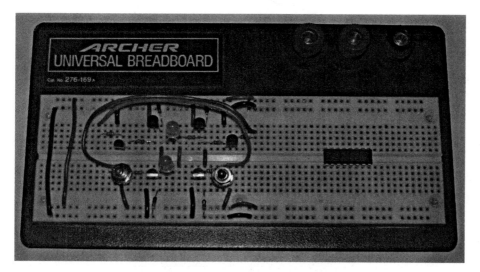

*Figure 1-22. This is a typical Breadboard found at Sparkfun.com (part #PRT-00112) or any electronics supply house.*

## Perforated Prototyping Board (Perf-Board)

After you get your circuit working on a breadboard, you will be ready to make a hard-copy to use as a prototype. This can be done fairly easily with perf-board and a soldering iron. Perf-board is a predrilled PCB (printed circuit board) with 0.1-inch hole spacing for easy integration with most through-hole components (See Figure 1-23). Each hole in the perf-board has its own copper pad for you to solder to, and each pad is separated from the next (except with special designs). This method requires the use of point-to-point wire connections, which can be tedious if the circuit is large in which case etching your own PCB might be a better solution (again, see Chapter 6). Perf-board can, however, be an excellent platform for the beginner circuit builder to test a variety of prototypes without having to design and etch a proper PCB.

*Figure 1-23. A standard piece of perforated prototyping board with an individual copper pad for each through hole. You can build complete circuits on this type of board using component parts, copper wire, and electrical solder. This type of board typically costs under $5.00 each, so they are useful for prototypes.*

## Printed Circuit Boards

After verifying that a circuit works as intended on your perf-board prototype, you might want to make 10 copies of the circuit board to sell or use in other projects. To hand-wire 10 of these boards is not only tedious, but the wire used in point-to-point soldering projects can break or snag, compromising reliability.

To avoid the tedious process of hand-wiring every circuit board that you attempt to build, you can alternatively make what is called a "printed circuit board" or PCB for short. A PCB can be handmade or made on a computer, but it involves creating a circuit design on a piece of copper coated fiberglass board called "copper clad," and dissolving the copper left around the design (see Figure 1-24). All of the wires on a PCB are contained in the copper traces that are created from the circuit design.

With a copper circuit etched onto the board, you can solder component parts directly to the copper—this is called a circuit board. The Arduino is printed on a piece of two-sided copper clad board and coated with a blue epoxy to protect the copper traces from short circuit. Using easy-to-find materials, you can make your own printed circuit boards at home in just a few hours (See Chapter 6).

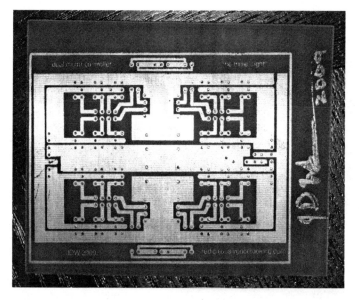

*Figure 1-24. The printed circuit board shown is one of my first few homemade motor-controllers designed on the computer. Using a total of 28 Mosfet switches to drive two DC motors, this is the original board used on the (200lb) Lawnbot in Chapter 10.*

Before completing an electronic circuit, you need to solder each component to the PCB.

## Soldering

Electrical soldering generally refers to the fusing of an electronic component to a PCB with the use of an iron and an electrical solder, which provides a secure connection to the PCB. The idea is to get both the component lead and the copper PCB pad hot enough that the solder will melt when it touches them. As tempting as it is, you shouldn't heat the solder wire with the soldering iron, because it will fuse only to the component lead and copper pad if they are hot as well.

There are many different types of solder available, but for electrical connections you should use a rosin-core electrical solder as shown in Figure 1-25. By using a thinner diameter solder wire, it does not require extremely high heat to fuse to the copper pad and component leads.

*Figure 1-25. This is a roll of rosin-core electrical solder used for circuit construction.*

It is best to let the iron heat up completely before attempting to solder. Soldering can be frustrating when the iron is not hot enough and the solder will not melt! You want only enough solder on the copper pad to completely fill any gaps around the component lead, but you don't want to use too much solder, because it will bubble out and possibly touch another component lead or copper trace.

You can get a soldering iron for under $10 at most hardware stores or Radio Shack. Though these work for most projects, they take awhile to heat up (around 10 minutes) and are difficult to solder in tight spots because they typically have a large tip.

An adjustable temperature soldering iron with multiple heating elements heats up in around 1 minute and typically has smaller available tips for soldering on small projects or tight spaces (see Figure 1-26). I highly recommend getting one of these if you can afford it: they are typically from $50-$150.

*Figure 1-26. I had been using cheap soldering irons for years, and then my wife decided to buy me a "nice" soldering iron. The Hakko 936 is probably not the nicest available, but it is immeasurably better than the $7-$10 soldering irons that I had been wasting my time with before. It heats up in a matter of minutes and can get much hotter than a typical iron, making soldering a breeze.*

Soldering can take some time to get used to, so I recommend buying some perforated prototyping board and using it to practice on before attempting to build your own PCBs. You can also buy electronic kits from various suppliers that come with all needed parts, PCB, and instructions–they only require that you have a soldering iron and an hour or two of assembly time. I bought several kits when I was learning to solder, and they provided both an entertaining project and valuable hands-on learning experience.

## Soldering Shortcuts

When soldering perf-board, we sometimes have a clear path on the copper-side of the board from one electrical lead to another. To make soldering easier and to keep the circuit free from cluttered wires, we can use some soldering shortcuts to simplify the connections (see Figure 1-31).

- *Option 1—Pooling solder.* You will notice that if you heat adjacent (but separated) copper pads and apply solder, the solder will tend toward both pads while avoiding the gap between them. This is because the solder cannot stick to the fiberglass PCB without any copper coating. If you add "too much" solder to these two pads, you will notice that the molten solder will try to jump the gap over to the other pool of molten solder on the other pad. If you are careful, you can let the solder solidify between the two pads creating a simple solder connection. This can be a helpful method of creating a jumper-wire between two or three adjacent pads. This is not, however, an acceptable method for high-power connections because the solder is not capable of transferring large amounts of current.

- *Option 2—Wire traces.* You can alternatively use a piece of solid bare copper wire (16-20awg), placed directly on the copper pads that you would like to connect (see A, B, and D in Figure 1-27). If the connection will span several pads, it is desirable to apply a small amount of solder to each pad that the wire touches to ensure that it will not move after the circuit is complete. You can also bend the wire around other components to make a curved or angled line. This method yields results similar to a homemade PCB trace. Because each wire is connected directly from one lead to another, there can be no crossing wires from other components on the underside of the PCB. This method is acceptable for higher-current applications, though an appropriate wire gauge should be used for the amount of current to be transferred.

*Figure 1-27. How to create traces using copper wire*

Trace A is a bare wire with no insulation, but is soldered only at each end. Trace B is bare wire, but is soldered at each copper pad, making it far more secure than trace A. Trace C is does not even have a wire–it just solder that is pooled across all six pads. Trace D is a wire that has its insulation in tact, but soldered only at each end. Trace C is difficult to accomplish across more than two or three pads and is not acceptable for hacceptable for high-power applications.

# Building a Robot

The actual hands-on building of the robot is my favorite part of the process. This is where you get to express your creativity by designing and building whatever you can imagine. This process usually starts with a few pieces of metal or wood and some nuts, bolts, screws, glue, tape, and whatever else you can find to make your bot come to life.

First you need to decide what you want your robot to do and set an objective (even if it is simply wandering around). You can build an autonomous robot that uses sensors for guidance or a radio-controlled bot that uses your inputs for control. If you have never built a robot before, you should probably start small. Several of the chapters in this book use hobby-type servo motors to drive the robot, which are easily interfaced directly to the Arduino without needing a motor-controller. By incorporating fewer parts in a project, it is easier and quicker to assemble and modify if needed.

Whatever you do, don't try to be perfect the first time around. It is better to have a decent idea and a prototype than to have only a bunch of *really good ideas*. As good as an idea might sound in your head, you won't know if it actually works until you try it. Several of the bots in this book went through MULTIPLE frames before finding one that worked and that I liked. If your bot does not work as expected on the first try, take notes and try it again; this is how great robots are built.

Make, test, tinker, break, remake–tis' the cycle of design.

## Hardware

Having the right tools available can make the building process much easier, but not everyone has a fully stocked workbench. Because nice tools are expensive, you will probably want to buy tools as you find that you need them. This way you don't have tools you will never use.

## Basic Building Tools

Although many of the power tools are mostly optional, the following are a few basic tools that I would recommend getting before you get started. You can go as far as you want with this, but these items should make your list (see Figure 1-28):

- Hammer
- Crescent-wrench
- Pliers (standard and needle-nose)
- Wire-strippers and crimpers
- Vice-grip pliers

- Screwdrivers—Phillips-head and flat-head
- Measuring tape

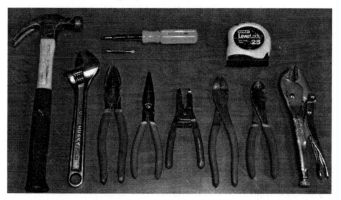

*Figure 1-28. My basic tool kit: multi use 6-in-1 screwdriver (top-center), 25-foot tape-measure (top-right), (from left to right) hammer, crescent wrench, lines-man pliers, needle-nose pliers, wire strippers, wire-crimpers, wire-snippers, and vice-grip pliers.*

After you have a basic tool set, you can begin to acquire more advanced tools as you need them (or as you can afford). You will also likely need the following items to build *every* project in this book–you don't have to own each tool as long as you have access to them.

- *A computer:* Although not typically found on your workbench, you need a computer to run the Arduino software and upload code. Your computer does not have to be the latest and greatest to run the Arduino IDE, pretty much any computer with a USB port will do. Both the Arduino software and Eagle Cad can be used on Windows, Linux, or Mac.

- *Voltage-meter (multi-meter):* This does not have to be expensive, typically the cheapest one you can find will measure AC/DC voltage, resistance, and around 250mA of DC current. I prefer an Analog meter so I can see every movement of the needle and how it is reacting to the signal I am testing–my digital meter jumps straight to the reading, which makes reading precise values easy, but changing voltages more difficult.

- *Electric drill:* If you don't already have one, you need to get one. You can get an electric drill for under $20 at just about any hardware store. If you want to spring for something nice, pick up an 18v cordless drill kit for about $75. It is also helpful to have a drill press if you plan to etch your own PCBs. A drill press can usually be purchased for around $60. You also need some drill bits if you are planning on using metal.

- *Saw:* You will likely need multiple saws, but their type depends on how much work you want to do. The cheapest saw you can get away with using to cut metal is a hacksaw, but cutting through thick metal pieces takes some patience. A reciprocating saw (sometimes called a saber-saw or saws-all) is a good choice for cutting just about anything from metal to wood to PVC. A jigsaw works if you already own one. Although they are slightly less versatile for robotics projects, there are times when a jigsaw will be handy.

- *Soldering-iron:* If you plan to make any of the circuits in this book, you need one. Remember to keep the tip clean with a wet sponge or wire brush periodically while soldering. You can use a $7 iron from Radio-Shack, but I highly recommend an adjustable temperature controlled model if you plan on soldering often. They heat up much quicker and get much hotter, but can cost from $50-$150.

- *Welder:* This is not required, but it can be helpful with the larger projects. A standard 110-volt wire feed type works well. Always remember to wear a welding mask to avoid damaging your eyes, and never look directly at the welding arc!

# Materials

We will be working with several different materials in this book including wood, metal, plastics, and fiberglass. It is always a good idea to wear protective eyewear and gloves when cutting any of these materials. You can work with whatever you feel comfortable using, though I personally prefer metal.

- *Wood:* Wood is the easiest and cheapest material that is also strong enough to support the weight of a large robot. As tempting as it is to use a few 2x4s from the lumberyard for the frame of a robot, they have a tendency to warp and split, which makes the idea less appealing for a project that we put a lot of time into. It can, however, be useful for prototyping.

- *Plastics:* I like to use acrylic Plexiglas sheets in place of glass for transparent applications and small robot bases because it is easy to drill and tap and can be cut with a jigsaw. PVC (pipe) can be useful for projects where lightweight strength is needed. Plexiglas, PVC, and most other plastic can be formed or shaped using a heat gun.

- *Metal:* It is hard to beat metal for building a robot frame. It is extremely strong, durable, and can be joined by either welding or using bolts/nuts. Cutting is a bit more difficult, requiring either a hacksaw (and some elbow grease) or a reciprocating saw with a fine-tooth metal blade. Once built, a metal frame will last for years and will not warp or change shape. Most hardware stores sell 48-inch long sections of assorted angle-iron and metal rods from $5-$25 depending on size and thickness.

- *Fiberglass:* Fiberglass is an outstanding material for creating specific shapes that would be nearly impossible to make from metal or wood. It is also extremely strong and rigid once set, as well as waterproof. The process involves laying a fiberglass cloth and then applying a two-part resin on top of the cloth. It only takes about 1 hour to harden, but it does make some strong fumes. A 1-gallon can of fiberglass resin is around $25 from most hardware stores (this lasts a long time) and the special fiberglass-cloth (sometimes called "mat") is around $5 for 8 sq. ft.

# Work Area

Ideally we have unlimited space to work in, but usually your space is dependent on your living arrangements. When I lived in an apartment, I had parts of projects laying around everywhere and used my back porch as a metal-working station, much to the dismay of my neighbors. Now that I have a house, I try to keep all of my projects confined to the garage and do most of my cutting/grinding/noise-making outside where there is good airflow.

There are several things that you should consider when selecting where to build your projects. These considerations are often overlooked, but are important to your safety and those around you.

- *Testing space*: Things don't always go according to plan, so it is a good idea to have plenty of room whenever you are testing an active robot that can pose a physical threat to others. Several of the robots in this book are large enough to seriously injure people and pets if it were to lose control. Do not test large robots inside or near people!

- *Ventilation*: Breathing in contaminants can be harmful to your lungs and brain. Breathing in sawdust might simply be uncomfortable, but breathing acid etchant fumes or solder smoke might prove to be a health hazard. Always work in a well-ventilated area or outside. If you are soldering, etching, welding, or working with fiberglass, it might be a good idea to use a respirator mask to protect your lungs and a fan to extract the dangerous fumes from your work area.

- *Safety*: Always mind your bots. It is a good habit to disconnect a power wire from the bot anytime that it is not used to prevent accidental startup and possible danger. Don't underestimate the capability of your bots to wreak havoc and destruction (even if that is its purpose) on unsuspecting items nearby.

- *Children*: If you have a work space that children can access, make sure you keep your soldering iron out of reach and unplugged, keep any blades or sharp objects out of reach, keep small components away from those who might mistake them for a new type of candy, and make sure any robots capable of harming a small person are disabled beyond turning Off the kill-switch (i.e., disconnect the battery supply). Several of the projects in this book use motors intended to carry a person. These motors are strong enough to do physical harm to people if the robot were to get out of control. For this reason, I suggest that you keep people and pets at least 20 feet away from your moving bots (unless thoroughly tested), for their own safety.

# Summary

To recap this chapter, we first discussed the basics of electricity including an electrical flow analogy, electrical properties, circuits, and types of connections. After talking about electricity, we moved into electronics and discussed semi-conductors, data sheets, integrated circuits, and IC packages.

Then a small introduction to the Arduino micro-controller including the Arduino IDE, two main Arduino variants (Standard and Mega), the components of a sketch, and finally the different types of common signals available on the Arduino.

With a brief discussion about electronics circuit design and some of the different types of schematic symbols used for various electronic components, we went over the basic tools you need for the projects in this book and the materials that are used.

In the next chapter, we discuss how to interface the Arduino with a variety of different devices.

# CHAPTER 2

# Arduino for Robotics

With some of the basics of electricity, Arduino, and general robot building out of the way, we jump right in to some of the specific interfacing tasks that are needed to complete the projects in this book. In Chapter 1, the code examples use low-power components that can be connected directly to the Arduino (LEDs, potentiometers, R/C receivers, button switches, and so on). This chapter focuses on how to interface your Arduino to mechanical, electronic, and optical switches, as well as some different input control methods, and finally some talk about sensors.

First we discuss the basics of interfacing relays, transistors, and motor-controllers to the Arduino. We then discuss the various methods of controlling your Arduino—focusing on the popular methods of wireless control. Lastly, I give you my two cents about the many different types of sensors available for robotic use.

There are no code examples in this chapter, but the information presented is useful to understand the interfacing methods, control types, and sensors used throughout this book. Let's start by introducing some switching components that can enable the Arduino to control high-powered devices.

## Interfacing Arduino

Because the Arduino can supply only around 40ma of current through any one of its Output pins, it is severely limited to what it can power by itself. A typical 5mm red LED requires about 30ma of current, so the Arduino has no problem lighting it up to 100%—but anything more, and it will struggle. To use the Arduino to control a high-powered device requires the use of an "amplifier." Also called a "signal-buffer," an amplifier simply reproduces a low-power input signal, with a much higher output power to drive a load.

A basic amplifier has an input and an output—the input is a low-power signal (like the Arduino) and is used to drive the larger output signal that will power the load. A perfect amplifier is able to switch the high-power signal as quickly and efficiently as the Arduino switches the low-power signal. In reality, amplifiers are not perfectly efficient and some heat is dissipated in the switching process, which often requires the use of a heat sink on the switching device and possibly a fan to remove heat (like the CPU in your computer).

There are different types of amplifying circuits that can be interfaced with the Arduino depending on the type of signal output used. For slow-switching signals using the digitalWrite() command, you can interface the Arduino to a high-power relay. For fast-switching PWM signals using the analogWrite() command, you must use a solid-state switch, which allows for full 0-100% digital output control. You can also purchase a preassembled electronic speed controller and use the Arduino to provide the input control signals.

First let's talk about an electrically activated switch called a relay, which can conduct very large amounts of current and can be controlled using the Arduino.

# Relays

A *relay* is an electrical switch that uses an electro-magnetic solenoid to control the position of a mechanical power contactor. A solenoid is similar to a motor because it uses a magnetic field to produce physical movement of the solenoid cylinder—but instead of spinning like a motor output shaft, the solenoid cylinder moves back and forth in a linear motion. Most relays are encased in a plastic or metal housing to keep the moving parts free from outside interference and dust (see Figure 2-1).

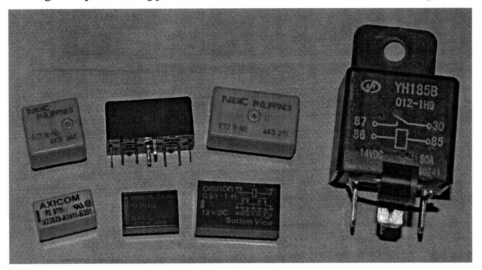

*Figure 2-1. Here you can see a variety of relays in small to large sizes. The three smaller relays on the bottom row are called "signal" relays, meaning their contacts are rated for less than 2 amps of current. The three relays on the top row are called "power" relays, ranging from 5 amp to 25 amp contact ratings. Lastly, the mammoth relay on the far right is an automotive power relay, which is rated at 60 amps.*

There are two parts to a relay: the solenoid and the contactor, and each is electrically isolated from the other. These two parts can essentially be treated as separate (but related) parts of a circuit, because each has its own ratings. The solenoid inside a relay has an electrical coil with a magnetic plunger that provides the movement needed to flip the contactor switch on and off. The relay coil should have the coil resistance listed as well as the operating voltage so that you can calculate how much current it will consume when in use. The contactor in a relay is where the high-power signal is switched. The contactor switch also has a voltage and current rating that tells you how much power you can expect the relay to conduct before the contacts fail.

## Types of Relays

Relays are available with several different operation types depending on your application, so it is useful to understand how each type operates to make sure you get the right relay for the job.

- Normally-Open (NO): This simply means that the two power contacts of the relay are connected when the relay coil is turned on and disconnected when the relay coil is turned off.

- Normally-Closed (NC): This is the opposite of Normally-Open; the power contacts are connected when the relay is off and disconnected when the relay is on.

- Latching: This means that the contactor switch in the relay is not spring-loaded, and it stays in whatever position it is placed into until the polarity is reversed to the coil, which returns the contactor switch to its original position. This is comparable to a standard home light switch—it stays on until you turn it off.

- Non-latching: This is the "normal" type of relay that we use for failsafe switches. The relay contactor switch is spring-loaded and returns to the preset position unless power is applied to the coil. This is comparable to a momentary button switch—it stays on only while you press the button; otherwise, it springs back to the off position.

## Relay Configurations

In addition to having different operating types, relays can have their contacts arranged in various configurations depending on the use. There are four common types of relays that we briefly discuss—each of these relays has only solenoid coil, but a varying number of power contacts. Any of these relay configurations can be Normally-Open or Normally-Closed as well as latching or Non-latching as described.

- Single Pole, Single Throw (SPST): This type of relay uses one coil to control one switch with two contacts—there are four total contacts on this relay (see Figure 2-2).

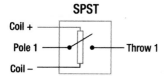

*Figure 2-2. This SPST relay has one pole, with one contact (a simple switch).*

- Single Pole, Double Throw (SPDT): This type of relay uses one coil to operate one switch with three contacts (see Figure 2-3). The middle contact is for the load, the upper contact is for Voltage1, and the lower contact is for Voltage2 (or GND). This relay has five total contacts and is useful for switching one contact (Pole 1) between two different sources (Throw 1-1 and 1-2) —also called a three-way switch.

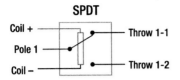

Figure 2-3. *This SPDT relay has one pole, with two contacts (a three-way switch).*

- Double Pole, Single Throw (DPST): This type of relay uses one coil to operate two independent SPST switches at the same time (see Figure 2-4). This relay has six total contacts and is useful for switching two loads at the same time—the two loads being switched can be associated (like a set of motor wires) or separate (like a dual-voltage power switch).

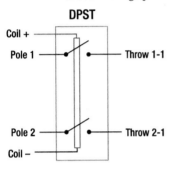

Figure 2-4. *This DPST relay has two poles, and each pole has one contact (a double switch).*

- Double Pole, Double Throw (DPDT): This type of relay uses one coil to operate two independent DPDT switches at the same time (see Figure 2-5). This relay has eight total contacts and can be configured as an H-bridge circuit, which is discussed in Chapter 3 (for controlling the direction of a load).

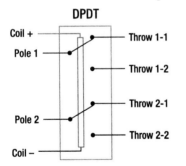

Figure 2-5. *This DPDT relay has two poles, and each pole has two contacts (a double three-way switch).*

## Uses

Relays have the advantage of using thick copper contacts, so they can easily be used to switch high currents with a relatively small amount of input current. Because the solenoid takes some time to move the contactor, PWM does not work with a relay. The PWM signal appears to the relay as an Analog voltage, which is either high enough to turn the relay coil on or it just stays off—but it is not generally a good idea to use a PWM signal on a relay.

You can, however, use a relay to switch high-power loads using the Arduino—including AC and DC lighting, motors, heaters, appliances, and almost anything else that uses electricity. The relay is extremely useful in robotics, because it can both switch a high-power load and be controlled electronically (and thus remotely), which opens many possibilities for its use. You can use a power relay as an emergency power disconnect on a large remote-controlled robot or a remote power switch for an electric motor or lights.

Using two SPDT (three-way) relay switches, we can control the direction of a DC motor. In Figure 2-6, you can see that if both relay coils (control 1 and control 2) are activated, the upper motor terminal will be connected to the positive voltage supply and the lower terminal will be connected to the negative voltage supply, causing the motor to spin in a clockwise direction. If power is removed from both relay coils, the upper motor terminal will be connected to the negative voltage supply and the lower terminal to the positive voltage supply, causing the motor to spin in a counter-clockwise direction.

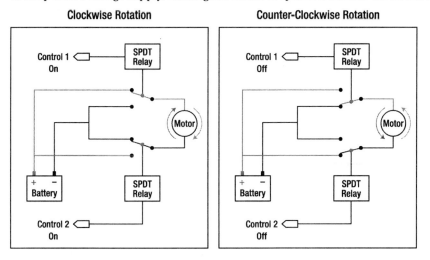

*Figure 2-6. These figures show how a DC motor can be controlled using two SPDT relay switches (or one DPDT relay switch).*

Before we can use the relay, we need to calculate how much power is needed to drive the relay coil. If the relay coil draws more current than 40mA that the Arduino can supply, an interface switch will be needed to turn on the relay coil using the Arduino.

## Calculating Current Draw

To determine the amount of current that a relay draws, you must first determine the coil resistance by checking the relay datasheet. If this information is not available, you can measure the resistance with a multi-meter. Using the coil resistance and voltage rating of the relay, use Ohm's law to calculate the current draw from the coil.

In Figure 2-7, you can see a sample of the datasheet from the Omron G5-CA series relays. As you can see, the relay is available with three different coil voltages (5v, 12v, or 24v). The coil resistance for each model is listed below along with the rated current. The 5v version of this relay coil has a rated current of 40mA, which is low enough to be powered by the Arduino without using an interface circuit.

## Specifications

### ■ Coil Ratings

| Item | Standard, high-capacity, or quick-connect terminals | | |
|---|---|---|---|
| | 5 VDC | 12 VDC | 24 VDC |
| Rated current | 40 mA | 16.7 mA | 8.3 mA |
| Coil resistance | 125 Ω | 720 Ω | 2,880 Ω |
| Must-operate voltage | 75% of rated voltage (max.) | | |
| Must-release voltage | 10% of rated voltage (min.) | | |
| Max. voltage | 150% (standard)/130% (high-capacity, quick-connect terminals) of rated voltage (at 23°C) | | |
| Power consumption | Approx. 200 mW | | |

Note: 1. The rated current and coil resistance are measured at a coil temperature of 23°
 2. The operating characteristics are measured at a coil temperature of 23°C.
 3. The "maximum voltage" is the maximum voltage that can be applied to the rela

### ■ Contact Ratings

| Item | Standard | | |
|---|---|---|---|
| | Resistive load | Inductive load (cosφ = 0.4, L/R = 7 ms) | |
| Contact form | Single | | |
| Contact material | Silver alloy | | |
| Rated load | 10 A at 250 VAC; 10 A at 30 VDC | 3 A at 250 VAC; 3 A at 30 VDC | |
| Rated carry current | 10 A | | |
| Max. switching voltage | 250 VAC, 125 VDC | | |
| Max. switching current | 10 A | | |
| Max. switching power (reference value) | 2,500 VA, 300 W | 750 VA, 90 W | |

*Figure 2-7. This is a sample portion of a relay datasheet; you can see both the coil and contact ratings.*

Even though this particular datasheet displays the rated current of the relay coil, some relays have only the operating voltage listed. In this case, you must manually measure the resistance of the relay coil using your multi-meter and then use Ohm's law to calculate the current draw.

From the datasheet in Figure 2-7, we use Ohm's law to verify the current draw for a 5v relay with a coil resistance of 125 ohms.

$$V = I * R$$

$$I = V / R$$

$$I = 5v / 125 \text{ ohms}$$

$$I = 0.040 \text{ amps (40mA)} —\text{The datasheet is correct!}$$

## Back-EMF Considerations

Remember from Chapter 1 that a relay coil (solenoid) is an inductive type load and produces a jolt of Backwards Electro-Motive Force, anytime the solenoid is turned off. This Back-EMF can severely damage electronic switching components that are not protected with a standard current rectifying diode, like the 1n4004 diode used in Figure 2-8. The diode is placed across the terminals of the load (in this case, the relay coil) to prevent the Back-EMF from damaging the Arduino output pin.

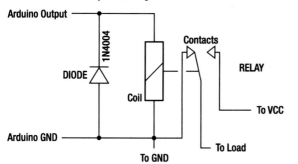

**Figure 2-8.** *This schematic shows the use of a diode around the relay coil to protect the Arduino output pin or other switching device from Back-EMF produced by the relay coil.*

Although the relay in Figure 2-7 *can* be driven directly by the current available from the Arduino, most power-relays require a bit more than 40mA to turn on. In this case, we need a signal interface switch to provide power to the relay coil using the Arduino. To do this, we first need to discuss solid-state (electronic) switches.

## Solid-State switches

A *solid-state switch i*s one that switches an electrical load using doped silicon chips that have no moving parts. Transistors, Mosfets, photo-transistors, and solid-state relays are all examples of solid-state switches. Because solid-state electronics have no moving parts, they can be switched much faster than mechanical ones. You should check the manufacturer's datasheet for the part you are using, but PWM signals can typically be applied to these switches to provide a variable output to the load device.

There are two places that we can put a switch in the circuit to control power to the load. If the switch is between the load and the positive voltage supply, it is called a *high-side switch*. If the switch is between the load and the negative voltage supply, it is called a *low-side switch*, as shown in Figure 2-9.

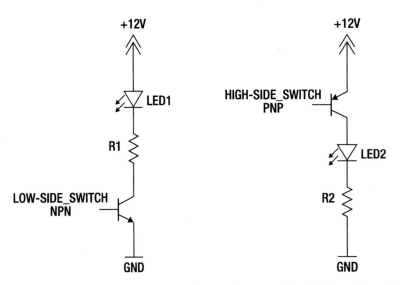

*Figure 2-9. Here you can see the difference between a high-side and low-side switch.*

# Transistors

A *transistor i*s an electronic switch that uses a small input signal to switch a large output signal, using a common voltage reference. Transistor switches differ from normal switches (like relays) because they cannot be placed just anywhere in the circuit. A low-side switch must use a negatively doped transistor, whereas a high-side switch must use a positively doped transistor.

There are three common types of transistors that we use: the Bipolar Junction Transistor (BJT), the Metal-oxide Semi-Conductor Field Effect Transistor (MOSFET), and the photo-transistor. All of these devices are transistor (electronic) switches and operate as such, but each is activated using a different means. The BJT is activated by supplying a specific amount of electrical current to its base pin. The MOSFET acts like a BJT, but instead of current, you must supply a specific voltage level to the MOSFET gate pin (usually 5v or 12v). The photo-transistor is the most different of the three, because this transistor is not activated by an electrical signal, but by light. We can interface all three of these types of transistors directly to the Arduino.

All types of transistors have a voltage and current (amperage) rating in their datasheet—the voltage rating should be strictly adhered to, because going over this limit will likely destroy the transistor. The current rating should be used as a guide to determine at what point the switch becomes unusably hot. As mentioned, you can install a heat sink and cooling fan to remove heat from the transistor, which increases its current rating.

## Bipolar Junction Transistor (BJT)

The most common type of transistor, the BJT, is a current-driven amplifier/switch whose output current is related to its input current, called "gain." It is usually necessary to use a current-limiting resistor between the Arduino and BJT transistor to keep it from receiving too much current and overheating. Transistors also have no diode protection in case of Back-EMF from an inductive load, so if driving a motor or relay solenoid, you should use a protection diode as shown in Figure 2-10. If no Back-EMF protection diode is used, the Arduino output pin can potentially be damaged if the transistor switch is harmed.

A basic BJT has three pins: the **Base** (input), **Collector** (output), and **Emitter** (common). The emitter is always connected to either the positive or negative voltage supply (the polarity depends on the type of transistor) and the collector is always connected to the load. The base pin is used to activate the switch, which connects the emitter and collector pins together. There are two types of BJT transistors that are labeled by the arrangement of the three doped silicon layers on the semi-conductor chip.

- Positive Negative Positive (PNP): Intended to be used as a high-side switch, the emitter of a PNP transistor connects to the positive voltage supply, the collector connects to the load, and the base is used to activate the switch. To turn this transistor off, its base pin must be equal to its emitter pin (positive voltage supply, or simply remove power to the base pin). Turning this transistor on is counter-intuitive because you have to apply a negative current, or a 0v (GND) signal to the base pin.

- Negative Positive Negative (NPN): Intended to be used as a low-side switch, the emitter of an NPN transistor connects to the negative voltage supply (GND), the collector connects to the load, and the base is used to activate the switch. To turn this transistor off, its base pin must be equal to its emitter pin (negative voltage supply). This transistor is turned on by applying a positive current to the base pin (see datasheet for specific transistor rating).

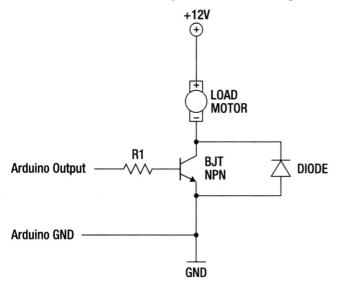

*Figure 2-10. This schematic shows a BJT used as a low-side switch to drive an inductive load (motor) with a Back-EMF protection diode around the switch. Notice that the transistor is driven through a current-limiting resistor (R1).*

Most BJTs require logic-level signals (+5v), to be applied to the base pin in order to activate the switch. Because a BJT is current-driven; when power is removed from its base pin the transistor quickly turns off. The current needed to switch on different transistors varies, but we will only use transistors that can be driven at levels provided by the Arduino. The common 2n2222a NPN transistor can be fully switched on with only a few milliamps of current and it can switch nearly 1 ampere, so it can be used as a simple low-side amplifier switch. The 2n2907a is the PNP counterpart to the 2n2222a that is commonly used as a simple high-side switch. Both of these parts are available at Radio Shack, Sparkfun.com, and Digikey.com and are inexpensive (less than $1 each).

## Mosfets

A MOSFET is a type of transistor that is voltage-driven instead of current-driven like the BJT. This type of switch is also capable of extremely high PWM speeds and typically has very low internal resistance, making them ideal for use in motor-controllers. Mosfets usually include an internal protection diode (as shown in Figure 2-11) to isolate the output voltages from the input signal and protect from Back-EMF produced by the load, so it is generally acceptable to interface the Arduino directly to a MOSFET switch; this is one less part that must be added into the circuit.

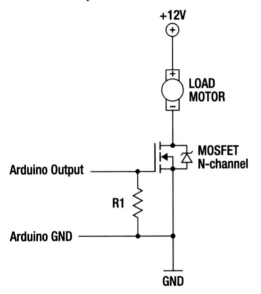

*Figure 2-11. This schematic shows a MOSFET switch (with built-in diode) used as a low-side switch to drive an inductive load (motor). Notice that there is no current-limiting resistor needed, but instead a pull-down resistor (R1) is used to keep the MOSFET switch turned off when not used.*

A MOSFET transistor is similar to a BJT transistor because they have corresponding pins and types. The MOSFET pins are labeled **Gate** (input), **Drain** (output), and **Source** (common), which correspond to the BJT transistors Base, Collector, and Emitter, respectively (see Figure 2-12). Also, a MOSFET is not labeled as NPN or PNP, but rather **N-channel** or **P-channel** to denote its mode of operation. For practical purposes, these terms are interchangeable. Because MOSFET switches are voltage-driven and consume very little current, it is not necessary to use a current-limiting resistor in series with the gate pin of a MOSFET (as with a BJT), but it is good practice to use a resistor from the gate to source pin (see R1 in Figure 2-11) to fully turn the switch off when not in use.

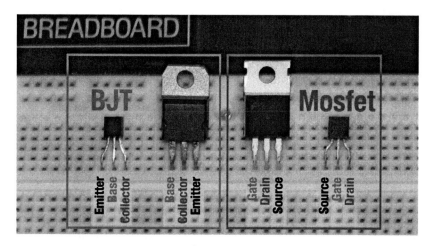

*Figure 2-12. Although they might physically look the same, the BJT (transistors) on the left are current driven, and the MOSFETs (transistors) on the right are voltage driven. Below each transistor, the pins are labeled—notice that the similar transistor packages have corresponding pins.*

## Logic-Level vs. Standard

A normal MOSFET requires around 10v applied to the Base pin to fully turn on. Because driving anything above 5v with an Arduino requires using a level-shifter or amplifier, we use what is called a logic-level MOSFET for direct integration. A logic-level MOSFET can be turned on with a 5v "logic level" signal, which can be easily interfaced to the Arduino. Remember that a MOSFET requires a specific voltage level to be activated, but little current.

Mosfets are also sensitive to excessive gate-to-source voltages. If the limit is exceeded for even a second, it can destroy the MOSFET, so care should be taken to work within the voltage limits of the MOSFET. The maximum voltage that can be applied to the gate pin is listed in the datasheet as the "Gate to Source Voltage" or "Vgs" —this number is usually between 18vdc and 25vdc.

To drive a standard gate MOSFET, there are many different MOSFET-driver ICs that use logic-level input signals and a secondary power source (usually 12v) to send the amplified output signal to the MOSFET gate pin. Many MOSFET drivers are intended to provide the MOSFET gate pin with large amounts of current very quickly to allow for high frequency PWM switching speeds. Because of the higher PWM frequencies available with a high-current driver, we use MOSFET driver ICs in several of the projects in this book.

## Mosfet Capacitance

Mosfets have tiny capacitors attached to their gate pins to maintain the voltage present at the gate. The capacitor charge enables the MOSFET to stay activated, even after the power is removed from the gate pin. Each time the MOSFET is switched, the gate capacitor must fully charge and discharge its current. For this reason, it is a good idea to ensure that the gate is forced to its off state by using a "pull-down" resistor to drain the capacitor when not actively powered by the Arduino (see R1 in Figure 2.11). Using a 10kOhm pull-down resistor from the gate pin to the source pin (gate to GND on n-channel, gate to VCC on p-channel) will be sufficient to keep the mosfet turned off when not in use.

As the PWM frequency that is applied to the MOSFET switch increases, the time allowed for the gate capacitor to charge and discharge decreases. As this happens, the gate-capacitor will require more current from the driver to fully charge and discharge in the shorter amount of time. If the current available from the driver is not sufficient to fully charge and discharge between switching cycles, the gate will be left in a partially conducting state, which can result in excess heating.

Saying that a MOSFET needs a lot of available current to switch quickly might seem confusing, because MOSFETs require a specific voltage to turn on and typically very little current. Although the 40mA that the Arduino PWM output pin can supply is plenty of current to fully switch a MOSFET on or off slowly, it is not enough to fully charge and discharge the MOSFETs gate-capacitor at high PWM frequencies where the MOSFET capacitor needs to be fully charged and drained 10,000 to 32,000 times per second!

Using a MOSFET driver IC (specialized signal-buffer) is the best way to drive a MOSFET switch because it can provide much more current during each switching cycle than the Arduino is capable of. A MOSFET driver can deliver enough current to the MOSFET to completely charge and drain the gate capacitor even at high PWM frequencies, which is important to reduce heat that is generated in the switch when it is not driven efficiently. You can also omit the pull-up or pull-down resistors from the gate pin when using a MOSFET driver to control a MOSFET—instead you should use a pull-down resistor at each input pin on the MOSFET driver IC, being driven from an Arduino PWM output pin.

## On-State Resistance—Rds(On)

One of the most important properties of a MOSFET is the internal resistance between its Drain and Source pins (Rds) when the switch is on. This is important because the resistance of the switch determines the amount of heat that it will create with a given power level. We can determine the maximum Rds(On) value by checking the manufacturer's datasheet. The maximum power that is dissipated is determined using the Rds(On) resistance and the continuous current (in amps) that will pass through the switch.

## Calculating heat using Rds(On) and amperage of DC motor:

How much total power will be passed through a MOSFET with an Rds(On) = 0.022 ohms (22 milliohms) and a continuous current draw of 10 Amperes? Use the Ohm's law pie chart from Figure 1-3 in Chapter 1—we want to know the heat produced in Watts, and we know the resistance of the MOSFET and the continuous current level passing through the circuit. So we need to use the formula: Watts = Current$^2$ x Resistance.

$$W = I^2 * R$$

$$W = 10 \text{ amps}^2 * 0.022 \text{ ohms}$$

$$W = 100 \text{ amps} * 0.022 \text{ ohms}$$

$$W = 2.2 \text{ watts}$$

This means that a single MOSFET with an Rds(On) = 0.022 ohms dissipates 2.2 watts if you try to pass 10 amperes through the switch. In my experience, dissipating more than 2 watts from a MOSFET in the TO-220 package results in excessive heating of the MOSFET. Any time more heat dissipation is needed, it is a good idea to add a heatsink or cooling fan to reduce the operating temperature and get rid of more heat. A good heat sink and fan can greatly increase the amount of power (or heat) allowed to safely pass through the MOSFET. If cooling methods do not suffice, you can arrange multiple identical MOSFETs in a parallel circuit to multiply the amount of current the switch device can handle. If you place multiple MOSFETs in parallel, it still operates only as one switch because they are opened and closed simultaneously, and their common pins are connected.

## Parallel Mosfets

One of the most useful features of a MOSFET is the capability to arrange multiple switches in parallel for increased current capacity and decreased resistance. This is done by simply connecting the Drain terminals together and the Source terminals together (see Figure 2-13). The Gate terminals should be driven by the same control signal, but each MOSFET should have its own gate resistor to divide the total available current equally to each MOSFET used in parallel—these resistors can be a very low value from 10 ohms to 330 ohms.

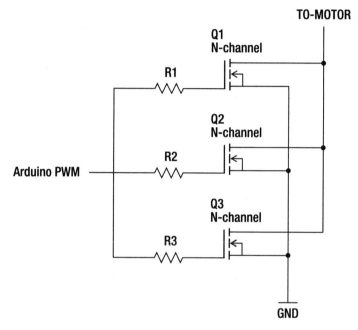

*Figure 2-13. Three MOSFETs (Q1, Q2, and Q3) are arranged in a parallel circuit (all like pins tied together) to allow three times the current flow and a third of the resistance as using only one MOSFET. The resistors (R1, R2, and R3) are in place only to evenly distribute the available current from the Arduino, but are not required.*

■ **Note** The voltage limits of the MOSFETs do not change even when using the parallel method. If the voltage limit is exceeded, you will likely blow up every MOSFET that is connected!

The total current that can be transferred through a parallel set of MOSFETs is equal to the amount of current that can be passed by a single MOSFET, times the number of MOSFETs used in parallel. In addition, the total resistance of the parallel set of MOSFETs is equal to the Rds(On) rating divided by the number of MOSFETs in the parallel circuit. This means that by using two MOSFETs in parallel, you decrease the resistance by half—and when the resistance is decreased, so is the heat dissipation.

## Photo-Transistors

A photo-transistor operates like a standard NPN transistor, except that it is activated using infrared light from an LED instead of electrical current. These transistors are commonly used for line-following robots to detect reflective light differences on colored surfaces. If the infrared emitter and detector are enclosed in an IC package, the device is an optical-isolator, because the low power device (infrared emitter) is electrically isolated from the high power switch (photo-transistor), enabling the input and output circuits to be separated (they have different power sources).

This type of switch is like a transistor/relay hybrid; it has electrical isolation like a relay, but the switch is interfaced as a transistor; the unique feature that you get with a photo-transistor is an electrically isolated switch with PWM switching capabilities. In Figure 2-14, the base is driven using light from an infrared LED connected to the Arduino (using current-limiting resistor R1), the collector (pin 4) is connected to the negative load terminal (as a low-side switch), and the emitter (pin 3) is connected to the GND supply.

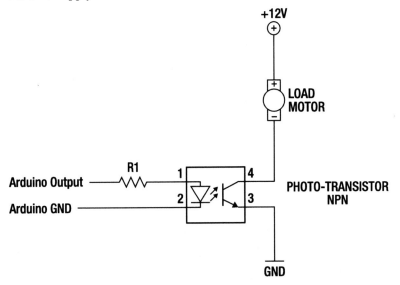

***Figure 2-14.*** *This optical-isolator (IRED and photo-transistor pair) is used as a low-side switch to drive a motor. Because the only thing connecting the Arduino to the Load is a beam of infrared light (no common GND signal), it is not required that you use a protection diode on the switch (though it is recommended).*

# Interfacing a Motor-Controller

The term *motor-controller* refers to an amplifier that is designed to control the speed and direction of a motor using a specified set of signal commands. There are two types of motor-controllers that we discuss: motor-controller ICs and Electronic Speed Controllers (ESC).

A motor-controller IC is an integrated circuit chip that is designed to use a low-power input signal to provide a high-power output signal commanding both speed and direction to a DC motor. These usually require a few extra components (a few resistors, a capacitor, and a +5v power supply from Arduino) but take care of the motor-control.

An ESC is a complete motor speed controller circuit that accepts one or more types of input signals and outputs an appropriate speed and direction to the motor using PWM. These usually prepackaged units that cost more to buy, but require less work to get going. If you are in a hurry, these are handy. The majority of ESCs are made for use with hobby airplane, car, and boat equipment and use a Servo pulse input signal. There are also an increasing number ESCs that are geared toward use in robotics, with a variety of different interfacing options.

## Motor-controller ICs

There are several packaged IC chips that are inexpensive and easy to build into a circuit. The common L293D dual motor-controller is a 16-DIP IC chip that contains two protected driver circuits capable of delivering up to 600mA of continuous current to each motor at up to 36VDC (see Figure 2-15). The L298N is a similar chip that can deliver 2 amps to each motor. These chips (and others) accept standard 0-5v input signals and have internal logic gates to prevent accidental overloading and commanding the controller into a destructive state.

Notice in Figure 2-15 that there are four sets of inputs and outputs, labeled 1A (input) and 1Y (output) through 4A and 4y. The digital state of these input pins determines the digital state of their corresponding amplified output pin. In practice, when you apply a 5v signal (VCC1) to pin 1A, you get a 12v signal (VCC2) at pin 1Y. There is also an "enable" pin for each set of input/outputs. The 1-2 Enable pin controls the state of both 1Y and 2Y output pins simultaneously, and the 3-4 Enable pin controls the 3Y and 4Y outputs. You can use digital pins on the Arduino to control the four input pins and set the motor direction, while using a PWM signal on each Enable pin to set the speed of each motor.

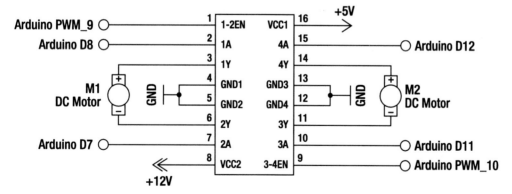

*Figure 2-15. A schematic of the L293D dual 1-amp motor-controller IC and how it can connect to the Arduino*

If a motor-controller IC fits your needs but you don't want to build your own circuit, there are several commercial kits and preassembled circuits available that use small motor-controller ICs. The AdaFruit motor-shield in Chapter 4 features two L293D motor-controller ICs (see Figure 2-16) capable of powering up to four DC motors with 600mA of continuous current each. Simply plug the shield onto your Arduino and go—this shield is also wired for two Servo motor connectors (see Chapter 3 for more information) that can be used in addition to the four DC motors.

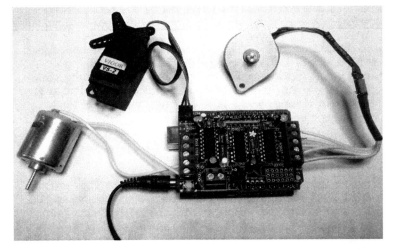

*Figure 2-16. The Adafruit motor-shield is an easy-to-use motor-driver for the Arduino that can drive a variety of different motors, from left to right: DC motor, Servo motor, Stepper motor.*

## Electronic Speed Controllers (ESCs)

An ESC is a motor-controller with its own control circuitry. These are intended to be driven using a specified input signal and do not require a micro-controller. There are many different preassembled ESCs for use with both hobby type vehicles (cars, boats, and planes) and robotics that accept a specific input signal and command the motor appropriately. Though many of these units are designed to accept a Servo pulse signal from a standard hobby R/C system or an analog voltage from a potentiometer, you can use the Arduino to emulate a Servo pulse or analog potentiometer value. This can enable you to control a specialized ESC motor-controller with the Arduino, using any input method.

The Sabertooth 2x25 motor-controller from Dimension Engineering (see Figure 2-17) is a versatile replacement for any of the motor-controllers made in this book. You can use the Arduino to send control signals to the Sabertooth to command each motor, using a variety of different signals. Over-current protection is built in to the board, so it simply shuts itself down when it gets too hot.

*Figure 2-17. This is the Sabertooth 2x25 dual 25-amp motor-controller. Though it doesn't look like much, it can provide two DC motors with enough power to move several hundred pounds with decent speed.*

There are many different speed-controllers available, each requiring a different control interface; some are PWM controlled, some use Serial commands, and others use analog voltages. Many hobby ESCs use a Servo pulse as the input signal to control each motor. There are four main motor-control interfacing methods that we will use, and I will briefly describe each:

- Simple PWM control: Uses a PWM signal to determine the 0-100% output of one motor. The duty-cycle of the PWM signal determines the proportional output speed of the motor, in one direction. This is a common control method with homemade motor-controllers that interface directly to the transistor switches and with some types of MOSFET driver ICs. You either need two PWM signals or a high-speed signal inverter to drive the motor in both directions.

- Bi-directional Analog control: Uses a 0-5v analog (or PWM) signal to determine the speed and direction of a motor. In this mode, the center position of 2.5v is considered Neutral. Below 2.5v spins the motor proportionally in Reverse with a 0v value yielding 100% Reverse. Above 2.5v spins the motor Forward with a 5v value yielding 100% Forward—this is called "Analog."

- R/C control: Uses a special "Servo" pulse signal that encodes the position of an R/C transmitter control stick. The signal is a pulse of electricity that has a specific on time, which ranges from 1 millisecond to 2 milliseconds where the neutral position yields a 1.5 millisecond pulse. This type of interface is meant to directly connect to most hobby R/C radio systems.

- Serial command: Uses a serial cable connected to a computer (USB) to receive a series of serial control pulses used to control the motors.

# User Control

There are many different views of exactly what defines a "robot." Some people think that it isn't a robot unless it has some intelligence, such as the capability to make decisions based on its environment. Most industrial robotic equipment is designed to do a specific task with good accuracy, over and over again—but these robots are controlled by a humans and do not have decision-making capabilities. Some consider robotics to include the automation of a process, even if it is human controlled. In the interest of variety, we extend the scope to include all of these things as robots.

A robot's control method varies depending on its application. A stationary robot might need only commands when the user wants a specific action to be carried out, whereas a fast-moving mobile robot needs several control updates each second. An autonomous robot can also have R/C control to allow for multiple uses. The Arduino chip has enough room to code multiple control methods on the same robot. The control method can be as simple as a set of buttons mounted to the bot or as complex as using a GPS chip to guide the bot to a set of latitude and longitude coordinates on its own (see the section, "The Robo-Boat," in Chapter 9). There are many different methods of control but we discuss only a few common types.

## Tethered (Wired) Control

Tethered control is easy to interface to an Arduino because you simply connect wires from each button, switch, or potentiometer directly to the Arduino input pins. You can even build your own controller box using a few potentiometers, some button switches, and a few feet of 8-conductor Thermostat wire from the hardware store. Using an 8-conductor wire and a common GND signal, you can easily have six or seven independent analog or digital channels on a tethered controller.

A medical power wheelchair typically has a joystick controller for the operator to control its movements, with a few other buttons to adjust anything from the top speed of the motors to the incline of the seat. The variable resistors and buttons in these controllers are wired directly into the micro-controller of the chair. The project in Chapter 11 is a ridable segway style bot that you can activate and steer from the handlebar—all of the connections are hard-wired into the Arduino.

Sometimes using a tethered controller is not possible on a robot, and you must look for a wireless solution. There are several to choose from with different applications and cost, so let's discuss a few.

## Infrared Control (IR)

A set of infrared sensors can be used to control a robot, just like you use a remote control to change the channel on your TV. A TV remote control sends a specific infrared code for each button that is pressed, that way your TV set knows what to do depending on what button is pressed (i.e., Volume up/down, channel up/down, and so on). Using this same concept, you can read infrared codes on your Arduino using an IR receiver IC (see Figure 2-18) and use these codes to command a robot with a different robotic action for every different button that is pushed.

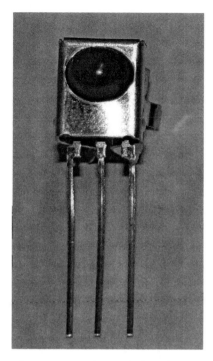

*Figure 2-18. Using an infrared receiver IC pulled from an old VCR (pictured), you can send signals to the Arduino with your TV remote control.*

This type of control uses light emitted from an infrared emitting diode (IRED) that looks and operates just like an LED, except you can't see any visible light (with your naked eye) when the IRED is turned on. Because infrared devices use light to transfer the signal, this type of control method must have a clear line of sight between the emitter and receiver. With a clear transmission path, an IR sensor has an effective range of around 20 feet. There are even some R/C cars, indoor micro-helicopters, and robot toys that use an infrared wireless link, like the popular Robosapien from WowWee robotic toys (`www.wowwee.com`).

## Radio Control Systems

Let me start by saying that I am by no means a radio expert, so I am not qualified to go into detail about the many different possibilities of radio signal transmission—but I have tried several different popular radio control methods and I can tell you which have worked best in my experience for robot use.

Radio control is probably the most common method for human control of a robot, because it is not strictly limited to line of sight operation and has an effective range of up to several miles. Most radio control equipment is intended for use in hobby airplanes, boats, and cars, but the Arduino makes an excellent interface to implement R/C control of a robot. A typical hobby grade radio control system consists of a "transmitter" that is used to capture your inputs and send them through the air, and a "receiver" that is used to capture these signals from the air and convert them into usable electrical signals (see Figure 2-19).

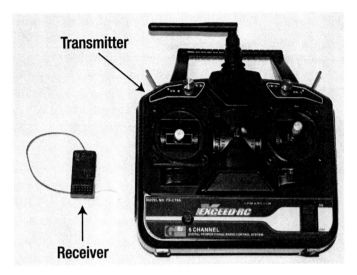

*Figure 2-19.* This hobby grade 2.4GHz radio system includes a six-channel transmitter and receiver pair for under $40 from HobbyPartz.com (part# 79P-CT6B-R6B).

There are three types of radio systems that can be used for robot control: Amplitude Modulation (AM), Frequency Modulation (FM), and Spread Spectrum (2.4gHz). Although each of these types of signal modification is different, each one accomplishes the same goal: send the transmitter values to the receiver. For more advanced projects, there is also Xbee, a popular 2.4GHz wireless link.

## Amplitude Modulation (AM)

AM radio systems are probably the most widely used, but mainly for remotely controlled toy cars and boats (27mHz and 49mHz are popular). These radio systems use long wire antennas to transmit their signals and are affected by interference from buildings, trees, and other radios nearby (on the same frequency). AM radio systems typically have no more than three usable control channels, making them less popular for use with robots. These systems can be used for small robots, but should be avoided where extreme reliability and range is required. These systems can be interfaced to the Arduino, but should be avoided unless you already own one.

## Frequency Modulation (FM)

In the USA, all FM 75mHz radio systems are intended for use on ground vehicles (such as cars and boats) and all FM 72mHz radio systems are intended for use on air vehicles (such as airplanes and helicopters). These radio systems usually require a matching set of crystals placed into the transmitter and receiver to determine what "channel" the radio is operated on—the crystals simply tune the radio Tx and Rx to the same specific frequency so they can operate without interference. FM radio systems usually have a good range in open areas (up to 1 mile) and are not as prone to interference as AM systems, making them usable for robotics.

## Spread Spectrum 2.4gHz

The 2.4GHz frequency range is common for wireless data transmission. Not only is this frequency band large enough to transmit large amounts of data (like audio, video, and Web), it can also provide a secure connection for R/C systems that is free from interference. There are many devices that use this frequency including wireless camera systems, wireless network routers, R/C systems, and even the Bluetooth wireless protocol. Spread Spectrum radios operate at 2.4gHz frequency, which is typically above the level of interference from metal fences and motor noise and they have no usage restrictions, making them suitable for use on any type of robot.

2.4gHz R/C systems use a process called "binding" to establish a semi-permanent connection between the transmitter and receiver. Binding is the replacement for matching frequency crystal pairs, used in legacy R/C systems. The spread spectrum standard uses a process called "frequency hopping" to constantly change frequency channels (both the transmitter and receiver simultaneously) to prevent any other nearby radios from crossing signals. An R/C system is the cheapest way to get a secure 2.4GHz connection that can be interfaced directly to the Arduino.

## Xbee

Xbee operates as a wireless Serial data connection (with selectable data rates), capable of both sending and receiving data. Xbee radios are made by Digi International (`www.digi.com`) and use the "Zigbee" wireless communication protocol. With a variety of applications, these radios are easy to interface to the Arduino, requiring only a 3.3v power supply and a connection to the Arduino Serial tx and rx pins (D0 & D1).

Using a set of Xbee radios, you can create your own custom programmable R/C controller or telemetry link to obtain information about your bot during operation (i.e., battery voltage, amperage draw, speed, and so on). You can even use a pair of Xbee radios to wirelessly program an Arduino! Xbee radios are available with different power levels to accommodate longer distance transmissions, providing an effective range that is comparable to the common 2.4GHz R/C link. Because of the versatility of this robust wireless link, there are several chapters that discuss using a pair of Xbees for both robot control and monitoring (see Figure 2-20).

**Xbee Radios**

**Sparkfun Xbee
Explorer Regulated**

**Sparkfun Xbee
Explorer USB**

*Figure 2-20. A pair of 2.4GHz Xbee radios (center) with breakout boards from Sparkfun.com*

There are many retailers that sell Xbee radios and shield adapter boards to enable easy interfacing with the Arduino. A basic Xbee radio costs about $25 each and the adapter boards can range from $10–

$25 each. An adapter board is needed because the pin spacing of each Xbee radio is 0.05 inch, which is not compatible with a breadboard or perforated prototyping boards, which use 0.1 inch spacing. In Figure 2-20, you can see two standard Xbee radios (Sparkfun.com part# WRL-08665), a Sparkfun Xbee Explorer Regulated breakout board (Sparkfun.com part# WRL-09132) to connect to the Arduino, and a Sparkfun Xbee Explorer USB breakout board (Sparkfun.com part# WRL-08687) for connecting to your computer. The makers of the Xbee radios have also created a software program called X-CTU, which is used to change settings on the Xbee radios while connected to your computer—the X-CTU software is free to use, but currently works only in Windows.

# Sensor Navigation

Although creating a control link that converts user input into robotic output can be extremely useful, there are some tasks that require the robot to make decisions of its own without consulting a human. The first three robotic projects in this book (chapters 4, 5, and 7) use some type of external awareness to direct the robot to its destination without using any user guidance.

Believe it or not, you are actually an autonomous (self-controlled) being that uses several different "sensors" to help determine the environment around you. Your eyes, ears, nose, hands, and mouth each have their own sensation that your brain can interpret into some form of intelligence. From these sensors, your brain is able to make informed decisions about how your body should proceed and keep you safe from harm. Along the same lines, a robotic sensor is a device that is attached to a robot to gather information about its surrounding area. Without sensors, the robot would not have any way of knowing what is around it or how to proceed. This is the easiest way to add intelligence to your bot.

There are many types of sensors and each reads the environment differently, so it is common to add several types of sensors to one robot to effectively navigate around obstacles and gather important information. A sensor can measure light, distance, proximity, heat, gas, acceleration, angle, humidity and moisture, contact, and rotational position (among others). We focus on the sensors that are readily available and offer the most versatility for the price.

# Contact Sensing

The most simple type of sensor that can be implemented is the contact switch, which simply tells the robot whether or not it is touching something. This type of sensor is commonly called a "bump-switch" and is used on the iRobot Roomba robotic vacuum cleaner to determine when it has bumped into a wall or other object. The main caveat of this sensor type is that it requires the robot to make physical contact with an object before it is detected.

# Bump Switch

The bump switch is a simple form of sensor because it consists of as few as two electrical contacts (see Figure 2-21). If the contacts are touching, the switch is closed; otherwise, it is open. We use this form of switch as a method of telling the robot when it has run into something. If we place them at several spots on the bot, we not only know when the bot has bumped into something, we can also determine the best direction to travel to keep from hitting the same objects again.

This type of sensor is also useful as an over-travel switch. These are commonly installed on garage-door openers. When the door opens to a certain point, it touches the over-travel switch and the main board receives a command to stop the lifting motor. This is how it knows where to turn it off.

*Figure 2-21. A typical tactile bump-switch with lever*

This type of sensor (or any switch) is read as a digital input using the digitalRead() command (see Listing 1-1 in Chapter 1).

# Distance and Reflection Sensing

Range detection is useful when trying to determine whether an object is near without the robot having to touch it. A good range detector can calculate the distance from an object with accuracy down to the nearest inch. Range detection sensors use reflected sound or light waves to measure the distance between the sensor and any obstacle within range. Different range detection methods result in different effective ranges, accuracy, and prices. Range detection sensors can have an effective sensing range from 1 centimeter to 25 feet and cost anywhere from just a few dollars for an IR range finder to several thousand dollars for a Laser range finder. We use infrared detection for Linus in Chapter 4 and ultrasonic range finders on Wally in Chapter 7.

## IR Sensor

IR detectors use an infrared emitter to send out IR light "packets" and a detector to check for reflections of that light that have bounced off any nearby objects. By measuring the amount of time that the light takes to return to the detector, the sensor can determine the distance from that object. IR finders can detect objects at distances up to 5 feet away—use an ultrasonic range finder for farther distances. The Sharp GP2 series of infrared proximity sensors are available at Sparkfun.com (part# SEN-08958) for under $15 and can be used for short-range object detection up to 5 feet (see Figure 2-22).

*Figure 2-22. This is the Sharp GP2 IR finder (Sparkfun.com part# SEN-08958).*

A simple infrared emitter and detector pair can be used at close ranges (under 3 inches) to determine the approximate reflectivity of a surface to infrared light. These simple IR emitter and detector pairs are the basis for the line-following robot in Chapter 4. The emitter and detector are mounted side by side and facing the same direction. The emitter is constantly sending a stream of infrared light toward the ground, whereas the detector is constantly reading the reflections of the light that is bouncing off the ground.

We use a piece of reflective tape as a guidance track for the bot to follow. As the bot moves away from the reflective tape, the IR sensors on each side begin to receive less IR light and therefore adjust the motor outputs to keep the bot centered on the tape. Using this simple guidance scheme, we can easily modify the path that the bot will follow by altering the path of the reflective tape. There are several different types of infrared emitter and photo-transistor packages that work for a line-following robot (see Figure 2-23).

*Figure 2-23. These are three different types of infrared emitter and detector pairs. The IR pair on the far right is the type used in Linus, the line-following robot from Chapter 4. These sensors range in price from $1 to $3 each from Digikey.com.*

■ **Note** Many household appliances that use a remote control contain a useful IR receiver like the one you can find at Radio Shack or Digikey. If you happen to have a broken VCR, DVD player, TV, or stereo that you don't mind dismantling, you can de-solder the IR sensor from the PCB and save a few bucks. They typically only have three pins: +5v, GND, and Signal.

## Ultrasonic Range Finder

The ultrasonic range finder uses high frequency sound waves that are reflected off nearby objects to calculate their distance. Some ultrasonic sensors require a microprocessor to both send and receive a signal from the sensor, whereas other sensors calculate the distance within the sensor and have a proportional output signal that is easily read by the Arduino.

Ultrasonic range finders are available in a variety of beam angles that determines the width of the detectable area. A narrow beam angle is better suited to detect objects farther away, whereas a broad beam angle better detects objects at short distances. These sensors are typically between $30–50 and can be easily read by the Arduino.

The Maxbotix brand of ultrasonic range finders have built-in processing that enables it to output independent serial, analog, and PWM signals at the same time to increase interfacing flexibility (see Figure 2-24). These range finders accurately measure distances from about 6 inches to 25 feet, and are well suited for obstacle avoidance and detection on robots. I prefer to use this brand of ultrasonic range finder because it is reliable and easy to interface to the Arduino using any of the three built-in output signals.

*Figure 2-24. The MaxBotix LV-EZ0 ultrasonic range finder with an effective range of 6 inches to 25 feet (Sparkfun.com part# SEN-08502)*

## Laser Range Finder

This type of range finder uses a laser to scan the objects around it, much like a laser scanner at the grocery store checkout. A laser range finder can have a viewing angle of up to 240 degrees, giving it a much wider view of its surroundings than other sensors. Each time the laser makes a rotation, it takes distance readings at set intervals. When the rotation is complete, the signal is compiled to create a snapshot of the surrounding area. Although this sensor has advanced features, the maximum detection range is around 15 feet and they are expensive (usually costing around $1,000). Until the price comes down a bit, we won't test any of these units.

## Orientation (Positioning)

There are several different sensors that can determine one or more aspects of a robot's position or orientation. A GPS sensor can tell you where the sensor is on a map using latitude and longitude coordinates, whereas an accelerometer and gyroscope can tell you the angular position (tilt) or rotational speed of your robot. Using these sensors, we can create an auto-leveling platform for a Segway type robot or upload a set of GPS coordinates for a robot to navigate to.

### Accelerometer

An accelerometer measures gravitational force or acceleration. By tilting an accelerometer along its measured axis, we can read the gravitational force relative to the amount of tilt. Accelerometers are available with up to three axis of sensing and can be directly interfaced to the Arduino with an Analog output signal. Many devices currently use accelerometers for input control, shock detection, stabilization platforms, and auto-leveling or tilt interfaces—you can find these devices inside of digital cameras, cell phones, laptop computers, and Nintendo Wii controllers to name a few.

Most accelerometers available today are small surface mount components, but there are many different breakout boards that have the sensor and all necessary filtering components (resistors and capacitors) soldered into place, so you can easily interface them to an Arduino. Sparkfun.com has a large selection of these "Arduino-ready" sensor boards in different configurations ranging from $20 to $50.

There are three axes that can be measured by an accelerometer and they are labeled X, Y, and Z, which correspond to the roll, pitch, and yaw respectively (see Figure 2-25). A single axis accelerometer measures either the X or Y axis, a dual axis accelerometer measures both X and Y axes, and a triple axis accelerometer measures all three axes. Each measured axis represents a separate Degree of Freedom (DOF) from the sensor—thus a triple axis accelerometer might be labeled as 3 DOF.

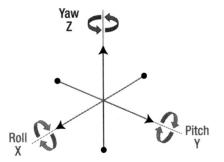

*Figure 2-25. This figure shows the three axes of rotation: roll, pitch, and yaw with their corresponding accelerometer symbols X, Y, and Z.*

Accelerometers are used for measuring gravitational changes, but they are also extremely sensitive to vibrations and sudden movements or shocks, which can cause the output signal to become distorted.

If an accelerometer is used for angle approximation, it is helpful to have another device that can correct for its short-term errors caused by vibrations. A "gyroscope" sensor can measure angular changes, but using a different method that is less susceptible to sudden gravitational changes.

## Gyroscope

A gyroscope is a sensor that is used to detect changes in rotational speed along its measured axis. These devices are often used in conjunction with accelerometers to produce a stable angle approximation of a robot for auto-leveling projects. Like an accelerometer, gyroscopes are also labeled by what axis they measure: X, Y, or Z.

Gyroscopes take excellent measurements in the short term, but suffer from a long-term mechanical error called "drift" that leads them away from their starting point, even without moving. To correct this drift, we need to use an accelerometer with a stable long-term angle reading to use as a reference point for the gyroscope.

## Inertial Measurement Unit (IMU)

To get around the hassle of buying a separate accelerometer and gyroscope, manufacturers combine multiple accelerometers and gyroscopes on the same circuit board to save space and cost. A circuit board that incorporates multiple sensors that are physically aligned with each other is called an inertial measurement unit (or IMU). The IMU shown in Figure 2-26 has two gyroscopes and one accelerometer to measure a total of six axes. By combining the readings from the accelerometer X axis and the gyroscope X axis, we can create a filtered angle measurement for a single axis auto-leveling platform in Chapter 11.

*Figure 2-26. This is the Sparkfun Razor 6 DOF inertial measurement unit (part# SEN-10010) used in Chapter 11. This IMU contains two gyroscopes and one accelerometer that together provide six separately measured aspects of the IMUs orientation.*

Sparkfun.com has an excellent tutorial/buying guide for accelerometers, gyroscopes, and IMUs, explaining their features and capabilities. If you are interested in learning more about these sensors, it is definitely worth reading:

Sparkfun.com IMU tutorial: http://www.sparkfun.com/tutorials/167

# Global Positioning Satellite (GPS)

Global Positioning Satellite (GPS) systems are sensors that use the signals from multiple tracking satellites in space to calculate its own position, and then outputs a specific set of latitude and longitude coordinates. The GPS sensor must be able to pick up at least three GPS satellite signals to determine its own position, though most connect to as many as 20 satellites at a time to get the best signal. The sensor itself can be purchased from $50–$150 and provides position, time, and speed detection. Most units need only a power and ground signal to begin outputting a serial data stream, which can be read by the Arduino.

The signal output by the EM406 GPS sensor (shown in Figure 2-27) is a NMEA standard string that must be decoded to obtain the valuable information like the latitude, longitude, speed, and direction. This signal is transmitted through a standard Serial connection to the Arduino and can be used in conjunction with other sensors to autonomously guide a robot from one point to another. Although a GPS can provide information about the speed and direction of your bot, it must be moving to calculate these values. By simply taking the difference between two position readings, we can determine what direction the bot is traveling and adjust its power accordingly to steer it to the correct ending coordinates.

***Figure 2-27.*** *The EM406 GPS sensor from Sparkfun.com (part# GPS-00465) can be connected directly to the Arduino to create an autonomously navigating vehicle (like the Robo-boat in Chapter 9).*

GPS is unique in that the satellites can be accessed from almost anywhere in the world, but because the satellites that it connects to are in space (really long way away!), the ground-level accuracy can vary from 10–30 feet. This means that you can't expect your bot to stop at the same spot each time using only standard GPS guidance. Your robot might end up 10 feet away from where you intended and its path might vary a few feet from your expectations. GPS also cannot detect movable objects or trees that might be in its path, so if your robot is to travel on the ground, it is a good idea to have other object detecting sensors installed to assist the GPS guidance (like ultrasonic range finders or bump sensors).

## Real Time Kinetic (RTK) GPS

To eliminate the gap in accuracy from a standard GPS system, there is a system called Real Time Kinetic (RTK) GPS, which uses a separate "base station" with a known position to calculate the exact position of the GPS receiver down to 1 centimeter! This type of GPS typically requires more setup to get it running, placing it above the scope of this book. If you need 1 centimeter accuracy from a GPS unit, it is possible.

# Non-Autonomous Sensors

Some sensors are not used for autonomous control, but rather to enable a user to do things not otherwise possible. A wireless camera for instance can enable a robot operator to be in one location, while the robot is operated in a different location. You can also use ultrasonic range finders, bump sensors, GPS positioning, temperature sensors, or hardware monitoring devices to assist your operation of the bot.

In Chapter 8, we build a dual motor-controller for a large mobile robot that has built-in current sensors installed to monitor the amount of power going through the controller. If the amperage exceeds a level that is pre-defined in the code, the Arduino immediately shuts down power to the motors (for a few seconds) to prevent overheating. This type of protection is essential for any robot that will have an unknown workload. Having your robot stop responding for a few seconds to cool down is better than it getting overheated and failing (requiring repair).

## Camera

By far the most instantly rewarding sensor to put on your bot is the wireless camera. There are several systems for under $100 that include both the wireless color camera (with audio) and the receiver that plugs into a TV, computer, or a small LCD monitor mounted to your R/C transmitter. These systems are commonly built on either a 900MHz or 2.4GHz radio link that can transmit a video signal anywhere from 300–800 feet depending on the strength of the radio and obstructions between the transmitter and receiver.

You can use a 2.4GHz wireless camera (see Figure 2-28) with a microphone to transmit an audio and video signal from your bot to a command station where you watch and control. This keeps you safe while the bot goes where you need it to. Again, this sensor is best utilized with other types of sensors to notify the robot if it has hit something or if it is approaching an object that the camera cannot see.

*Figure 2-28. This 2.4GHz wireless camera from Sparkfun.com (part# WRL-09189) is an excellent way to add a remote set of eyes and ears to your robot for about $75.*

## Current Sensor

A current sensor is used to measure the amperage passing a given point at a given time. If either motor draws an excess amount of current, we can program the Arduino (which controls the motor-controller) to stop driving that motor for a specified amount of time (1–2 seconds) to keep from overheating. By protecting the motor-controller, it is far less likely to fail.

There are several types of current sensors, but I prefer to use a current sensor IC, like the ACS-712 (5 amp) or ACS-714 (30 amp) from Allegro MicroSystems (Figure 2-29). Although only available as an 8-SOIC (Small Outline IC) surface mount package, it is easily interfaced to both the Arduino and a motor. The IC only needs +5v and GND signals to begin outputting an analog voltage at the VOUT pin, which is easily read using the Arduino on any analog input pin—you can even use the Arduino regulated +5v supply to power the current sensor IC.

*Figure 2-29. The ACS-712 bi-directional current sensor can be used in series with one of the load terminals to measure the amperage level. It can easily be read using an Analog input on the Arduino.*

In Figure 2-30, you can see a simple schematic depicting how you might connect the ACS714 current sensor to your Arduino. The current sensor IC needs a 5v power supply and a bypass capacitor connected from the filter pin to GND. You must then route at least one of the motor supply wires through the current sense pins of the sensor (as shown in Figure 2-30).

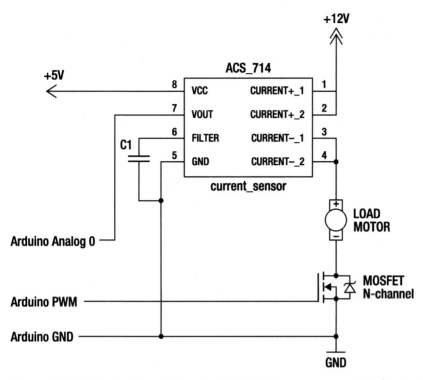

***Figure 2-30.*** *A simple schematic for the ACS-712/714 current sensor IC in a circuit*

In Chapter 8: The Explorer-Bot, we use the ACS-714 bi-directional 30-amp current sensor (big brother to the ACS-712 shown in Figure 2-29) to sense the current passing through either drive motor. Using the Arduino to monitor the analog output voltage of the current sensor, we can tell the Arduino to stop sending motor commands if the reading from the current sensor is above a certain level—this is called "over-current" protection and can keep a motor-controller from destroying itself.

# Summary

This chapter briefly discussed the various interfacing and control methods that are used in this book, as well as some of the different sensors.

Relays are reliable and easy to interface, but produce Back-EMF and must use a protection diode to drive directly from the Arduino. Transistors are available in several forms and can be driven directly by the Arduino, but must be specifically placed as either a high-side or low-side switch. ESCs are available for those who do not want to build their own circuits, but typically cost more to buy than building a similar motor-controller using transistors or relays.

We then talked about some various control methods using both wired and wireless links, including infrared controllers and radio control. Radio control is implemented using a variety of different methods, the most common of which is 2.4GHz. We use 2.4GHz hobby radio control systems and Xbee wireless serial links to both control and monitor robotic functions. Wireless radio control is used on the Explorer-bot, Lawnbot, and Battle-bot projects in this book.

Lastly, we explored some of the sensor types to create an autonomous (self-guided) robot. We use contact switches on the Bug-bot, infrared detectors on the Line-bot, ultrasonic sensors on the Wall-bot, and GPS on the Robo-boat to guide these four bots around their course without any user input. Sensors can also be used to assist a human for easier or improved control, as with the Explorer-bot or the Seg-bot.

In the next chapter, we discuss the various types of electric motors, batteries, and wheels that are popularly used in robotics.

# CHAPTER 3

# Let's Get Moving

At this point, you are probably sick of blinking LEDs and want to use your Arduino to start driving some motors, right? Well, this chapter discusses some of the important robotic parts that we must use in order to get an Arduino robot moving. First we start with the various types and applications of electric motors, then we discuss the circuits that make them move. Lastly this chapter includes a brief description of the materials that we need to use to complete the projects in this book.

## Electric Motors

There are many different types of robots that have different levels of intelligence and mobility, but the common thread that you will find in almost every robot is a motor of some kind. An electric motor is used to convert electrical heat into rotational motion using a carefully arranged set of magnets and coil windings. By energizing the magnets with electricity, the coil winding spins—a motor typically has an output shaft attached to this magnet, so you can mount a wheel or gear on the end.

A motor has several ratings such as speed (RPM), voltage, amperage, and total power. We can usually determine whether or not a motor will suit our particular needs by combining the specifications that are important to our project. The speed in RPM of the motor gives us an idea of how fast it will be able to move, the voltage determines its potential power, and the watt rating tells us what combination of voltage and amperage we can use to power the motor without overheating it.

This book focuses on mobile robotics, so only DC power sources are used. Although AC motors are useful (washing machines, air conditioning equipment, kitchen appliances, power tools, and so on), they are most efficiently operated when plugged into an appropriate AC power source. Because we use DC batteries for all of our bots, we use only motors that use DC power (though there are several types— see Figure 3-1).

*Figure 3-1. DC motors come in all shapes and sizes. The large motor is made for an electric scooter, the 2 in the center are small hobby motors, and the 2 on the right are DC servo motors.*

Each different type of DC motor is used for a specific range of applications, though they can also be manipulated for use in a variety of different robotic tasks. The simplest of electric motors is the standard brushed DC motor, which is commonly used for high-speed applications, or high torque when gearing is used. Brushed DC motors are not only used in many of the projects in this book, but they are also commonly used in gear motors and servo motors.

There are also DC motors that do not have brushes, but operate by constantly changing the electro-magnetic field around the output shaft using a special driving sequence. Both stepper motors and brushless DC (BLDC) motors use this concept and typically have between three and six wires for operation. These types of motors cannot be driven directly by a constant power source; they instead require the use of a series of amplifiers and a micro-controller input signal.

## Brushed DC Motor (Permanent Magnet Type)

The Permanent Magnet Direct Current (PMDC) motor, commonly known as just a brushed DC motor, is used in electronic devices, robotics, and toys (see Figure 3-1). The typical DC motor has only one motor coil with two wires for operation. This is by far the easiest type of motor to drive, control, and manipulate. You can also reverse the rotational direction of a DC motor output shaft by reversing the polarity of the voltage to the motor terminals.

Most DC motors have brushes that physically touch a set of spinning electrical contacts, called *commutators* that are electrically connected to the motor coil winding. When each brush touches a different commutator, the electrical current is passed through the motor coil, which forces the motor output shaft to spin about its axis. Permanent Magnet DC motors typically have two magnets attached to the inside of the motor casing and the coil winding and commutator mounted to the output shaft—the brushes are typically spring loaded to keep them securely mated to the commutator contacts while spinning (see Figure 3-2).

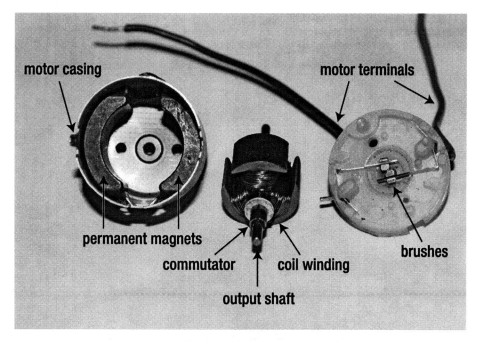

*Figure 3-2. A typical DC motor disassembled for viewing. The inside of the motor casing (left) has two permanent magnets attached and a hole for the output shaft to come through. The coil winding (center) is wrapped around the commutator, which is mounted to the output shaft. The brushes (right) are attached to the ends of the motor terminals, which are mounted to the motor's plastic end cap.*

A DC motor consumes as much power as it needs at a given voltage and consumes more (current) as its workload increases. A typical DC motor draws anywhere from 50mA to 50 amps of current and have speeds ranging from 1,000RPM to 20,000RPM. Using gears, we can transform the available power of a motor from high-speed, low-torque (ideal for flat grounds) into low-speed, high-torque (ideal for hills), or vice versa, which can extend the usability of the motor's power.

Because brushed DC motors use physical contact to transfer power from the motor terminals through the coil, periodic changing of the motor brushes is necessary for frequently used motors. Many DC motors have easily accessible brushes that can be replaced in a matter of minutes.

## Brushless Motors

A brushless DC (BLDC) motor uses an electro-magnetic field created by energizing one of three common motor coils in sequence in order to spin the output shaft. The fact that there are no brushes means that these motors have a longer life cycle and higher reliability, giving them an advantage over the standard brushed DC motor. Because of their abnormal coil setup, they cannot be operated with the same simplicity of a standard brushed DC motor, and instead must use a specialized three-phase driver circuit.

Hobby grade BLDC motors are rated by how many RPMs they produce per volt that is present at the motor terminals, denoted "Kv". For instance, a brushless motor with a 1000Kv rating operated at 12 volts, produces 12,000RPM (12 volts × 1000Kv = 12,000RPM). These motors are commonly used to replace brushed DC motors where longevity and reliability are preferred over being easy to drive and inexpensive. They have almost completely replaced DC motors for use in computer hard drives, cooling fans, and CD/DVD ROM drives (see Figure 3-3). We use a brushless DC motor to power the Robo-boat in Chapter 9.

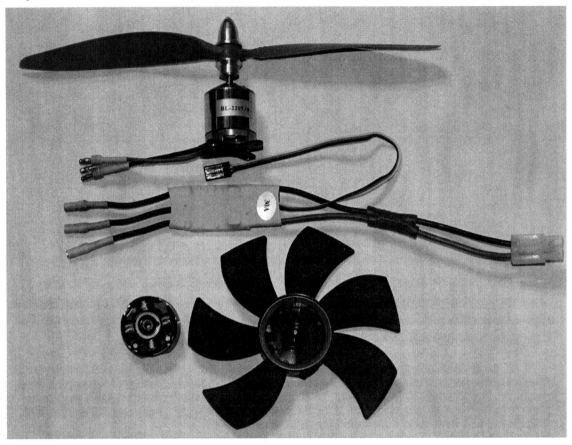

*Figure 3-3. Brushless DC motors are commonly used for PC cooling fans and hobby airplanes. The brushless PC fan in this picture was dismantled due to a broken fan blade. You can also see the brushless DC hobby airplane motor with a BLDC 30A motor controller.*

## Stepper Motors

Stepper motors are brushless DC motors that have two or more independent coils instead of three common coils like a BLDC motor. These coils must be energized at set intervals to keep the motor shaft spinning, much like the BLDC motor. This means that you cannot simply apply power to the wires and watch the motor spin. These motors must be driven using a special sequence and timing provided by the Arduino.

Stepper motors have a defined number of steps or magnetic intervals; each time a coil is switched in sequence, the motor shaft rotates one step. The number of degrees per step determines how many steps are in each rotation of the output shaft. The more steps the motor is capable of, the higher the resolution or more precision it has. This is common with Computer Numeric Controlled (CNC) machines that use two or more stepper motors to control the exact X and Y coordinates of the machine head—they can return to any exact spot on the grid by counting the X and Y steps to that position.

Stepper motors are available in the following two basic types:

- *Bipolar.* These stepper motors have two coils that are typically identified by having exactly four wires (see Figure 3-4). Each set of wires is connected to a motor coil and can be identified by measuring the coil resistance with a multi-meter. Each coil in the stepper motor must be switched in a special sequence in order to turn the output shaft—requiring that each of the four motor wires must be driven by its own signal amplifier to operate the motor (or a dual motor-controller).

- *Unipolar.* These stepper motors also have two coils, but they additionally have two windings in each coil—so this motor has three wires per coil (x2), totaling six wires. You can usually connect the two common wires from each coil together, resulting in a five-wire motor—some motors have this already done internally. This motor has a constant positive power supply to the common wire from each coil and an N-type transistor switch at each of the negative coil wires. With the appropriate switching sequence from the Arduino, this type of stepper motor is easy to drive.

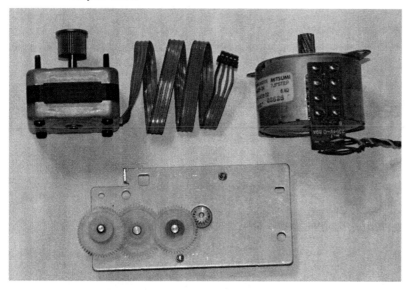

*Figure 3-4. A few bipolar stepper motors, noted as having four wires on each motor*

Stepper motors are commonly used for high-precision applications like computer printer heads, CNC machines, and some robotic applications.

# Gear Motors

The power of a motor at a given energy can be arranged to have either high speed or high torque. Think of an 18-speed mountain bike to visualize how this works: If you put the bike in first gear, your pedaling will provide a high torque that can enable you to ride up a steep hill with ease at the expense of going slowly. If you put the bike in eighteenth gear, it will be nearly impossible to pedal up a steep hill but will yield excellent speed on flat ground or going downhill.

The power produced by an electric motor can be manipulated in the same way. To convert the power, we must use a series of gears connected to the motor's output shaft or buy a motor with gears built onto the output shaft, called a *gear-motor*. A gear motor reduces the speed of the motor output shaft from its normally high speed (1,000–20,000RPM) to a slower output speed that is more manageable for a mobile robot (see Figure 3-5).

*Figure 3-5. Here you can see a small DC gear motor (left) and again with the DC motor removed from the plastic gear box.*

A gear motor can be any type of electric motor, as long as it has a gear box that reduces the output speed of the motor shaft. Each gear motor should have what a *gear ratio* that specifies the ratio of input speed to output speed of the motor output shaft. For instance, a gear motor with a 100:1 gear ratio implies that the actual DC motor output shaft must spin 100 times to make the geared output shaft complete one revolution.

# Servo Motors

A servo motor is a special type of DC motor that uses an encoder to determine the position of the output shaft. Hobby servo motors consist of a small DC motor, speed-reducing gear box, potentiometer shaft encoder, and motor drive circuitry, making them easy to interface directly to the Arduino (see Figure 3-6). The motor drive circuitry is not only used to decode the input signal (R/C servo pulse), but also to drive the DC motor.

These motors can move to a specific position quickly and require only three wires to interface with the Arduino (signal, power, and ground). The signal used to operate the servo is a precisely timed pulse of electricity that ranges from 1 milliseconds to 2 milliseconds – where a 1.5mS pulse yields the center position of the servo motor. The servo motor looks for an update with a new pulse about 50 times per second, or every 20 milliseconds.

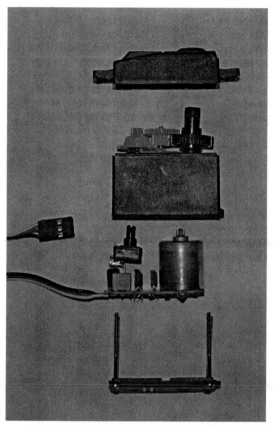

*Figure 3-6. A dismantled view of the larger Servo motor from Figure 3-1 reveals the gears, potentiometer, circuit board, and DC motor that are normally packed inside the plastic casing.*

These motors are intended for use in hobby cars, planes, boats, and helicopters, but have made their way into robotics for their precision, durability, and ease of use. You can find a general-purpose servo motor at your local hobby store for around $15 or at several online retailers for around $5 each.

Hobby servo motors were designed to emulate the position of an R/C transmitter control stick. If the control stick is moved to its upward most position, the servo motor output shaft will likewise move 90 degrees in one direction. If the control stick is moved to its downward most position, the servo motor output shaft will move 90 degrees in the other direction. The total range of most hobby servo motors is about 180 degrees total (1/2 of a complete rotation). Trying to make the output shaft move any farther than its stopping point will likely result in a stripped gear.

## Continuous Rotation

It is true that the output shaft of most hobby servo motors can rotate only from 0–180 degrees—but by hacking the internal components of the servo, we can alter its operation to rotate continuously like a normal gear-motor. To do this, we simply disconnect the shaft encoder (potentiometer) and place a resistor divider in its place (a pair of resistors connected together), which tells the controller board that the motor is at the center position at all times. If any pulse signal above 1.5ms is received, it will move the motor forward continuously—likewise if the pulse is below 1.5ms, it will spin in reverse. This can give us the ability to control either forward or reverse continuous rotation of a servo motor.

You can also modify a hobby servo motor to operate as a standard DC gear motor (as in the Chapter 4) by completely removing the servo control circuitry and building your own. This method requires removing the potentiometer and all the electronic components, leaving only the two wires from the DC motor itself and all of the gearing. If there are any plastic stops that keep the output shaft from rotating completely, they should be removed as well. This enables you to drive the motor with full-speed control using a simple transistor amplifier.

## Linear Actuators

A linear actuator is an electric DC motor that converts rotational motion into a linear motion. This is usually accomplished using an Acme threaded rod or other screw drive mechanism. These motors are useful for vertically lifting loads or moving an object back and forth (like a steering wheel). These can be used to automatically open a door or gate, raise/lower a hinged load, or move an object back and forth (see Figure 3-7).

*Figure 3-7. Linear actuator motor from a power wheelchair, used adjust the incline of the seat*

The stroke of a linear actuator refers to the maximum distance it can extend. The speed of the actuator tells you how fast it will travel, usually rated in inches/second. The power of the actuator is determined by the power rating of the motor that is driving it and is usually rated by the maximum load capacity in pounds that the actuator can lift. It is typically fine to use a relay to control a linear actuator for simple On/Off control, unless you need extremely precise control in which case you should use a motor-controller.

## Calculating Power

Because the amperage of a motor varies depending on the load, most DC motors list the voltage level at which it can safely operate. Although DC motors are usually forgiving and can be slightly over-powered without causing problems, an excess voltage level can burn up the motor coil.

As discussed in Chapter 1, the amperage that is consumed by a motor is dependent on the voltage level and the internal resistance of the motors coil. After the operating voltage is decided, you can measure the motor's coil to determine its resistance, and lastly use the voltage and resistance to calculate the amperage of the motor. With the amperage and voltage known, you can select a properly sized motor-controller for the motor.

## Driving

The DC motor is the simplest motor to power; apply a positive signal to one wire and a negative signal to the other and your motor should move, as shown in Figure 3-8. If you swap the polarity of the wires, the motor will spin in the opposite direction.

The speed of the motor is dependent on the positive supply voltage level—the higher the voltage, the faster the motor shaft spins. The power of the motor is its capability to maintain its speed, even under a load and that is determined by the amperage available from the power source—as the workload of the motor increases, more amperage is drawn from the batteries.

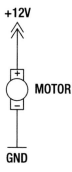

*Figure 3-8. To power a DC motor, simply connect one wire to the Positive supply and the other wire to the Negative supply.*

Some of our robots have powerful motors that can operate at up to 24vdc—if the entire 24 volts is applied to the motor all at once, it is likely to spin the tires or pop a wheelie! We don't want to break any of our equipment or hit anyone nearby because our bot launches when we turn the motors on, so we will use a motor-controller to vary the voltage to the motor from 0v to the power supply voltage (in most cases, 6v, 12v, or 24v). This enables the bot to start slowly and work its way up to full speed, which causes less strain on the batteries during start-up and provides more precise control.

We can vary the voltage level to the motors by using a pulse-width modulation PWM signal to determine the output duty-cycle, or percentage of On time. Because using PWM means that the output is either fully on or fully off, the motors receive as much amperage as the power supply allows for the given duty-cycle, and the power can be varied from 0% to 100% for full speed control.

## Finding the Right Motor

DC motors are in virtually any device that has moving parts—you can harvest useful DC motors from old cassette tape players, VCRs, toys, and cordless tools. Salvaging a DC motor is usually easy because they are rarely ever soldered to a printed circuit board (PCB), so you simply unplug the wires and remove any fasteners that are holding the motor in place. If the wires are soldered into place, just cut them leaving as much wire connected to the motor as possible (unless you plan on soldering your own wires to the motor terminals). Once removed, you can test the motor by powering it with a 6v or 12v battery (depending on its size).

As previously mentioned, gear-motors reduce the speed of a motor shaft to a usable RPM for driving a robot. When salvaging parts, you might come across a motor assembly that has plastic or metal reducing gears attached to the motor; you can re-use these gears and create your own makeshift gear-motor. Gear-motors and gear assemblies can also be found at surplus and commercial websites.

Surplus:

- www.allelectronics.com

- www.goldmine-elec.com

- www.alltronics.com

Commercial:

- www.Sparkfun.com

- www.trossenrobotics.com

- www.pololu.com

- www.superdroidrobots.com

- www.robotmarketplace.com

You can find 12v automotive windshield-wiper motors at your local junkyard that can be used as drive motors for a medium-sized bot. You can also find powerful motors at your local thrift-store by looking for cordless drills that have bad battery packs or cosmetic blemishes, but working motors and gear boxes.

## The H-Bridge

When driving a DC motor in only one direction, we do not need any special circuitry to switch the motor on or off; a simple switch in series with one motor terminal will do. But to reverse the polarity of the voltage of the motor terminal, we need a *half-bridge* circuit or push-pull driver. This circuit uses two switches (S1 and S3 as shown in Figure 3-9) to provide a path from one motor terminal to either the Positive voltage supply or the Negative voltage supply (Ground). By using only one of these switches at a time, a short-circuit is avoided—the other motor terminal is permanently connected to either VIN or GND

## Half-Bridge Configurations (2 Switches)

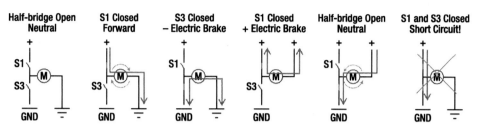

*Figure 3-9. Various half-bridge states*

The bridge is used to route the correct polarity to the motor terminals at the appropriate time. To avoid a short-circuit, you should *never* close both switches on the same side of the bridge (both the positive and negative) at the same time (see Figure 3-12). To control the polarity to both motor terminals, we need two identical half-bridges arranged in an H-bridge (see Figure 3-10).

### H-bridge with 4 switches

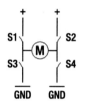

*Figure 3-10. Notice how the circuit looks like the letter "H," which is why they call it an H-bridge.*

For the motor to spin, the battery current must flow from the Positive supply, through the Motor, and to the Ground supply to complete the circuit. To make this happen we must open one switch from each side of the bridge, one Low-side and an opposite High-side—that means we can either turn on S1 and S4 to go Forward, or we can turn on S2 and S3 to go in Reverse. The direction of the current flow through the motor terminals determines the direction that the motor spins. We can manipulate the flow of the current by closing the two corresponding switches together to give us directional control of the motor. If all four switches are open (disconnected), the motor is *coasting*, meaning there is no path for the current to travel.

## Generating a Brake

There is also an acceptable condition called *electric-braking*, which refers to connecting both motor terminals to the same voltage supply—as opposed to leaving them disconnected. Because most DC motors act as a generator if you spin the motor shaft, by connecting both terminals to either the Positive supply or the Ground supply, we are essentially trying to force the generated electricity back into the same supply (see Figure 3-11). This results in the motor resisting to spin—that is, it will keep the motor shaft from moving by forcing opposing voltages into the same supply. We can tell the Arduino to keep both Low-side switches closed to form an electric brake when the bot is in Neutral to make sure it does not roll down a hill or move without being commanded. Alternatively, if all switches are left open in Neutral (coasting), there will be no resistance to the motor generating electricity—so if it is on a hill, it will roll.

### Full-Bridge Configurations (4 Switches)

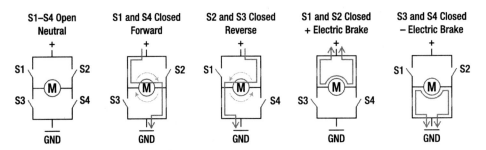

*Figure 3-11. Acceptable H-bridge states*

### Shoot-Through Conditions
### NOT OK!

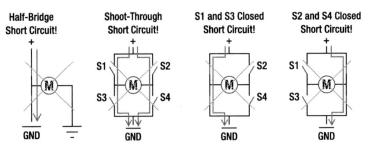

*Figure 3-12. Shoot-through H-bridge states—bad!*

## Implementation

To create an H-bridge circuit, we simply need four switches—two of the switches must control the path of the current from the positive supply to each motor terminal, and the other two must control the path of the current from the negative supply to each motor terminal. These switches are labeled as S1, S2, S3, and S4 in the illustrations. We can use any type of switch that we want in the H-bridge, depending on our application. Relay switches work fine for single speed (On/Off) operation, whereas bipolar transistors or mosfets are more appropriate for full-speed control using PWM.

If you are making a smaller H-bridge with BJT transistors, you should include protection diodes from the drain to source of each transistor to protect them from Back EMF. Mosfets have built-in "body diodes" that are capable of handling the same voltages and amperage as the mosfet itself, so these are usually safe to interface directly to the Arduino.

There are four different homemade approaches to building an H-bridge circuit that we discuss, each with their own benefits and drawbacks. We start with the most simple implementation and progress to the most complex.

## Method 1: Simple Switches

We can make a full H-bridge using (2) three-way (SPDT) switches from the hardware store, a DC motor, and a 9v battery. This simple bridge has built-in short-circuit protection so it cannot be commanded into a shoot-through state. It can, however, be placed into any acceptable H-bridge state: forward, reverse, electric brake (positive), electric brake (negative), or neutral. Each switch in the circuit has three positions, On/Off/On, and switches the center contact between the two outer contacts (or in this case, the positive and negative battery wires).

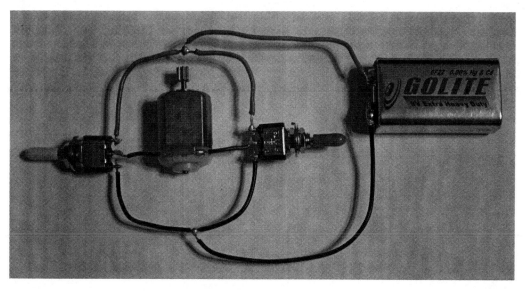

*Figure 3-13. Here you can see a basic H-bridge circuit using two SPDT switches, a DC motor, and a 9v battery. Notice how the top terminals of each switch share a common positive supply wire, while the bottom terminals share a common negative supply wire. The center terminals of each switch are used to route the power signals to the motor terminals.*

This method shows the simplicity of a basic H-bridge circuit, but does not provide speed control (it is either on or off). Although this might be a rugged circuit, its use is limited, so it is usually only good for testing and educational purposes.

## Method 2: DPDT Relay with Simple

This method is wired the same as Method 1, but we combine the two SPDT switches and use one DPDT Relay, so it can be controlled by the Arduino. Also we can use the Arduino to provide a simple PWM signal for speed control of the motor (see Figure 3-14). The simplest way to do this is to add a Logic-level N-channel mosfet (or several in parallel) to control the entire circuit's path to ground. By using a PWM signal on the Ground supply to the H-bridge (Relay), we can control the speed of the motor from 0–100%, whereas the relay switches the motor's direction. The relay acts as both the High-side and Low-side switches in the bridge, so there are actually two low-side switches in this configuration—the relay used to route the power terminals and the N-channel mosfet used to provide the PWM speed control.

This provides complete 0–100% speed control and requires as few as four parts other than the relay: (2) logic level N-channel mosfets, (1) diode (for relay coil), and (1) small prototyping PCB (or you can make your own). Depending on the mosfet, you can expect to carry about 10 amperes at 24vdc with no heatsink or fan; an n-channel logic-level mosfet can be found at Digikey.com for between $0.50–$5.00 each and with an amperage rating from 100mA–200amps. I usually select power mosfets with the highest amperage rating in my price range (anything above 75 amps), a higher voltage rating than I plan to use in my project (usually 30v–55v is good), and the lowest possible on-state resistance (check the datasheet for Rds(On)).

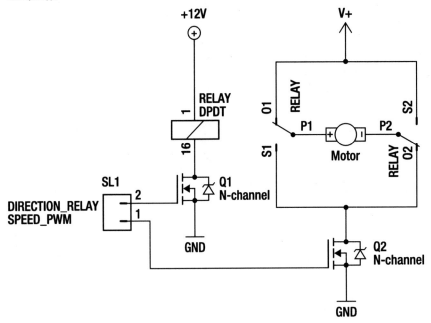

*Figure 3-14. A relay-based PWM speed control circuit*

We can build this circuit with (2) FQP50N06L N-channel mosfets from Digikey. One mosfet is needed to provide PWM speed control, and the other mosfet is needed to interface the relay coil to the Arduino for direction control.

The relay mosfet can be controlled by any Arduino digital output pin, whereas the speed control mosfet should be controlled by an Arduino PWM output. Next we connect the mosfet Drain pin to the Relay as shown in Figure 3-14, and the mosfet Source pin to the main Ground supply. The prototyping PCB makes this easier to put together and you can add screw-terminals for easy wiring. The voltage and current limits of this circuit are dependent on the mosfet and relay ratings, giving this circuit potential despite using a mechanical relay switch.

## Method 3: P-Channel and N-Channel Mosfets

Moving up, we have a basic solid-state H-bridge that uses P-channel mosfets for the high-side switches and n-channel mosfets for the low-side switches. This H-bridge has no internal protection against short-circuit, so you must be careful not to open both switches on the same side of the bridge because this will result in a shoot-through condition. This design can easily be implemented on a prototyping PCB as well as adding multiple mosfets in parallel to increase the current capacity. This H-bridge can be built using only two p-channel power mosfets, two n-channel power mosfets, two n-channel signal mosfets, and a few resistors (see Figure 3-15).

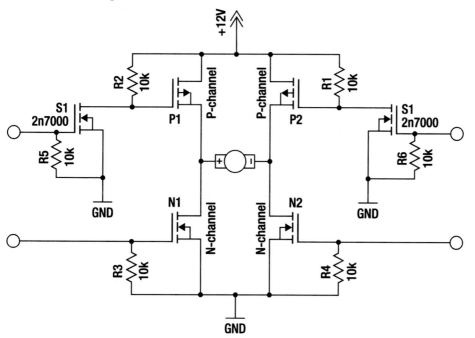

*Figure 3-15.* Notice the 10k pull-up resistors on the P-channel mosfets and the 10k pull-down resistors on the N-channel mosfets. This keeps the mosfets in the off state when not in use.

This method enables for a full solid-state circuit without using any mechanical switches or relays. If this circuit is operated within the voltage and current limits of the mosfets, it will easily outlast either of the previous methods. Even though this bridge is more complex than the previous two, it still has limitations; this design is not optimized for high PWM frequencies or high voltages, but costs little and is easy to build.

## Method 4: N-Channel H-Bridge

Most p-channel mosfets have higher Rds(On) values, lower amperage ratings, and higher prices than their n-channel counterparts, making it difficult to design a symmetrical H-bridge.

As you might recall, to turn on an n-channel mosfet (logic-level), the Gate pin must be 5v higher than the Source pin (usually Ground). By connecting an n-channel mosfet backward, we can get it to conduct as a high-side switch. To do this, we connect the mosfet Drain pin to the Positive voltage supply and the Source pin to the motor or load. The only catch is that we must now get the Gate pin to be at least 5v above the Positive supply voltage through boot-strapping.

So how do we make a voltage that is higher than the Positive supply voltage of the batteries? A charge pump is used to collect voltage through a diode and into a capacitor each time the PWM signal is cycled. This is called a *bootstrap circuit* and is effectively a simple voltage doubler used to provide the mosfet Gates with an elevated voltage level. There are several H-bridge driver ICs that include all of the circuitry needed for this operation and require only an external capacitor and diode. We use this type of driver chip to enable the Arduino to control each switch in the H-bridge individually. This type of H-bridge allows for high current capacity and fast PWM switching speeds, which are useful features for a robot motor-controller.

For more information about n-channel H-bridges and circuit diagrams, check out the Open Source Motor Controller (OSMC) project. You can download complete circuits and PCB files, ask questions, or design your own variation and submit your progress to share with the group.

```
http://www.robotpower.com/products/osmc_info.html
```

# H-Bridge ICs

To build your own H-bridge, but leave the designing to a professional, you might be interested in an H-bridge IC. An H-bridge IC is a complete H-bridge circuit that is contained on a tiny integrated circuit chip. These are usually fitted into a circuit with very few extra components, typically only a few resistors and a regulated power supply for the logic controls. When using an H-bridge IC, you can usually expect shoot-through protection, thermal overload protection, and high frequency capabilities. Although these H-bridge chips are far less likely to be destroyed by user error than a completely homemade design, they also have much lower power ratings than a homemade H-bridge, typically under 3amps of continuous current.

There are several H-bridge IC chips that include all four switches and a method of controlling them safely. The L293D is a Dual H-bridge IC that can handle up to 36 volts and 600 milliamp per motor. The L298N is a larger version of the L293D that can handle up to 2amps (see Figure 3-16). There are a few ICs that can control up to 25amps, but they are expensive and hard to find. There are several H-bridge ICs that work for some of the smaller projects in this book, but the larger bots require a higher powered H-bridge capable of conducting 10amps or more.

*Figure 3-16. Here is the popular L298N dual 2amp H-bridge motor-controller on a homemade PCB. The other components include a 7805 5v regulator, a few EMF protection diodes, a capacitor, and some direction LEDs. This board can be used to control the speed and direction of two independent DC motors.*

## Changing PWM Frequencies

We talked about how higher PWM frequencies eventually lead to switching losses and cross-conduction, so what is a good PWM frequency to use? If you leave your Arduino alone and don't change anything, the PWM outputs will run at 1kHz (pins 5 and 6) and 500Hz (pins 11, 3, 9, and 10). This is considered a relatively low PWM frequency for motor-controllers because at this frequency, there is an audible "whine" that you can hear from the motor coils being switched.

Because most motor-controllers can easily handle a 1kHz PWM signal, you might want to leave the Arduino at its default values. If however, you want your motors to be silent during operation, you must use a PWM frequency that is above the audible human-hearing range, typically around 24,000Hz (24kHz). A problem arises because some motor-controllers are not capable of switching at such high frequency—switching losses increase as the PWM frequency increases. Because it is a difficult design task, motor-controllers that can operate at silent switching speeds (24kHz or higher) are usually more expensive and well built.

The frequency of each PWM output pin on the Arduino is controlled by one of three system timers that are built into the Arduino. Think of each system timer in the Arduino as a digital metronome, that determines how many beats will be in each second. The value of each timer can be changed using one line of code and a specific setting selected from Table 3-1.

To change the frequency of a PWM pin, select an available frequency from Table 3-1 and replace the <setting> in the following code with the appropriate setting from the chart. Then add the following line of code into the setup() function of your sketch, depending on the timer you want to change:

```
TCCR0B = TCCR0B & 0b11111000 | <setting>; //Timer 0 (PWM pins 5 & 6)
TCCR1B = TCCR1B & 0b11111000 | <setting>; //Timer 1 (PWM pins 9 & 10)
TCCR2B = TCCR2B & 0b11111000 | <setting>; //Timer 2 (PWM pins 3 & 11)
```

*Table 3-1. Available PWM Frequency Settings for Each Arduino System Timer*

| Arduino Timer | <setting> | Divisor | Frequency (Hertz) |
|---|---|---|---|
| 0 (pins 5 and 6) | 0x01 | 1 | 62500 |
| 0 (pins 5 and 6) | 0x02 | 8 | 7812.5 |
| 0 (pins 5 and 6) | 0x03 | 64 | 976.56 |
| 0 (pins 5 and 6) | 0x04 | 256 | 244.14 |
| 0 (pins 5 and 6) | 0x05 | 1024 | 61.04 |
| 1 (pins 9 and 10) | 0x01 | 1 | 31250 |
| 1 (pins 9 and 10) | 0x02 | 8 | 3906.25 |
| 1 (pins 9 and 10) | 0x03 | 64 | 488.28 |
| 1 (pins 9 and 10) | 0x04 | 256 | 122.07 |
| 1 (pins 9 and 10) | 0x05 | 1024 | 30.52 |
| 2 (pins 3 and 11) | 0x01 | 1 | 31250 |
| 2 (pins 3 and 11) | 0x02 | 8 | 3906.25 |
| 2 (pins 3 and 11) | 0x03 | 32 | 976.56 |
| 2 (pins 3 and 11) | 0x04 | 64 | 488.28 |
| 2 (pins 3 and 11) | 0x05 | 128 | 244.14 |
| 2 (pins 3 and 11) | 0x06 | 256 | 122.07 |
| 2 (pins 3 and 11) | 0x07 | 1024 | 30.52 |

This tableTable 3-1 shows the available frequencies with their corresponding settings—you might notice that some frequencies are available only on certain timers, making each PWM pin unique. For example, to change the frequency on PWM pins 9 and 10 from the default 500Hz to an ultra-sonic switching speed of 32kHz, change the setting for system timer 1 in the setup() function, as shown in the following:

```
void setup(){
    TCCR1B = TCCR1B & 0b11111000 | 0x01;
}
```

By changing timer 1 to a setting of "0x01", PWM pins 9 and 10 will now operate at 32kHz frequency anytime the analogWrite() command is used on either pin. Alternatively, you can set these same PWM pins to operate at their lowest available frequency (30Hz) by changing the <setting> to "0x05".

If you operate the PWM output at a too low of a frequency (below 100Hz), it will significantly decrease the resolution of the control—that is, a small change in the input will cause a drastic change in output and changes will appear choppy and not smooth as they do at higher frequencies. If in doubt, simply stay with the Arduino default PWM frequencies because they are sufficient for most robotics projects, even if you can hear your motors.

---

▓ **Note** Changing the Arduino system timer 0 affects the output of certain Arduino timing functions that rely on timer 0, such as the delay(), millis(), and micros() functions.

---

## Back EMF

*Back Electro-Motive Force (Back EMF)* is the term used to describe the energy that must be disposed of when the electro-magnetic field of an inductor collapses. This collapse happens each time the motor is stopped or changes directions. If the voltage cannot escape through a rectifying diode, it can damage an unprotected transistor and possibly damage the Arduino pin that is driving it. A simple rectifier diode (1n4001) works for most relay coils and small BJT transistor-based H-bridges up to 1amp.

A protection diode should be placed between the motor terminal and the power supply. If using an H-bridge, a diode must be placed between each motor terminal and both the positive and negative power supply for a total of four diodes (see Figure 3-17). If you have an H-bridge that has no protection diodes, you can add the diodes directly onto the motor terminals as shown in Figure 3-18.

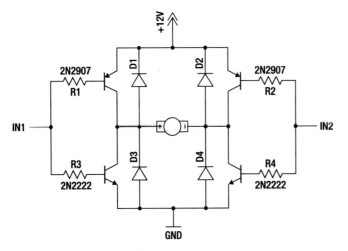

**Figure 3-17.** *Protection diodes should be placed around the switches to protect them from motor back EMF, D1–D4 in the image.*

**Figure 3-18.** *Notice this implementation of Back-EMF protection diodes, soldered directly onto the motor terminals—this alleviates the need for diodes built in to the motor-controller.*

# Current Sensing

Sometimes, the best way to protect a homemade H-bridge is to install a current-sensing device to monitor the level of amperage that is passing through the H-bridge. By reading the output of a current-sensor with the Arduino, we can send a stop command to each motor if the current level exceeds a given point. The over-current protection feature uses current sensing to disable the driver if the power reaches an unsafe level to protect it from overheating. Using this feature nearly eliminates user errors that can result in a destroyed motor-controller.

The simplest way to measure the amperage level in an H-bridge is to measure the voltage drop across a power resistor. This resistor must be placed in series with motor and the positive voltage supply, and the motor must be powered and running while you are measuring the voltage across the resistor (see Figure 3-19). Knowing the exact value of the resistor in ohms and the measured voltage across the resistor, we can use Ohm's law to calculate the amperage that is passing through the resistor, and therefore the circuit.

The only problem with this method is that the resistor creates heat in the process (wasting electricity). For this reason, it is ideal to pick the lowest value resistor possible (0.01–1 ohm) and it must have a power rating that is sufficient for the amount of current you will pass through it.

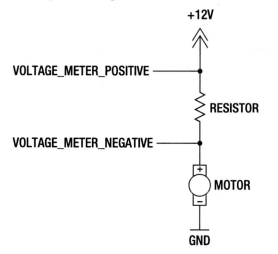

*Figure 3-19. By measuring the voltage across a current-sensing resistor, we can calculate the amount of current that a motor is using.*

For example, if the voltage drop across a current sensing resistor is 0.5 volts, and the resistor value is 0.05 ohms, how much current is passed through the resistor, and what will the power rating need to be for the resistor?

First we measure the current through the resistor:

$V = I * R$

$0.5v = I * 0.05 \text{ ohms}$

$I = 0.5v / 0.05 \text{ ohms}$

$I = 10 \text{ amps}$

If you measure 0.5 volts across a 0.05-ohm current sensing resistor, the amount of current that is passing through the resistor is 10amps.

Now to calculate the power dissipation of the resistor:

$W = I^2 * R$

$W = (10amps * 10amps) * 0.05$ ohms

$W = 5$ watts

As you can see, the resistor must be rated for 5 watts to be able to handle 10 amperes flowing through it without failing.

There are better options available for current sensing in an H-bridge, like the hall-effect based ACS-714 current sensor that can accurately measure up to 30amps in either direction, and outputs a proportional analog output voltage that can be read using the Arduino. This sensor is mentioned in Chapter 2 as a non-autonomous sensor. It is available on a breakout board for use with an existing motor-controller or as an IC that can be soldered directly into a motor-controller design (like the ones used on the Explorer bot in Chapter 8). With this motor feedback mechanism, we can use the Arduino to monitor the motor output current and create a custom over-current protection method to keep the motor-controller from overheating.

## Commercial H-Bridges (Motor-Controllers)

If you do not plan to build your own motor-controller, you will still need to decide which one to buy. It is important to select a motor-controller with a voltage limit that is at least a few volts above your desired operating voltage, because a fully charged battery is usually a few volts higher than its rating. This is important because if the maximum voltage limit is exceeded even for a few seconds, it can destroy the mosfets, which will result in a broken H-bridge. The amperage rating is a bit more forgiving, in that if it is exceeded the H-bridge will simply heat up. Remember that using a heat sink or cooling fan can increase the maximum amperage limit by removing the dangerous heat, so many commercial units have heatsinks or fans built-in to aid in heat dissipation.

A commercial H-bridge can range in price from $10–$500+, but we will assume that you are not made of money, and focus mainly on the budget motor controllers. Most units accept PWM, Serial, or R/C pulse signals and some have the capability to read several different signal types using on-board jumpers to select between modes. You can find units that handle anywhere from 1amp to 150amps of continuous current and have voltage ratings from 6VDC to 80VDC.

### Small (Up to 3amps)

This size H-bridge powers small hobby motors, typically not larger than a prescription medicine bottle. There are many different H-bridges available from online retailers that can handle several amps and range in price from $10–$30 (see Table 3-2). The L293D and L298N are two common H-bridge ICs that many small commercial motor-controllers are based on. The Sparkfun Ardumoto is an Arduino compatible dual motor-controller shield that is based on a surface mount version of the L298N H-bridge IC shown in Figure 3-16, and is capable of handling up to 2amps per channel (see Figure 3-20).

*Figure 3-20. The Sparkfun Ardumoto is a motor-controller shield that is built around the L298N dual H-bridge IC.*

This class of speed controllers also includes hobby Electronic Speed Controller (ESC. These H-bridges usually work only with voltages up to around 12v, because most hobby vehicles do not operate above 12v. They can, however, handle quite a bit of current, but accept only R/C servo pulse signals for control. These are available for both brushed and brushless DC motors, and are usually inexpensive and compact.

*Table 3-2. This Chart Shows the Pricing of Some Small Commercial H-Bridges*

| Company | Model | Channels | Amperage Rating | Price |
|---|---|---|---|---|
| AdaFruit Industries | Motor-Shield | 4 | 1-A | $19.50 |
| Sparkfun.com | Ardumoto | 2 | 2-A | $24.95 |

## Medium (Up to 10amps)

This power range accommodates motors up to the size of a soda can. These begin to pack some real power but are usually useful for only robotics as gear-motors to provide more torque and lower speeds. There are also several different commercial H-bridges to choose from in this category, usually ranging from $30–$100 (see Table 3-3). At this power level, the motor-controller can generate a lot of heat, so it might be a good idea to use a heat-sink or fan to keep things cool and extend your operating range.

After you get above 5amps, the options for packaged ICs start to get thin—most medium-powered commercial H-bridges use an H-bridge driver IC and a set of four n-channel power mosfets.

*Table 3-3. A List of Suggested Medium-Sized Commercial Motor-Controllers*

| Company | Model | Channels | Amperage Rating | Price |
|---|---|---|---|---|
| Pololu.com | 24v12 | 1 | 12A continuous | $42.95 |
| Dimension Engineering | Sabertooth 2x12 | 2 | 12A continuous | $79.99 |
| Basic Micro | Robo Claw 2x10A | 2 | 10A continuous | $79.95 |

# Large (Over 10amps)

This class of H-bridge powers the largest DC motors that we use, in the range of 15amps to 150amps. This type of motor is found in electric scooters, power wheelchairs, and power tools and can be used to power larger robots weighing as much as 500 pounds! This means it can probably carry you around.

There are several options for large H-bridges ranging from around $60 to $500+ (see Table 3-4). These motor-controllers are usually full-featured and include heat-sinks or fans to keep them cool. You will want to be careful when connecting the power to these bridges because most do not usually include reverse-polarity protection and connecting the wires incorrectly is not covered under the warranty!

*Table 3-4. A List of Sugd Large-Sized Commercial Motor-Controllers*

| Company | Model | Channels | Amperage rating | Price |
| --- | --- | --- | --- | --- |
| Pololu.com | 24v23 CS* | 1 | 23A continuous | $62.95 |
| Basic Micro | Robo Claw 2x25A | 2 | 25A continuous | $79.95 |
| Dimension Engineering | Sabertooth 2x25 | 2 | 25A continuous | $124.99 |
| Dimension Engineering | Sabertooth 2x50 | 2 | 50A continuous | $249.99 |
| RobotPower.com | OSMC (assembled) | 1 | 160A continuous | $219.00 |

*\* This H-bridge has a built-in Current Sensor IC that can be read using the Arduino.*

## The Open Source Motor Controller (OSMC)

The OSMC is an open-source H-bridge based around the Intersil HIP4081 H-bridge driver. This chip has built-in logic to control an all N-channel mosfet H-bridge at up to 1MHz PWM frequencies (that's 1000kHz!). It cannot be commanded into a destructive state, so you can use a variety of input techniques.

The driver chip can handle input voltages from 12v to 80v and supply around 2amps of current to the mosfets. This is enough to drive the 16 mosfets used on the current OSMC design at around 16kHz PWM frequency. The use of four parallel mosfets per leg of the H-bridge brings the total current rating up to 160amps at up to 48vdc (voltage rating limited by mosfets). A single OSMC can drive only one DC motor and costs around $219 pre-assembled, but it can be used for any of the robots that we build. We provide a completely through-hole design that you can build yourself for less than half of the price as a standard OSMC, if you want to build your own.

There is a Yahoo! Group devoted to the development of this design as well as several variations that users have contributed. Because the OSMC is open-source, you can edit, modify, and altogether change the design to fit your needs. If your design works, it is always polite to share your new design with the OSMC community.

http://tech.groups.yahoo.com/group/osmc/

Because 160amps might be a bit more than most people need, you can install only as many mosfets as you need. I built two homemade OSMCs and only installed two mosfets per leg (eight total per board) on a 150lb bot, and I can run the bot continuously for several hours without the H-bridge heating up.

Because the OSMC design does not use heat-sinks, it is a good idea to add a cooling fan above the mosfets if you will push much current through them.

Now that we have a better idea of what type of motors and motor-controllers we need, let's take a closer look at the power supply that move the motors—batteries.

# Batteries

The type and size of battery you choose for you robot determines not only how long it will run between charges, but also how fast it will drive the motors, and how much current can be discharged at once. Batteries are rated by their output Voltage and Amp/Hour rating, which tells us how long the battery will supply power given a particular load. It is important to know that most rechargeable batteries can supply voltage levels that are around 10%–15% higher than their rated voltage when fully charged. For this reason, it is a good idea to choose a motor-controller with a voltage rating that is several volts above your project's maximum operating voltage.

You might recall that arranging the batteries with both series and parallel connections can provide multiple output voltages and higher Amp/Hour ratings. We often use these techniques to achieve a specific voltage with several smaller battery cells. Different battery compositions have varying cell voltages: NiCd and NiMh are 1.2v per cell, LiPo batteries are typically 3-7v per cell, and Lead Acid batteries are 2v per cell. We discuss only re-chargeable batteries, because they are more efficient for robotics projects.

## Nickel Cadmium (NiCad)

NiCad batteries have been around for several years and offer good performance and a life cycle of several thousand charges. These batteries are also used for cordless power tools, older cordless telephones, and consumer rechargeables (see Figure 3-21). NiCad is, however, prone to a condition called "memory" that occurs when it is repeatedly charged before being allowed to fully discharge. This causes the battery life to be reduced considerably and is different than reduced battery-life due to age. If you have any of these batteries that are still good, they can be used for small- to medium-sized robots—otherwise, NiMH batteries are generally a better option for around the same price.

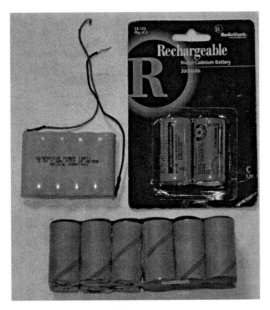

*Figure 3-21. NiCad batteries are typically available in standard alkaline battery sizes: AA, AAA, C, D, and so on, but have a cell voltage of 1.2v instead of 1.5v like a standard alkaline battery cell.*

## Nickel Metal Hydride (NiMH)

These rechargeable batteries are commonly used with cordless power tools, cordless telephones, cell phones, toys, and many consumer rechargeable batteries (AA, AAA, and so on) are still made using NiMH. These batteries offer high amp-hour ratings for their size, often in the range of 1000mAh to 4500mAh, and can typically be found in 1.2v cells, which can be arranged in a series to produce whatever voltage you need (see Figure 3-22). They can be re-charged many times but are prone to decreased output as they get older.

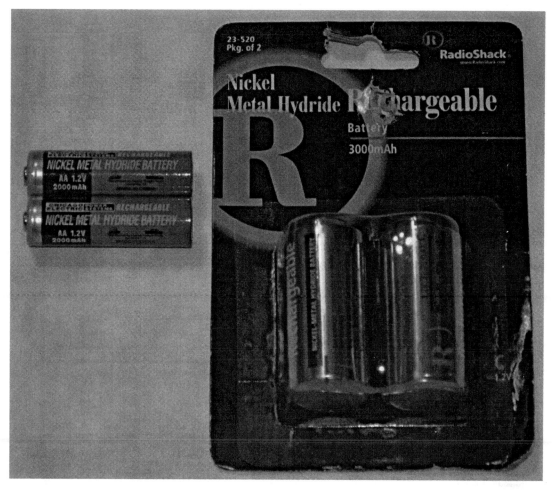

*Figure 3-22. NiMh batteries are also available in standard.*

## Lithium Polymer (LiPo)

Lithium Polymer batteries are one of the newer battery types used for their high power to weight ratio. With a typical cell voltage of 3-7v, these batteries are lightweight yet powerful and are able to deliver large amounts of current very quickly. LiPo batteries have recently become much more affordable, making them a viable option for many robotic projects, though proper charging and discharging is required to prevent overheating. They are typically arranged in series packs with up to six cells, totaling 22.2v (see Figure 3-23).

*Figure 3-23. A few different sizes of hobby LiPo battery packs that I use for robotics projects. Shown are two 7.4v packs (2-cell), two 11.1v packs (3-cell), and one 18.5v pack (5-cell).*

If a Lithium Polymer cell is discharged below 3-0 volts, it can become volatile and possibly catch fire. LiPo batteries must also be charged properly or again risk catching fire. For this reason, it is recommended that you learn more about lithium batteries before using them in a project. Although LiPpo's are lightweight and pack a lot of power, they can be dangerous if the proper precautions are not taken. Many people shy away from using these batteries in favor of a more forgiving chemistry.

## Lead-Acid

This is the type of battery you can find in your car, boat, Power-wheels, solar power systems, and backup power applications. They are typically heavy and bulky, but have excellent power output and the highest amp/hour ratings that we use, usually ranging from 5AH to around 150AH. These batteries are typically available only in 6v, 8v, 12v, and 24v cells of which the 12v variety is the most common. They have internal lead plates arranged in series, each producing around 2 volts. The thickness of these plates determine the use of the battery.

There are several different types of lead-acid batteries to choose from, though we are interested only in the deep-cycle and AGM types for use on our bots.

- *Deep-cycle:* This type of battery has thick lead plates that are designed to provide smaller amounts of current for longer periods of time, and they can be drained and re-charged many times. These are commonly used for powering lights, radios, pumps, and other accessories on boats, RVs, solar, and backup power systems. A typical deep-cycle battery has a rating from 20Ah to 150Ah. This type of battery works well for powering large robots for several hours between charging.

- *Starting*: This type of battery has a lot of thin lead plates that can deliver massive amounts of current very quickly. This is ideal for powering automotive starters that draw larger currents in a short amount of time in order to start an engine. If this type of battery is allowed to completely drain several times (more than 5%–10% discharge), it can render it useless! These batteries are *not* suitable for draining and re-charging very many times, so we avoice this type for our robotics projects.

- *Wet-cell battery*: This includes most automotive batteries because they have removable caps that enable you to add water or acid if needed. These batteries are by far the largest and heaviest and must be mounted upright to keep them from spilling, but are good for larger robots where extended run-time is required.

- *Gel-cell battery*: This battery is similar to the wet-cell in terms of power, capacity, and size. These batteries, however, are sealed from the manufacturer to keep them from spilling—this enables them to be mounted in almost any position. A gel-cell battery is typically more expensive than a standard wet-cell battery but also has a longer life.

- *Absorbed Glass Mat (AGM):* This battery is typically used for medium applications including backup lighting and some solar power setups. These batteries are sealed from the manufacturer and can be mounted in any position. They are also commonly referred to as Sealed Lead Acid or SLA batteries (see Figure 3-24). They are affordable and typically rated from 2Ah to 75Ah. These are similar in operation to deep-cycle batteries and are designed to be recharged many times. These are usually a bit heavy for small bots, but are an excellent choice for a medium- to large-size robot and have the best run-time for the price.

*Figure 3-24. A few standard AGM sealed lead-acid batteries. Pictured are two 6v, 4.5AH batteries (top) and one 12v, 7AH battery (bottom).*

Each battery type has its own advantages. Notice in Table 3-5 that although NiCad and NiMh batteries are good choices for most projects, LiPo batteries are the lightest and lead-acid are the cheapest. Each has its own place in our projects, and we will use each type throughout this book.

*Table 3-5. Battery Comparison*

| Type of Battery | Voltage | Volts/Cell | Cells | Price | Weight | Amp/Hours |
| --- | --- | --- | --- | --- | --- | --- |
| Lithium Polymer | 11.1v | 3-7v | 3 | $32.00 | 14oz | 5000mAh |
| NiCad | 12v | 1.2v | 10 | $49.99 | 32oz | 5000mAh |
| NiMH | 12v | 1.2v | 10 | $49.99 | 32oz | 5000mAh |
| Lead Acid (SLA) | 12v | 2.0v | 6 | $15.99 | 64oz (or 4lbs) | 5000mAh |

# Charging

It is best to buy a good battery charger that has multiple charging voltages and currents. A typical adjustable automotive battery charger is selectable from 6v–12v and has several amperage levels, usually 2amps and 15amps.

As a rule of thumb, a normal charging rate is not more than $1/10^{th}$ of the Amp/Hour rating. This means that a battery that is rated for 5000mAh should not be charged with a current that is more than 500mA (5000mAh / 10 = 500mA). If an automotive battery charger delivers too much current for your batteries, you might need to use a hobby-type charger that it compatible with multiple types of batteries.

I use a Dynam Supermate DC6 multi-function battery charger to charge all of my NiCad, NiMh, LiPoly, and small lead-acid batteries, because it offers both balance charging and selectable current levels for charging a variety of different battery types (see Figure 3-25). It requires a DC power source from 11V–18V, and can charge batteries up to 22.2V. Most hobby chargers also come with several different charging adapters to accommodate for the various plug types commonly found on rechargeable batteries.

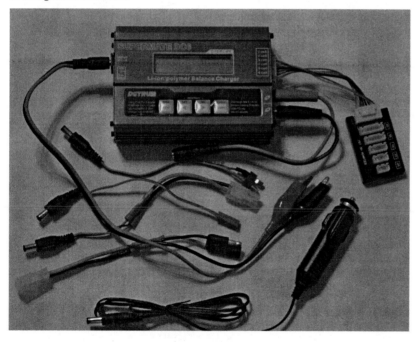

**Figure 3-25.** *A Dynam DC6 multi-battery charger. This charger is compatible with LiPo, NiMh, NiCd, and Lead-acid—as well as having an adjustable charging rate.*

Lithium batteries require special attention to keep them from overheating and catching fire, so it is recommended that you buy the appropriate charger for the battery pack you have chosen. Lithium batteries have no "memory" effect, so you can charge them as often as you like without completely discharging them.

# Materials

As with everything else, there are several different materials you can choose from to build your robot. Each has its own place and you shouldn't count any one material out of your supply, because it might be the best solution to a future problem. My theory is that the more tools that you have available, the more solutions you have to a given problem. I consider the term "tools" to go further than just hammers and drills to include your materials, creativity, and general skill-set—welding, woodworking, plastic-molding, fiberglassing, 3-d printing, sewing, machining, PCB fabricating, or whatever moves you.

## Wood

Wood is by far the easiest material to come by. You can theoretically make a robot from tree limbs if you were so inclined, or plane the limbs into planks and make a finished wood frame. Wood is generally used only for cheap prototyping and proof-of-concept project, because it is susceptible to bending and warping without proper treatment (not good for precisely mounted parts). Sheets of wood can be used to build a platform for holding electronics, because it is non-conductive and easy to drill holes in when mounting PCBs. Wood is also good for making wedges or spacers that might be too difficult to make using steel.

## Metals

There are two types of metal that are of special interest to any robot builder: steel and aluminum. Both of these make strong and rigid frames that are resistant to warping and if properly painted, should last for many years. They can be either bolted together or welded and are strong enough for even the largest robots.

- *Steel*: This metal can be put together using bolts (requires drilling holes) or welding (requires welder). Either way can be very strong and likely outlast all other parts on the bot. Steel is however heavy, so it is generally not good to use for smaller bots because smaller motors won't be able to carry a steel frame around. Large bots benefit from a steel frame because it is strong and can support quite a bit of weight.

- *Aluminum*: This meatl has the same general uses as steel, but it is much lighter. You can build small, medium, and large bots with aluminum. Welding aluminum requires special equipment, so you might have to plan on bolting these pieces together.

If using bolts, you need to pre-drill holes the same size as the bolts you use. You should buy drill bits made for drilling through steel and use the highest speed setting on your drill. You can also drill aluminum, wood, and plastics with a steel drill bit. Metals can also be "tapped" to add screw threads to a drilled hole, which can be helpful to decrease the number of bolts needed to secure each piece together.

If you need to cut steel or aluminum, you can use an angle-grinder, reciprocating-saw (with steel blade), cutting-torch, metal miter saw, jigsaw, or hacksaw depending on your tool selection. A reciprocating saw is usually the fastest and cleanest cutting of the saws (it is my personal choice for quick cuts), whereas an angle-grinder is good for cleaning up rough edges.

## Nuts and Bolts

Regardless of what material you choose to build your robot, you are going to need some nuts and bolts to hold everything together. Using a nut and bolt to secure two pieces of metal, wood, plastic, or fiberglass together can provide excellent strength in addition to being removable if needed.

A bolt is a metal rod with precision threads, and is available in almost any length and diameter that you can think of, in both metric and SAE sizes. You can find bolts with various shaped heads and thread types but they all serve the same purpose—holding two or more objects together.

A nut is the threaded metal ring that mounts to the bolt. Like bolts, nuts are also available in various shapes and sizes, and with different thread types. You will likely need a pair of pliers or a wrench to tighten a nut to a bolt, and it is advisable to use a lock-washer to prevent the nut from loosening during use.

*Figure 3-26. Here you can see a variety of nuts and bolts, like the ones used throughout this book.*

## Plastics

PVC is a commonly available plastic that can be cut, drilled, tapped, and even welded using a stream of hot air. We use PVC plastic to make a motor-mount in Chapter 9, and clear plexiglass (clear acrylic) sheets in multiple projects as a non-conductive mounting base and protective cover.

## Chain and Sprockets

Chain is used to transmit power from a drive sprocket on the motor, to a receiver sprocket mounted on the wheel. Chain comes in several different sizes, but we use only #25 roller chain plexiglass also labeled as 1/4in pitch. This type of chain is commonly found on electric scooters. Sprockets are also labeled by their pitch, so it is important to get matching sprockets and chain or they won't fit together. You can choose a gear-ratio for the motor sprocket and wheel sprocket pair by selecting the number of teeth on each sprocket. Using a small motor sprocket and a large wheel sprocket is a good way to gear down a drive-train, allowing for reduced speed and increased torque.

Chains are usually sold with universal connecting links so you can size the chain to fit your needs. When using a chain and sprocket setup, it is important to maintain proper chain tension. Too much tension can result in a broken chain and not enough tension creates a slack in the drive transmission that can result in broken sprockets teeth. Each of the projects that use chain drive transmissions need to have adjustable motors or wheels to tension the chains plexiglass this can complicate the building process, so it is usually desirable to use motors with the wheels attached when available.

## Wheels

The wheel is the final stage of the drive-train. It is what makes contact with the ground to propel the robot. As you might know, a larger wheel diameter travels farther than a shorter wheel diameter. Logically, this makes sense because each time the motor output shaft makes one complete revolution, the bot must travel the same distance as the outer circumference of the wheel. So a larger wheel travels faster than a smaller one, using the same motor RPM.

For smaller bots, you can make your own wheels from plexiglass or wood, or buy a toy car from your local thrift-store that has a salvageable set of wheels on it. Larger bots require finding wheels typically manufactured for a lawnmower, wheel-barrow, lawn-tractor, or other similarly sized vehicle that can carry the same payload. Wheels often require modification to fit onto a motor output shaft or attach a sprocket.

## Summary

At this point you should be able to identify the various types of DC motors and determine what type of motor you need for your project. In this chapter you learned that standard brushed DC motors are usually identified by having two wires and are by far the most common and the easiest to drive, but have brushes that wear out after extended use. Brushless motors typically have three wires and require special circuitry to operate, but have excellent high-speed durability and reliability. Stepper motors have four, five, or six wires and also require a special drive circuit to operate, but have a specific number of steps in each rotation, making them ideal for position tracking applications. Servo motors use an encoding device to determine the location of the output shaft, making them ideal for angular position emulation. A linear actuator is a DC motor that converts rotational motion into linear movement. Any of these motors can be mated to a gear box to convert its energy from high-speed/low-torque to low-speed/high-torque.

We then discussed the various types of H-bridge motor control circuits and their allowed states. You should now understand how to command a simple H-bridge circuit into Forward, Reverse, or Electric-braking (positive or negative), and how *not* to command a Shoot-through condition (short-circuit). We then moved on to discuss how to change the PWM frequency for each timer on the Arduino as well as how to deal with Back-EMF and the benefits of current sensing in an H-bridge. We finished talking about H-bridges with a few suggestions for various sizes of commercial H-bridge motor-controllers.

Lastly, we talked about the various types of batteries and materials that we will use in our projects. Although NiCad and NiMh have a high-energy capacity, are commonly available, and easy to work with, they can also be expensive. Lead-acid batteries are inexpensive and provide excellent power, but can be heavy and thus are not suitable for small bots. Lithium Polymer (LiPo) batteries are extremely lightweight, provide excellent power, and have come down considerably in price since becoming available, but are sensitive to over-discharging and thus require more complex circuitry to ensure that they are not completely drained.

Enough talk, let's start building some robots! First up is a small autonomous robot that loves to follow lines... I named him Linus because I'm a Linux geek (Thanks, Mr. Linus Torvalds!) and it seemed to fit his behavior.

# CHAPTER 4

# Linus the Line-Bot

Let's begin with a small robot for our first project that introduces the basic concepts of automated control. This robot decides where to go based on its surroundings and can change its path if the environment is changed. Linus' purpose is to follow a black line on a white surface (see Figure 4-1). His aspirations are quite low, but he is still fun to experiment with and easy (and cheap) to build.

*Figure 4-1.* The mostly finished Linus sitting on his track

The cost of this project as shown is around $80. This includes a commercial motor-driver board, two hobby servo motors, a homemade IR sensor board, and several other items that might be used for multiple robots (Figure 4-2).

You also have the option to substitute your old usable parts like previously used servo motors (or gear-motors), or maybe you already have a motor-controller, at which point the price for this bot will drop quite a bit. If you want to save some money, you can also skip ahead to Chapter 6 to find out how to make your own PCBs on your PC with free software. You can also build these circuits on prototyping board from Radio Shack.

We start by making an infrared sensor board so that Linus can detect the color of the surface beneath him, and then go through the process of modifying a hobby servo motor for continuous rotation. Next we fit the rear wheels onto the motor output shafts and make a bracket for the front caster wheel. We then modify a tin container for use as our frame, and install the motors, infrared sensor board, Arduino with motor-controller shield, and batteries. After everything is wired up, we load the code onto the Arduino, make a track for Linus to follow, and start testing to see how fast we can get him to go around the track without losing his path. With Linus complete, you can then add LED interior lighting, a speed adjustment potentiometer, or paint his frame to add some style. Let's look at the parts required to build Linus.

# Parts List for Linus

For every project in this book, you are expected to have an Arduino ($35), so we won't include that in each project price. In Chapter 6, we build a "poor-man's Arduino" that is intended to replace your main Arduino when a project is completed so you don't have to keep buying new Arduinos–unless you are rich. The price per board to build yourself is around $8-$15 each, but they can be programmed only with an FTDI cable ($15 from Sparkfun.com), because there is no USB interface built onto the homemade boards.

I also do not include tools or other standard materials (like wire) into each project price, because these will last for several projects. A roll of solid 22AWG wire should get you through most of the book, as should a roll of rosin-core solder. It is also handy to have a few pieces of scrap metal or aluminum on hand. A 36-inch long piece of flat aluminum stock enables you to make several brackets, supports, or motor mounts, so I keep a few different sized pieces in my parts bin.

This project uses some basic robotic components: sensors, motors, wheels, a frame, batteries, a motor-controller, and your Arduino micro-controller (Figure 4-2). If you already have a robot base with several of these components, you might complete this project for as little as $15 to build the infrared sensor board.

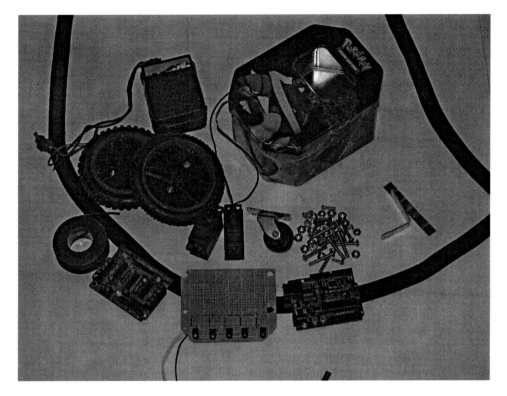

*Figure 4-2. Here you can see the unassembled parts used to build Linus.*

You can also substitute parts to save money as you please: a set of gear-motors you might have for the servo motors I used, a homemade H-bridge for the AF motor-controller, or pre-built IR sensors from Sparkfun.com (item: ROB-09453) instead of building your own. With a little tweaking, any of these alternatives should work. You can also save money by ordering some parts from Digikey.com, because you will get far more in quantity for nearly the same price as buying from Radio Shack. See Table 4-1 for a complete list of parts. This chapter presents one way to build a line-following robot.

*Table 4-1. The Parts List*

| Part | Description | Price |
| --- | --- | --- |
| AF motor-shield | AdaFruit.com (part# 81)–This Arduino shield is capable of driving up to four DC motors. | $19.95 |
| (2) hobby servo motors | HobbyPartz.com (part# EXI-Servo-B1222) –Standard sized EXI hobby servo motors | $6.45 ea. |
| (5) IR emitter/detectors | Digikey (part# TCRT5000L)–These are standard infrared emitter/detecter pairs. | $1.06 ea. |

| Part | Description | Price |
|---|---|---|
| Perforated prototyping board | Radio Shack (part# 276-158)–Or similar, any piece of 0.1-inch perforated copper clad prototyping board will work. | $2.99 |
| (5) 10k ohm resistors | Digikey (part# P10KBACT)–50 pack of resistors | $1.78 |
| (7) 150 ohm resistors | Diglkey (part# P150BACT) –50 pack of resistors | $1.78 |
| Frame | Thrift store–I used a tin keepsake box from a children's card game; cookie tins work, too. | $0.39 |
| (25) nuts and bolts | Hardware store–#6 bolts with nuts, 1/2 inch to 2 inch in length | $3.00 |
| (2) drive wheels | Thrift store–Salvaged from toy motorcycle | $1.99 |
| Caster wheel | Hardware store–Used for rolling cabinets, and so on. | $1.99 |
| Battery | Clearance rack–6v, 1000AH or equivalent. Can be NiMh, NiCd, or non-rechargeable. | $1.00 |
| Power switch | Radio Shack (part# 275-612)–Standard SPST switch to toggle power | $2.99 |
| (2) LEDs | Digikey (part # C503B-BAN-CY0C046) –I used two Blue LEDs connected to the motor output terminals. Use any color you like. | $1.08 |
| 5k Potentiometer | Radio Shack (part # 271-1715) –This is used to adjust the speed of Linus without reprogramming. | $2.99 |
| Spray paint | Hardware store–Used to add some color, not required. | $5.00 |
| **Grand total** | **As tested** | **$67.12** |

This, of course, includes the AdaFruit motor-shield, the batteries that can be removed to use in other projects, and the spray paint that will last for several bots. These parts should be used for easy prototyping, whereas handmade circuits should replace the Arduino and AF motor-shield after the Line-bot is fixed for permanent use (after testing is complete). After you finish the projects in this book, you will easily be able to build an Arduino and motor-controller replacement at home and for far less than buying a new Arduino and AF motor-shield.

# How Linus Works

The infrared emitter sends a continuous beam of infrared light that is reflected from the ground back to the infrared detector. Depending on the reflectiveness of the ground color, the detector receives varying amounts of reflected infrared light. The detector is actually an infrared photo-transistor that uses infrared light to activate the transistor base. The more infrared light that gets to the detector, the more the transistor conducts. We use five IR sensors in a straight line to determine the exact position of the non-reflective line beneath the robot. By adjusting the two drive motors based on the line sensor readings, we can keep the bot centered on the line as it drives around the track.

## The Track

The track must be a solid color with no variations. A few pieces of white poster-board work best with black electrician's tape for the line (see Figure 4-3). The line provides a contrast of color that the sensors can differentiate. You can make whatever line shape you want for your bot to follow: it can be twisty, have intersections and loops, or be a simple circle. The neat thing about Linus is that he responds differently each time around the track. Because he responds to his sensors, if there is a split in the track, he might go left the first time around and right the next! It is interesting to watch the decision-making processes of this little machine.

*Figure 4-3. This is the first track I designed to test Linus, which worked very well.*

Now that you know how Linus maneuvers around the track, let's get started building the infrared sensor board.

# Building the IR Sensor Board

The IR sensor board consists of five infrared emitter and detector pairs. You can make your own IR emitter/detector pairs using individual IR LEDs and IR phototransistors from Radio Shack (part # 276-142), but they are over $3 per pair, which is about $15 for the all five sensors! Digikey.com has several different IR emitter/detector pairs for about $1 each–that cuts the cost down to $5 for the infrared sensors (see Figure 4-4).

*Figure 4-4. The parts needed to build the IR sensor board: (5) IR sensors from Digikey.com, (5) 150 ohm resistors, (5) 10k ohm resistors, some wire, and a piece of prototyping board from Radio Shack*

The infrared emitter LED (the blue or clear one) sits next to an infrared phototransistor detector (that looks like a black LED) with a small divider between them. The small divider makes sure no IR light is read by the detector that is not first reflected from the surface (in our case, the floor or track). The sensors should not be placed directly beside each other (without a gap) in order to avoid interference from the next sensor. They should also not be placed so far apart that there are "dead spots" in between that are not read by any sensor. See Figure 4-5 for a view of the completed infrared sensor board.

*Figure 4-5. The IR sensor board with all five sensors installed*

I chose to place my sensors about 0.5 inch apart, which works well. If you place the black line between sensor 2 and sensor 3, you will see both outputs affected (the output value of those sensors will be lower than the rest). If you, however, place the black line directly under sensor 3, only sensor 3 will show an altered value–sensors 2 and 4 are just far enough away from sensor 3 to not detect any of the black line. If the sensors were closer together, both sensor 2 and sensor 4 would pick up on the black line, even if it was centered directly beneath sensor 3. Determining the spacing of each sensor is a matter of testing–if you don't feel like testing it, start by spacing the sensors 0.5 inch apart.

To make things easier, I chose to use a piece of Radio Shack perforated copper clad prototyping board that is wide enough to enable proper spacing between each IR sensor. This board is approximately 2 3/4 inch by 3 inch and most of it is unused except the top and bottom few rows. To get started building this circuit, you first need to see the schematic diagram (see Figure 4-6) that shows how each sensor should be connected in the circuit as well as a pinout of the actual IR sensor, shown in Figure 4-7.

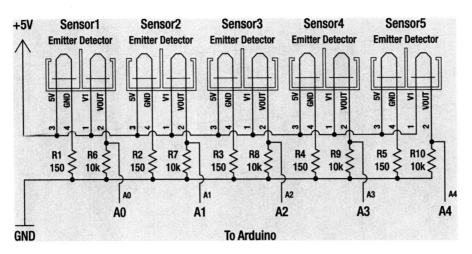

*Figure 4-6. This is the schematic of the IR sensor board.*

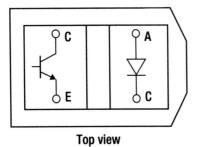

**Top view**

*Figure 4-7. IR sensor schematic (detector or photo-transistor = Left, Emitter = Right)*

The following nine steps will walk you through building the IR sensor board:

1.  Place IR sensors on prototyping board. Each IR pair has two LEDs with four total leads. The top of the pair is the Emitter (the blue-colored LED), and the bottom is the Detector or photo-transistor (the black-colored LED). The *indented* end of the sensor package should be closest to the edge of the board. as shown in Figure 4-8.

*Figure 4-8. Placing the sensors*

The Anode of each Emitter diode (marked "A" in Figure 4-7) and the collector of each photo-transistor (marked "C" in Figure 4-7 on left) should both be tied directly to +5v. The cathode of each IR Emitter (marked "C" in Figure 4-7 on right) should be connected to Ground through a 150 ohm resistor, and the emitter pin of each photo-transistor (marked "E" in Figure 4-7) should be connected to Ground through a 10k ohm resistor–the output for each IR pair is also tied to this pin.

2. After placed, solder each lead to the PCB to secure it down as shown in Figure 4-9. To avoid overheating any one sensor, it is recommended to solder the first leg of each sensor, then go back to the beginning and solder the second leg of each sensor, and so on. This gives each sensor some time to cool down between soldering each leg to the prototyping board.

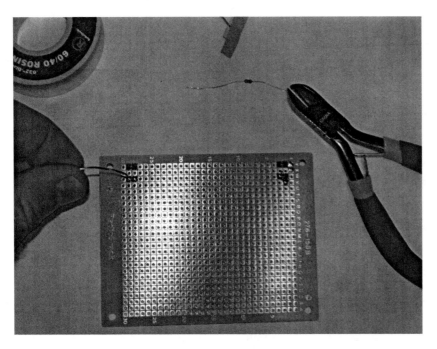

*Figure 4-9. Soldering each sensor into place on the prototyping board*

3.  After securing each sensor, solder the two pins together on the right side of each sensor pair, the anode of the emitter and collector of the photo-transistor (see Figure 4-10). You can bend the right-side leads until they are touching each other flat against the board–then solder them together, clipping off the extra with a set of plier snips.

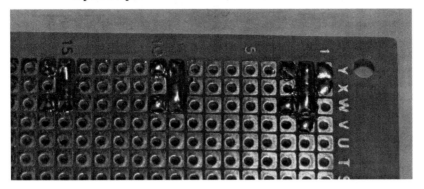

*Figure 4-10. Make a "solder-bridge" between the anode of the emitter and the collector of the photo-transistor*

4. Next add 10k pull-down resistors from the photo-transistor (Detector) output pin to Ground (see Figure 4-11). By placing the pull-down resistors on each sensor output pin, we are ensuring that the Analog inputs of the Arduino will be defaulted to a value of 0, unless there is IR light activating the photo-transistor. We do this because the IR photo-transistor acts as a simple switch, enabling +5v to pass through it when turned on. When the switch is in the off state, we need to use a pull-down resistor to give the Arduino analog Input a default value (GND) so it is not left "floating."

**10k Ohm Resistors**

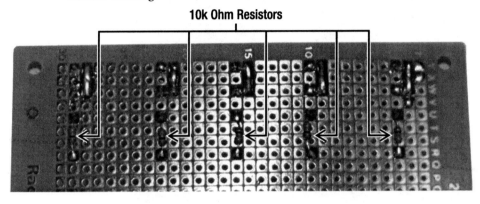

*Figure 4-11. Install the (5) 10k ohm resistors from the emitter pin of each photo-transistor to a common Ground.*

5. Add 150 ohm current-limiting resistors for the IR Emitter LEDs. Supplying 5v through the 150-ohm resistor enalbes 33mA to go to each IR Emitter, which is just below the maximum current rating. Place each 150-ohm current limiting resistor from the cathode pin of each IR emitter to Ground as shown in Figure 4-12.

**150 Ohm Resistors**

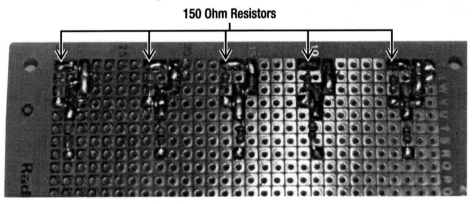

*Figure 4-12. Install the (5) 150 ohm resistors from the Emitter's Cathode pin to Ground.*

6.  Connect all +5v pads together. You must use some jumper wires to connect each +5v pad to the next, and finally to the power wire (white wire) soldered to the bottom-right of the board (see Figure 4-13). Looks are not important because this board will be hidden in the frame, but make sure each connection is secure.

*Figure 4-13. Run red wire to each +5v pad, down to the white +5v supply wire. On the other side of the board, connect all of the Ground pads together, down to the black Ground supply wire.*

7.  Connect Ground wires together. I connected the Ground wires together on the other side of the board, but you can place them on the same side as the other wires if you prefer. The ground wires should likewise connect each Ground pad together and then finally the Ground supply wire at the bottom-right of the board (black wire), as shown in Figure 4-14.

***Figure 4-14.*** *The top-side Ground supply wires can be routed on the bottom side if you like, as long as each Ground pad is connected.*

8. Connect signal Input wires. I found a five-wire plug from an old VCR that easily plugs in all five sensors at once. You can also use plain solid wire, each wire should be about 8 inches long to give enough length to reach the Analog ports on the Arduino. These signal wires should be soldered to the top of each 10k resistor (between the resistor and the photo-transistor output) in order, as shown in Figure 4-13.

9. Lastly, I put some black electrical tape over the exposed wires on the front of the board to keep from shorting anything out when face down in the metal tin frame (see Figure 4-15).

   Electrical tape is an excellent insulator and can easily cover nearly any electrical connection. I always keep several rolls of this tape on hand.

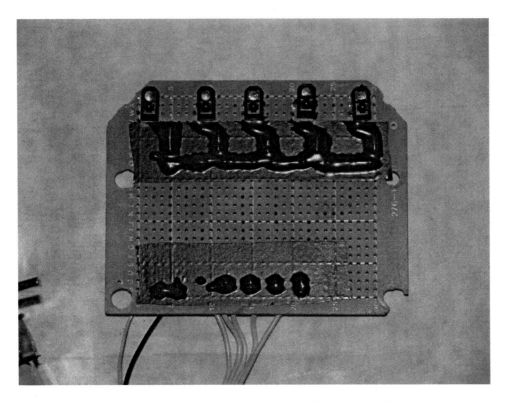

*Figure 4-15. Electrical tape to cover the Ground and signal wires from shorting out on the tin frame*

The IR sensor board is now ready to be tested and then installed into Linus. To test the IR board, simply plug the power wire into the Arduino +5v and the Ground wire to Arduino Ground. Now point your digital camera at the sensors and look through the viewfinder. You should see the infrared LED's showing a pale blue color, which means they are working.

All that is left to do is connect the sensor output wires into the Arduino analog inputs. I programmed Linus such that when the IR board is facing down (as it does when installed), the far left IR sensor is 1 and the far right sensor is 5–the center is 3 and so on. Sensor 1 goes to Arduino analog input 0, and go in order from there (i.e., Sensor 3 goes in analog input 2, and 5 goes in analog input 4).

# Modifying a Servo for Continuous Rotation

Servo motors are intended to operate with a range of about 180 degrees. This means that they will not spin in a complete circle without modification. By modifying these motors, you will not be able to use them as they were intended, because this procedure is mostly non-reversible. I chose to do this because you end up with small, reliable gear motors that cost around $6 each and is available at most hobby shops.

---

▦ **Note** If you have some other gear motors that you want to use, that is fine. You might have to adjust the speed of the motors or battery voltage of the circuit, but it should work the same.

---

There are two methods that you can use to modify a servo motor. Both methods involve physically removing the plastic "stops" that keep the servo shaft from rotating beyond 180 degrees. These are here because the shaft is attached to a potentiometer and if rotated beyond 180 degrees, the potentiometer shaft would break. Both methods also involve removing the potentiometer from operation, either by physically removing it altogether and soldering two resistors in its place, or by pushing it down so it is not moved by the rotating of the servo output shaft.

## Method 1: Direct DC Drive with External Speed Controller

The first method (the one I used) involves removing all electronics inside the servo motor, leaving only the DC motor and the gearing. The three-wire pigtail is soldered directly to the motor terminals (red and white wires soldered to one terminal, black wire soldered to the other terminal). This is straightforward and easy to do, but requires using an external motor-driver to power the motors. These motors consume little current, so even an L293D dual motor controller IC will work (under $3 from Sparkfun.com–sku: COM-00315).

If you want to modify your servo motors to be standard gear motors, the following six steps guide you through this process.

1. Remove four screws from the rear of the servo motor housing as shown in Figure 4-16. You need a small Phillips head screwdriver. Be careful when pulling the motor housing apart because the gears tend to fall out.

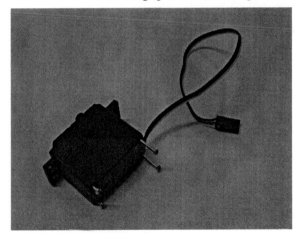

*Figure 4-16. Remove servo motors rear screws and cover using a small Phillips head screwdriver.*

2. Remove motor with PCB and potentiometer as shown in Figure 4-17. This might take some finesse to keep from breaking any plastic pieces on the housing, but be gentle and you should have no problems.

*Figure 4-17. Remove circuitry, and de-solder motor from PCB, then cut the red, white, and black wires from the PCB.*

3. Remove plastic stop. This is located under the output shaft. You have to remove the protruding piece of plastic that keeps the shaft from spinning 360 degrees. I used a soldering iron to melt the protruding piece of plastic away from the output shaft (gently). The idea here is to make sure the motor shaft can spin freely (see Figure 4-18).

*Figure 4-18. Using a soldering iron, melt away the plastic stop from the main black gear. It protrudes from the rest of the gear and keeps it from spinning continuously.*

4.  De-solder motor from PCB. The motor terminals on the Futaba S3003 Servo are soldered to the PCB and must be de-soldered. You can probably do this with a soldering iron if you don't have a de-soldering iron–though Radio Shack sells a decent de-soldering iron for around $12. You can save the circuitry boards if you want to try reversing this procedure in the future, though I have not tried this.

5.  Solder servo wires directly to motor terminals as shown in Figure 4-19. I soldered the red and white wires to the terminal with the red dot beside it and the black wire to the other terminal.

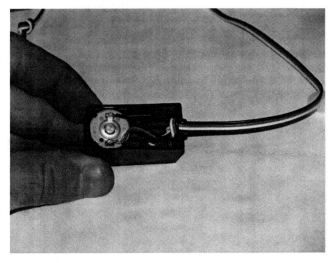

*Figure 4-19. Solder the red and white wires to the motor terminal with the red dot beside it, and the black wire to the other terminal. Now it is ready to be re-assembled.*

6.  Re-assemble and test. Make sure you have all the gears in their respective places (as in the picture), then tie a knot in the motor wire so that you make sure and keep some slack inside the motor compartment (see Figure 4-19). This keeps you from accidentally ripping the wires from the motor terminals. Now power the two terminals with +5v and Ground to make sure the motor output shaft spins.

## Method 2: Servo Pulse Drive with Internal Motor Driving Circuitry

The second method involves removing only the potentiometer and soldering (2) 2.5k ohm resistors in its place, in the form of a resistor divider. This tells the servo circuitry that the motor is *always* at the center position. The servo circuitry determines which direction to spin the motor based on the value of the potentiometer. If the servo receives any pulse above 1.5 milliseconds it moves forward, and any pulse below 1.5 milliseconds make it reverse. Because it will never reach its destination on the potentiometer (remember we replaced it with fixed resistors), it will spin continuously until a different pulse is received.

To modify your servo motors to operate as DC gear motors that still use the servo drive circuitry, the following six steps guide you through this process.

1. Remove four screws from rear of servo motor housing. You need a small Phillipshead screwdriver. Be careful when pulling the motor housing apart because the gears tend to fall out.

2. Remove motor with PCB and potentiometer. This might take some finesse to keep from breaking any plastic pieces on the housing.

3. Remove plastic stop. This is located under the output shaft. You have to remove the protruding piece of plastic that keeps the shaft from spinning 360 degrees. I used a soldering iron to melt the protruding piece of plastic away from the output shaft (gently). The idea here is to make sure the motor shaft can spin freely.

4. Remove potentiometer from PCB (see Figure 4-20). You can either clip the leads or de-solder it completely. Either way, you want to place two 2.5k-ohm resistors in its place. You need to solder the first resistor from the center potentiometer pin to the left pin. The second resistor goes from the center pin to the right pin. This outputs a neutral 2.5v signal at all times to trick the servo motor into running continuously in the direction commanded.

*Figure 4-20. You can cut the leads on the black potentiometer or de-solder them. Then, solder (2) 2.5k-ohm resistors from each outer pin to the center pin and solder together.*

5. Replace PCB into servo housing. Make sure the gear teeth slide in without force, or remove the gears first and replace them after the motor/PCB are in place.

6. Re-assemble and test. Make sure you have all the gears in their respective places.

To test the servo motor using its own circuitry, you need to use a servo command. Upload the code in Listing 4-1 to your Arduino and test the servo modified with method 2.

*Listing 4-1. Test a Servo Motor Connected to Arduino Pin 2*

```
// Connect servo motor signal wire to Arduino pin 2, red wire to +5v,
// and black wire to GND - then upload to test.

#include <Servo.h>              // Include the Arduino Servo library

Servo Servo_Motor1;             // create servo called "Servo_Motor1"

void setup()
{
  Servo_Motor1.attach(2);       // attaches the servo to pin 2
}
```

```
void loop()
{
    Servo_Motor1.write(0);       // tell the Servo_Motor1 to go in Reverse
    delay(1000);                      // wait 1 second
    Servo_Motor1.write(179);   // tell the Servo_Motor1 to go Forward
}
```

The advantage of using method 2 is that because you did not remove the servo driver circuitry, you do not need a motor-controller to power the motors. You can control them with a simple pulse from any Arduino digital pin. This can save you $20 on the parts list.

The downside is that to keep the servo spinning the correct direction, you must send a pulse from the Arduino about every 20ms. Because this can complicate the coding somewhat, I chose to modify my servo motors using method 1 and drive them with a motor-driver. This way any gear-motor can be used with the same code.

Regardless of how you chose to modify your servo motors, we still need to attach wheels to them. Now we discuss how to connect the wheels to the servo adapter plate.

## Fitting the Drive wheels

I have had extremely good luck finding old R/C toys at my local thrift store. Each car, boat, or motorcycle usually yields several DC motors, wheels, gear-boxes, and sometimes a servo motor or other interesting piece. This is where Linus' wheels come from (see Figure 4-21).

*Figure 4-21. Some wheels from a thrift-store R/C car with the servo mounting bracket*

Though there are many wheels you can buy that mount directly to a servo motor, I opted to use the mounting hardware that came with my servo motors (the four leg cross shape bracket) and mounting them to two large wheels that I pulled from an old R/C motorcycle from the thrift store. You can use any diameter wheel you like (larger = faster), as long as you can attach the servo-mounting bracket to it. I used small #6 bolts to hold the bracket to the wheel and it is quite secure with only two bolts, as shown in Figure 4-22.

*Figure 4-22. Both wheels with the servo brackets mounted and the motors next to them*

If using a salvaged set of wheels, follow the following four steps to mount the wheels to the servo mounting brackets.

1. Line up the bracket in the center of the wheel and mark two holes–one at each end of the bracket.

2. Drill holes through both the bracket and the wheel.

3. Secure bolts tightly with screwdriver. Make sure the bracket hub points out so it can mount to the servo output shaft.

4. Repeat for other wheel.

With the rear wheels installed, we only need a front caster wheel to have a rolling frame. In the next section, we focus on making a bracket to use when mounting the front caster wheel.Making a Caster bracket

The tin I used was relatively small and space was fairly tight, so I chose to mount the front caster wheel to the front of the tin using an "L" bracket made from aluminum pieces. My first attempt uses two pieces of aluminum strips that I bent using a vise. I later used the same process for a piece of 2-inch wide piece of flat aluminum to make one large bracket instead of two small ones, but either way will work.

To build a caster wheel-mounting bracket, perform the following steps:

1.  Make sure the bracket gives the wheel enough room to completely spin around without hitting anything. Then bend the brackets to length in a vise or with a pair of pliers, leaving about 1 inch-1.5 inches on the back side of the bracket to mount to the tin frame (see Figure 4-23).

*Figure 4-23. Bend the brackets so that there is enough room to swing the caster completely around. Then mark the mounting brackets, using the caster wheel-mounting holes with a permanent marker.*

2.  Drill holes for the caster mounting plate to mount to the aluminum brackets, as shown in Figure 4-24. My caster wheel required (2) 1.75 inches by 1.25 inches "L" brackets.

***Figure 4-24.*** *Drill holes through "L" bracket where marked.*

3. Use bolts or rivets to secure the caster wheel to the "L" brackets, as shown in Figure 4-25. With the brackets mounted, the caster wheel is ready to be mounted to the frame.

*Figure 4-25. The caster wheel with all four bolts secured to the mounting bracket.*

At this point, the two rear wheels should be able to mount to the servo motors and the front caster wheel should have a bracket mounted and ready to install onto the frame. Next, we need to build the frame.

# Making a Frame

I actually modified an aluminum tin from the thrift store to use as Linus' frame. Anytime I build a robot, I look through my current stock of materials and scraps to see whether anything can be re-used for my new bot. If not, I make a trip to the local thrift store to check out their supply of used goods. This trip, I found a pile of old cookie tins that are now empty and sold for around $0.39 each! As it turns out, a cookie tin can serve as an excellent lightweight metal frame for a small robot. I bought several of different shapes and sizes to give myself some options later.

The tin I decided to use was a Poke'mon children's card game tin that has a nice little clear plastic window on the lid, so you can see the electronics neatly tucked away inside. The lid serves as a stabilizer for the rest of the frame, tying the whole thing together–but also allows for easy access to the electronics if needed.

There are several modifications needed for the tin in order to mount motors, the Arduino, and the IR board inside, which are outlined in the following steps:

1. First, we need to measure, mark, and cut the holes for the drive motors. The bottom of the tin should sit about 0.25 inch above the ground so that the frame does not scrape when driving. First, measure the radius of the wheel, and then subtract 0.25 inch from that measurement. This tells you exactly how high on the tin that the center of the wheel axle (motor output shaft) should be mounted. Use a permanent marker to mark this spot, measured from the bottom and toward the rear of the frame.

   Next it is time to measure the servo motor and mark these dimensions, centered around your previous mark. The dimensions of my motor mounting holes were 0.75 inch W by 1.625 inches L, though I added a little padding to make sure I could move the motor around slightly if needed. Measure the same distance on the other side of the tin.

   Now using a Dremel rotary tool or similar, carefully cut the holes that you marked using a metal cutoff wheel (see Figure 4-26). This metal is sharp when cut, so wear gloves and don't cut yourself!

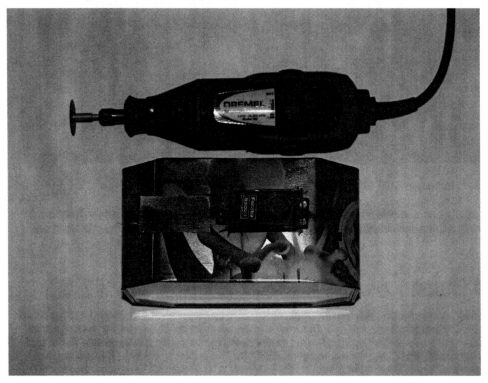

*Figure 4-26. Using a Dremel rotary tool (or similar), cut holes the size of your motors.*

2.   Test fit the servo motors into the mounting holes. If they fit, place the wheels onto the motors and make sure there is about 0.25 inch clearance between the bottom of the frame and the ground (this should be the same on each side). After proper clearance is achieved, you can mount the motors with (4) #6 bolts and nuts (see Figure 4-27). You can also mount the wheels to the motors at this time, using the screws that came with your servo motors. Simply slide the wheel onto the output shaft, and insert the screw through the center of the wheel hub. Tighten the screw down so that the wheel cannot wobble or move side to side.

*Figure 4-27. The wheel holes have been cut, the wheel test-fitted, and the rear ground-clearance looks good (about 0.25 inch to 0.5 inch).*

3.   Now we mount the caster wheel assembly to the front of the frame, as shown in Figure 4-28. Drill a hole in the back of the bracket on each side to mount into the tin frame. Now center the caster wheel bracket on the front of the frame and adjust the height until it is the same as the rear (0.25 inch) and mark each caster bracket mounting hole to the frame. After marked, drill holes through the frame and mount the front caster wheel.

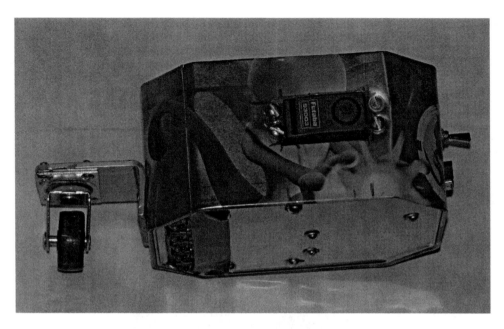

*Figure 4-28. The caster wheel assembly is mounted in the frame along with the motors.*

---

■ **Note** I went back and removed the 2 "L" brackets I previously made with a single 2-inch wide piece of aluminum flat bar (shown in Figure 4-28). I cut it to length and bent it in a vice as I did the previous brackets. I felt that the new piece looked nicer, but you can use whichever method you like.

---

4. Next we need to cut an access hole for the IR sensors to peek through the bottom of the frame. This hole enables us to mount the sensor board inside of the frame. I had to clip the edges of my IR sensor board PCB with a pair of pliers to make it fit inside the odd-shaped tin. Measure the total outline of the IR sensors and mark a rectangle on the bottom of the tin (I positioned my sensor board at the front of the frame). This is where the IR sensors will poke through the bottom of the frame and detect the Line on the ground. Carefully cut this shape out with a Dremel tool (see Figure 4-29).

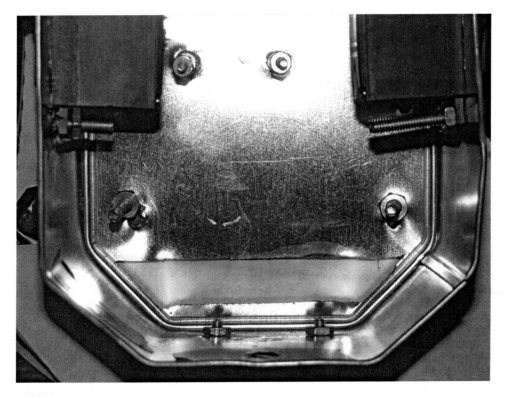

*Figure 4-29. The hole cut for the IR sensor board to fit through the frame toward the ground*

5.  Place the IR board with the sensors down, into the frame and through the access hole that you cut in the front base of the frame. With the sensors poking through the access hole, mark four mounting holes in the IR board with a marker. You can place mounting holes anywhere that does not interfere with the wires in the circuit. Drill the marked holes with a 1/8-inch bit and mount #6 bolts through the frame, from the bottom pointing upward. Now place the IR board onto the bolts and secure it with another nut on each side (see Figure 4-30). Make sure the IR sensors are evenly protruding from their access hole in the base–they should each be about 0.25 inch from the ground.

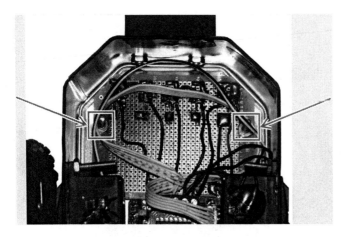

*Figure 4-30. Mount the IR sensor board into the frame, face down, and tighten nuts.*

6.  Mounting the Arduino. Now we need to add some mounting bolts to the base of
    the frame to hold the Arduino. Place your Arduino in the bottom of the tin
    (centered), and mark a hole for the USB programming port to protrude from the
    back of the frame (you might also want to mark a hole for the DC power port).
    Using a 1/2-inch bit, drill a hole for each port at the marked spots. With the USB
    port extending slightly through its new access port in the back of the frame, mark
    the three mounting holes on the base of the frame with a permanent marker. Drill
    these holes with a 1/8-inch drill bit and mount (3) #6 bolts (0.5 inch-1 inch long),
    securing each tightly (see Figure 4-31).

*Figure 4-31. Install mounting bolts for Arduino in the frame.*

7. Now place the Arduino on the mounting bolts and secure with one more nut. The USB port should poke through the back of the frame for easy programming.

8. Install Adafruit motor-shield. This simply plugs on top of the Arduino. You should connect the VIN jumper that enables the Arduino to use the same power supply as the motor-controller, which will simplify the wiring.

Congratulations, you are finished building a basic Linus, the Line-bot. It is now time to make the electrical connections (see Figure 4-32).

*Figure 4-32. Bottom view of the finished Line-bot*

# Making Connections

It is time to connect each of the sensor signal wires into the Arduino analog ports, according to Table 4-2. Each analog input pin is accessible from the top of the AF motor-shield. By connecting each infrared sensor to an analog input of the Arduino, Linus will have five different points of detection.

*Table 4-2. Where to Connect Each Sensor to the Arduino*

| Sensor Number | Arduino Analog Port |
|---|---|
| Sensor 1 | A0 |
| Sensor 2 | A1 |
| Sensor 3 | A2 |
| Sensor 4 | A3 |

| Sensor Number | Arduino Analog Port |
| --- | --- |
| Sensor 5 | A4 |
| Speed control Potentiometer (if used) | A5 |

With the sensors connected, we still need to connect them to a power source. The Arduino is an excellent option here, because it has a built-in 5v regulator–simply connect the IR sensor board power wires to the Arduino +5v and GND pins.

Lastly, we need to connect both motors to the motor-controller. The left motor should connect to M1 on the AF motor-shield, and right motor should connect to M3 on the motor-shield. If the motor does not spin forward when powered, you need to reverse the polarity of the motor by swapping the terminal wires connected to the motor-shield. With all of the electronics installed, we need to find a battery to fit in our frame (see Figure 4-33).

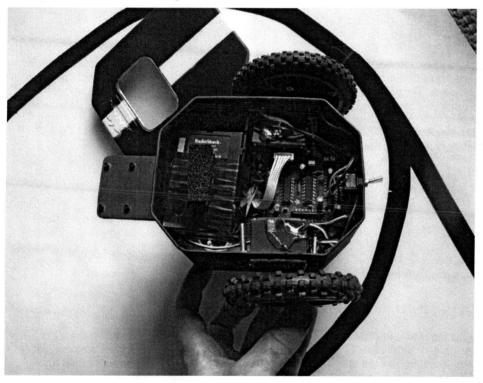

*Figure 4-33. Inside view of the Line-bot*

With all of the electronics mounted inside of Linus, we need to add only a power supply to get him moving.

# Installing Batteries

You can use any *type* of batteries that you can find, provided that they are between 5v–8v, and fit inside the frame. I am using (2) 6v 1000mAH NiCad rechargeable R/C batteries packs from Radio Shack. They were on clearance for $0.50 each with a charger, so I bought a few and arranged them in parallel (positive terminals tied together and negative terminals tied together) to produce 6v with 2000mAH–that means it will run at the same speed as one battery pack (6v), but with twice the run time (1000mAH × 2).

I placed my batteries into the front of the frame above the IR shield. They fit nicely in front of the motors, though I wedged a small piece of styrofoam between the battery pack and the inside of the frame to keep everything secure.

If you don't want to use a battery pack, you can buy a battery holder from Radio shack, which enables you to place four "AA" batteries (either re-chargeable or regular) into the pack to produce between 4.8v–6v depending on the batteries used (Radio Shack part #270-391-$1.79).

Keep in mind that servo motors were designed to run on voltages from 4.5v – 7.5v. Using a voltage above this level can damage the servo motor.

## Install Power Switch

I used a SPST toggle switch to switch the positive supply wire between the batteries and electronics. By mounting the switch at the rear of the frame above the Arduino USB port, you can easily kill the power with the flip of a switch. The positive wire coming from the battery should be soldered to one post the switch, and the other post should be connected to the power supply of the AF motor-shield. If you set the VIN jumper on the AF motor-shield, your Arduino will be powered using the same source as the motor-controller. The Arduino ground wire can be connected directly to the battery ground supply.

With everything installed in the frame, it is time to load the code and start testing.

# Loading the Code

Now that we are done with the hard part, it is time to load the code to your Arduino. First open the Arduino IDE and copy the code to a blank sketch (you can also download the code so you don't have to type it all out). After copied, press the Compile button to make sure there are no errors. Now select your Atmega chip from the "Tools • Board" menu (I am using the Arduino Duemilanove with the Atmega328 chip). Now plug in the Arduino to your PC USB port and press the Upload button. Instead of

Download Code: https://sites.google.com/site/arduinorobotics/home/chapter4_files

The plan is for Linus to try to line up his center IR sensor (sensor 3) directly on top of the black line on the track (Listing 4-2). If the value of sensor 3 is below the threshold (reading a black surface), we know that the bot is centered on the line and we can command it to drive both motors straight forward.

If sensor 3 rises above the threshold value, we will then check both the left-center sensor (sensor 2) and the right-center sensor (sensor 4) to see whether either is below the threshold. If so, we proceed forward with both motors, and if not we proceed to the next test.

If by some chance, sensors 2, 3, and 4 are all above the threshold, we proceed to check sensors 1 and 5 (the far left and far right sensors) to see whether either of them are below the threshold value. If so, we turn back from that direction to return to center.

You might have to calibrate your Max and Min values for each sensor, because they might differ from mine. They are denoted as "s1_min" and "s1_max" for sensor 1, and so on. To test the max value, place the assembled bot onto your white poster-board track–with no black tape beneath it, which should enable all five sensors to read their highest value. Now place each sensor above the black tape, and record both the minimum and maximum values for each sensor. Remember, sensor 1 should be the far left sensor, and sensor 5 is the far right (see Table 4-1 for the parts list).

*Listing 4-2. Full code listing for Linus.*

```
// Linus the Line-bot
// Follows a Black line on a White surface (poster-board and electrical tape).
// Code by JDW 2010 - feel free to modify.

#include <AFMotor.h>  // this includes the Afmotor library for the motor-controller

AF_DCMotor motor_left(1);   // attach motor_left to the Adafruit motorshield M1
AF_DCMotor motor_right(3);  // attach motor_right to the Adafruit motorshield M3

// Create variables for sensor readings

int sensor1 = 0;
int sensor2 = 0;
int sensor3 = 0;
int sensor4 = 0;
int sensor5 = 0;

// Create variables for adjusted readings

int adj_1 = 0;
int adj_2 = 0;
int adj_3 = 0;
int adj_4 = 0;
int adj_5 = 0;


// You can change the min/max values below to fine tune each sensor on your bot

int s1_min = 200;
int s1_max = 950;

int s2_min = 200;
int s2_max = 950;

int s3_min = 200;
int s3_max = 950;

int s4_min = 200;
int s4_max = 950;

int s5_min = 200;
int s5_max = 950;
```

```
// this threshold defines when the sensor is reading the black line
int lower_threshold = 20;

// value to define a middle threshold (half of the total 255 value range)
int threshold = 128;

// this threshold defines when the sensor is reading the white poster board
int upper_threshold = 230;

// this value sets the maximum speed of linus (255 = max).
// using a speed potentiometer will over-ride this setting.


int speed_value = 255;

// end of changeable variables

void setup()
{
  Serial.begin(9600); // start serial monitor to see sensor readings

// declare left motor
  motor_left.setSpeed(255);
  motor_left.run(RELEASE);

// declare right motor
  motor_right.setSpeed(255);
  motor_right.run(RELEASE);
}

void update_sensors(){

// this will read sensor 1
  sensor1 = analogRead(0);
  adj_1 = map(sensor1, s1_min, s1_max, 0, 255);
  adj_1 = constrain(adj_1, 0, 255);

// this will read sensor 2
  sensor2 = analogRead(1);      //  sensor 2 = left-center
  adj_2 = map(sensor2, s2_min, s2_max, 0, 255);
  adj_2 = constrain(adj_2, 0, 255);

// this will read sensor 3
  sensor3 = analogRead(2);            // sensor 3 = center
  adj_3 = map(sensor3, s3_min, s3_max, 0, 255);
  adj_3 = constrain(adj_3, 0, 255);

// this will read sensor 4
  sensor4 = analogRead(3);      //  sensor 4 = right-center
  adj_4 = map(sensor4, s4_min, s4_max, 0, 255);
  adj_4 = constrain(adj_4, 0, 255);
```

```
// this will read sensor 5
  sensor5 = analogRead(4);   // sensor 5 = right
  adj_5 = map(sensor5, s5_min, s5_max, 0, 255);
  adj_5 = constrain(adj_5, 0, 255);

// check value for speed potentiometer if present  (to read the pot, uncomment line below)
//speed_pot = analogRead(5) / 4;

}

void loop(){

  update_sensors(); // update sensors

  //speed_value = speed_pot;   // Leave commented out, unless using potentiometer


// first, check the value of the center sensor
  if (adj_3 < lower_threshold){

// if center sensor value is below threshold, check surrounding sensors
    if (adj_2 > threshold && adj_4 > threshold){

      // if all sensors check out, drive forward
      motor_left.run(FORWARD);
      motor_left.setSpeed(speed_value);

      motor_right.run(FORWARD);
      motor_right.setSpeed(speed_value);
    }
    // you want the bot to stop when it reaches the black box.

    else if (adj_1 < 1){
      if (adj_2 < 1){
        if (adj_3 < 1){
          if (adj_4 < 1){
            if (adj_5 < 1){

          //  if all sensors are reading black, stop Linus.
            motor_left.run(RELEASE);
            motor_right.run(RELEASE);

            }
          }
        }
      }
    }
  }

// otherwise, the center sensor is above the threshold
// so we need to check what sensor is above the black line
```

```
else {

  // first check sensors 1
  if (adj_1 < upper_threshold && adj_5 > upper_threshold){
   motor_left.run(RELEASE);
   motor_left.setSpeed(0);

   motor_right.run(FORWARD);
   motor_right.setSpeed(speed_value);
  }

  // then check sensor 5
  else if (adj_1 > upper_threshold && adj_5 < upper_threshold){
    motor_left.run(FORWARD);
    motor_left.setSpeed(speed_value);

    motor_right.run(RELEASE);
    motor_right.setSpeed(0);
  }

  // if not sensor 1 or 5, then check sensor 2
  else if (adj_2 < upper_threshold && adj_4 > upper_threshold){
    motor_left.run(RELEASE);
    motor_left.setSpeed(0);

    motor_right.run(FORWARD);
    motor_right.setSpeed(speed_value);
  }

  // if not sensor 2, then check sensor 4
  else if (adj_2 > upper_threshold && adj_4 < upper_threshold){
    motor_left.run(FORWARD);
    motor_left.setSpeed(speed_value);

    motor_right.run(RELEASE);
    motor_right.setSpeed(0);
  }


}

///// Print values for each sensor

/////sensor 1 values
Serial.print("sensor 1:  ");
Serial.print(sensor1);
Serial.print(" - ");

Serial.print("Adj 1:  ");
Serial.print(adj_1);
Serial.print(" - ");
```

```
/////sensor 2 values
Serial.print("sensor 2:   ");
Serial.print(sensor2);
Serial.print("  -  ");

Serial.print("Adj 2:   ");
Serial.print(adj_2);
Serial.print("  -  ");

/////sensor 3 values
Serial.print("sensor 3:   ");
Serial.print(sensor3);
Serial.print("  -  ");

Serial.print("Adj 3:   ");
Serial.print(adj_3);
Serial.print("  -  ");

/////sensor 4 values
Serial.print("sensor 4:   ");
Serial.print(sensor4);
Serial.print("  -  ");

Serial.print("Adj 4:   ");
Serial.print(adj_4);
Serial.print("  -  ");

/////sensor 5 values
Serial.print("sensor 5:   ");
Serial.print(sensor5);
Serial.print("  -  ");

Serial.print("Adj 5:   ");
Serial.print(adj_5);
Serial.print("  ");

Serial.print("speed:   ");
Serial.print(speed_pot);
Serial.println("  ");


}

// end of code
```

Lastly, we need to make a track to test Linus on. The track will only require a roll of black tape and your imagination.

# Making the Track

The track is the fun part, because it can be any shape or size that you want. I chose to use two pieces of white poster-board from the craft store, using black electrical tape for the line (Figure 4-34). I placed the poster-board together end-to-end and taped the underside with clear packing tape. You can add as many pieces of poster-board as you want, the bigger the better. You can make different tracks on each side of the poster-board, so you might want to buy a few rolls of electrical tape.

*Figure 4-34. Track 1: Linus continuously drives around making different decisions at each turn. If he ever makes it into the black box, he gets to rest.*

Although it is fun to watch the bot meander around the track at its own will, at some point you want to give it a break. So I wrote a section of code that tells the motors to stop if all sensors are reading black–then by placing a black square of electrical tape about (4 inch × 4 inch) at the end of the track, the bot will stop when it reaches this point.

The track in Figure 4-34 lets Linus wander around for as long as he wants and his path changes depending on what angle he enters each line intersection. The only drawback is that it takes Linus a long time to pick the path leading to the black box.

Unlike the above track, the track in Figure 4-35 is a definite length and might be better suited for calculating speed and tweaking Linus' settings. This track is also reversible, so when you get to the center black box, you can turn around and go back to the beginning black box.

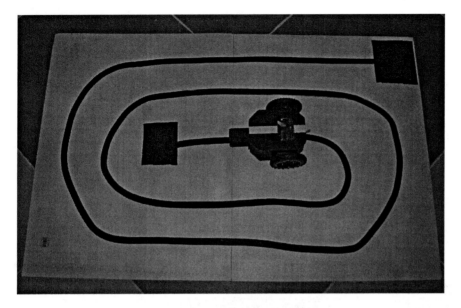

*Figure 4-35. Track 2: This track starts at the top and ends in the middle. You can turn Linus around and have him go back the way he came, but he will stop either way. This track is good for lap time testing (to see whether modifications in the code result in a faster lap time).*

# Testing

After you have your track designed, place your bot on the line and turn on the power. You should see Linus start moving, and if everything is wired up correctly, following the black line. You can hold the front of the bot with the IR sensors just above the black line while the rear wheels slightly off the ground. When sensor 3 is directly above the black line, you should see both wheels spinning. If you move the bot to the right slowly, you should see the left wheel stop while the right wheel spins at full speed attempting to correct the position. If you move the bot to the left, you should see the right wheel stop while the left wheel spins.

   If you want to experiment, you can change the following variables to see Linus exhibit a different behavior on the track:

```
// this threshold defines when the sensor is reading the black line
int lower_threshold = 20;

// value to define a middle threshold (half of the total 255 value range)
int threshold = 128;

// this threshold defines when the sensor is reading the white poster board
int upper_threshold = 230;

// this value sets the maximum speed of linus (255 = max).
// using a speed control potentiometer will over-ride this setting.
int speed_value = 255;
```

These variables determine how far from the black line the bot will allow before trying to correct its position and the maximum speed of Linus. If you mess it up, you can always re-download the original.

# Add-ons

Now that you have your line-bot assembled and working, you can start adding whatever you want. I added two blue LED lights (one on each motor) that light up whenever that motor is turned on. I also painted the frame with flat black spray paint, and added a white "racing-stripe" down the center of the lid. I later added a potentiometer to the front to easily adjust the "speed_value" variable mentioned previously without re-programming.

## LED Lights

To add LEDs to each motor, simply connect the LED to the motor terminals. You can buy pre-biased LEDs (that already have a resistor built-in), but you want to make your own by, soldering a resistor (330 ohm to 1k ohm) to either lead of the LED. After the resistor is installed, connect one LED to each motor terminal (see Figure 4-36). You have to connect the LED's positive lead to the motor's positive lead and negative to negative. If you plug it in backwards, it shouldn't hurt the LED at 6 volts, but it won't light up.

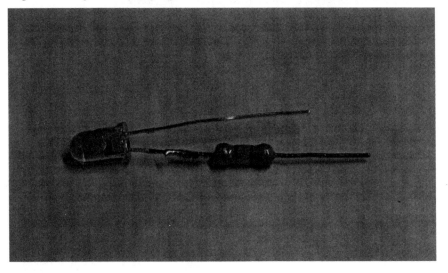

**Figure 4-36.** *LED with resistor soldered to one leg*

After soldering the LED leads and resistor, and connecting it to the motor terminals, you need to secure the LED in place so it doesn't wobble around (see Figure 4-37 and 4-38). You can drill a small hole on each side of the tin just above the motor and mount the LED pointing outside so you can see them light up.

*Figure 4-37. LED with resistor hot-glued to the top of the servo motor casing*

*Figure 4-38. Both blue LEDs lit up as the bot is driving forward with both motors*

As I mentioned, my tin has a small clear plastic window in the lid, so I chose to mount my LEDs on top of each Servo motor inside the tin. The LEDs can be seen through the plastic window as each motor spins (see Figure 4-39). To keep them secure, I used a hot-glue gun with a few dabs on each LED lead to keep it secure to the top of the motor. This glue holds very well but with a flat head screwdriver, but can be removed if desired in the future with no harm to your motors.

*Figure 4-39. Both blue LEDs lit up with the lid on top–you can see through the plastic window.*

## Painting

I decided that I didn't really want Linus to sport a Poke'mon paint job, so I took his rear wheels off, taped him up, and spray painted his frame (see Figure 4-40). I thought I would keep it simple, so he got a gray primer coat, then a flat black base coat (see Figure 4-42), then a stripe down the center with some flat white paint. I also sprayed the bottom black to make sure nothing reflected from the bottom of the silver Tin.

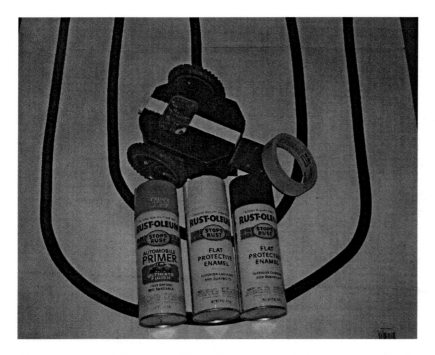

**Figure 4-40.** *I used three cans of Rust-oleum spray paint. Each can of paint lasts for several different projects, so they are worth buying.*

Prep the bot for painting with some white paper to cover the electronics and green painters tape to cover the motors, caster wheel, IR sensors, and anywhere else paint might get on something it shouldn't (see Figure 4-41). I had to tape off the clear plastic window on the lid so it would still be see-through.

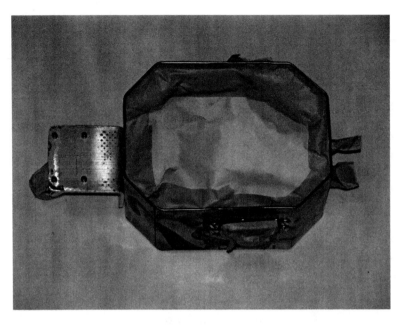

*Figure 4-41. The bot is prepped with tape and ready for spraying.*

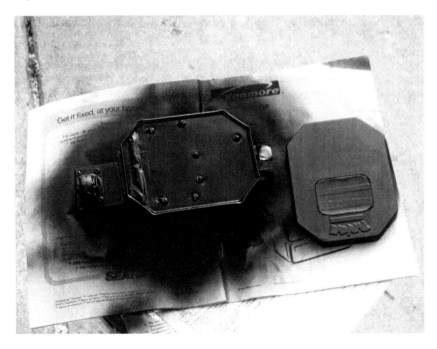

*Figure 4-42. The first coat of flat black paint, after the gray primer*

You should spray thin, light coats with the spray paint and wait about 30-40 minutes before re-coating. Lastly, adding a stripe to the lid means putting tape everywhere, except where you want the line to be (see Figure 4-43). In this case, I wanted my stripe to be about the same width as the line on the track, so I did a rough measurement with a roll of electrical tape on each end and put masking tape everywhere else. I then primed the stripe gray, and then painted it white when that was dry. When the last coat of paint dries, you can put Linus remove all masking tape and mount the wheels back on to the motor output shafts, as shown in Figure 4-44.

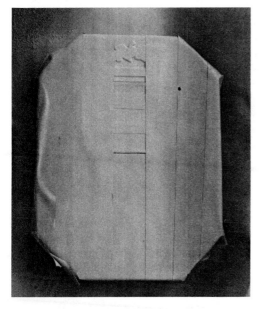

**Figure 4-43.** *Priming the stripe on the lid*

And here is the finished product of the spray paint job.

*Figure 4-44. The finished paint job for Linus*

## Adding Speed Regulator (Potentiometer)

Because our five sensors are only using up five of the six Arduino analog inputs (A0-A4), we still have one available (A5). The speed of the bot can be changed in the code by adjusting the value of the "speed_value" variable, but by adding a potentiometer connected to last remaining analog pin, we can adjust the top speed of the bot on the fly without re-programming the Arduino. The speed control potentiometer is not necessary, though it makes testing the line-bot much easier.

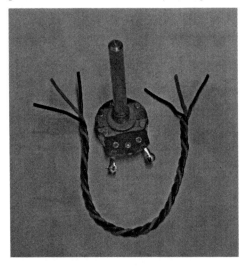

*Figure 4-45. A potentiometer and three strands of solid copper wire to use for the speed control*

If you choose to add this potentiometer, you will need to plug the left pin into Ground, the center pin into Arduino analog pin 5 (the last one), and the right pin to Arduino +5v, according to Table 4-3. Then simply remove the comment lines beneath the "update_sensors();" line at the beginning of the main loop as shown in the following code. This tells the Arduino to update the "speed_value" variable to equal the potentiometer reading, each time the sensors are updated.

Change this:

```
void loop(){

  update_sensors();

  // speed_value = speed_pot;
```

to this:

```
void loop(){

  update_sensors();  // this line remains unchanged.

  speed_value = speed_pot;  // removed comment lines from beginning of this line.
```

*Table 4-3. Potentiometer wiring chart.*

| Wire | Potentiometer Pole | Arduino Connection |
|------|--------------------|--------------------|
| Red | Left pole | Arduino +5v |
| Green | Center pole | Arduino A5 (analog input 6) |
| Black | Right pole | Arduino Ground |

To mount the potentiometer, use a 3/8-inch drill bit (or the recommended size for the potentiometer you are using) to drill a hole in the front of the frame, just above the caster wheel bracket (see Figure 4-46). Slide the potentiometer through the hole, and use the washer and nut to secure it to the frame.

*Figure 4-46. The speed control potentiometer mounted through the front of the frame*

Now adjusting the top speed of the bot is as simple as turning a knob. This comes in handy if you are using a battery pack above 6v, and find that the bot moves too quickly or you would like to test it at a slower speed.

You can see the finished Linus in Figure 4-47.

*Figure 4-47. Top view of the finished Line-bot with the potentiometer mounted*

# Summary

In this chapter, we used infrared light to detect the reflectivity of a surface. We found that darker colored surfaces (like black tape) reflect less infrared light than a lighter colored surface (like a white poster-board). Using a homemade infrared sensor board with five basic IR emitter/detector pairs, Linus is able to determine what sensor is directly above the black line.

We also discovered how to modify a standard hobby servo motor for continuous rotation, as well as how to remove the servo circuitry to operate as a standard DC gear motor. We then mounted the drive wheels to the servo adapter plates to secure to each motor, and made a mounting bracket for the front caster wheel.

The frame for this robot is a tin container that was used to hold a children's card game, and was modified using a Dremel rotary tool using a metal cut-off wheel attachment. The motors, front caster wheel, and Arduino were then mounted into the frame. After completing the frame, we installed the AdaFruit motor-shield atop the Arduino, a 6v battery for power, and made the connections from the IR sensor board and battery to the Arduino, and the motors to the motor-controller.

With everything installed, we loaded the code to the Arduino, made a track using poster-board and electrical tape, and began testing Linus. By changing the speed variables and light thresholds, we are able to change the way the robot responds to the track. After we got Linus working, we added accent lighting inside the Linus frame, a speed control potentiometer, and finally gave him a nice paint job. In the next chapter, we build another autonomous robot using ultrasonic "ping" sensors to detect and maintain a specific distance from the wall, as the maneuvers around a room autonomously...let's get ready to build Wally the wall-bot.

# CHAPTER 5

# Wally the Wall-Bot

In the previous chapter, I showed you a simple use of infrared sensors to detect the color variations of the floor surface and choose a direction accordingly. Although an IR sensing robot is autonomous, you must place a line on the ground for the bot to follow. Using a different type of sensor called an Ultrasonic range finder, you can measure distances from 6 inches to 25 feet. In this chapter, we create a robot named Wally (Figure 5-1) that uses these sensors to autonomously navigate around a room without touching anything other than the floor.

First we build a homemade motor-controller on perforated prototyping board, using N-channel and P-channel mosfets to form a dual H-bridge. We then modify the base of a dual motor toy to be controlled using the Arduino. Here you will be able to choose any robot base that you want. After selecting a base, we modify it to hold the motor-controller, Arduino, three ultra-sonic sensors, and a battery pack. After assembled and wired, we can load the code and start testing.

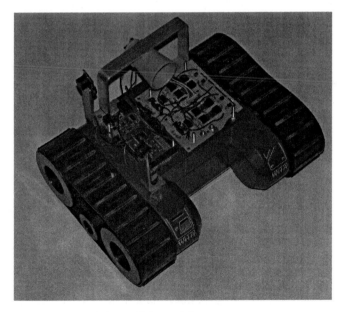

*Figure 5-1.* Wall the Wall-bot ready to go

# How Wally Works

Wally the wall-following robot attempts to determine the distance of a nearby wall and follow the wall to its end point. This is accomplished by using three independent ultrasonic range finding sensors to determine the distance from the robot to the wall, and adjusting the speed and direction to keep these readings within the specified range. Two of the sensors are mounted on Wally's right side—one at the front corner and the other at the rear corner, both facing the wall (right). By placing two sensors on the right side, we not only know how far Wally is from the wall, but we can determine when the two sensors are parallel to the wall.

From the sensor placement we can determine that if the front-right and rear-right sensor readings are equal, the bot is parallel with the wall. If the front-right sensor is less than the rear-right sensor, the bot is heading toward the wall. Lastly, if the front-right sensor is greater than the rear-right sensor, the bot is heading away from the wall (see Figure 5-2).

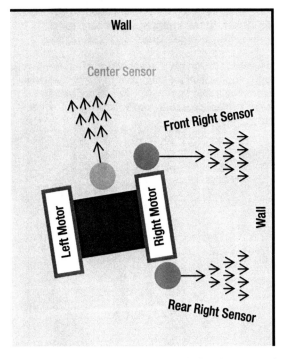

*Figure 5-2. This image shows Wally heading away from the wall.*

Because we want the bot to sense the wall without actually touching it, I set the desired distance to be around 8 inches from the wall. This tells Wally that if he is more than 8 inches from the wall, he needs to steer back toward the wall. If he is closer than 8 inches to the wall, he should steer away from the wall. When both right sensors are equal to 8 inches, Wally will drive straight forward until the wall path changes. The idea is to stay exactly 8 inces from the wall, using it as the path around the room.

The center sensor is used to determine when a wall ends and serves to keep Wally from hitting anything in front of him. When the front center sensor falls below 12 inches (i.e., he is approaching the corner of a room), Wally is instructed to turn left a bit and see whether the path is clear. If so, he will continue following the new wall; if not, he will keep turning until there is enough room.

The end result is a small robot that will autonomously drive around a room, staying approximately 8–10 inches from the wall. When the bot reaches a corner (inside or outside corner), he will determine which direction to turn to keep following the wall. You can add obstacles to the wall to try and confuse Wally, but when properly tweaked, he will not be fooled and will continue on his journey around your room until he runs out of battery power.

The sensors used on Wally can be any type that can calculate precise (+/– 1 inch) distance measurements from 6 inches to 5 feet. Though there are several range finders to choose from (using both IR and ultrasonic ranging), I selected some ultrasonic range finders from Maxbotics (Sparkfun part #SEN-00639) that have an built-in signal processor and output a simple Analog voltage that can be easily read by the Arduino using the analogRead(pin) command. The Analog output signal of each sensor is calibrated to centimeters, so if you want to convert the output to inches, simply divide by 2.54 (because there are 2.54 centimeters in 1 inch).

To read this sensor on your serial monitor, upload the following code to your Arduino, power the sensor with +5v and GND, and connect the Analog signal from the sensor into the Arduino A0 pin.

```
void setup(){
Serial.begin(9600);
}
void loop() {
int center_sensor = analogRead(0) / 2.54; // read sensor from pin A0 and convert to inches
Serial.println(center_sensor);  // displays the sensor reading in inches.
}
```

Though these sensors produce mostly reliable readings, it is recommended that you install a 100uF capacitor between the sensors +5v and GND to reduce glitches in the readings caused by unstable supply voltages. The capacitor acts as a small battery that supplies power to the sensor during power dips and voltage spikes, smoothing the overall operation.

The parts for Wally were mostly scavenged or homemade, with the exception of the ultrasonic sensors and the Arduino. Wally's frame came from a tank-steering toy with tracks (yes, tank tracks) from the thrift store. The term "tank-steering" refers to the use of two independent motors (one left and one right) that control both the speed and direction of the bot—there is no steering wheel on this type of drive-train. The frame does not have to have actual "tank tracks" on it (Linus was a tank-steering robot). I have found at least 10 different tank steering R/C cars at my local thrift store that work for Wally (all for under $3 each), though the gearing of the frame you choose is important. A slower moving drivetrain works better for Wally.

The motor-controller is a high-speed dual H-bridge made from 12 mosfets (8 power and 4 signal), 16 resistors, and 2 mosfet driver ICs. The mosfet drivers are simple high-speed signal buffers—they have 2 inputs, 2 outputs, VCC, and Ground. The mosfet drivers act as an amplifier for driving the low-side N-channel mosfets with a 0–100% PWM signal for full-speed control. The high-side P-channel mosfets use a small signal transistor to turn them on, but they are controlled by digital pins, not using PWM.

This simple H-bridge (x2) provides access to control all four switches of each H-bridge independently (called four-quadrant control), allowing for electric-braking (through either the high- or low-side mosfets), but incorporates no shoot-through protection so you must make sure you connect everything properly to avoid problems. Because the bridge uses a mosfet driver, you can switch the mosfets at ultrasonic PWM frequencies for silent operation (32kHz on the Arduino).

■ **Note** Without the mosfet drivers, the H-bridge will still work, but the Arduino cannot supply the required current for such high PWM frequencies, so the switching speed is limited to around 1kHz.

# Parts List for Wally

We need to order a handful of parts from an online electronics supplier, a few ultrasonic sensors from Sparkfun.com, and find a robot "base" or salvaged frame with wheels and motors (see Table 5-1). This project should work well with any tank-drive robot base.

*Table 5-1. The Parts List for Wally*

| Part | Description | Price |
|---|---|---|
| (3) Ultrasonic sensors | Sparkfun (part #SEN-00639)—Maxbotics LV-EZ1 ultrasonic range finder. Range is 6 inches to 20 feet. | $25.95 ea |
| Frame | Thrift-store. I found a slow-moving toy with tank-steering for $3. It happens to have tank tracks (not required). Your frame should include both drive motors and all gearing. DFRobot.com (part #ROB0037). | $3.00–$41.00 |
| Batteries | 6–12v, rechargeable recommended—at least 1Ah capacity. | $5.00 |
| Arduino | I used my Arduino MEGA, though any Arduino will work. | |
| Hot-glue gun | This is not required, but makes mounting the sensors extremely easy. It is also removable without much effort for testing sensor placement. | $3.00 |
| Aluminum bar | I used three small pieces of 1/8-inch thick x 3/4-inch wide aluminum flat bar from the hardware store. Total length used is 24 inches. | $3.00 |
| Nuts and bolts | I use #4 or #6 nuts and bolts, approximately 2 inches long, to mount the Arduino and motor-driver boards to the robot frame. These nuts/bolts are sold in 5 pcs/pack for under $1 each—I bought 2 packs. | $2.00 |
| Power switch | Radio Shack (part #275-634). This is optional, but recommended. Simply place it in series with the positive supply from the battery. Digikey (part #EG4810). | $2.99 |
| Male header pins | Sparkfun (part #PRT-00116) —I used these to connect the motors to the H-bridge. 40 pins per unit, I only used 6, but they are handy to have around. | $2.50 |

| Part | Description | Price |
|------|-------------|-------|
| Motor-driver | This board controls both drive motors forward/reverse, with full-speed control at up to 32kHz PWM. Parts can be purchased at Digikey and Radio Shack. | |
| (4) N-channel signal transistors | Digikey (part #2N7000) —These are 200ma logic-level N-channel mosfets used to interface the P-channel power mosfets. Almost any logic-level N-channel mosfet will work here. | $0.39 ca |
| (4) N-channel power mosfet | Digikey (part #FQP50N06L) —Any N-channel power mosfet will work. Rated for 52 amps at 60 volts. | $1.25 ea |
| (4) P-channel power mosfet | Digikey (part #FQP47P06) —This mosfet has a high Gate-to-Source voltage (Vgs) of +/–25v, though any P-channel power mosfet will work. Rated for 47 amps at 60 volts. | $2.26 ea |
| (2) TC4427 mosfet drivers | Digikey (part #TC4427) —This mosfet driver is used to switch the N-channel power mosfets at high PWM speeds (32kHz) for silent operation. | $1.33 ea |
| (4) 10k resistors | Digikey (part #ERD-S2TJ103V) —Sold in 10 packs for under $1. These can also be purchased at Radio Shack in a 5 pack for $0.99. | $0.78 |
| (4) 150-ohm resistors | Digikey (part #ERD-S2TJ151V) —Sold in 10 packs for under $1. These can also be purchased at Radio Shack in a 5 pack for $0.99. | $0.78 |
| (2) 8-pin IC sockets | Digikey (part #A24807) —These can also be purchased at Radio Shack. | $0.33 ea |
| (2) Female 6-pin headers | Digikey (part #3M9516) —These headers are the same type that are used on the Arduino analog A0-A5 pins, and make wiring the motor-controller to the Arduino easy. | $0.94 ea |
| Perforated PCB prototyping board | Radio Shack (part #276-147) or (part #276-168). | $3.99 |

# The Motor-Controller

The motor-controller is important because without one your robot won't move. You can use any type of motor-controller that can support the motors on your bot, though I built a simple dual H-bridge on Radio Shack perforated copper-clad board with some components ordered from Digikey.com.

Wally requires forward and reverse control of each motor in order to turn fully at the end of a wall, so a full H-bridge must be used to control each motor. The simplest of solid-state H-bridges can contain as few as four transistors, but limitations in PWM frequency and heat generated from cross-conduction quickly make this type of bridge unappealing. Adding a few extra parts to the simple four-transistor H-bridge can provide a versatile and inexpensive motor-controller.

I decided to build the H-bridge for Wally to meet the following minimum criteria:

- Continuous amperage = 5 amps
- Voltage rating = 12vdc
- Speed control capable (PWM)
- Easy to build
- Silent PWM switching speed (32kHz)

## The High-Side Switches

The H-bridge uses P-channel mosfets for the high-side switches and N-channel mosfets for the low-side switches. Remember that a P-channel mosfet (like a PNP transistor) is turned on by supplying a voltage to the Gate pin that is around *5–10v below* the positive supply voltage, usually Ground. To invert the signal required to turn the P-channel mosfets on, I used small N-channel signal mosfets to provide the GND supply to turn them on, whereas a 10k-ohm pull-up resistor (to V+) keeps them turned off when not used. These mosfets are intended to be controlled using a digital output pin and are not set up to be driven using a PWM signal.

## The Low-Side Switches

The N-channel mosfets on the low-side of the bridge are the logic-level type and can be driven directly by the Arduino, but the 40mA supplied by the Arduino PWM pins is hardly enough to drive the mosfets at higher PWM frequencies. To remedy this, I used a mosfet driver chip that amplifies the Arduino PWM signal to supply around 2 amps to the mosfet Gate pins—that's about 100 times more current than the Arduino can supply! Because of this, the N-channel mosfets can be driven at much higher frequencies without causing any problems.

The motor-controller schematic shown in Figure 5-3 illustrates the operation of each H-bridge in the circuit. Because the circuit contains two full H-bridges, you must build two of the circuits in the schematic onto your prototyping board.

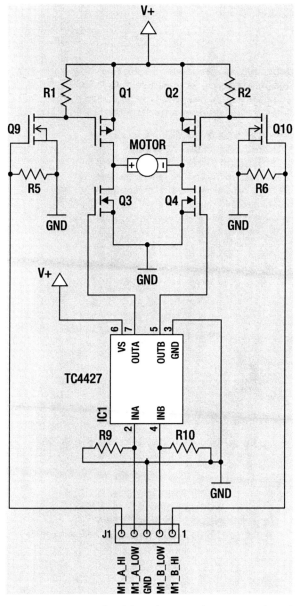

*Figure 5-3.* *One side of the schematic for our simple H-bridge motor-controller. The complete circuit contains two of these schematics side by side, using a common V+ and GND.*

The mosfet driver uses the positive voltage supply from the batteries to power the N-channel mosfet Gate pins, and the voltage limit of the TC4427 mosfet driver IC is only 18v, so the maximum voltage of this circuit is 18vdc. I tested this circuit with both 6v and 12v battery packs with excellent results.

Using the parts list and circuit schematic, we can start building the motor-controller.

# Building the Circuit

To get started building this dual H-bridge, you need the following materials: a soldering iron, rosin-core solder, wire, a prototyping board, two 8-pin IC sockets, two female 6-pin headers, four N-channel power mosfets, four P-channel power mosfets, and four N-channel signal mosfets. After you have the motor-controller parts together (refer to Table 5-1), the following steps guide you through the building process.

1.  *Place the 8-pin IC sockets (onto the prototyping board and solder each tab):*
    Next connect the pin 3 of each IC socket (bottom row, center right pin)
    together with a black wire because this is the Ground pin for each IC. Also tie
    the pin 6 of each IC (directly above the GND pin) to each other with a red wire
    because this is the V+ for each IC. I tied the two sets of wires into the center of
    the board between the IC sockets (see Figure 5-4).

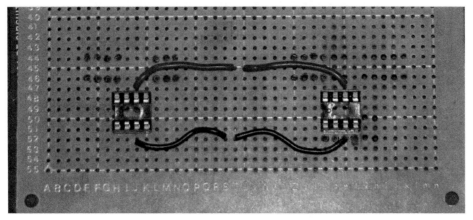

*Figure 5-4. You should start building the H-bridge by placing the two IC sockets onto the prototyping board and connect the common V+ and GND pins of each to the center of the board.*

2.  Pins 1 and 8 (the top left and bottom left pins) of the TC4427 mosfet driver IC
    are not internally connected to anything—there are only six active pins in this
    8-pin package. To further illustrate this, I clipped the leads from pins 1 and 8
    completely off to show that they are not needed (see Figure 5-5).

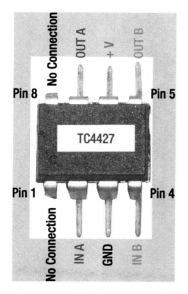

**Figure 5-5.** *The TC4427 mosfet driver IC uses six of its eight pins. To prove that they are not needed, I clipped pins 1 and 8 from the IC. If you solder these pins onto the board, they serve only as anchors to keep the chip secure.*

3.  *Install mosfets*: Repeat these instructions for each side of the motor-controller.Start by placing the N-channel power mosfets (FQP50-N06L) about 4–5 holes above the IC sockets—pin 5 (top right) of the TC4427 IC controls the lower right mosfet Gate pin, whereas pin 7 controls the lower left mosfet Gate pin. I used a 150-ohm resistor (each) between these pins and the mosfets Gate pin—these resistors are not required. Space the lower mosfets about 3–4 holes apart to give them room (you want to leave some room on the bottom to solder), as shown in Figure 5-6.

4.  Next place the P-channel power mosfets directly above the N-channel power mosfets, such that their tabs can be soldered together. The tab of a mosfet is almost always tied to the center pin (drain) of a TO-220 mosfet. By soldering the corresponding P and N channel mosfets drain tabs together, there is no need to connect the center pins of the mosfets beneath the PCB (you can even clip them off), though I soldered them to the PCB pad to help hold the mosfet in place. The motor terminal wires are soldered directly to these tabs (see Figure 5-6).

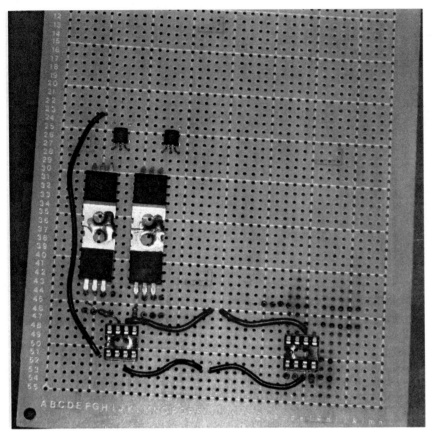

**Figure 5-6.** *All of the mosfets in the left H-bridge are installed—the same should be done for the right H-bridge.*

5.   Lastly place the N-channel signal mosfets (2n7000) above the P-channel power mosfets (FQP47-P06). The drain pin from the 2n7000 should connect to the Gate pin of the FQP47-P06, the Source pin of the 2n7000 should connect to Ground, and the Gate pin of the 2n7000 should be connected to the Arduino Input. I ran out of color coded wire, so I had to use black wire for the (4) 2n7000 connections—they are the wires going from each side of the IC sockets upward toward the 2n7000 signal mosfets in Figure 5-7.

6.   *Install resistors.* Remember that the mosfets have tiny capacitors inside of them that must be drained each time it is switched in order to fully turn off. This is easily done with a pull-up or pull-down resistor. Resistors can be installed any direction.

7.   The P-channel mosfets are turned off by setting the Gate pin voltage equal to the Source pin, which is connected to the positive voltage supply. So you want to place a 10k pull-up resistor from the Gate pin to the Source pin of each P-

channel power mosfet. This ensures that unless turned on, these mosfets will stay off.

8. Next install the 10k pull-down resistors to the N-channel signal mosfets (2n7000) from the Gate (center) to the Source (left), which keeps the signal mosfets off unless turned on by the Arduino.

9. The pull-down resistors for the N-channel power mosfets are placed at the inputs of the TC4427 driver IC, from each input (pins 2 and 4) to Ground (pin 3) to ensure that they are turned off by default. Pull-down resistors at the Gate pins of the N-channel power mosfets are not necessary now that the mosfet driver IC will not leave them floating.

10. Figure 5-7 shows where I placed the resistors on my prototyping board. The exact hole that each part goes through is not terribly important—just stick to the schematic to make sure you are connecting each part correctly. It is helpful to keep a list of the parts and their descriptions handy to reference while building. I constantly double-check the manufacturer's datasheet pinout diagrams of each part to make sure I know what pin goes where (the datasheet can usually be downloaded from the manufacturer's website).

**Figure 5-7.** *The top set of resistors are used to keep the P-channel power mosfets and N-channel signal mosfets turned off when not used. The bottom set of resistors are used to keep the mosfet driver IC outputs turned off unless commanded on by the Arduino.*

11. The top and bottom boxes in Figure 5-8, show where the pull-up and pull-down resistors go (all 10k ohm). The center boxes show the optional Gate resistors (150 ohm) for the N-channel power mosfets. These are not required and can be replaced with jumper wires. The bottom boxes show the TC4427 input pull-down resistors.

12. *Install headers and make connections:* I used (2) 5-pin female headers from Digikey for easy connections to the motor-controller.

    - *Header Pin 1 (far left):* Controls the AHI (A high-side input) of each bridge, which turns on the P-channel power mosfet using the N-channel signal mosfet. This input should be connected to the Gate pin of the 2n7000.

    - *Header Pin 2:* Connects to the TC4427 pin 2 (IN-A), which controls the ALI (a low-side input) of each bridge. You should use a PWM signal to control this input.

- *Header Pin 3*: Connects to Ground.

- *Header Pin 4*: Connects to the TC4427 pin 4 (IN-B), which controls the BLI (B low-side input) of each bridge. You should use a PWM signal to control this input.

- *Header Pin 5 (far right)*: Controls the BHI (B high-side input) of each bridge, which turns on the P-channel power mosfet using the N-channel signal mosfet. This input should be connected to the Gate pin of the 2n7000.

After connecting the Header Pins, make common connections like the + Voltage and the Ground supply. The + Voltage wire should run from the P-channel mosfets Source pins down to the + Voltage supply of each TC4427 IC (pin 6). This supply wire should then connect to the positive battery power supply. I made some of these connections on the bottom of the board as shown in Figure 5-8. The Ground wire should connect all of the N-channel mosfets (power mosfet and signal mosfet) Source pins, as well as the Ground supply of each TC4427 IC (pin 3) —this wire can then also be connected to the negative battery power supply.

After completed, the motor-controller should look similar to Figure 5-9.

*Figure 5-8. The underside of the perforated prototyping board*

*Figure 5-9. The completed dual H-bridge that will serve as the motor-controller for this project*

As you can see in Figure 5-10, using perf-board looks a bit messy because there are several wires running on the top of the board, but if each connection is soldered properly, it will work just as well as an etched PCB.

## Building the Frame

Using a tank steering setup, you can control the direction of the bot by varying the speed to each motor. By powering both motors equally, the bot travels forward. To turn right, reduce the speed of the right motor. Likewise reducing the speed of the left motor forces the bot to turn left. With bi-directional control of each motor, you can turn each wheel opposing directions to achieve a zero-turn radius (meaning it can turn 360 degrees without moving forward or backwards).

To achieve this type of control, you simply need a frame with two drive wheels, one on each side of the bot. You can build your own tank steering setup with two gear motors or continuous rotation servos as we did with Linus the line-bot, or you can use a tank steering toy or robot base, like the one I was able to find at my local thrift-store. If you cannot find a frame to salvage, you might be interested in one of the several robot bases from DFRobot.com, like the RP5 mobile tank platform for a reasonable $41.00 (see Figure 5-11).

I was able to find an R/C toy with tank tracks for $3 from the thrift-store. The base of the toy was the perfect size for Wally, so I removed everything but the base of the frame with the tank treads and motors mounted inside. The top of the frame had enough room to mount the Arduino and motor-controller, whereas the bottom of the frame was large enough to mount (2) 6v rechargeable batteries.

1. *Strip frame down to motors and base.* If salvaging an old toy, you can remove all of the **electronics** because you will build your own motor-controller and the Arduino will provide the control signals. All that is needed, is access to the terminal wires of each motor. In Figure 5-10, the battery compartment is in the center of the base and a 6-pin plug is used to connect both motors and the power supply wires to the main board.

*Figure 5-10. Here you can see the underside of the frame base, including both drive motors attached into the black gear boxes and the wiring harness.*

*Figure 5-11. The DFRobot RP5 Mobile Tank Platform includes two drive motors with gearing, wheels, and tank tracks. You can easily mount your Arduino, batteries, motor-controller, and sensors to this frame.*

2. *Mount the motor-controller and Arduino:* used a marker to mark the mounting holes onto the frame, and a drill to make the holes. After drilling the holes, secure four bolts to hold the motor-controller and three or four bolts to hold the Arduino (three holes for a regular Arduino and four holes for the Arduino Mega). Secure a nut to each bolt with the bolts pointing upward through the frame. I had to use #8 bolts for the motor-controller board and #4 bolts for the Arduino (see Figure 5-12).

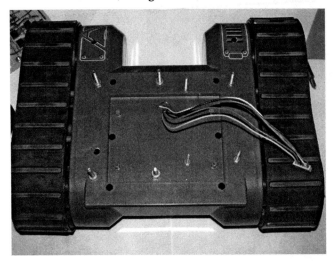

**Figure 5-12.** *The frame with mounting bolts installed*

3. *Making connections:* Now you can install the Arduino and motor-controller onto the bolts and wire up the Arduino to the motor-controller (see Figure 5-13). You need (4) PWM outputs and (4) digital outputs to control both bridges. Use Table 5-2 to connect each motor-controller input to the Arduino outputs, double checking each wire when you are done.

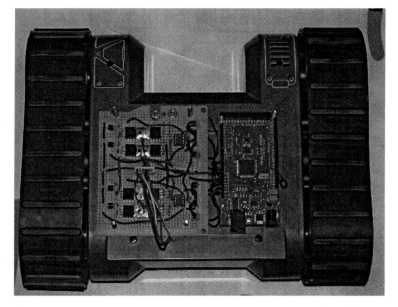

**Figure 5-13.** *The frame base with motor-controller and Arduino mounted*

In the code, we will change the Arduino system timers 1 and 2 in the setup() function to allow for silent PWM switching at 32kHz. On a regular Arduino, this changes PWM outputs 9, 10, 11, and 3. On the Arduino Mega, this will change PWM outputs 9, 10, 11, and 12. The digital outputs (AHI and BHI for each bridge) can be assigned to any available pins.

You can use either board, but it *does* matter how you connect each bridge. That is, you must take care to connect the A High-side input (AHI), A Low-side input (ALI), B High-side input (BHI), and B Low-side input (BLI) connections for each bridge correctly, as shown in Figure 5-14. If not connected properly, the bridges can be commanded into a short circuit. Make sure you have everything connected according to the circuit schematic, and take a moment to look at Table 5-2, to make sure each connection is wired properly to the Arduino.

**Table 5-2.** *Motor-Controller Connections to Arduino*

| Bridge Connection | Arduino Code | Arduino Pin | Arduino Mega Pin |
| --- | --- | --- | --- |
| Motor 2 - AHI | M2_AHI | 8 | 8 |
| Motor 2 – ALI (PWM) | M2_ALI | 9 | 9 |
| Motor 2 - BLI (PWM) | M2_BLI | 10 | 10 |
| Motor 2 - BHI | M2_BHI | 7 | 7 |
| Motor 1 - AHI | M1_AHI | 2 | 2 |

| Bridge Connection | Arduino Code | Arduino Pin | Arduino Mega Pin |
|---|---|---|---|
| Motor 1 - ALI (PWM) | M1_ALI | 11 | 11 |
| Motor 1 - BLI (PWM) | M1_BLI | 3 | 12 |
| Motor 1 - BHI | M1_BHI | 4 | 4 |

▪ **Note** If using a standard Arduino, M1-BLI should connect to PWM pin 3. If using the Arduino Mega, M1-BLI should connect to PWM pin 12. The other connections are the same regardless of what board you use.

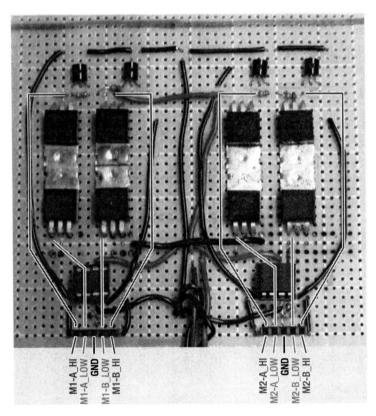

*Figure 5-14. Here you can see the labels for each connection on the motor-controller. Use Table 5-2 to make these connections to the Arduino.*

With both H-bridges connected to the Arduino as per Table 5-2, we lack connecting only the sensors and batteries to finish Wally. Let's begin by making a few mounting brackets to secure the ultrasonic range sensors to Wally's frame.

## Installing the Sensors

With the bot ready to move, you now need to install the sensors to guide it along its path. Start by finding a place on the frame to mount each sensor.

Two of the ultrasonic sensors should be placed on the right side of the bot facing the wall—one mounted on the front corner of the frame and the other mounted on the rear corner. The third sensor should be placed on the rear of the bot facing forward (straight ahead), so that the bot will know when it is getting close to the end of the wall. They must be placed high enough that their view of the wall is not obstructed by anything, so you will likely need to make some mounting brackets.

I used a piece of 3/4-inch wide, 1/8-inch thick aluminum flat bar to make a few mounting brackets for the sensors. I started by cutting three identical 4-inch long pieces of the aluminum flat bar. Then measure 1 inch from the end of each piece and bend at a 90-degree angle, as shown in Figure 5-15. This makes an "L" shaped bracket (1 inch x 3 inches) that is easily mounted to the frame to hold a sensor.

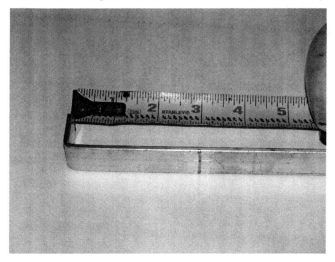

*Figure 5-15. The side sensor brackets were made from a piece of 3/4-inch wide aluminum flat bar.*

I used an all-purpose hot-glue gun to secure the sensors to the brackets and the brackets to the frame. A standard crafting hot-glue gun is an excellent tool for prototyping, because you can easily make semi-permanent connections quickly. I glued the sensor to the top of each mounting bracket as shown in Figure 5-16, and then glued the bottom of each bracket to the top of the frame deck. Remember, the side sensors should be mounted at the front and rear corners of Wally's right side, facing the wall (see Figure 5-18). The rear sensor should be mounted somewhere in the center of the bot, facing forward.

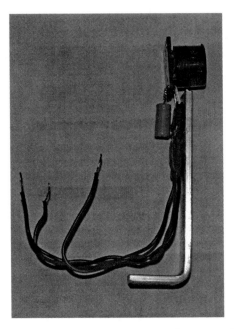

*Figure 5-16. This image shows the sensor glued to the sensor bracket.*

The backside of the sensor shows the labeling for each output pin (see Figure 5-17). The Analog output is the easiest pin to read with the Arduino. You need only three wires to operate each sensor: GND (pin 1), +5v (pin 2), and the Analog output, marked "AN" (pin 5). I used a 6-pin female header with long pins soldered to the sensor, then bent downward at a 90-degree angle to allow for easy mounting. Because these sensors are so lightweight, I chose to mount them to the aluminum brackets with a hot-glue gun. Just a dab of glue on the black header should securely hold the sensor to the top of the bracket. The hot-glue holds securely, but is also removable with a little prying or a razor knife.

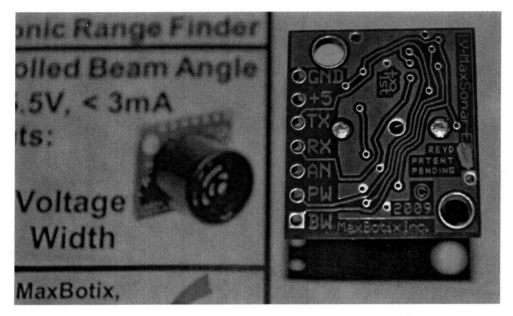

*Figure 5-17. The Maxbotics MaxSonar LV1 series ultrasonic range finder*

The third sensor should be mounted to the rear of the bot, facing toward the front to prevent it from hitting anything. Because the distance that the bot will stay from the wall is determined in the code and can be changed to fit your course, exact sensor placement is usually not required. You are able to check the readings of the each sensor on the Serial monitor in the Arduino IDE, in order to calibrate the desired distances.

The manufacturer (Maxbotix) recommends installing a 100uf capacitor between the GND and +5v pins of each sensor to smooth the sensor output during any power supply dips, resulting in more accurate readings. Simply solder the capacitor terminals to the rear of the sensor. Make sure the voltage rating of the capacitor is at least double the working voltage (in this case, a 10v rating or better).

*Figure 5-18. This is a photo of all three sensors installed on Wally. The two side sensors are a different model than the larger center sensor, but they are all three made by Maxbotix and have the same output pins, meaning that they are read by the Arduino in the same way.*

For the center range finder, I used a larger Maxbotics sensor (Sparkfun part #SEN-09009) that I purchased to use on a different robot—it is a nicer, all-weather version of the other two Maxbotics sensors that has a 25-foot range (about 5 feet farther than the others), but costs quite a bit more at around $100 each. Any of the Maxbotics sensors will work in the place of the center sensor.

## Installing the Battery and Power Switch

With the Arduino, motor-controller, and sensors installed on the frame, you need only a power source and switch (optional) to finish the building process and start testing. You can use any type of battery pack that you have handy from 6v to 18v, because we can adjust the top speed of the PWM output in the Arduino code to limit the voltage to the motors. Because Wally will likely require some tuning to fit your setup, it is recommended that you have batteries with at least 1 Amp/Hour (1000mAH) rating or higher to allow a decent run-time before recharging.

Battery packs can be found at garage sales, thrift stores, and even clearance sections at Radio Shack and hobby stores. During a sale a few years ago, Radio Shack was clearing out its 6v–1AH NiCd battery packs commonly used in R/C cars, to replace them with the newer NiMh equivalents. For some reason, it priced each battery pack at $0.50 each including a wall charger, so I bought about 10 of them for $5.00. They have been a valuable purchase for powering various bots that I have built. I usually either arrange two packs in series to produce 12v–1Ah for higher speed, or two in parallel to produce 6v–2Ah for longer run-time at slower speeds.

You can also buy battery holders from Radio Shack (part #270-391—about $2 each) to use with standard AA or rechargeable AA batteries, that have two wire leads for you to wire into your project. The holders are wired in series, so the four AA pack produce 6v using standard 1.5v batteries, or 4.8v using rechargeable 1.2v batteries. The eight AA pack produce 12v with standard batteries or 9.6v with rechargeable batteries. Although almost any battery pack between 3v–18v will work, the voltage level of the battery pack determines Wally's overall speed. I recommend using a battery pack voltage of 6v–12v, and if you find that Wally is a bit too fast, you can adjust his top speed in the code.

I used (2) 6v–1Ah rechargeable NiCd battery packs wired in series to produce 12v for this bot. The motors have plenty of power to turn and add top-speed if needed, but is also slow enough to get accurate readings from each wall while driving.

## Installing a Power Switch

A power switch is needed to easily turn off the power to the bot without removing any wires. A simple SPST switch works—just connect the positive lead from the battery to one pole of the switch and the other pole should connect to the Arduino and motor-controller power supply (see Figure 5-19). The Ground wire from the battery can be permanently connected to the Ground supply of the Arduino and motor-controller and does not need to run through a switch.

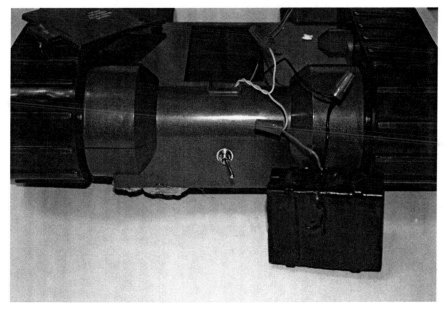

*Figure 5-19. The power switch (SPST) is wired in series with the positive battery supply.*

In Figure 5-19 you can see how the positive lead (red wire) from the battery connects to the switch (yellow wire), which then goes through the switch and connects to the main power supply. The negative black wire connects directly to the main ground supply. The switch is mounted at the rear of the bot (top of the picture).

With the batteries, sensors, motor-controller, and Arduino mounted to the robot base, it is time to discuss what we want Wally to do, and how to write that into the code.

## The Code

In this chapter, we must control eight different Arduino output pins to command both H-bridges. To make this easier, we use a *function()* in the Arduino language. You can create a function that is a specific set of commands with a function name—and anytime this function name is called in the main loop, the specific set of commands will be processed.

For example, to get both motors to go forward, you have to type all of the commands in Listing 5-1, each time you want to change speed, direction, or stop.

*Listing 5-1. Required Code to move Forward at varying speeds*

```
Void loop(){

    // Command motor 1 forward at speed 255
    digitalWrite(m1_AHS, LOW);
    digitalWrite(m1_BLS, LOW);
    digitalWrite(m1_BHS, HIGH);
    analogWrite(m1_ALS, 255);
    // Command motor 2 forward at speed 128
    digitalWrite(m2_AHS, LOW);
    digitalWrite(m2_BLS, LOW);
    digitalWrite(m2_BHS, HIGH);
    analogWrite(m2_ALS, 128);

    delay(1000);

    // Command motor 1 forward at speed 64
    digitalWrite(m1_AHS, LOW);
    digitalWrite(m1_BLS, LOW);
    digitalWrite(m1_BHS, HIGH);
    analogWrite(m1_ALS, 64);
    // Command motor 2 forward at speed 192
    digitalWrite(m2_AHS, LOW);
    digitalWrite(m2_BLS, LOW);
    digitalWrite(m2_BHS, HIGH);
    analogWrite(m2_ALS, 192);

    delay(1000);

}
```

By defining these common sets of commands into functions once using the void() declaration (see Listing 5-2), we can simply call the function name anytime we want to use that particular set of commands. This code is the same as Listing 5-1, but instead uses functions() to declare the cumbersome coding sequences once. The function() names are then called throughout the loop() as they are needed. This makes the loop() function much less cluttered, easier to read, and is also less prone to coding errors.

**Listing 5-2.** *Using Functions to Declare Coding Sequences*

```
void loop(){
        // In the loop, we will call the function names declared below
        // Remember to include a speed value into the parentheses for int x or int y.
        m1_forward(255); // drive motor 1 forward at full speed of 255
        m2_forward(128); // drive motor 2 forward at half speed of 128

        delay(1000);

        m1_forward(64); // drive motor 1 forward at full speed of 64
        m2_forward(192); // drive motor 2 forward at half speed of 192

        delay(1000);

}

// motor functions
void m1_forward(int x){
  digitalWrite(m1_AHS, LOW);
  digitalWrite(m1_BLS, LOW);
  digitalWrite(m1_BHS, HIGH);
  analogWrite(m1_ALS, x);
}
void m2_forward(int y){
  digitalWrite(m2_AHS, LOW);
  digitalWrite(m2_BLS, LOW);
  digitalWrite(m2_BHS, HIGH);
  analogWrite(m2_ALS, y);
}
```

Just remember that you must call the function each time you want to use it—simply declaring the function does not cause it to be used. I have declared several functions in this sketch to define repetitive actions like commanding each motor separately to go forward, reverse, or stop. Each function is declared separately at the end of the sketch (placement of the function declaration does not matter).

You will notice that there is a number in parentheses after the forward or reverse commands, this is called an *argument*. The *argument* is used to declare the PWM speed that you want the motors to receive (defined by the variables "int x" and "int y" in the motor functions below the loop). The number can be between 0 (stopped) to 255 (full-speed) PWM range. The stop command for each motor does not require a number in the parentheses because stopping does not have a speed.

There are also several "if/else" conditional statements used in this code to test the sensor readings against the defined threshold values. The code can look confusing, but I tried to explain each line so you can figure out what is happening as you read through it.

## Code Objectives

Wally's main goal is to keep his right side parallel with the wall, while traveling around the room. If one of the side sensors reads higher or lower than the other, the code will adjust the outputs of each motor to correct his position and make the sensor readings equal again. The third center sensor is used to "keep an eye on the road" and make sure he doesn't accidentally hit anything. If the center sensor reading falls below a set threshold, Wally will turn left and continue along the next wall. Wally's course is adjusted by reducing the power to the motor in the direction you want him to turn. I mentioned that if you power both motors equally (M1 and M2), the bot will travel in a straight line. If you want to turn left, reduce the power to (or stop) the left motor (M1) and Wally will turn left; if you want to turn right, reduce the power to (or stop) the right motor (M2).

In Figure 5-20, Wally is heading toward the wall—when the front-right sensor reads 7 inches and the back-right sensor reads 9 inches, Wally knows that he is no longer parallel to the wall and should reduce the power to M1 while applying full power to M2 to correct his orientation.

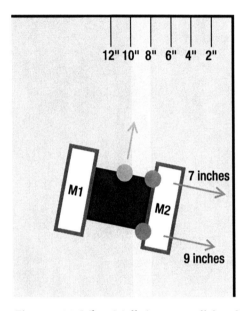

*Figure 5-20. When Wally is not parallel to the wall, his side sensor readings will not be equal and he will attempt to correct his position.*

To keep the side sensor readings equal, pick a range in which to travel. We do this by selecting a minimum and maximum threshold. The minimum threshold determines when the bot is too close to the wall and should move away. Likewise the maximum threshold determines when the bot is too far away from the wall and should return. In Figure 5-21, I chose 8 inches as the lower threshold and 10 inches as the upper threshold (leaving a 2-inch padding). This tells Wally that if both of his side sensors are within this range, go straight ahead, and if either of the two side sensors are out of this range (either above or below) check and correct this error by adjusting the motors.

This means that Wally has a 2-inch padding to compensate for irregularities in the wall and still continue straight. If he wanders outside this 2-inch padding zone, the Arduino will correct his position until both of his right-side sensors are between 8 and 10 inches from the wall. You can adjust the lower and upper limits for the right sensors from 8 and 10 to whatever you want; they can even be the same if you want a tight tolerance with no padding.

The center sensor is used to determine when Wally is approaching the end of a wall, and prevents him from running into it. As long as the center sensor reading is above the threshold (in this case, 12 inches), the Arduino will use the right-side sensors to adjust the motor output and keep Wally on track. If the center sensor falls below the threshold, Wally will stop, turn left, and then continue following the next wall (see Figure 5-21). If the wall is an outside corner, when Wally's side sensors reach the corner of the wall, they will instruct him to turn right and continue following the wall.

Ideally, Wally would travel parallel to the wall with his side sensors both within the shaded line (8–10 inches from wall) while traveling forward. Realistically, small bumps in the drive-train and irregularities in the walls cause his path to be somewhat less than a perfectly straight line. But after some tweaking, Wally is able to maneuver around most of the house without assistance (or touching any walls).

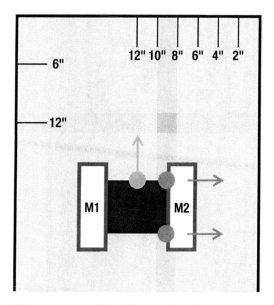

*Figure 5-21. Wally will stop when the center sensor falls below its threshold; I tested Wally with a center threshold between 12–20 inches.*

Now that we understand how Wally should work, let's upload the code.

Uploading the code in Listing 5-3 provides the code to use with the standard Arduino. If you use the Arduino Mega, change "m1_BLS 3" to "m1_BLI 12, and use Table 5-2 to make sure that you have the H-bridge connected properly before proceeding.

*Listing 5-3. The Main Code for Wally*

```
// Wally the wall-bot.
// Follow a right-hand wall and traverse obstacles, using 3 ultrasonic sensors
// Connect Maxbotics ultrasonic sensors to Arduino analog inputs A0, A1, and A2.
// H-bridge motor pins are listed below and shown in Figure 5-14

// create variables for each sensor reading
int front_right_sensor = 0;
int back_right_sensor = 0;
int center_sensor = 0;
```

```
// define pins for motor 1
int m1_AHI = 2;
int m1_ALI = 11;
int m1_BLI = 3;   // 12 on Ardiuno Mega
int m1_BHI = 4;

// define pins for motor 2
int m2_AHI = 8;
int m2_ALI = 9;
int m2_BLI = 10;
int m2_BHI = 7;

// variables to hold upper and lower limits
int threshold = 20;  // Use this to adjust the center sensor threshold.
int right_upper_limit = 10; // Use this to adjust the upper right sensor limit.
int right_lower_limit = 8;  // Use this to adjust the lower right sensor limit.

// speed variables
int speed1 = 64;  // setting for 1/4 speed
int speed2 = 128; // setting for 1/2 speed
int speed3 = 192; // setting for 3/4 speed
int speed4 = 255; // setting for full speed

// end of variables

void setup(){

  // change the PWM frequency for Timer 1 of Arduino
  // pins 9 & 10 on standard Arduino or pins 11 and 12 on Arduino Mega
  TCCR1B = TCCR1B & 0b11111000 | 0x01;
  // change the PWM frequency for Timer 2 of Arduino
  // pins 3 & 11 on standard Arduino or pins 9 & 10 on Arduino Mega
  TCCR2B = TCCR2B & 0b11111000 | 0x01;

  Serial.begin(9600);

  // set motor pins as outputs

  pinMode(m1_AHI, OUTPUT);
  pinMode(m1_ALI, OUTPUT);
  pinMode(m1_BHI, OUTPUT);
  pinMode(m1_BLI, OUTPUT);

  pinMode(m2_AHI, OUTPUT);
  pinMode(m2_ALI, OUTPUT);
  pinMode(m2_BHI, OUTPUT);
  pinMode(m2_BLI, OUTPUT);

}
```

```
void gather(){
  // function for updating all sensor values
  // Divide each sensor by 2.54 to get the reading in Inches.
  back_right_sensor = analogRead(0) / 2.54;
  front_right_sensor = analogRead(1) / 2.54;
  center_sensor = analogRead(2) / 2.54;
}

void loop(){

  gather();  // call function to update sensors

  // first, check to see if the center sensor is above its threshold:
  if (center_sensor > threshold) {

    // is the Front Right Sensor (FRS) below the lower threshold value?
    if (front_right_sensor < right_lower_limit){
      // if so, check to see if the Back Right Sensor (BRS) is also below lower threshold:
      if (back_right_sensor < right_lower_limit){
        // Wally is too close to wall, go back:
        m1_stop();
        m2_forward(speed3);
      }
      // otherwise, see if BRS is above the upper threshold:
      else if (back_right_sensor > right_upper_limit){
        // Wally is heading toward wall - correct this:
        m1_stop();
        m2_forward(speed3);
      }
      // (else) If BRS is not above upper threshold or below lower threshold, it must be↲
within range:
      else{
        // Wally is just slightly off track, make minor adjustment away from wall:
        m1_forward(speed2);
        m2_forward(speed3);
      }
    }

    // else, if FRS is not below the lower threshold, see if it is above the upper threshold:
    else if (front_right_sensor > right_upper_limit){
      // FRS is above upper threshold, make sure it can still detect a wall nearby (use↲
center sensor threshold value):
      if (front_right_sensor > threshold){
        // Wally might be reading an outside corner wall, check BRS:
        if (back_right_sensor < right_upper_limit){
          // If BRS is still within range, make minor adjustment:
          m1_forward(speed3);
          m2_forward(speed2);
        }
        // Otherwise, check to see if BRS is also above the threshold:
        else if (back_right_sensor > threshold){
```

```
            // Wally has found an outside corner! Turn right:
            m1_forward(speed4);
            m2_reverse(speed1);
         }
      }
      // FRS is above upper threshold, see if BRS is below lower threshold:
      else if (back_right_sensor < right_lower_limit){
         // if so, bring Wally back toward the wall
         m1_forward(speed3);
         m2_forward(speed1);
      }
      // if not, check to see if BRS is also above the upper threshold:
      else if (back_right_sensor > right_upper_limit){
         // if so, bring Wally back towards wall:
         m1_forward(speed2);
         m2_stop();
      }
      // Otherwise,
      else{
         // else, make minor adjustments to bring Wally back on track
         m1_forward(speed3);
         m2_forward(speed2);
      }
   }

   // else; FRS is within both side thresholds, so we can proceed to check the BRS.
   else {
      // see if BRS is above the upper threshold:
      if (back_right_sensor > right_upper_limit){
         // is so, make adjusment:
         m1_forward(speed1);
         m2_forward(speed3);
      }
      // if BRS is within upper threshold, check to see if it is below lower threshold:
      else if (back_right_sensor < right_lower_limit) {
         // if so, make opposite adjustment:
         m1_forward(speed3);
         m2_forward(speed1);
      }
      // otherwise, BOTH side sensors are within range:
      else {
         // So drive straight ahead!
         m1_forward(speed2);
         m2_forward(speed2);
      }
   }

}

// If center sensor is not above the upper threshold, it must be below it, time to STOP!
else {
   // If center sensor is BELOW threshold, turn left and re-evaluate walls
```

```
    // Stop Wally

    m1_stop();
    m2_stop();
    delay(200);
    // Turn Wally left (for 500 milliseconds)
    m1_reverse(speed4);
    m2_forward(speed4);
    delay(500);
    // Stop again
    m1_stop();
    m2_stop();
    delay(200);
  }

  // Now print sensor values on the Serial monitor
  Serial.print(back_right_sensor);
  Serial.print("            ");
  Serial.print(front_right_sensor);
  Serial.print("            ");
  Serial.print(center_sensor);
  Serial.println("          ");

  // End of loop

}


// Create functions for motor-controller actions

void m1_reverse(int x){
  // function for motor 1 reverse
  digitalWrite(m1_BHI, LOW);
  digitalWrite(m1_ALI, LOW);
  digitalWrite(m1_AHI, HIGH);
  analogWrite(m1_BLI, x);
}


void m1_forward(int x){
  // function for motor 1 forward
  digitalWrite(m1_AHI, LOW);
  digitalWrite(m1_BLI, LOW);
  digitalWrite(m1_BHI, HIGH);
  analogWrite(m1_ALI, x);
}


void m1_stop(){
  // function for motor 1 stop
  digitalWrite(m1_ALI, LOW);
  digitalWrite(m1_BLI, LOW);
```

```
    digitalWrite(m1_AHI, HIGH); // electric brake using high-side fets
    digitalWrite(m1_BHI, HIGH); // electric brake using high-side fets
}


void m2_forward(int y){
    // function for motor 2 forward
    digitalWrite(m2_AHI, LOW);
    digitalWrite(m2_BLI, LOW);
    digitalWrite(m2_BHI, HIGH);
    analogWrite(m2_ALI, y);
}


void m2_reverse(int y){
    // function for motor 2 reverse
    digitalWrite(m2_BHI, LOW);
    digitalWrite(m2_ALI, LOW);
    digitalWrite(m2_AHI, HIGH);
    analogWrite(m2_BLI, y);
}


void m2_stop(){
    // function for motor 2 stop
    digitalWrite(m2_ALI, LOW);
    digitalWrite(m2_BLI, LOW);
    digitalWrite(m2_AHI, HIGH);  // electric brake using high-side fets
    digitalWrite(m2_BHI, HIGH);  // electric brake using high-side fets
}


void motors_release(){
    // function to release both motors (no electric brake)
    // release all motors by opening every switch. The bot will coast or roll if on a hill.
    digitalWrite(m1_AHI, LOW);
    digitalWrite(m1_ALI, LOW);
    digitalWrite(m1_BHI, LOW);
    digitalWrite(m1_BLI, LOW);

    digitalWrite(m2_AHI, LOW);
    digitalWrite(m2_ALI, LOW);
    digitalWrite(m2_BHI, LOW);
    digitalWrite(m2_BLI, LOW);
}
```

After loading the code onto your Arduino, and double-checking all of your connections to the H-bridge and sensors, power on your bot and place it near a wall. If all the sensors are connected properly and the motors are spinning in the correct direction, the bot should start following the wall.

I verified that it would stay the set distance from the wall by letting it follow a long (15 foot) wall with no obstructions. After completing a few runs without any issues, I began adding some obstacles for it to traverse. A box or piece of wood placed perpendicular to the wall forces Wally to stop and go around the obstacle, staying the set distance from the obstacle as it does from the wall. The size, shape, and thickness of the obstacles determines how well the ultrasonic sensors will be able to "see" them and react properly.

You can adjust the threshold settings and speeds to tweak your wall-bot for varying motor speed, battery voltage, and turn radius to get it working the way you want. See Listing 5-4 for a list of the variables that can be adjusted to Wally's performance.

*Listing 5-4. Variables that Can Be Changed During Testing*

```
// variables to hold upper and lower limits
int threshold = 20;  // Use this to adjust the center sensor threshold.
int right_upper_limit = 10; // Use this to adjust the upper right sensor limit.
int right_lower_limit = 8;  // Use this to adjust the lower right sensor limit.

// speed variables
int speed1 = 64;  // setting for 1/4 speed
int speed2 = 128; // setting for 1/2 speed
int speed3 = 192; // setting for 3/4 speed
int speed4 = 255; // setting for full speed
```

The speed variables are simply there to provide several options to play with when testing. You can change these throughout the code (or insert your own speed values to test 0-255). To see the readings from Wally's sensors, plug him into your PC and hold him next to a wall.

# Summary

In this chapter, we used ultrasonic range finders to detect nearby objects and avoid hitting them, while the robot travels around a room. Because most rooms have walls, I decided to use the wall as a guide for the robot to use. Using the three sensors strategically mounted around the robot frame, we are able to detect objects to the right and in front of the robot.

To save some money on parts, I went on a salvage trip to the local thrift store and found an old robotic toy with tank tracks on its base. I bought the toy, removed the top, stripped out the electronics, and began prepping it for my own electronics. If you cannot find a second-hand toy that will work, there are several robot bases available online including one that is a perfect substitute for the base used on Wally—DFRobot.com (part #ROB0037).

We built our own dual H-bridge motor-controller on perforated prototyping board, which receives its commands from the Arduino. The motor-controller requires several component parts from Digikey.com and some patience for assembly. After completed, we mounted the motor-controller and Arduino on the base using several small nuts and bolts. We then wired each connection from the motor-controller to the Arduino according to Table 5-2, double-checking each connection.

The sensor brackets were made from 3/4-inch wide aluminum flat bar, and attached to the frame using glue. The sensors were glued to the top of each mounting bracket, and then wired to the Arduino analog inputs (A0, A1, and A2). Lastly, we installed the power switch and battery pack to the base of the frame.

In the next chapter, we discuss the process of designing circuits on your computer using (freeware) CAD software, and then make printed circuit boards from your designs at home in your back yard! All you need is a clothes iron, some basic chemicals, access to a laser printer, and some magazine paper, and you can have long-lasting circuit boards that are easy to replicate and can be custom tailored to any project. We also learn how to build our very own Arduino-compatible programming boards to use in future projects.

# CHAPTER 6

# Making PCBs

In this chapter, we change direction and instead of building a robot, we focus on the production of an Arduino board (and other electronic circuits) for use in the next few chapters. Although there are many commercially available robot parts, sometimes you either cannot find the perfect part, or it is more cost effective to build your own. This chapter covers some basic concepts to help you get started designing your own electronics circuits using a computer aided design program (CAD). You might think printing your own circuit boards requires expensive equipment and special training, but you can design and build your very own Printed Circuit Board (PCB) for under $25 and in only a few hours time. I guide you through the process that I found to be inexpensive, effective, and easy enough to do in the garage or backyard.

You have probably seen a dark green PCB from a computer or other electronic device, and stared in amazement. Each electronic device has a unique circuit board that is created for a specific purpose. These boards are extremely helpful for creating a circuit in a much more compact area than using perforated board and wire. The reason the board can be smaller is because each wire is replaced with a copper *trace*. Traces are flat pieces of copper that are glued to an insulated fiberglass board. The traces are created using a computer program that simulates a circuit board layout, and enables you to place components on the board to see how everything fits before creating the PCB.

This chapter covers three basic steps of making a PCB: creating a circuit design using a CAD program, transferring the design from your computer to the copper-coated board, and etching the copper board with an acid solution to leave only the finished wire traces hidden under the design. Of course, each of these main steps have their own detailed set of instructions, but if followed correctly you will also be able to reproduce any circuit design that you want.

## PCB Basics

A PCB is made using a piece of fiberglass board about 1/16-inch thick, which is coated with a thin layer of copper on one or both sides. All that you need to create traces on a copper clad board (bare PCB) is an ink, toner, or paint that can resist the etchant chemicals and protect the thin copper coating. This coating can be a black permanent marker, toner from a laser printer, or even fingernail polish.

---

**Note** Make sure you use a laser printer with black toner; inkjet printers do not work for this method.

---

You can create a circuit design on the computer using one of several open-source or freeware circuit design programs, or find an existing open-source circuit design file to download and print. To transfer a design from paper to copper, you need to print the design on a piece of glossy magazine paper, place it face down onto the copper board, and heat the back of the paper with a clothes iron for a few minutes. The iron melts the toner from the paper and transfers it on the copper board. When it cools, the board is soaked in warm water until the paper backing is easily removed and the toner is left printed on the copper.

After transferred, the toner from the printer acts as a plastic coating on the copper that protects it from the acid etchant solution. The etchant is a chemical used to dissolve the copper (or any other metal) that is not coated with plastic toner, leaving only the fiberglass board and any copper that is beneath the transferred toner. After the etching process completes, the transfer coating (toner) is removed with a solvent (like acetone) to reveal the remaining copper traces beneath. Each board needs to have tiny holes drilled to place any through-hole components so that each pin can be soldered to the appropriate copper trace.

---

■ **Caution** Always wear eye and skin protection when working with muriatic acid or other etchant chemicals, because they can burn you! If your eyes or skin comes in contact with the acid, immediately wash with water.

---

Making PCBs at home is a fun way to learn more about electronics—forcing yourself to learn the names of the pins on each component and seeing how they connect together is an invaluable learning experience. After you complete your first board, you will likely feel confident enough to start designing your own circuits and producing them yourself at home. Don't worry if you mess up a board, a $5 PCB will typically be large enough to make several small circuits, and a $12 gallon of muriatic acid will be enough to etch 100 or more PCBs. After you get a few base supplies, the cost to produce additional boards drops considerably. You might also be able to find some bulk or surplus packs of less-expensive, thin copper clad board, which is perfect for learning and building low-power circuits.

## What You Need to Get Started

You do not need to purchase anything to get started designing a circuit, because there are several open-source circuit design programs. Even the popular circuit design program Eagle has a freeware version that is available for personal use. You need to download one of these programs to complete the projects in this chapter (even if you are just downloading a circuit file for printing).

You must use a black laser printer for the method presented in this book. If you don't own a laser printer, find a friend that does or visit your local copy shop for help. Using normal paper does not work for transferring the toner to the copper board, so you must use a glossy type paper like the pages of a magazine. This usually means manually feeding each piece of paper into the printer.

Transferring the design requires a clothes iron, copper clad board (PCB), an abrasive (Scotch-brite) scrub pad, and some acetone or lacquer thinner. These items can be found at your local convenience store, except for the PCB, which can be purchased at Radio Shack or Digikey.com.

The etching process requires an acid solution that dissolves any unprotected copper from the fiberglass board. There are two types of etchant solution that I have tried with success: a pre-mixed ferric-chloride solution (available at Radio Shack) and a homemade solution of muriatic acid and hydrogen peroxide (my personal preference). Although either works, the ferric-chloride solution takes longer to etch and yields only approximately two PCBs per bottle (16oz = $10). The muriatic acid and hydrogen peroxide solution is quicker to dissolve the copper, easier to find, and less expensive than the pre-mixed solution for multiple boards.

Table 6-1 lists the items you need to get started making your own PCBs. You can find most of the parts and materials at the hardware store, grocery store, or Radio Shack.

*Table 6-1.* *PCB Parts and Materials List*

| Part | Description | Price |
|------|-------------|-------|
| Black laser printer | Newegg.com—Almost any laser printer that uses black toner works. Color laser toner does not work, nor does black or color inkjet printers. If you don't have a black laser printer, you probably know somebody who does, or you can go to a copy shop and have someone print your design for you. I use a Brother 7020 | $59.99 |
| Glossy magazine paper | Recycle—I use my wife's old *Cosmopolitan* magazines with great success. I have tried other magazines with mixed results. Pages with only writing and no pictures are ideal. | Recycled |
| Copper clad PCB | Radio Shack (part #276-1499) —This is the copper-coated fiberglass board that will be etched. It can be bought as a double-sided board, approximately 4.5 inches x 6 inches. You can cut this board before using if your design is smaller than the total size of the board. One piece should make several small circuit boards. Digikey also sells copper clad PCBs. | $3.99 |
| Scotch-brite abrasive pad. | Hardware store—It has a light abrasive grit and makes the copper surface shiny and clean before transferring the design. | $2.00 |
| Acetone | Hardware store—Fingernail polish remover, painter's acetone, lacquer thinner—I have used them all with success. It simply needs to clean the surface and later remove the toner after etching. | $3.00 |
| Iron | Recycle—Any old iron should work, you must put it on its highest heat setting with no steam. You should remove any water from the iron just to make sure.<br><br>If you don't have one, check a thrift store or garage sale for a used one. It does not need to be nice. | $5.00 |
| Muriatic acid | Hardware or paint store—It comes in a gallon jug for etching (cleaning) concrete. I picked mine up at Sherwin Williams paint store—1 gallon is enough to etch at least 100 boards. If they have a smaller/cheaper size, get it. | $12 per gallon |
| Hydrogen peroxide solution | Pharmacy—This is the same solution that you buy at the grocery store to put on minor cuts and scrapes. One bottle is enough to etch about three to five boards. | $1 per bottle |

| Part | Description | Price |
|------|-------------|-------|
| Rubber gloves | Hardware store—You need rubber gloves to protect your hands from the etchant solution. Because the etchant reacts only with metal, rubber gloves are a good barrier. Any rubber gloves work, though chemical gloves are ideal. | $1.00 |
| Etching container | Recycle—Any plastic or glass container will do. DO NOT USE A METAL CONTAINER, because the etchant will eat through it. I use a recycled plastic food container (sour cream, butter, and so on) with a lid. | Recycled |
| Drill | Harbor Freight Tools (item #38119) —I use a drill press to drill the holes for each component in the PCB after etching. You can use a hand drill, but it will be more difficult to line up each hole precisely. | $20–$60 |
| Micro drill bits | Harbor Freight Tools (item #44924) —These should be very small, because the holes should be only large enough for the component lead to fit through. Too large and they will be extremely difficult to solder. | $6.00 |
| Soldering iron | Any soldering iron will do. I have used both the cheap Radio Shack irons and an expensive temperature controlled irons, and both work. I do not say equally, but they do both get the job done. Amazon is a good place to look, or your local electronics shop. | $8–$70 |
| Paper towels | These are for cleaning the PCB and later removing the black toner from the etched board. You need about 2–4 clean sheets. | $2.00 |
| Air pump | Pet store—An aquarium air pump works fine. This is not required, but it tremendously speeds up the etching process. You also need about 2 feet of rubber air tubing. | $10.00 |

Now that we have the general parts list and the basic steps laid out, we should go into more detail about the circuit design process.

First we discuss a few important details about the design software, and then we dive in by designing and building a few circuits.

# Circuit Design

Before the PCB can be etched, it must first have a circuit design applied to the copper. Though there are many different programs that you can use to create electronic circuits on your computer, I focus on using the popular program Eagle, from CadSoft. Eagle can be used on Linux, Mac, and Windows, and has a freeware version available for personal (hobby) use. The freeware version is limited only by the size of the PCB that it lets you design (4 inches x 3.2 inches). Many useful circuits can be designed in this space, like an Arduino clone that requires only a 2.5-inch x 3-inch PCB. If you decide that you really like using Eagle and want to start building PCBs to sell or you want to build PCBs with an unrestricted size, you can purchase a license for a full-featured version of Eagle from its website.

CadSoft USA website: http://www.cadsoftusa.com/

You can install Eagle by downloading the file for your operating system and following the directions on the following website:

http://www.cadsoft.de/download.htm

For more software options, the following other circuit design programs are worth checking out (these might not work on all operating systems):

Geda: http://www.gpleda.org/index.html

Fritzing: http://fritzing.org/

KiCad: http://www.lis.inpg.fr/realise_au_lis/kicad/

# Searching for Open-Source Designs

If you are thinking that this is way over your head, I suggest starting slow. Instead of committing to design your own circuit, start by downloading the circuit design program and a few files from the book website. You can open the files with the design program and see what you think—it might make more sense if you get a good look at the program and a file that we use in this chapter.

Many open-source electronics projects available on the Internet include layout files for you to build the design yourself, as is the case with many of the products from Sparkfun.com. These files can be downloaded, opened, and printed for use in your project. Most of the project files that I have come across were created in Eagle, which is another reason I prefer to use it. If you do not want to spend any time designing your own boards but you want to save a little money, downloading layouts that someone else has already tested is usually a safe bet. With a good parts list and schematic (so you know the orientation of each component), you should be able to tackle almost any PCB design.

Because the Arduino is open source, all of the files (schematics, boards) needed to build your own PCB are also available for you to download and use free of charge. There are many different variants of the Arduino board, so you can pick one that fits your needs.

You can view the different Arduino variants in the following website:

http://arduino.cc/en/Main/Hardware

When searching Google for H-bridge circuits, schematics, and Eagle board files, I found several good designs that are available for download. If you are feeling adventurous, you can also find a plethora of schematics for H-bridge motor controller circuits that you can use in Eagle to create your own board layout.

Among the many options, the Open Source Motor Controller (OSMC) stands out as an excellent H-bridge with plenty of documentation, online support through the OSMC Yahoo! Group, and an extremely robust power range (160amps at 48vdc). Because it is an open-source project, many people have joined in and designed variants of the OSMC to fit their needs, posting the design files of their version for others to use. These designs are available for download to anyone who joins the OSMC Yahoo! Group.

You can find more information about the OSMC project, including the files needed to build your own by visiting the following website:

http://www.robotpower.com/products/osmc_info.html

# Making Your Own Designs

There are two main functions of any circuit design program: a *schematic editor* and a *board editor*. The schematic editor is used to create a working diagram of the circuit using component symbols, and to determine proper orientation and placement of each component part in the circuit. The board editor uses a compatible schematic file to add each component in the circuit to a virtual PCB, enabling you to re-arrange each component for optimum placement. Using various tools in the design program, you can re-size the width of each trace on the PCB (depending on the power requirements of the trace).

The schematic editor is not concerned with proper sizing or placement of components, it can be considered the blueprint that shows the builder what goes where. In order to keep things neat, you will often see Ground and +VIN pins in the schematic connected to their respective symbol (GND, +12v, and so on) instead of connected to each other. That is, traces that will be connected together in the board file might not always be visibly connected in the schematic (though they will have the same name if connected). This is done so there are fewer wires crossing in the schematic, which makes it easier to read.

To make a board layout in Eagle, you should start with a schematic, so that the program will know what parts are supposed to be connected in the final board layout. Eagle can convert a compatible schematic file (.sch) into a board layout file (.brd), which is what you will use to print out and transfer to the copper PCB.

# Schematics

Schematics use electrical symbols for each component part in the circuit to show the orientation and connection of each part. These symbols are discussed in Chapter 1 with a few pictures of the symbols for various popular component parts. The electrical symbol for each component part should be in the manufacturer's datasheet to show the pinout diagram.

The Eagle schematic editor has a Net tool, which enables you to draw virtual wires between component parts that should be connected.

After each part is connected in the schematic, Eagle transfers the parts to the board layout editor for you to configure. It is up to you to place each component piece where you want it to go, but Eagle can help with routing the wires. Remember that some parts are available in multiple packages (TO-220, TO-92, 28-DIP IC, and so on). When you add parts to the schematic editor, choose the part with the package type that you intend to use in the actual circuit. Any pin connection changes in the circuit must be done in the schematic editor—changes made in the schematic editor immediately show up on the board editor as well. After you have a workable schematic, you can transfer to the circuit board editor.

# Board Layouts

After you have a schematic file, denoted by the *.sch file type, you can switch to the board editor from the schematic editor by selecting File   Switch to Board. This opens the board editor window with all of the parts (shown to scale) used in the schematic. Any connection made using the Net tool in the schematic shows up as an air-wire in the board editor (shown as a thin yellow line) to denote a connection between two parts.

You will notice that the parts are not in the layout area by default (denoted by the box). You must place them into the layout area either one at a time, or by using the Group tool to select all components at once and then use the Move tool by right-clicking your mouse on the schematic and selecting Move Group. After all the parts are placed inside the layout area, you can begin arranging them so that each trace will be as short as possible. Using the Tools   Ratsnest feature shortens each virtual wire to be as short as possible and connects to the nearest like wire, this gives you a better idea of where the traces will end up as you are placing parts.

After you feel satisfied with your component layout, hopefully avoiding any crossing wires, you can select the Tools Auto feature, which automatically routes the traces on the board. After the auto router is finished, you might need to tidy up some of the traces. If you want to re-run a trace, simply use the Edit Ripup tool to remove a wire on the board editor, which returns the connection to a virtual wire until you re-route it using the Wire tool by selecting Edit Wire.

Before you get started with Eagle, take a moment to look at these various tool shortcut symbols and their descriptions in Table 6-2. These tools are available along the left side of the screen in both schematic and board editors. By selecting one of these buttons with your mouse, you are able to use the tool to edit your design.

*Table 6-2. Commonly Used Tools in the Eagle Schematic and Board Editors*

The Move tool is used to grab a wire, component, or a group and move it. The move tool settles only on a grid line, so if you can't move something to the spot you want to, change the grid spacing to something a bit smaller by selecting View Grid from the menu bar. Common grid spacings are 0.1 inch, 0.05 inch, and 0.025 inch.

The Copy tool is used to copy a part of group of parts. In general, this tool should be used only in the schematic editor.

The Mirror tool is used to flip a component around. In general, this tool should be used only in the schematic editor (unless you know what you are doing).

The Rotate tool is used to rotate a component, wire, or group of objects. Selecting an object with the Move tool and clicking the right button on the mouse also rotates the selected object.

The Group tool is used to draw a box (or other shape) around a set of wires or components in order to move, copy, or flip the entire group. This tool is useful to grab an entire circuit and move it without disrupting any of the inner connections. If the mouse button is pressed and held, it begins to shape a rectangle. If it is pressed once, you are allowed to draw a shape around any set of objects you want, left-clicking to end the shape.

The Change tool is used to change a component, wire, or other object in the editor. You must first select the Change tool, and then a box pops up with a list of options. After selecting the option that you want to change, click on the object in the editor and the change will be made. This is helpful to change the size of a group of traces or the diameter of a hole.

The Delete tool is used to delete a wire, component, or group. If you make a mistake, use this tool to get rid of the error. You can delete a single wire or a group of wires, after using the Group tool to define the group.

The Add tool is used to add component parts to the schematic. You can search through the available libraries by simply entering a phrase in the search bar and pressing Enter. Note that the specific part numbers can be found only when using the schematic editor. The parts available in the board editor are usually package types (i.e., TO-220 or T0-92).

The Name tool is used in both the board and schematic editor to name a component or wire. The name of a wire does not only enable you to identify what you are working with, but Eagle will keep track of wires and components with the same name to make sure they are connected. The name of a component stays the same regardless of its value.

The Value tool is used to enter the value or part number of a component so you will know what component goes where. A common part like a resistor should have the value of the component (i.e., 10K or 330 ohm) whereas a specific component like a 5v regulator should use its part number (i.e., LM-7805 or LM-2675).

The Ripup tool is used to return a wire into an unrouted wire (or virtual wire). If you use the Auto-router tool and don't like the way it places the wires, you can use this tool to remove the wire and run it manually using the Wire tool.

The Wire tool is used to draw a line on the board editor. These lines are what make up the PCB traces on a finished board. Use this tool to place wires on the board to connect components as needed. You can change the width of a wire using the drop-down menu after selecting the tool—the default width is 0.016 inch, which is fine for low-power traces, but high-power traces should be 0.07 inch or larger.

The Text tool is used to create a label on either the schematic or board editor. You can change the size of the font or layer that the text is shown on.

The Rectangle tool is used to draw a rectangle of solid wire on the board. This should be used if you want to fill in a large portion of the board with a rectangle of wire. It is better to use the Wire tool to draw PCB traces because their length and width can later be changed without deleting.

The Polygon tool is used to draw a shape around the circuit to define a Ground-plane. By using the Name tool to re-name the polygon shape to the same name as the Ground trace (typically "GND"), Eagle fills in all empty spaces with a pad that is connected to Ground. This is helpful for filling in unused space to cut down on the amount of copper that needs to be etched.

The Net tool is used to make connections in the schematic editor. This tool creates virtual wires and should be attached to the component pins in the schematic. The size of the wire in schematic view does not affect the actual PCB trace size. You can delete these wires if you make a mistake.

The Via tool is used to place a pad with a hole in the PCB. The diameter of the via can be changed from the toolbar after it is selected (.07 inch is a good size). If you drill the holes directly in the center of each via, your finished PCB will be spaced perfectly and placing components will be easy. You can connect wires directly to the vias or the pads of a component part.

The Ratsnest tool is used to optimize virtual wires and fill a polygon plane (like a GND plane). This tool is useful to tidy up the wires as you place parts on the board editor, making it easier to arrange the components.

The Auto tool is used to enable Eagle to automatically route the virtual wires on the board editor into PCB traces. If you use a single-sided design, you will want to change the setting "1 TOP" to equal "N/A" under the Preferred Directions in the General tab of the Autorouter setup (you will see this box when you select the Auto-router tool)—otherwise, just click OK and watch Eagle route the wires.

Now that you have an idea of some of the tools and their functions, let's make our own design using Eagle.

Let's create a design. If this is your first PCB making attempt, you should start out simple. We make a 1 amp H-bridge using NPN and PNP transistors. We briefly run through how to create a schematic in Eagle and then transfer the schematic to the board editor, where we can rearrange the parts to create a usable PCB file. Start by opening the circuit design program, Eagle, on your computer and getting a cup of coffee or tea—you will be at your computer for a while (probably about an hour or two).

## Working with the Schematic Editor

We begin our design using the schematic editor. The following steps guide you through creating the schematic:

1. *Open schematic editor.* Open the Eagle program on your computer and select File New Schematic from the menu bar as shown in Figure 6-1.

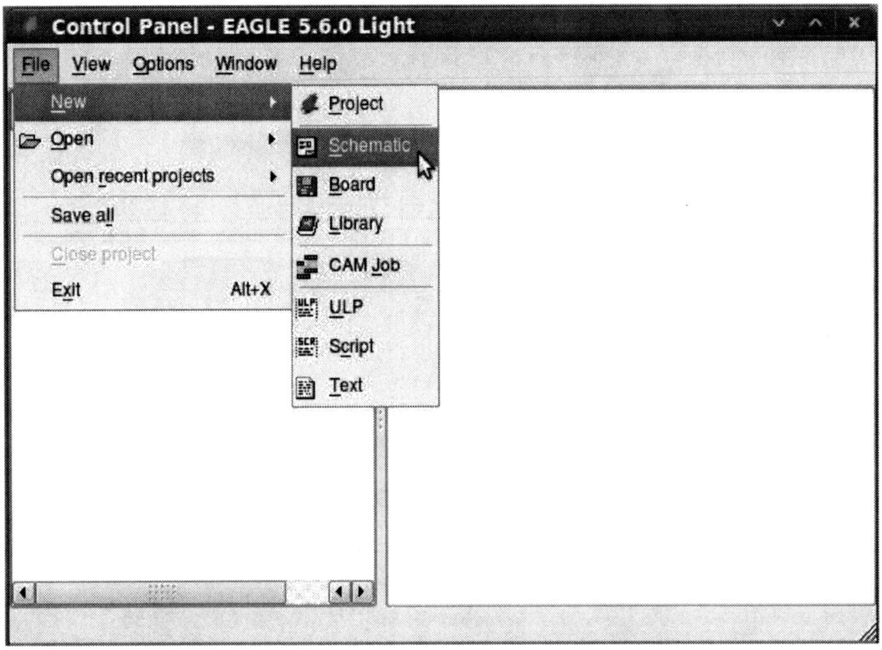

***Figure 6-1.*** *Selecting a new schematic from File  New  Schematic*

2.  *Add supply symbols*: With the schematic editor open, select Edit  Add(see Figure 6-2). Type **supply** into the search bar and press Enter on your keyboard. Scroll down until you see the "+24v" symbol and select it, placing it on the schematic. Next select Add again and find the "GND" symbol, placing it on the schematic.

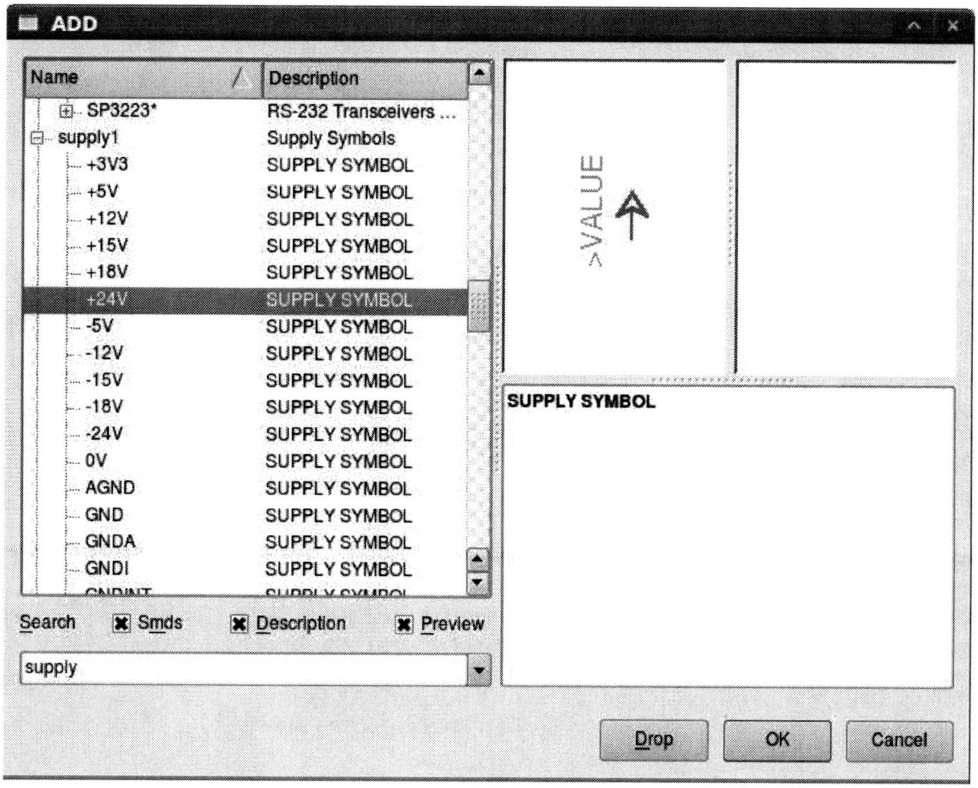

*Figure 6-2. Adding supply symbols for +24v and GND*

3. *Add transistors:* Select the Add tool and search for "2n2907" (PNP transistors) and add (2). Select the Add tool again and search for "2n2222" (NPN transistor) and add (4). You need to use the Mirror tool to change the direction of the three transistors on the right side of the schematic as shown in Figure 6-3.

---

▒ **Tip:** Pressing the middle mouse button (the mouse wheel) before placing a component activates the Mirror tool, effectively inverting its direction. You can do this as needed in step 3, when placing the transistors on the right side of the schematic.

---

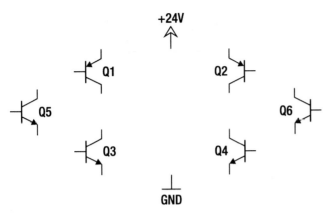

**Figure 6-3.** *Q1 and Q2 are PNP transistors used as the high-side switches in the H-bridge, Q3 and Q4 are NPN transistors used as the low-side switches, and Q5 and Q6 are NPN transistors used to invert the control signal to the PNP transistors.*

4.  *Add resistors:* These resistors are used to limit the amount of current allowed to each transistor, so we will place one in front of each transistor base pin (the middle pin, as shown in Figure 6-4). The datasheet for the 2n2222 NPN transistor recommends between 1mA and 10mA of current to be applied to the base pin to get the most efficient current gain. To do this using the +5v produced from each Arduino output pin, we will use standard 1k-ohm resistors that will provide 5mA to each transistor base pin (Ohm's law).

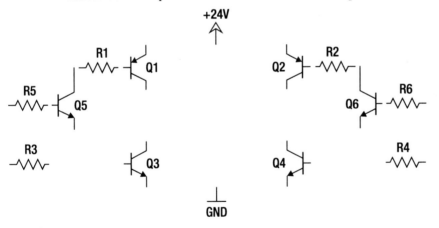

**Figure 6-4.** *The current-limiting bias resistors are added to each transistor in the schematic, represented by components R1 through R6.*

5.  *Add diodes:* Place (4) 1n914 diodes between the motor terminals and the positive and negative power rails, with the Cathodes (striped end) facing the

positive voltage supply (see Figure 6-5). These diodes protect the transistors from Back-EMF.

6.  *Make connections:* Using the Net tool, connect each component pin to its appropriate connection as shown in Figure 6-5. Add (2) GND supply symbols to the emitter pins of Q5 and Q6. These can be copied from the GND symbol that you already placed in step 1. I added a motor symbol to the center of the H-bridge, to denote where the motor terminals should be connected—this is not required.

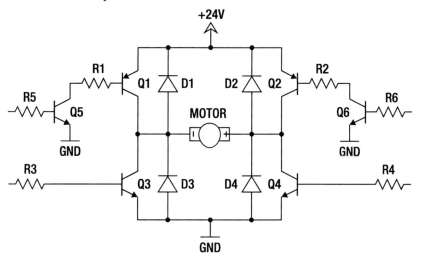

*Figure 6-5. The H-bridge schematic with transistors, resistors, diodes, and wires in place*

7.  *Tie common inputs together:* We now tie the inputs connected to R6 and R3 together to ensure that when this input is HIGH, the motor will spin forward. We then need to tie the other inputs together from R5 and R4, so that when this input is HIGH, the motor will spin in reverse.

    To tie these inputs together in the schematic, use the Name tool to give them both the same name. I chose to name the inputs from R3/R6 = ARDUINO_DP10, and the inputs from R4/R5 = ARDUINO_DP9. By tying common inputs together, only two wires are needed to drive the bridge in either direction.

---

■ **Note** The only catch is that you *must not* bring both inputs HIGH at the same time, because this will cause a shoot-through condition and possibly damage the bridge if no fuse is in place.

---

8.  *Add connectors:* Select the Add tool and type MTA02-**100** in the search bar. Adding these connectors adds a set of pads arranged in a straight line with

standard 0.1-inch spacing, so you can add male-pin headers or similar connector.

I placed three of these connectors into the schematic to provide a connector for the power wires (J1), motor terminals (J2), and the control inputs (J3).

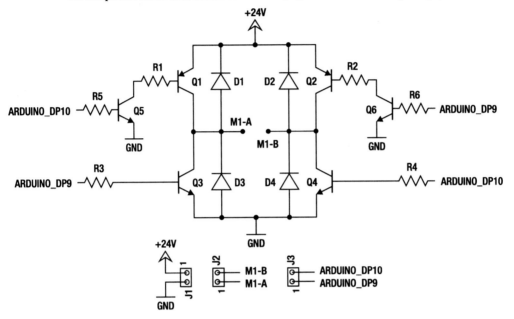

***Figure 6-6.*** *After wiring each part in the schematic, you should name each signal (inputs, outputs, and power traces) to ensure that they will be connected in the board editor.*

Now that you have a workable schematic to use, you should be ready to switch from the schematic editor into the board editor, where Eagle will supply you with the physical components you will be using to make your board. Don't worry about making everything perfect in the schematic editor before switching to the board, because you will be able to make changes to the schematic even while working on the board editor (changes are immediately updated between the two editors).

## Working with the Board Editor

The object of using the board editor is to lay out the physical components used in the schematic, onto a virtual circuit board for you to arrange. Your challenge is to place the components in such a way that none of the signal wires will cross each other. If you must cross two wires, and you cannot find a resistor or diode to act as a bridge (to route the wire trace beneath), you will have to use a jumper wire to make the connection. First, we convert our schematic file into a circuit board layout file.

The following steps guide you through the layout design process:

1. *Switch to the board editor.* When your schematic file is ready, select File Switch to Board from the schematic editor menu (see Figure 6-7). When selecting this option, Eagle warns you that no board file exists for the schematic you are working on, and it asks you whether you want to create

one—answer "yes" and the board editor will open with all of the components from the schematic and virtual wires connecting each component pin according to the schematic.

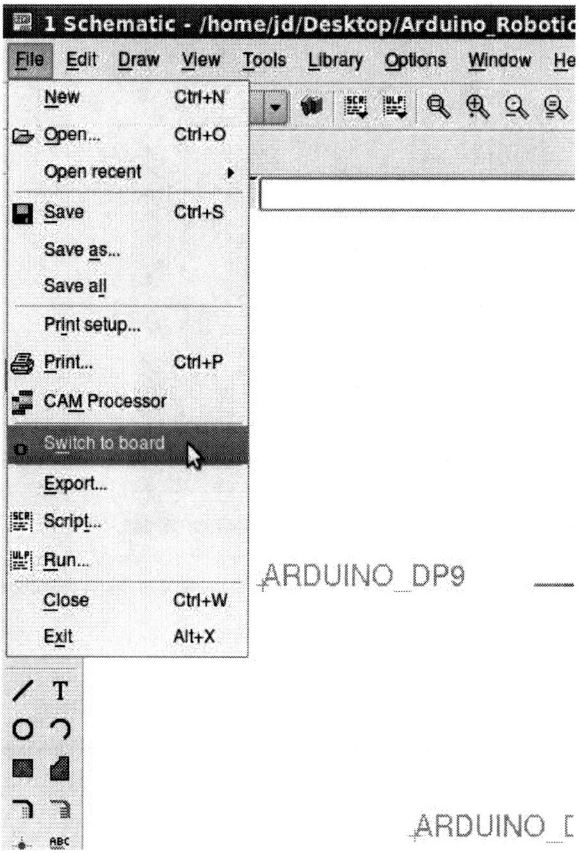

*Figure 6-7. Select the File menu from the schematic editor and choose the Switch to board option.*

2. *Move components:* With all the components now placed on the board editor screen, move each part into the working layout area, which is in the box on the board editor screen, as shown in Figure 6-8.

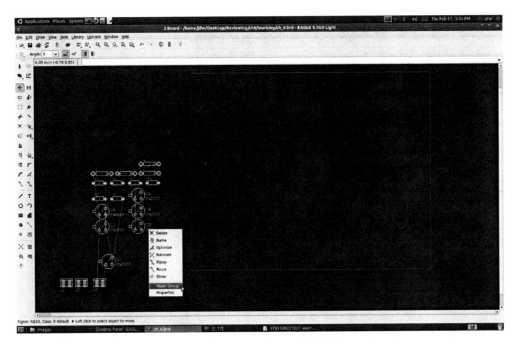

**Figure 6-8.** *Each component needs to move into the workable layout board area.*

3. *Arrange parts on board editor.* The arrangement in Figure 6-9 won't allow crossing wires when we route the traces. It helps to turn on the spacing grid in the board editor so you can make sure everything is aligned properly because this will be the way your PCB looks when it is finished. To enable, go to View Grid Display from the board editor and select the On box. The grid size should be 0.05 inch by default. The component outlines are accurately sized with the real components that you will place on the board, so make sure your component outlines are not overlapping in the layout, because they will also overlap when you try to assemble your board.

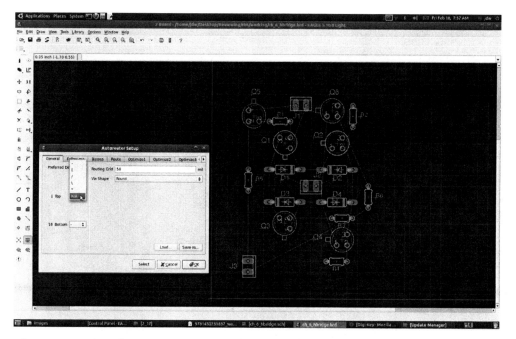

***Figure 6-9.*** *With each component placed on the board, you can start routing wire traces to replace the virtual wires (shown in yellow).*

4. *Wiring by hand*: Start by using the Wire tool from the Tools ▸ Wire menu, to connect the pads of components that are connected by the yellow air wires or virtual wires.

I routed the Power (+24v), GND, M1, and M2 motor terminal wires to replace the yellow air wires shown on the board editor. The power and motor terminal traces carry the majority of the power in this circuit, so we make their wire traces a bit larger than the rest. The default width for a wire in Eagle is 0.016 inch, which is suitable for a signal trace but not for the power traces in an amplifier circuit. To make a wire larger, you should click the Width tab with the Wire tool selected, and change the diameter to 0.05 inch before routing these traces—you can change it back to 0.016 inch or 0.024 inch for routing the signal traces (see Figure 6-10).

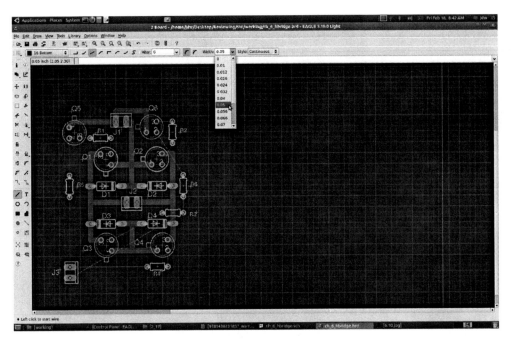

**Figure 6-10.** *Select the Wire tool, change the width to 0.05 inch, and route each power, GND, and motor terminal trace first.*

5. *Routing power:* Click the Ratsnest button to remove the yellow virtual wires periodically after replacing them with wire connections. Finish the routing by connecting the remaining wires. You can use the resistors and diodes on this board as bridges to route wires beneath, as done with R2, R3, and D3 in Figure 6-11. You might notice the Ground wire going from Q5 and Q6 to Q3 and Q4 is still unrouted—that wire will be connected using the Ground plane in step 8.

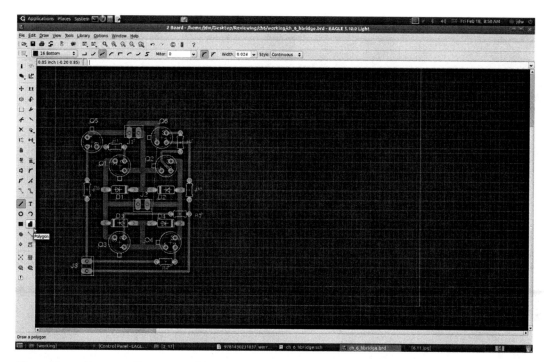

**Figure 6-11.** *Use a smaller wire width to finish the signal traces and then select the Polygon tool to create a Ground plane.*

6. *Make a Ground plane:* To fill all empty space on the PCB with a common GND pad of copper, you must select the Polygon tool from the Draw   Polygon menu (see Figure 6-11). Upon selecting the Polygon tool, draw a line completely around the circuit, giving a little padding around the edges. To finish the polygon (actually a rectangle in this example), double click at the starting point. When the line is finished, use the Name tool to change the name of the polygon to be the same as the Ground supply, usually GND (see Figure 6-12).

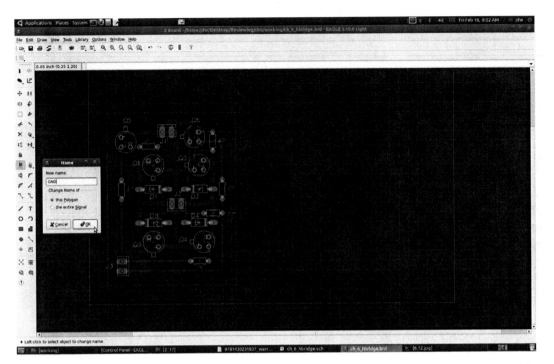

*Figure 6-12. After creating the polygon, use the Name tool to name the polygon "GND," effectively filling any open space on the PCB with a pad of copper that is connected to the GND signal of the PCB—this is called the Ground plane.*

7. *Set clearances:* Now you need to set the clearances of the Ground plane so the traces are not too close together. Changing the wire clearance makes transferring the design to the copper PCB much easier. Select Tools DRC from the menu and then go to the Clearance tab. From there, change the first three boxes (under the Wire column) from 8mm to 30mm as shown in Figure 6-13.

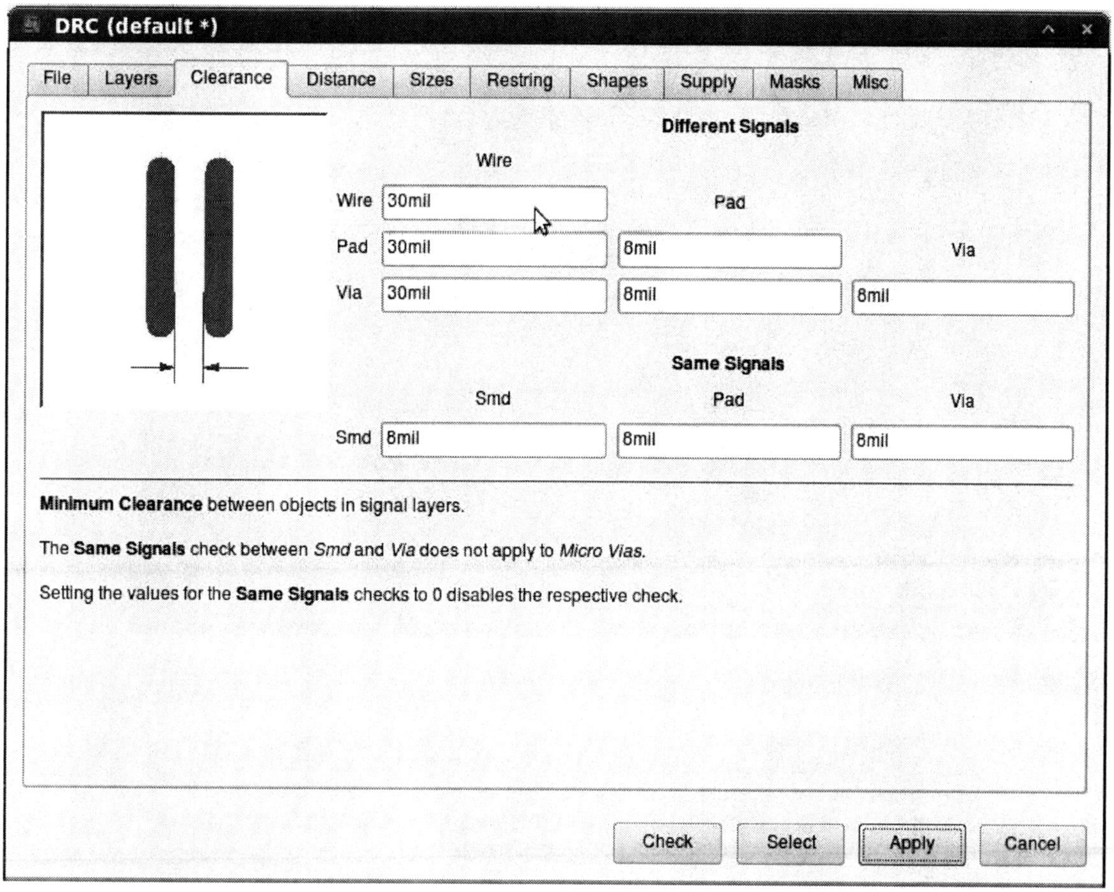

*Figure 6-13. Changing the clearances enables more room between traces and the Ground plane.*

8. *Filling in the Ground plane:* After the polygon is named and the clearances set, click the Ratsnest button once again to fill in the Ground plane (see Figure 6-14). This fills in all empty space with a large copper pad that is connected to all Ground connections in the circuit. Using a Ground plane is not always necessary, but it keeps you from having to remove an excess amount of copper from the board when etching, resulting in a much quicker etching time. You can play with the clearances if you want to add more space between the pads and traces. I selected 30mm clearances because it works every time; I have had trouble with the default 8mm clearance that tends to make the gaps so small that solder pools across them onto other traces, causing difficulties while assembling.

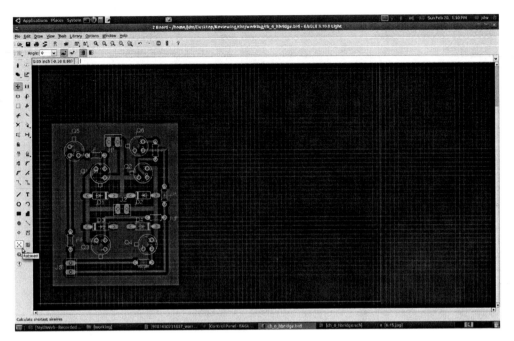

**Figure 6-14.** *Using the Ratsnest tool fills in the Ground plane.*

9. *Preparing for printing.* You are now almost ready to print the design onto the magazine paper and transfer it onto a PCB. Before printing, we should add four mounting holes using the Hole tool. I placed my mounting holes at each corner of the board. If you need more room around the edges, feel free to move the Ground polygon border to add some extra room.

You also need to turn off the unwanted layers before printing. Because we want to print only the copper traces onto the board with the toner, the other layers that show the component outlines, names, and values should all be temporarily turned off. Go to the View Display/hide layers menu and select only the following three layers: Bottom, Pads, and Vias as in Figure 6-15. The design is now ready to print.

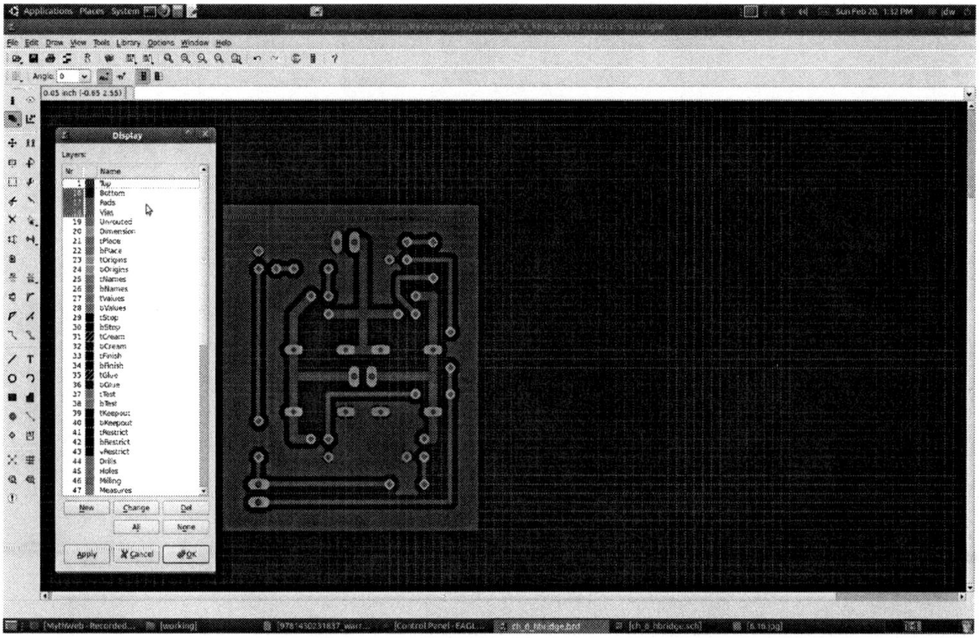

**Figure 6-15.** *When ready to print, make sure you have selected only the layers that you want to transfer. For a single-sided through-hole design like this one, we need only the Vias, Pads, and Bottom layers.*

10. *Printing the design*: To print, go to File Print and make sure the boxes are checked for Black and Solid in the Options box, as shown in Figure 6-16. Feed a piece of magazine paper into the manual feed tray of your laser printer, and press OK to print.

---

■ **Note** Because the ink used in most magazines is not toner, it will not transfer to the PCB when heated with the iron. Only the toner printed onto the paper with your design with will transfer, so you can select almost any page from the magazine that you want. Although a page with only black text on a white background is ideal (like the back of a pharmaceutical advertisement that explains the side-effects), pages with pictures and colorful text will also work, though they might make it more difficult to see your design until it is fully transferred.

---

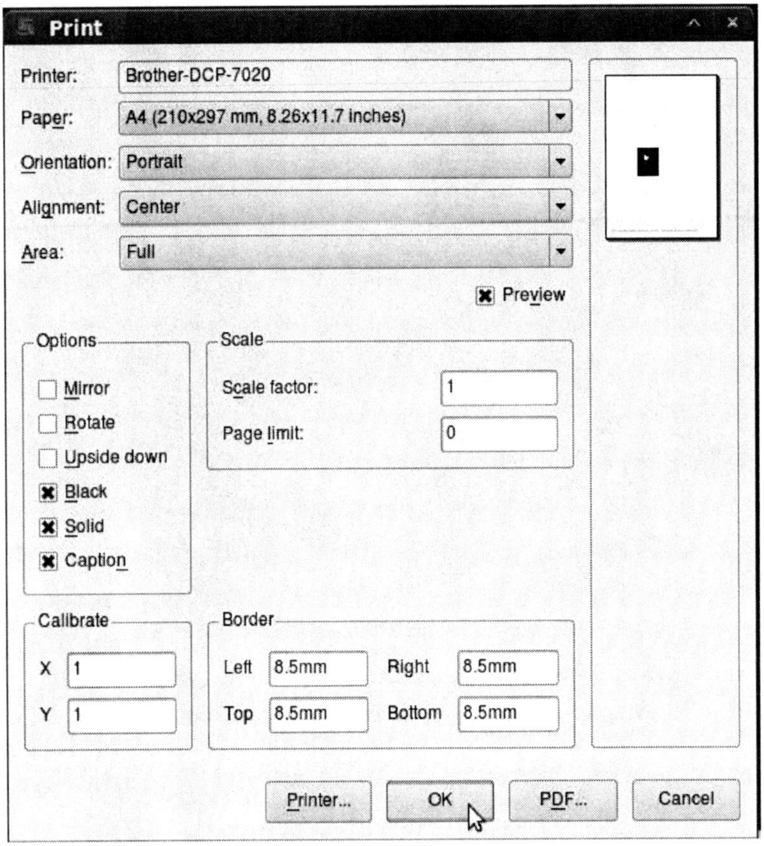

*Figure 6-16. When you are ready to print, make sure you select the Solid and Black options from the Print Setup menu.*

Assuming the paper feeds through properly and the print is not smudged (this happens occasionally), you are ready to iron your design onto the PCB. If you are planning on doing this now, go ahead and plug in your iron to let it pre-heat.

## Transferring the Design

The next step in the PCB-making process is to transfer the design that you have just made onto the blank copper clad board. If you want to etch the H-bridge, you will use only one side of the copper clad board, so a double-sided board is not necessary. I chose to make a single-sided board for the project because lining up the prints on each side of the board to transfer both layers is something that takes time and patience and might frustrate a first-time PCB maker.

We just described how to make a schematic and convert it into a board file, design the physical circuit board, and print the design in Eagle. We designed a simple H-bridge using PNP and NPN bipolar junction transistors to show the basics of the PCB design process. With the design procedure covered, we will move into the hands-on stage of the PCB building process, which can be done using any circuit board design file.

Before getting started with the PCB transfer, we will add an optional Arduino circuit design to build instead of the H-bridge design created previously. I will build both the H-bridge and the Arduino clone circuit simultaneously using the following steps.

# Let's Make an Arduino Clone: the Jduino

It isn't right to show you how to make PCBs without detailing how to make an Arduino clone. If you are like me and make lots of stuff, buying a brand new Arduino for each project can get expensive. Plus, after you get a project the way you want it, you probably won't re-programming it unless something breaks.

The good news is that it is fairly easy to get the brain behind the Arduino working by itself, after being removed from the Arduino main board. There are few parts that are required to get it running: the Atmega chip itself, a 16mHz resonator, and a 5v regulator with a few small capacitors. You can make this happen on a Radio Shack breadboard, but the Arduino has a strange 0.15-inch spacing between Digital pins 7 and 8, which will keep a perf-board Arduino from being able to accept shields. If you don't plan on using any shields in a certain project, you can throw out the Arduino pin positions altogether and make your own variant. There are many options for making and Arduino, but I will show you how to make a basic, shield compatible Arduino clone that lacks only a USB port. You must have an FTDI programming cable (the same one used for the Arduino Pro, Ardupilot, and many others) to program this Arduino.

I wanted to design my own poor-man's Arduino to use in my projects to save a little money and still experiment. It is a basic design, but works with other Arduino shields and has its own 5v regulator, a power LED, and an FTDI programming port.

If you don't want to invest in the FTDI programming cable, you can still use this Arduino by programming the Atmega chip in your main Arduino, and then transferring the programmed chip into the clone for use. I use the FTDI programming cable with many of my Arduino clones, because I can make programmable boards for around $10 each including the Atmega chip.

I don't go step by step on how to design the Arduino clone in Eagle (though I encourage you to try it from the schematic), but you can download the design files for this project from the Google hosting site for the Arduino Robotics book projects:

https://sites.google.com/site/arduinorobotics

The Arduino clone requires you to order some parts online, because your local electronics supply house might not carry the Atmega328 chips, 16mHz resonators, or male/female headers. Table 6-3 provides a complete list for the Arduino clone. Order from Sparkfun.com and you will be well on your way to making your own Arduino.

*Table 6-3. Parts List for Arduino*

| Part | Description | Price |
| --- | --- | --- |
| Copper clad PCB | Radio Shack (part #276-1499)—4.5 inches x 6 inches double-sided copper clad board. This is enough to make two or three Arduino clones. | $3.99 |
| Atmega328 | Sparkfun (part #DEV-09217)—Atmega328 chip with Arduino bootloader installed. | $5.50 |
| 16MHz resonator | Sparkfun (part #COM-09420)—Used for timing the Atmega chip correctly. | $0.50 |

| Part | Description | Price |
|---|---|---|
| 28DIP socket | Sparkfun (part #PRT-07942)—Socket to allow removal of Atmega chip. | $0.50 |
| FTDI programming cable (optional) | Sparkfun (part #DEV-09718)—Cable for programming the Arduino clone. This is not required, but makes the clone programmable without removing the Atmega chip. This programs all future Arduino clones that you build. | $17.95 (optional) |
| Female headers 40-pin | Sparkfun (part #PRT-00115)—These headers allow for plugging prototyping wires into your new Arduino. You can clip however many you need in a row. It comes with 40 sockets. | $1.50 |
| 7805 5v regulator | Sparkfun (part #COM-00107)—This provides a constant 5v to the Atmega chip. | $1.25 |
| Capacitors (2) 10uF, 25v | Sparkfun (part #COM-00523)—These values are minimum, but can be higher if you already have a stock of capacitors. | $0.45 |
| Reset button | Sparkfun (part #COM-00097)—This button enables you to reset the Arduino when programming or restarting. | $0.35 |

The H-bridge that we created earlier in this chapter requires a few parts that can be purchased from Radio Shack, Sparkfun.com, or Digikey.com (see Table 6-4).

*Table 6-4. Parts List for BJT H-Bridge*

| Part | Description | Price |
|---|---|---|
| (4) 2n2222 NPN transistors | Radio Shack (part #276-1617)—15 pack | $2.99 |
| (2) 2n2907 PNP transistors | Radio Shack (part #276-1604)—15 pack | $2.59 |
| (6) 1k ohm resistors | Radio Shack (part #271-004)—5 pack | $0.99 |
| (4) 1n914 Diodes | Radio Shack (part #276-1122)—10 pack | $1.49 |
| 1 pc. copper clad board | Use what you have left over from the Arduino clone. | |
| (6) Header pins | Sparkfun (part #PRT-00116)—You can also solder the wires directly to the PCB instead of using header pins. | $2.50 (optional) |

# Making the Transfer

Open Eagle on your computer and download the files for project 6. This includes both the completed H-bridge and the Arduino clone.

1.  *Open the file.* Open the "bjt_h-bridge.brd" or "jduino.brd" file depending on whether you are building the h-bridge or Arduino clone—or if you have your own .brd file that you want to try, you can still follow the steps for transferring and etching. Turn your iron on High to let it pre-heat.

    Following the directions described in the "Making a Design in Eagle" section for printing the designs (see Figure 6-16), select the Layers tool from the board editor menu and make sure that only the Bottom, Pads, and Vias layers are selected. You should now see only the blue bottom layer and the green pads and vias where holes will be drilled. Remember that when you open a design that has a Ground plane in Eagle, you must first select the Ratsnest tool to fill it in. After filled, the design is ready to print.

    Print the design on the magazine paper, manually feeding it into the printer. After it prints, make sure there are no runs or lines going through the toner print (see Figure 6-17).

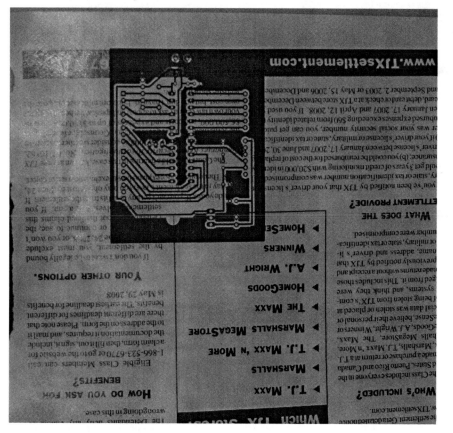

*Figure 6-17. The printed design on a piece of magazine paper*

2. *Re-sizing the design:* You should now have a printed design in the center of a piece of magazine paper. Look over the toner print and make sure the printer did not make any run marks through the design and that the toner is solid black throughout—if not, re-print! Be careful from this point on that you do not touch the toner or any part of the printed design because it might transfer oil or dirt from your fingers onto the print, which can keep it from transferring.

   Cut the prints about 1/8 inch larger than the toner design with razor-blade knife or a pair of scissors, being careful not to touch the toner. Place the re-sized design (toner side up) on the PCB to see how large it needs to be, and mark the corners with a marker (see Figure 6-18).

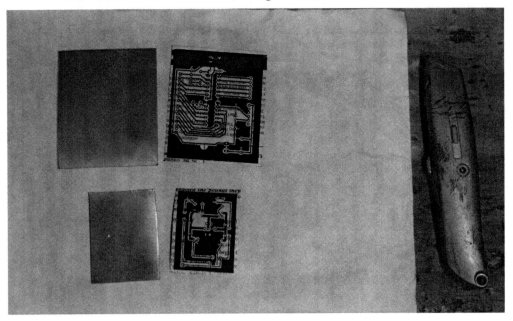

*Figure 6-18. Both designs printed and resized, ready to transfer to the copper clad*

3. *Resize PCB:* With the PCB marked, use a razor-blade knife to score the PCB on each side. Cut clean straight lines with the razor-blade, scoring several times to make a nice groove. If using a double-sided PCB, repeat on other side. Now snap the PCB along the scored line, it should break easily, though you might have to use your razor knife to clean up the edge. You have to do this for each PCB that you make to avoid wasting copper clad board (see Figure 6-19).

*Figure 6-19. The two pieces of copper clad board cut to size and ready for cleaning*

4.   *Clean PCB.* It is time to get out the Scotch-brite abrasive pad to clean the surface of the copper clad board. Using the pad, vigorously scrub the PCB until the entire surface is shiny—it helps to scrub the PCB either up and down or left and right, but not both.

With the PCB shiny and new looking, use a paper towel dabbed in Acetone or Lacquer thinner to remove any excess dirt or copper dust from the PCB. Clean the copper surface at least five times with a clean part of the paper towel, folding it after each cleaning. Each time you clean it, dab a little more Acetone on the towel to make sure you pick up all the remaining dust and until the paper towel has no visible dirt for at least two cleanings.

**Figure 6-20.** *Both boards after scrubbing with the Scotch-brite pad and cleaning thoroughly with lacquer thinner (acetone works, too)*

When I first started making my own PCBs, I had a terrible time trying to get the toner to transfer to the copper. I did everything correctly up to this step, but I was not thoroughly cleaning the copper ("thorough" being the key word), which resulted in partially transferred designs on the copper clad! I got frustrated the first few times until I realized the copper surface still had micro-dust on it. Over-cleaning the copper surface before transferring fixed this problem indefinitely. When in doubt, clean again.

5. *Iron design onto copper.* The PCB should now be as clean as it is going to get, so let it dry for about 1 minute (the acetone must evaporate completely). Now place the printed design face down, on the clean copper surface of the PCB.

Holding one corner with your finger, gently place the (hot) iron over the other half of the design for about 5 seconds, giving it just enough time to bond the toner to the copper (see Figure 6-21). Now release your finger and place the iron gently over the entire design, and do not move the iron back and forth while on top of the design. Make sure you place the center part of the iron over the design, so it heats the transfer evenly.

*Figure 6-21. Heat each board with an iron (on the highest heat setting), placing an extra sheet of magazine paper between the iron and the back of the actual design.*

After about 30 seconds directly on top of the design, remove the iron and place another sheet of magazine paper on top of the design to act as a buffer between the iron and the top of the design. Now you can apply pressure while slowly and gently moving the iron back and forth. I use the front of the iron and press firmly while moving front to back, making sure to get every part of the board. This makes sure each trace is pressed to the copper while being heated. After each part of the design has been pressed with the front of the iron, heat the entire board with the center of the iron for about 3 minutes, applying as much downward force as you can without moving the iron.

■ **Note** You do not want to move the iron *directly* across the design because it might rip the paper, causing any toner traces to be ripped as well. To prevent this, put another sheet of magazine paper on top of the design and then move the iron around on top of that—this way if you rip the paper, it won't rip the actual design.

6.  *Remove paper backing.* After ironing is complete, let the board sit for about 5 minutes to cool down. After the copper board has cooled to the point that you can pick it up by the edges without burning your hand, place the design in a plastic container with warm soapy water and let sit for 10–20 minutes (see Figure 6-22). The longer you let it soak, the easier the paper is to remove.

*Figure 6-22. Place the cooled boards into a plastic container and add warm water with some soap to dissolve the magazine paper.*

After soaking, remove the PCB from the water and lightly rub the paper with your thumb (not your fingernail). It should start peeling away as a wet pulpy mess, but the toner traces should remain. If the transfer went according to plan, the toner should stick to the copper and no amount of rubbing will remove the actual toner.

■ **Note** Do not use your fingernails to remove the paper! The toner is bonded to the copper, but it can still be scraped off fairly easy.

7.  *Inspect the transfer.* After all the paper is removed, inspect the design to make sure that all the toner transferred successfully. If there are any small spots that did not transfer, you can touch them up with a permanent marker or some fingernail polish. If too much of the toner failed to transfer, it is probably best to re-try the transfer process by repeating steps 4–6.

In Figure 6-23, notice the right edge of my design did not fully transfer. Because all the traces transferred nicely, I decided to fix this with a little fingernail polish. You can apply some fingernail polish, wait until it dries, then scrape away any excess before etching.

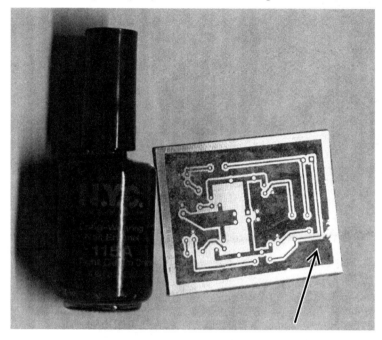

*Figure 6-23. The H-bridge design transferred successfully, with the exception of one spot in the Ground plane that I patched using fingernail polish.*

In Figure 6-24 the Arduino clone transferred successfully, with the exception of one small spot on the bottom left, which is contained in the Ground plane and can be fixed with a marker or fingernail polish.

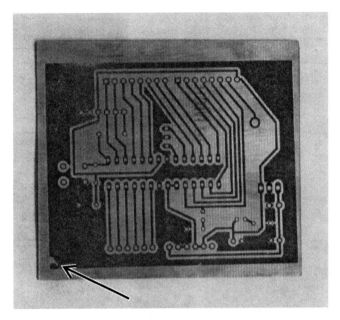

**Figure 6-24.** *The Arduino clone design transferred nicely, except for one small cosmetic spot near the corner—this was fixed using a black permanent marker.*

After you are satisfied with the transferred designs and have made any necessary corrections, it is time to etch the copper clad board to remove any copper that is not covered by toner, marker, or fingernail polish. At this point, you should be advised that the next step requires using a chemical mixture to dissolve metal. Although this is no more dangerous than adding chemicals to a swimming pool, anyone participating should use caution when near the chemicals (protective eye-wear and rubber gloves). You should also keep a supply of water nearby (bucket or hose-pipe) to rinse any chemicals that come in contact with your skin or clothes.

## Etching

Assuming your transfer worked correctly, you are ready to etch your board to reveal the copper traces that will be your circuit. Select a space to etch. Because the chemicals can be dangerous, it is a good idea to do this outside and with plenty of ventilation.

Gather the materials from the list in Table 6-1 and the transferred PCBs you are going to etch. Set up a fan to blow the fumes outside and away from you; make sure you wear your rubber gloves and goggles. Hydrogen peroxide is a topical skin disinfectant that is used to clean minor cuts and scrapes—you can also use this as an oral rinse to clean a tooth or sore. The muriatic acid on the other hand, is a chemical used to clean concrete or as a swimming pool cleansing agent, and can cause burns if it gets on your skin without being rinsed off. When these two chemicals mix, the solution slowly dissolves copper, aluminum, and most other metals, so it is advised that you use a plastic bowl as an etching container. Because muriatic acid is an etchant, it will discolor concrete. I use a cardboard box flattened beneath the etching container and equipment to keep it from getting on the ground.

# Measuring the Solution

With all of your parts together, it is time to measure the etchant solution. Use a plastic measuring cup to measure 8 ounces of hydrogen peroxide and pour it into the etching tank (the plastic container). Now carefully measure 4 ounces of muriatic acid and pour it into the etching tank. After the muriatic acid is placed into the hydrogen peroxide, some fumes will be created—**do not breathe these fumes!** It is now safe to place the copper clad PCBs into the etching tank.

In Figure 6-25, you see three different plastic tanks:

- The Glad plastic container in the center is used with the air bubbler as an etching tank (Method 1).

- The sour cream container that was cleaned out is used for a bubble-less etching tank (Method 2).

- The larger plastic tank on the right, which I fill with about 2 inches of water and place both etching tanks inside of while etching, is used to immediately neutralize any etchant solution that spills out of the etchant tanks.

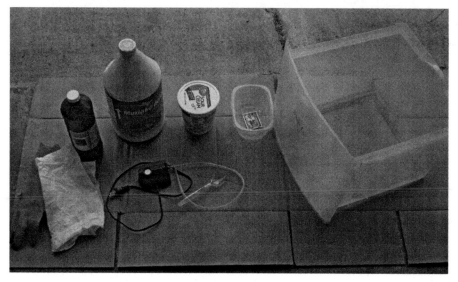

*Figure 6-25. The chemicals and materials needed to etch a PCB at home. The two smaller containers will be used for different etching methods.*

This makes sure there is always water nearby to dilute the acid etching solution. If the etchant touches water, it immediately loses its etching capability, so make sure you don't get any water in the etchant tank while etching.

There are several different ways that you can etch a PCB, so I offer the two in which I am most familiar. Method 1 might be considered safer, but requires the use of an air pump (aquarium bubbler), which costs about $10. Method 2 bypasses the need for an agitator by placing the PCB and etchant solution into a sealed container and spinning the container with your hand to agitate the solution—this method is more likely to spill or leak than Method 1.

# Etching: Method 1

Using any small plastic bowl and an air bubbler, you can etch a copper clad PCB in about 10 minutes. The air bubbler is used an agitator to help remove the dissolving copper more quickly. Place the end of the air tubing beneath the PCB submerged in the etchant. Place the design face down and the tube beneath the board—the bubbles should rise up the board flowing over the toner design. You might have to re-position the board every few minutes to enable the bubbles to reach every part of the board. Use a plastic spoon or fork to lift the PCB from the tank and position it, being careful not to scratch the toner (see Figure 6-26).

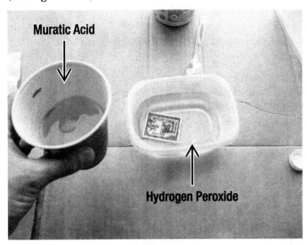

*Figure 6-26. Mixing the etchant solution requires two plastic containers (an etchant tank and measuring cup) and the PCB that you are etching.*

---

■ **Note** Etchant solution = 2 parts Hydrogen Peroxide + 1 part Muriatic acid

---

As the etchant reacts with the copper, it turns a bright green color (see Figure 6-27). Use the air bubbler to force bubbles to the bottom of the tank. As the bubbles rise past the board, they remove the excess copper that has dissolved, thereby speeding up the etching process—this is called an *agitator.*

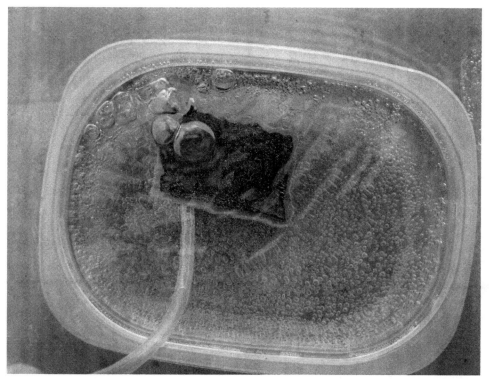

*Figure 6-27. The etchant solution changes colors from clear to green as the copper dissolves.*

If you do not have an aquarium bubbler or do not want to purchase one, you can use the alternate method of etching, and agitate the PCB manually by shaking.

# Etching: Method 2

The plastic recycled sour cream container is used for etching without an air bubbler. Instead of relying on movement from the bubbles created by the air pump, we make the movement manually by swirling the sealed container with the etchant and PCB inside. Because the container is circular, the board will not be able to lay flat against the sides of the container (which is good) and by perforating the lid with small pin-holes, we can fill the container 3/4 full with etchant and spin it around for about 5 minutes to agitate the copper without bubbles (see Figure 6-28).

This method should be done over a larger tank of water and with gloves, because it tends to spill some etchant out of the container while spinning. Do not try this method without perforating the top—the solution creates some fumes that must be able to escape from the closed container.

*Figure 6-28. The plastic container with the PCB inside, about half-way finished etching*

Fill the plastic container 3/4 full of etchant, and then place the perforated lid onto container. Gently shake or spin back and forth in a circular motion for about 3 minutes (you can take breaks). This method uses the constantly swirling liquid to remove the etched copper. Notice that the toner on the board cannot touch the sides of the container thus eliminating the risk of scraping the toner off the copper; only the sides of the PCB can touch the plastic container.

---

■ **Caution** Some etchant *will* come out of the perforated holes and possibly under the lid of your container. It is best to do this over a bucket that is 1/4 filled with water. This way if you spill any etchant, it neutralizes in the water without harming anything.

---

When the board is finished etching, you will be able to see through the board between the traces. Remove the board and wash with clean water.

Hold the board up to the light and make sure there are no traces touching. The light illuminates the fiberglass and enables you to see only the copper traces (see Figure 6-29).

*Figure 6-29. Use a light source to verify that all copper has been etched away except for the transferred traces. Light glosw through the fiberglass board, but not through the copper traces.*

When you are finished etching (using either method), you should have a circuit board with no visible copper, and only toner remaining on the fiberglass board. Figure 6-30 shows the BJT H-bridge next to the Arduino clone, both etched with the toner still on.

*Figure 6-30. Both PCBs after etching—notice the copper is now removed, leaving only the transferred toner.*

When you are finished etching your PCBs, pour the remaining etchant solution into a bucket of water to dilute it. Then pour the diluted solution in an inconspicuous area (the back of the yard or edge of the road) because it is an acidic water solution.

## Removing the Toner

Now that the copper has been etched from around the toner design, there is no more need for the toner. You need to remove the toner from the PCB to reveal the copper traces beneath (see Figure 6-31). The easiest way to remove the toner is with acetone or lacquer thinner and some paper towels.

*Figure 6-31. Using a paper towel dabbed in acetone, rub the toner from the back of the PCB. The acetone should dissolve the toner enabling it to be removed with little effort.*

Dab some acetone on a paper towel and begin rubbing the design until the toner begins to wipe off (see Figures 6-31 and 6-32). You might have to fold the paper towel halfway through and add more acetone; just make sure you remove all toner from the copper surface.

*Figure 6-32. Removing the toner from the Arduino clone*

You should now have a clean PCB with visible copper traces that is ready to have holes drilled for the pads and vias (see Figure 6-33). Each hole should be evident by a circle in the copper. If you have a hole that does not show up (maybe the toner was smeared), refer to the Eagle board file to make sure the board has each hole shown in the design file.

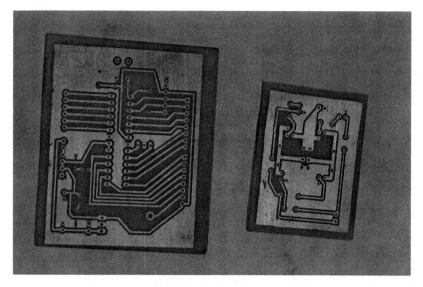

*Figure 6-33. The two PCBs after etching—only copper traces are visible with the toner removed.*

Don't look back; you're almost finished! All that is left to do for each PCB is to drill the holes for each component and solder the pieces into place. Drilling requires some patience, good light, and a steady hand.

# Drilling

Although there are many ways to drill a PCB, I like to use my handy bench drill press for this step. The drill press makes sure each hole is drilled perpendicular to the PCB, and enables precision control over the height of the drill head, meaning each hole can be perfectly placed. Hopefully you have a drill press (or access to one), because it is far easier to accurately place holes than with a hand-held drill (see Figure 6-34).

It is also helpful to use the right-sized drill bit—if the bit is too small, you won't be able to fit the component leads through the board; if the bit is too large, there will be a space between the component lead and the copper trace causing trouble during soldering.

Harbor Freight tools sells a set of small PCB drill bits for under $10 (item #44924) that will work with either a drill press or a hand-held drill. If you are not sure about the size of the drill bit, test the bit on a piece of scrap copper clad to see whether a component lead will fit through it. It is not uncommon to use several different sized drill bits on a PCB that has many different sized components.

*Figure 6-34. The Arduino clone PCB on the drill press*

After each hole is drilled, make sure they are spaced properly by fitting the IC socket, headers, and LEDs. The boards should now be ready to add components and solder together.

# Soldering

Soldering the components to the PCB is the final step in the building process, and in my opinion, the most fun. You need to refer to the schematic and board files for this chapter to make sure you place each part correctly. I always start soldering with the parts that are not easily damaged (IC socket and headers), and then move on to the more sensitive parts last (LEDs, capacitors, and ICs) —this way they are not exposed to much heat during soldering (see Figure 6-35).

*Figure 6-35. Start building the Arduino clone by placing the 28-pin IC socket, female headers, and LED with resistor on the PCB.*

When soldering, remember to heat the copper pad and component leads and let the solder bond to them. If you try to heat the solder onto the copper, you will likely make a mess and have cold solder joints that might fail later. A good solder joint appears shiny, silver, and smooth. When properly heated, the solder melts into all crevices and forms a neat puddle around the component lead.

We now begin building each board, starting with the Arduino clone. Make sure you have all of the parts from Table 6-2 for the Arduino clone and/or Table 6-3 for the BJT H-bridge.

## Building the Arduino Clone

The Arduino clone is an easy circuit to build, with all through-hole components and very few polarized parts (the voltage regulator, LEDs, and larger capacitors). The resistors, 16MHz resonator, ceramic capacitors, and headers can be installed in any direction.

1. *Install IC socket and headers*: Although the IC socket is symmetrical and works in either direction, it does have an indentation mark on one end of the socket—this is used to denote pin 1 of the IC socket and should point toward the reset button (away from the voltage regulator) in this circuit. Make sure each leg is inserted fully through the board and begin by soldering the four corners (see Figure 6-36). Check the socket to make sure it is sitting flat on the board, and then solder the remaining terminals.

***Figure 6-36.*** *When installing an IC socket or other component with several pins, always secure the corner leads first and inspect from the top before proceeding to solder the remaining pins.*

After soldering the IC socket, insert the (2) 8-pin headers and the (2) 6-pin headers on the sides of the Arduino clone, and solder them to the board. These headers are also symmetrical, so orientation does not matter.

2. *Install power LED (red) and test:* Insert the power indicator LED, which is tied into the +5v from the voltage regulator, through a 330-ohm resistor to ground. Insert the LED into the board with the long leg (positive cathode) of the LED toward the IC socket, and then insert the 330-ohm resistor and solder both into place. Because the LED positive is tied to the +5v pins of the Arduino clone, and there is no voltage regulator installed yet, you can power the Arduino clone with a separate +5v and Ground signal to test the LED, as in Figure 6-37.

Ground    +5V

**Figure 6-37.** *The Arduino clone with IC socket, headers, and power LED installed. Using another Arduino or any 5v power source, you can power the LED to test it before proceeding.*

3.  *Install remaining parts:* Now you must install the remaining parts to complete the Arduino clone (see Figure 6-38).

    - *16MHz resonator:* Install any orientation—it cannot be installed incorrectly. Bend down before soldering.

    - *Male headers:* Install the 6-pin male headers for the FTDI port and the 2-pin header for the power port. These can be installed in any direction.

    - *Capacitors:* The aluminum capacitors used for the voltage regulator are polarized and should be placed with the black stripe facing Ground. The ceramic capacitors used for the FTDI port are non-polarized and can be placed in any direction.

    - *Reset button:* The Reset button is rectangular and cannot be placed incorrectly. Also place 10k pull-up resistor between reset the button and IC socket.

    - *D13 LED (green):* The other LED is for digital pin 13; place longer lead (positive) toward IC socket and then a 330-ohm resistor. This LED lights up anytime Digital Pin 13 is driven HIGH.

- *Voltage regulator.* Lastly, place the 7805 voltage regulator on the board and bend down. You can use hot glue to hold down to the board if needed. If you want to connect the Ground pin next to digital pin 13, you should solder a wire from the via to the Ground tab of the 7805 voltage regulator as shown in Figure 6-38.

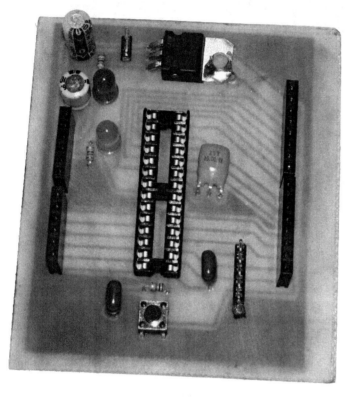

*Figure 6-38. The finished Arduino clone (jduino), ready for use*

## Building the BJT H-Bridge

The BJT H-bridge is quite simple requiring only six different types of components including the PCB. You need (4) NPN transistors, (2) PNP transistors, (6) 1k-ohm resistors, (4) diodes, (3) sets of male pin headers, and the PCB. The design is meant to be used as a learning tool because it is easy to etch, solder, and use. It can handle 1 ampere of continuous current at up to 30vdc with the 2n2222 NPN and 2n2907 PNP transistors pairs.

The following steps guide you through this process:

1. *Install the transistors and diodes.* These parts must be placed correctly in order to work. Install the transistors as shown in Figure 6-40. The emitter pin (pin 1) of each NPN transistor (2n2222) should connect to the GND plane, and the emitter pins of the PNP transistors (2n2907) should connect to the +VIN supply. The (4) NPN transistors should be placed at each end of the board, whereas the (2) PNP transistors should be placed in the center of the board. See Figure 6-39 for a pinout of the transistor pins.

   The two diodes on the left in Figure 6-41 (closest to the PNP transistors) should have their striped end (cathode) facing the center of the board, whereas the two diodes on the right should have their striped ends facing the outside of the board (see Figure 6-41).

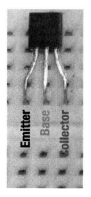

*Figure 6-39. A standard pinout of a BJT transistor in the TO-92 package. The emitter (left) is labeled as pin 1 in the schematic and board files, the base (center) is labeled as pin 2, and the collector (right) is labeled as pin 3.*

2. *Install header pins.* This board needs three sets of header pins to connect the motor, power supply, and inputs from the Arduino. These header pins can be male pin or female socket type as used on the Arduino clone. You can alternatively solder wires directly to each header pin location if you do not want to use headers. If using male pin headers, you need to cut them from the strip using wire snips as shown in Figure 6-40.

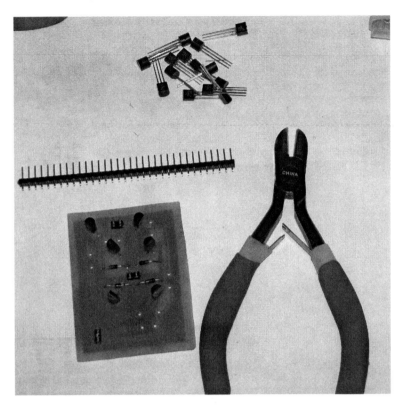

**Figure 6-40.** *Snip three sets of two header pins from the strip with pliers, and solder one set for the power terminals, one set for the motor terminals, and the last set for the input connections.*

3. *Install resistors:* The last components to install are the (6) 1k-ohm resistors that limit the amount of current allowed to each transistor base. Resistors are non-polarized and can be installed in any direction. When you are finished, verify that your board looks like the one in Figure 6-41 before testing your new PCBs.

**Figure 6-41.** *The finished BJT H-bridge PCB, ready for use*

---

⬚ **Note** The two NPN transistors at the top of the board are used to invert the signal to the PNP transistors and can be either 2n3904, 2n4401, or 2n2222 NPN transistors. All resistors should be 1k-ohm and as small as 1/8w is fine. The diodes can be any that they sell at Radio Shack—this includes the 1n4001 1-amp diodes and the 1n4148 200ma fast-switching diodes. Because the bridge is rated only for 1 amp, any of these diodes will work.

---

The only requirement of this bridge is that you do not bring both inputs HIGH at the same time—this will cause a shoot-through condition and likely blow a fuse or the bridge if no fuse is installed. You will notice that one of my resistors is a larger 1/4 watt type, but this is not important because the value is still 1k-ohm (I ran out of 1/8w resistors when building).

This H-bridge is perfect for controlling the speed and direction of small hobby motors up to 1 amp. This includes most DC motors used for front-end steering in R/C cars as well as servo motors and some gear motors.

# Testing

Now that you have completed both the Arduino clone and the BJT H-bridge, you can use them to control a DC motor. I added a single potentiometer (shown in Figure 6-42) connected to the Arduino Analog port 0. We use this potentiometer and the code in Listing 6-1, to control both the speed and direction of a DC motor. I decided to test the Arduino clone and H-bridge together to verify their operation (any small DC motor will do).

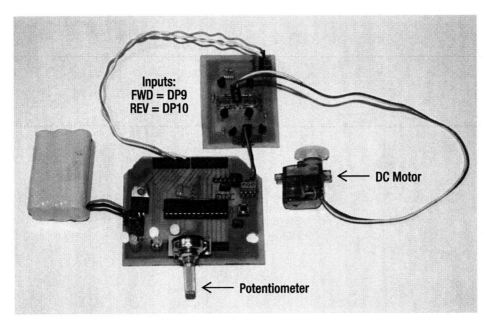

**Figure 6-42.** *Here we have the Arduino clone (jduino), the BJT H-bridge, a DC motor, 7.2v battery, and a potentiometer (connected to A0 of the Arduino clone) to control the speed and direction of the DC motor. I modified the Arduino clone a bit to be mounted in the robot from Chapter 7.*

If the potentiometer is centered, the motor will be turned off, and the green LED on D13 will turn on. If the potentiometer is moved to the right, the motor will spin proportionally forward with far right being full speed. If it is moved to the left, the motor will spin proportionally in reverse with far left being full speed. This type of control scheme uses one input to enable bi-directional control of the output, which is excellent for our testing purposes.

Upload the code in Listing 6-1, and connect the BJT H-bridge inputs to Arduino PWM Pins D9 = forward and D10 = reverse. The H-bridge power supply can be between 5v–30vdc. The Arduino power supply can be between 5v–12vdc. The potentiometer controls both the direction and the speed of the motor (any potentiometer will work)—I used what I had lying around. To test the green LED that we added to D13 on the Arduino clone, I commanded that LED to be turned on when the potentiometer is centered (in neutral) —this gives you a better idea of where to stop.

**Listing 6-1.** *Testing the JDuino*

```
//CODE
// Test the BJT H-bridge and the Arduino Clone.
// Connect inputs from BJT H-bridge into Arduino DP9 and DP10
// Connect Potentiometer to Arduino Analog pin 0.

int forward = 9; // use pin 9 for PWM forward
int reverse = 10; // use pin 10 for PWM reverse
int LED = 13; // use LED on pin 13 to indicate neutral
```

```
int potentiometer_value = 0; // read the potentiometer to determine direction and speed
int deadband = 20; // determines deadband from center - a higher number equals a larger↵
 neutral zone.

void setup(){

  Serial.begin(9600); // start serial monitor at 9600 bps

  // set PWM pins to be outputs
  pinMode(forward, OUTPUT);
  pinMode(reverse, OUTPUT);

  // set LED pin to be an output
  pinMode(LED, OUTPUT);

}

void loop(){


  // read potentiometer (0-1023) and divide by 2 = (0-511).
  // Now break that up into 255 either direction (0-255 = PWM value range).↵
  potentiometer_value = analogRead(0) / 2;

  if (potentiometer_value > 256 + deadband) {
    digitalWrite(reverse, LOW);
    analogWrite(forward, potentiometer_value - 256);
    digitalWrite(LED, LOW);

    Serial.print(potentiometer_value - 256);
    Serial.print("     ");
    Serial.print(potentiometer_value);
    Serial.print("     ");
    Serial.println("  Forward    ");
  }
  else if (potentiometer_value < 255 - deadband) {
    digitalWrite(forward, LOW);
    analogWrite(reverse, 255 - potentiometer_value);
    digitalWrite(LED, LOW);

    Serial.print(255 - potentiometer_value);
    Serial.print("     ");
    Serial.print(potentiometer_value);
    Serial.print("     ");
    Serial.println("  Reverse    ");
  }
  else {
    digitalWrite(forward, LOW);
    digitalWrite(reverse, LOW);
    digitalWrite(LED, HIGH);
```

```
    Serial.print(potentiometer_value);

    Serial.print("      ");
    Serial.println("   STOP   ");
  }

}

// open serial monitor to see potentiometer reading and motor direction
// end of code.
```

If you do not have a DC motor that is small enough to test, you can always use a voltage meter to test the motor outputs at M1-A and M1-B of the H-bridge (center header pins). The voltage reading at these pins should be proportional to the potentiometer position and the H-bridge positive voltage supply.

# Summary

In this chapter, we demonstrated how to use a circuit design program (using Eagle from CadSoft) to design and build a PCB from scratch. We started by creating a schematic for a simple H-bridge using bipolar junction transistors. After completing the schematic, we used the design software (Eagle) to convert the schematic into a circuit board layout. With the circuit board editor, we were able to rearrange the component parts from the schematic to fit on a virtual PCB.

After designing the circuit layout file, we walked through how to print the circuit design onto a piece of glossy magazine paper to be transferred onto the copper clad circuit board. First we thoroughly cleaned the copper board with a Scotch-brite pad, and then removed any dust with acetone and paper towels (clean thoroughly!). After cleaning, we heated up the iron and heated the design onto the copper board for about 3 minutes, making sure to press firmly on each part of the design for a complete transfer. After cooled, the circuit boards were placed in warm soapy water to dissolve the magazine paper, leaving only the toner melted to the copper.

After transferring the design onto the copper board, we carefully mixed a chemical solution of two-parts hydrogen peroxide to one-part muriatic acid in a plastic container, to make an etchant solution. The circuit boards were then submerged into the etchant solution for about 5 minutes (with intermittent agitation), until all of the copper was dissolved. After etching, the boards were washed in cold water and the toner was removed using acetone and paper towels.

We then discussed how to drill the PCBs for each pad and via in the circuit design, and finally placing each component and soldering into place. The finished circuit boards were then inspected and tested using a potentiometer and DC motor to verify that there were no short circuits or crossed traces. If everything went together correctly, the motor should spin with full speed control in either direction, and stop when the potentiometer is centered.

In the next chapter, we build another autonomous robot that guides itself around a room using only bump-sensors. We use the Arduino clone from this chapter to build the Bump-bot, as well as a few homemade bump sensors.

# CHAPTER 7

# The Bug-Bot

In this chapter you build a robot (the Bug-Bot) that uses *bump sensors* to navigate around objects and explore a room, much like an insect would. The bump sensor is nothing more than two wires pressed together when the bot bumps into something, to let the Arduino know that it needs to find a new path (Figure 7-1). These sensors are commonly used for object detection but require that the bot have physical contact with the object to detect it. Some robots incorporate several types of sensors for object avoidance and autonomous navigation; these usually include a bump sensor on the front and/or rear of the bot to stop it if the other sensors do not.

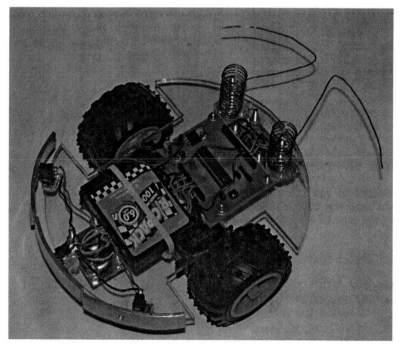

*Figure 7-1. The visible components of the Bug-bot: three bump sensors on the left, a battery and Arduino clone in the center, two antennae sensors on the right, and two hobby Servo motors with wheels attached beneath a simple, homemade plexiglass frame.*

The simplest of bump sensors can be constructed using a piece of wire, a nut, and a bolt. To illustrate this, I decided to build the bump sensors for the front of the Bug-bot from scratch. I then used SPST switches for the rear sensors, which have aluminum bumpers attached to them.

## Reading a Switch with Arduino

The majority of the code for this project involves reading the digital state of an Input pin. Recall from Chapter 1 that a digital Input can be read only as either HIGH (+5v) or LOW (GND). You can read the state of a digital switch from any Arduino pin using the digitalRead(pin) command. The default state of each pin can be either HIGH or LOW, depending on how you want to interface the switch. In this project, I focused on using as few parts as possible and keeping the design simple.

Connecting each bump sensor switch is simple: one pole of the switch connects to the Arduino Input pin; the other connects to GND. The Arduino has internal 20k ohm pull-up resistors on each pin that can be activated in the code if needed. To minimize the amount of parts needed (no extra resistors to buy), you can utilize these internal resistors to keep the Input pin HIGH unless the bump switch connects it to GND. Although it might make more sense (to me at least) to keep the input LOW using a pull-down resistor and only read HIGH (+5v) if the switch is activated because it would require slightly less power (but the Atmega168 pins are capable of holding only an input pin HIGH and not LOW), you must utilize the Arduino's internal pull-up resistors to avoid using external resistors.

To use the Arduino's internal pull-up resistors, you simply declare the pin as an INPUT using pinMode() in the setup() function; then digitalWrite the pin HIGH. With the pull-up resistor enabled, digital pin 2 in Listing 7-1 is HIGH by default unless driven LOW by some other source (that is, the bump switch). You can test the following example by running it on your Arduino and viewing the Serial monitor. Connect pin 2 to GND to see a 0 reading; otherwise, it reads 1.

*Listing 7-1. Reading a Contact Switch*

```
// Code Example 7-1: Reading a contact switch
// Switch wires should connect to GND and Arduino digital pin 2
// The LED on pin 13 will stay On, unless pin 2 is connected to GND
// The variable "button_state" will hold the value of the button
// The button value can be either HIGH (1) or LOW (0)

int LED = 13;  // use LED connected to pin 13
int button = 2; // use pin 2 to read the button switch
int button_state; // use this variable to hold the value of "button" (pin 2).

void setup(){
  Serial.begin(9600);  // Start serial monitor at 9600 bps.

  pinMode(LED, OUTPUT);   // declare "LED" (pin 13) as an OUTPUT.
  pinMode(button, INPUT);   // declare "switch" (pin 2) as an INPUT.
  digitalWrite(button, HIGH);   // Enable the internal Pull-up resistor on Pin 2.
}

void loop(){
  button_state = digitalRead(button); // read the button

    if (button_state == 0){    // if the button_state is equal to 0 (LOW),
    Serial.println("LOW");   // then serial print the word "LOW"
    digitalWrite(LED, LOW);   // and turn the LED on pin 13 Off.
```

```
  }
  else {                        // Otherwise, the input is equal to 1 (HIGH)
    Serial.println("HIGH");     // so serial print the word "HIGH"
    digitalWrite(LED, HIGH);    // and turn the LED on pin 13 On.

  }
}
```

# How the Bug-bot Works

This robot acts as an autonomous rover, driving around a room until it bumps into an obstacle. The idea is to place the sensors such that they have the widest detection area possible; this ensures that the bot does not drive into an obstacle without detecting it. It is also helpful if the sensors provide enough time to be activated and the robot stopped before it hits the obstacle. This way, your robot won't run around like a bull in a china shop, knocking things over as it rams into them.

## Antennae Sensors

When designing the front bump sensors for this project, I thought it might be fun to model their function after a real-life bump sensor—like an insect antennae. To feel their way around a room, many insects rely heavily on their antennae. One of the purposes of the antennae is to detect a change in the environment (that is, a wall or obstacle) before the bug reaches the change to give it time to adjust its path.

Along the same lines, I decided to make two antennae "feelers" on the front of the Bug-bot (see Figure 7-2) to detect a wall or an obstacle. The design is quite simple; the Arduino Input wire connects to a coiled wire (a home-made spring), and a bolt connected to GND runs through the center of the coil without touching it. If the coil spring is moved, it touches the bolt and connects to GND, thereby notifying the Arduino that it has bumped into something.

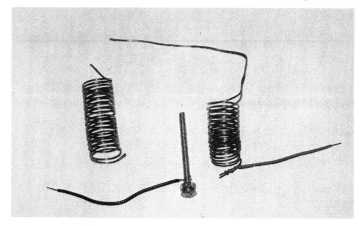

*Figure 7-2. The Antennae sensors are simple contact switches using a coiled copper wire attached to the Arduino input pin and a bolt attached to Arduino GND.*

I unwrapped about 5 inches from the top of the home-made wire coil and straightened it out in front of the robot to resemble the antennae of an ant or caterpillar. When the bot comes within a few inches of a wall or other object, the wire antennae touch the object, which moves the coil spring until it touches the GND bolt running through its center. When the switch is Closed, the Arduino immediately stops, reverses, and turns before heading in a new direction. This way, the robot can gently cruise the room without causing any damage.

## Bumper Sensors

The rear bump sensors are made using three lever switches with aluminum bumpers attached to broaden their bump detection range. These are simple SPST switches that cost approximately $2 each and act in the same way as the antennae switches that you mount to the front. I decided to break the rear bumper range into three parts, left, center, and right, so the robot knows where it was bumped.

Now that you understand how the bump sensors interface to the Arduino, review the complete parts list for the Bug-bot (Table 7-1) before building.

## Parts List for the Bug-bot

The parts list for this project should be a bit less expensive than the previous chapters (Table 7-1) because you build this robot "MacGyver style." To keep the cost down, make a simple acrylic frame. The Arduino clone was borrowed from Chapter 6. The antennae sensors are composed of just a few items you should have laying around, and you do not need to purchase a motor controller because of the modified Servo motors used.

*Table 7-1.* *The Bug-Bot Parts List*

| Part | Description | Price |
|---|---|---|
| Two Servo motors: continuous rotation | HobbyPartz.com (part# Servo_SG5010). These are cheaper Servo motors that | $4.90 each |
| Arduino Clone: from Chapter 6 (or other Arduino) | Home-made Arduino clone: Uses an FTDI cable for programming, has own +5v regulator, and accepts most Arduino shields. | $10-$15 |
| Three SPST limit switches | Sparkfun part# COM-00098: Switches are actually SPDT, but you use only two of the thee poles. | $1.95 each |
| 6v battery | Sparkfun part# PRT-08159: Four AA battery holder yields 4.8v (with 1.2v rechargeables) or 6v (with 1.5v alkalines). 6v rechargeable battery pack. | $2.00 |
| Two wheels | I pulled two wheels from an old thrift-store R/C car that I had laying around. | $1.00 |
| 12-inch × 16-inch plexiglass sheet, 1/4-inch thick (6mm) | Your local hardware store should sell sheets of 1/4inch-thick acrylic plexiglass, or you can order it online. | $7.00 |

| Part | Description | Price |
|------|-------------|-------|
| 3/4-inch wide aluminum flat bar: 1/8-inch-thick, 12-inch long | Again, your hardware store should sell assorted pieces of metal; if not, look online. | $3.00 |
| Two SPST power switches | Radio Shack part#275-324. These are standard SPST switches: one is used for power and the other to toggle the mode of the robot. These are optional but make things easier. | $2.99 ea |

Most of these parts should be locally available for you to purchase; although Servo motors are typically less expensive online. The bump sensors can be any momentary button switch that you can find, and the toggle switches can be recycled or mismatched as long as they work.

▒ **Note** If you don't want to build a new robot base, you can repurpose or add bump sensors to one of the previous robots: Linus or Wally. Although I build a different platform for each project to give examples of the many ways to build a robot, most of the concepts and examples used in this book can be hacked onto another robotic platform and should require only minor tweaking.

I bring this up to let you know that you do not have to actually build three robots to do three different things—if you can afford only the parts for one frame, you can still add several different sensors to it to make a multifunction robot. If you already have a frame, you can skip the frame-related parts and simply add the sensors to your existing robot.

# The Motors

For this bot, I again use hobby Servo motors modified for continuous rotation. You can either buy these motors from Sparkfun.com (part# ROB-09347 ) premodified, or you can modify a normal Servo motor using the steps this chapter provides.

These motors use little power and provide a large amount of torque for their size, but they need to have wheels mounted to them (as you did in Chapter 4). Luckily, most Servo motors come with a small bag with several adapter plates in various sizes that mount to the Servo output shaft. I try to find the two wheels (usually from a thrift store toy car) and then go through the Servo adapter plates to see which one has the best fit to the wheel—usually the largest one.

## Modifying the Servo Motors

When modifying the Servo motors in Linus the line-bot (Chapter 4), I removed the entire electronics circuit leaving only a DC gear-motor; this time with the bug-bot, I modified only the circuit to retain use of the built-in motor-controller. You might recall that this modification requires removing both the plastic stop piece on the motor's output shaft and the positioning potentiometer. Without removing these two pieces, the output shaft of the Servo cannot physically complete a full rotation (see Figure 7-3).

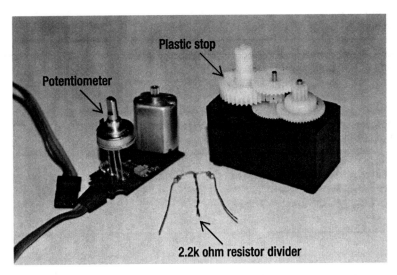

*Figure 7-3. On the left, you can see the potentiometer mounted to the Servo motor control board. In the center is the resistor divider created from two 2.2k ohm resistors to replace the potentiometer. On the right is the Servo motor gear box with the plastic stop piece that must be removed.*

Materials needed for continuous rotation are as follows:

- Small Philips-head screwdriver
- Soldering iron
- Pair of small wire snips
- Two 2.2k ohm resistors

The potentiometer reports the current position of the output shaft to the built-in motor controller so that it knows how to command the motor, so you just need to remove the potentiometer (by unsoldering) and replace it with a 2.2k ohm resistor divider. You can create the resistor divider by connecting one lead from each resistor to the outside holes previously occupied by the potentiometer, and connecting the other leads to each other and the center hole of the potentiometer (see Figure 7-4). The resistor divider creates a signal that mimics the center position of the potentiometer, thereby tricking the Servo motor into thinking that it is always centered, regardless of the actual position of the output shaft.

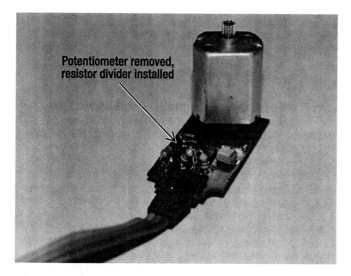

*Figure 7-4. The potentiometer has been removed and the resistor divider has been soldered in its place.*

To complete the continuous rotation process, you must also remove the plastic stop on the motor output shaft to allow it to spin 360 degrees. To access this stop, remove the black plastic gear-box cover to reveal the base of the output shaft (as done in Chapter 4). You should see a small 3mm × 3mm piece of plastic protruding from the output shaft that keeps the shaft from spinning 360 degrees. You must completely remove this piece of plastic using a small razor knife (see Figure 7-5). Test the output shaft after removing the plastic piece to make sure it spins all the way around before re-assembling.

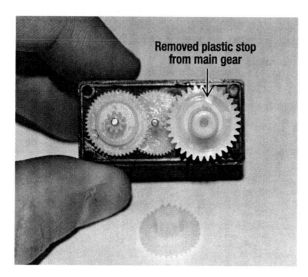

*Figure 7-5. The plastic stop removed from the largest plastic gear (which is also the gear box output shaft)*

This modification enables you to drive the Servo motor directly from any Arduino pin, using the internal motor-driver circuitry built in to the Servo. The servo now acts as a gear motor with a built-in motor controller that accepts pulse signal inputs.

## Controlling the Servo Motors

Remember that the Servo motor's drive circuitry is intended to use an input pulse signal from 1000 microseconds (uS) to 2000uS from an R/C receiver to direct the motor to the correct position. By replacing the potentiometer with two 2.2K ohm resistors (as a voltage divider), the Servo thinks that the motor shaft is always at the center position, regardless of where it is. If you command the Servo to full forward (2000uS pulses), the motor tries to spin indefinitely forward and never reaches its destination (that is, continuous rotation). To stop the Servo, you must provide it with a pulse signal that commands it to the position defined by the 2.2k ohm resistor divider. (This should be a pulse of approximately 1500 microseconds.)

After you replace the potentiometer with a resistor bridge, you should test the modified Servos not only to ensure that they work properly, but also to determine the stop pulse for each motor and record it for use in the final code. Using the example Code 7-2, you can connect the potentiometer removed from the Servo motor to Arduino A0 and open the Serial monitor to see the values. Simply turn the potentiometer until the motor stops spinning and record the value shown on the Serial monitor of your computer. To set up your Arduino and Servo motor to use the example test code, connect the Servo motor control wire (white or yellow) to the Arduino D9 and a potentiometer connected to A0, as shown in Figure 7-6. You also need to connect +5v and GND wires to the Servo and potentiometer.

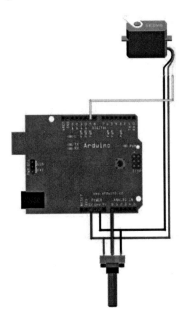

*Figure 7-6. The connections needed to test the modified Servo motors with the Arduino and a potentiometer*

# Converting the Pulse Value to Degrees

Use the Servo.h library for Arduino to make the code easier to read and follow. The library provides the necessary functions to drive the Servo motors with only one line of code in the loop, each time you want to change speed or direction. Instead of commanding the Servo with a specific pulse value, the library interpolates the 1000uS – 2000uS pulse range into the 0 degrees: 179 degrees range of a standard unmodified hobby Servo motor. To stop the Servo motor, you must command it to its center position (the position supplied by the 2.2k resistor divider) using a neutral pulse, typically 89 using the Servo library (halfway between 0 and 179).

Use Listing 7-2 to test each motor and find the neutral stop pulse. To avoid reuploading the code to the Arduino multiple times, I added the temporary use of the potentiometer to assist in finding this number for each motor.

The code in Listing 7-2 is intended to test a continuous rotation Servo motor using a potentiometer to control the speed and direction. If you try this code with an standard Servo motor that has not been modified, its angular position corresponds to the position of the potentiometer.

*Listing 7-2. Continuous Rotation Servo Test*

```
// Connect Servo motor signal wire (white or yellow) to Arduino D9
// Connect Servo +5v and GND wires to Arduino power source
// Connect potentiometer (center pin) to A0, outside pins to +5v and GND.

#include <Servo.h> // Include the Servo.h Arduino library

Servo servo1; // create "servo1"
int speed_val;  // use "speed_val" to hold potentiometer value

void setup() {
  Serial.begin(9600); // start serial monitor at 9600 bps
  servo1.attach(9);  // attach "servo1" to pin 9
}

void loop() {

  // read potentiometer, adjust to servo library angular value range (0-179)
  speed_val = map(analogRead(0), 0, 1023, 0, 179);

  // write adjusted potentiometer value to servo1
  servo1.write(speed_val);

  // print adjusted value to the serial monitor
  Serial.println(speed_val);
}
```

This code enables you to control any type of hobby Servo motor, standard or continuous rotation. If your Servo motor is not modified, it simply mimics the position of the potentiometer. If you have modified the Servo for continuous rotation, the potentiometer commands the direction and speed of the Servo motor.

With the Servo motors modified and tested, now proceed to mount the wheels to the Servo motor adapter plates and then to the Servo motors.

## Mounting the Wheels to the Servos

You can mount the wheels to the Servo adapter plates using either small bolts, hot glue, or both. You can pick just about any old toy with removable wheels to mount to the Servo motors, as long as you make sure they are aligned straight and do not wobble when spinning.

First drill the center of the wheel with a drill bit that is larger than the Servo set screw head, so you can screw the adapter plate onto the Servo output shaft after the adapter plate is mounted to the wheel (see Figure 7-7).

*Figure 7-7. Drill the center of each wheel using a 1/4-inch drill bit to make a hole for the set screw to pass completely through, so the Servo output shaft set screw fits snugly against the Servo mounting plate.*

Now mount the adapter plates to the wheels by lining them up as straight as possible before gluing them, as shown in Figure 7-8. Turn the wheel around backward, and look through the axle hole to make sure it is lined up properly with a adapter plate.

You can now test fit the wheels by mounting them on the Servo motor output shafts to make sure the adapter plates are mounted squarely. Test the Servo motor by commanding it full-speed in either direction; while spinning, check to make sure the wheels spin evenly without wobbling.

*Figure 7-8. Center the Servo wheel adapter plates on each wheel before gluing them. You can use Super Glue or high strength hot glue.*

With the wheels mounted to the motors, you can begin building the frame.

# Building the Frame

Build the frame as simple as possible, which requires only one piece of round plexiglass with holes cut for the motors and wheels. (I added a second piece of plexiglass as a top plate, which is optional.) You can cut plexiglass with a jigsaw and a fine-tooth jigsaw blade. The plexiglass should likely have a protective film coating on it when you buy it; this should be left on while you mark your lines and cut, to protect the clear finish from scratches. You can remove the film after you finish cutting to reveal the clear surface.

## Marking the PlexiGlass

I used an 8-inch round electric stove drip pan (see Figure 7-9) as a template to mark the plexiglass with a permanent marker. Because the frame will be whatever size you cut it, you can choose a larger template to build a larger robot. The round template I used was actually a small oven/stove drip pan, labeled as a 6-inch pan, but with the lip it measures 8-inch total.

8" Oven
Drip Pan

*Figure 7-9. Mark a circle on the plexiglass using a permanent marker and a 6inch to 8-inch round tin, bowl, or any object the size you would like your frame to be. If you are artistic, you might freehand a design to cut out for your frame.*

With the circle marked, you need to also mark the cutouts for the motors. Start by setting the wheel/motor pairs onto the acrylic sheet, with the wheels centered in the circle and parallel to each other, as shown in Figure 7-10. Mark two notches in the plexiglass large enough for the wheels to fit into. The wheels cannot stick out from the edge of the plexiglass because you want the bot to spin around without the wheels hitting anything.

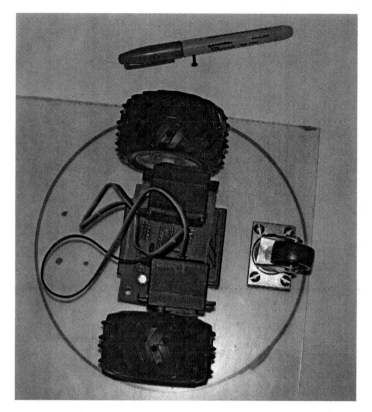

**Figure 7-10.** *Lay the motors and caster wheels onto the plexiglass, and mark the outline of the drive wheels and the mounting holes for the caster wheels.*

Now that you have everything marked on the plexiglass frame, it is ready to be cut.

## Cutting the PlexiGlass

With the frame marked, it is now time to cut the circular template line with the jigsaw. As you cut the plastic sheet, move the jigsaw slowly with the motor at full speed to ensure a clean cut and avoid cracking. If you move slowly and keep your eye on the blade, making sure it stays on the outside edge of the marked line, it should take only about 2 to 3 minutes to cut this piece (see Figure 7-11).

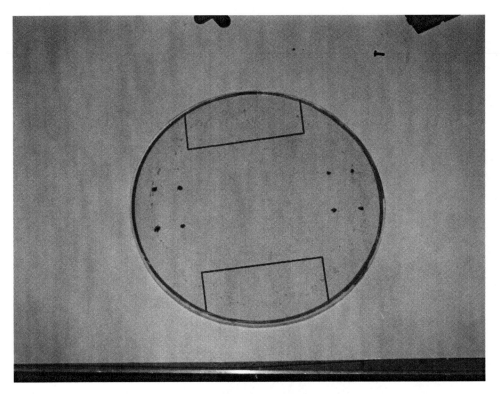

***Figure 7-11.*** *The circular shape has been cut, the caster wheel mounting holes have been marked, and the outline for the drive wheels has been marked.*

In Figure 7-11, you can see the circular piece of plexiglass after cutting with the jigsaw along the template line. Cut on the outside of the marked line because you can always go back and cut more, but it is hard to do accurately if you have already cut the marked line completely off. (That is, you cut the inside edge of the line.)

You can now cut out the sections for the motors and drill holes for the caster wheels, as shown in Figure 7-12.

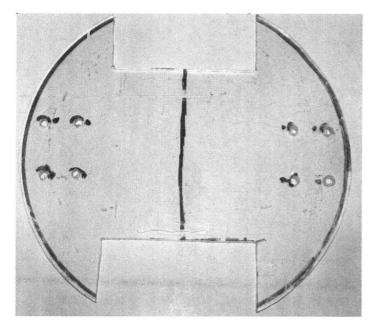

*Figure 7-12. After cutting with a jigsaw (fine-tooth blade) and drilling holes for the caster wheels, the frame base plate is ready to mount the motors and wheels.*

In Figure 7-12, you can see the circular frame that has been cut to allow for the wheels to poke through. I lined the motors up with the wheels attached and marked their silhouette with a red permanent marker, aligning them as centered as possible. At this point, you can also drill the mounting holes for the two caster wheels.

## Mounting the Motors

Mount the motors to the plexiglass using hot glue to keep them in place. Apply enough glue to cover the majority of the Servo motor casing; then press each motor to the frame, making sure the motors are parallel to each other and the cuts. The motor shafts should poke out from the plexiglass, as shown in Figure 7-13.

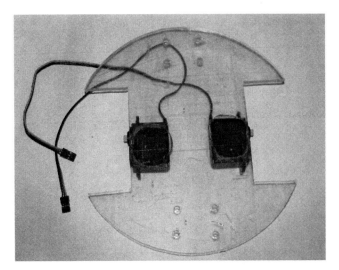

*Figure 7-13. Using a high-temperature glue gun, glue each motor into place onto the plexiglass frame. Center the motor output shafts in the gap on each side of the frame, accessible to mount the wheels.*

You can now mount the wheels with adapter plates to the Servo motor output shafts. Simply place the adapter plate onto the Servo; then insert the set screw and tighten it down.

---

■ **Note** If the motors are not mounted parallel to each other, the wheels will either point toward or away from each other, and the robot will not drive completely straight.

---

## Mounting the Caster Wheels

With the motors mounted, you need to mount the two caster wheels to the front and back of the bot; this keeps the bot balanced going either direction. I used 8 small bolts to secure the caster wheels to the plexiglass, using 3 nuts on each bolt to both secure and adjust the height of the caster wheels. You need 8 bolts and 24 nuts total to mount both of them.

Use the first nut to secure each bolt tightly to the caster wheel mounting plate. Use the second nut to set the height of the caster wheel from the frame; it should be placed on the bolt about halfway down (for starters). The third nut secures the plexiglass to the second height adjusting nut. If you need to adjust the height of the caster wheel, loosen nuts two and three, adjust to the desired height, and then retighten nuts two and three to the plexiglass frame (see Figure 7-14).

**Figure 7-14.** *Use three nuts on each bolt to make both caster wheels adjustable in height.*

The motors and caster wheels are the only things mounted to the bottom of the frame (see Figure 7-15). The Arduino, battery, and sensors are all mounted to the top for easy access. I drilled a large 1/2-inch hole through the frame to get the Servo motor wires from the bottom to the top where I needed to plug them into the Arduino.

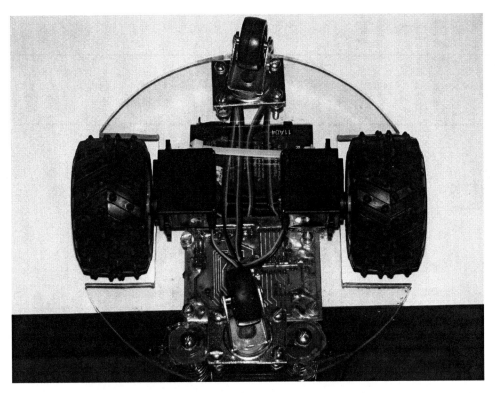

*Figure 7-15. From the underside of the frame, you can see the motors mounted with wheels attached.*

With the bottom of the frame finished, now focus some attention to the top, where the Arduino, front and rear sensors, toggle switches, and battery will be mounted.

## Mounting the Arduino

Mount the Arduino on top of the plexiglass frame. I used four bolts to mount my Arduino clone to the frame of the Bump-bot; although if you use a standard Arduino, you need only three.

The easiest way to mount the Arduino is to use #6 size nuts and bolts (1-inch or longer) to secure it to the frame. I placed the Arduino where I wanted to mount it and used a permanent marker to mark the mounting holes onto the plexiglass. When marked, drill holes through the plexiglass, install the bolts pointing upward, and secure tightly with one nut each (see Figure 7-16). These bolts should now fit nicely through the Arduino mounting holes, and you can then use a few more nuts on top of the Arduino to hold it down securely to the frame.

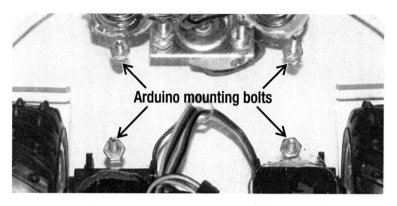

*Figure 7-16. Measure and mark four holes to mount the Arduino onto the frame base' then drill the marked spots and use #6 bolts to hold the Arduino into place.*

When the Arduino is in place, you still need to mount the battery pack and build the sensors before making connections.

## Installing the Battery

You can mount the battery anywhere there is room; although because it is usually the heaviest part of the robot, place it above the wheel axis or as close as possible.

To hold the battery in place, I marked and drilled one hole on each end through the plexiglass and secured it down with two zip ties, as shown in Figure 7-17). You can be easily cut and replace the zip ties if needed, but they can retain their secure hold for many years if left alone. Alternatively, you can use a few dabs of hot glue from a glue gun to secure the battery to the top of the plexiglass frame.

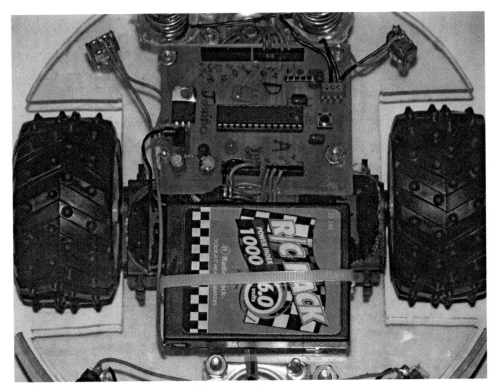

*Figure 7-17. The 6v battery strapped to the frame with a zip tie*

I used another 6v 1000mAh NiCad battery pack from Radio Shack (one of my $0.47 clearance bin finds) and the motor speed was right on par. For longer run time, you can add multiple battery packs in parallel.

Installing the power and mode switches, I used a power switch (SPST) between the battery and Arduino, allowing for easy power switching (see Figure 7-18). The power switch can be any size but should have a current rating of 5 amps or higher to ensure that it does not overheat.

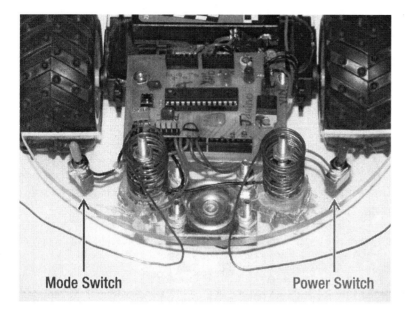

**Figure 7-18.** *To complete the basic construction of the robot, install the power switch and optional mode switch to change the direction of the Bug-bot.*

To add a mode switch, you need to mount a second toggle switch to the frame. This is a SPST mode switch used to switch the default direction of the Bump-bot, depending on which sensors you use. Connect the two pins of the mode switch to the Arduino digital pin 4 and GND.

Now that you have a powered Arduino, make a few sensors and get the Bug-bot on its way.

# Making the Sensors

This robot has two different types of bump sensors: antennae feelers and bump switches. Make the antennae feelers from materials you find around the house, whereas the bump switches are small-limit switches with aluminum bumpers attached to them.

## The Front Antennae Sensors

The antennae sensors are quite easy to make. You need a 4-foot to 6-foot strand of 14awg-18awg solid copper wire (bare or stripped) and a 3/4-inch round rod or pipe to wrap it around (see Figure 7-19). Start by stripping any rubber insulation from the copper wire, leaving it in a single long piece. When stripped, place the 3/4-inch round pipe or rod into a bench vise with the end of the copper wire secured to it. Begin wrapping the copper wire as closely as possible until the wire runs out, periodically tightening the wire as you wrap. Do this twice because you have two front antennae sensors.

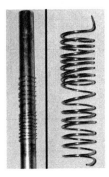

*Figure 7-19. This image shows the wire wrapped around a 3/4-inch rod to give it a coiled shape (left), and when removed it retains the coils (right).*

You can unwrap the end of the coiled wire about 6-inch at the top and straighten it out. This is where the shape of the antennae comes from; bend it as you want. Then solder a signal wire to the bottom of the coil to plug into the Arduino. The GND wire should be soldered directly to the bolt that you place in the center of the coil, as shown in Figure 7-20.

Activate the internal pull-up resistors on the Arduino pins used to read each sensor, and the inputs read HIGH unless you close a switch and connect to GND.

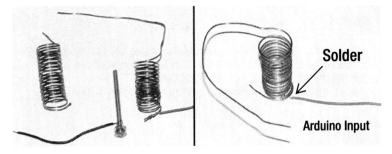

*Figure 7-20. Solder a GND wire to the bottom of each bolt and solder a signal wire to the base of each coil.*

Drill a hole in the plexiglass on each side of the front caster wheel to mount the GND bolts for the antennae sensors. Tighten the nut down securely on the GND bolts, and place the coiled wires around them with the antennae at the top. If you use a 3/4-inch round rod to wrap your antennae around, you should have plenty of space between the antennae and the bolt. Then position the coiled wire as close to center as you can, and hot glue the base of the coil to the plexiglass frame, quite liberally. It does not hurt to glue the bottom two spirals of the coil, but try not to get glue on any of the other copper spirals because it might hinder the flexibility of the sensor.

## The Rear Bump Sensors

The bump sensors on the rear of the bot are small limit switches from Sparkfun.com that detect when the bot bumps into something. There are three of these bump switches, each with its own small bumper to expand each sensor's bumpable range.

Figure 7-21 shows the parts needed for the rear bumper: three SPST switches and a 12-inch piece of aluminum flat bar, 1/8-inch thick, 3/4-inch wide. Bend the flat bar to fit the contour of the rear of the plexiglass frame. Use a vise and slightly bend the aluminum bar every two or three inches; then place it against the rear of the frame to make sure it fits.

***Figure 7-21.*** *The three contact switches used for the rear of the robot, with a piece of 3/4-inch wide aluminum flat bar, bent to the curve of the frame.*

When fitted with the rear of the bot, you can cut the aluminum rear bumper with a hack saw into three equal pieces to mount on each sensor (see Figure 7-22). Together, the sensors create a rear bumper capable of detecting left, center, and right impact. I also made three small "L" brackets, each from a piece of aluminum about 1/2-inch wide and 2-inch long. Glue these brackets to the switches to help secure them to the plexiglass frame.

**Figure 7-22.** *The aluminum bumper bar, cut into three equal sections for each contact switch and the small "L" brackets used to mount the rear bump switches to the frame*

With the aluminum bar cut into three pieces, mount the bump switch sensors onto the robot frame and attach the bumper levers. Start by hot gluing the small "L" brackets to the sides and bottom of each bump switch.

Next, glue the bottom of each "L" bracket to the frame; one center and the other two equally spaced between the center and each drive wheel. Make sure there is about 1/2-inch between each sensor to allow movement when pressed without touching each other.

Finally, hot glue the aluminum bumpers to the limit-switch arms (see Figure 7-23). You can use Epoxy, a small bolt, hot glue, solder, or any combination of these to mount the bumpers to the switch levers, so long as they stay attached when bumped.

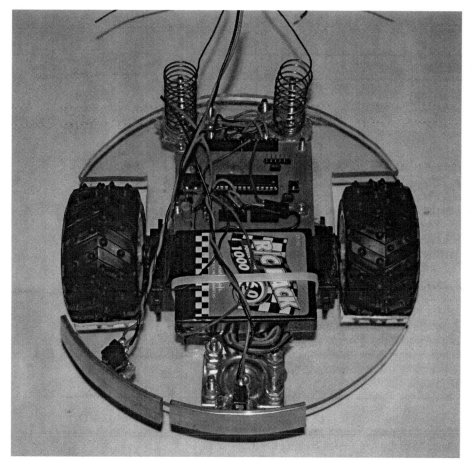

**Figure 7-23.** *Two of the three rear contact switches and aluminum bumpers installed. Make sure the wires soldered to the contact switches are long enough to reach the Arduino.*

With all sensors installed and the bumpers mounted, this robot should have all the hardware that it needs, but you still need to wire it up.

## Making Wire Connections

You need to connect five sensors, two motors, and a battery to connect to the Arduino before loading the code and testing. The two antennae sensors in the front connect to digital pins 2 and 3. The bumper sensors in the rear connect to analog pins 0, 1, and 2, which are also called digital pins 14, 15, and 16 respectively, when used as a digital input or output. Again, the analog input pins are used only as digital inputs because they were closer to the rear bumper sensors. Use Table 7-2 to make sure each wire connects correctly before proceeding.

*Table 7-2. Connections that need to be made from the motors, mode switch, and each sensor to the Arduino.*

| Component | Connection | Arduino connection |
|---|---|---|
| servo_L | Control wire (white, yellow, orange) from the Servo plug. | D9 |
| servo_R | Control wire (white, yellow, orange) from the Servo plug. | D10 |
| mode_pin | SPST switch: Wire one terminal to GND and the other to the Arduino digital input pin. | D4 |
| antennae_L | Coiled, bare copper wire with a separate wire connecting the coil base to the Arduino digital input pin. | D3 |
| antennae_R | Coiled, bare copper wire with a separate wire connecting the coil base to the Arduino digital input pin. | D2 |
| bumper_R | SPST switch: Wire one terminal to GND and the other to the Arduino digital input pin. | D14 (A0) |
| bumper_C | SPST switch: Wire one terminal to GND and the other to the Arduino digital input pin. | D15 (A1) |
| bumper_L | SPST switch: Wire one terminal to GND and the other to the Arduino digital input pin. | D16 (A2) |

Remember to connect the power signals to the Servo motor connectors (VIN+ and GND from battery) and the GND signals for each sensor and input switch. After you connect everything (see Figure 7-24), you can load the code to the Arduino and bring the Bug-bot to life!

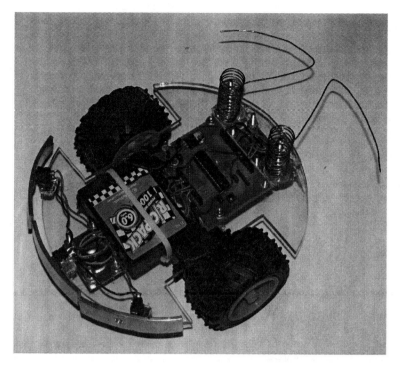

*Figure 7-24. The Bug-bot with all sensors installed, ready to test*

With the necessary building steps out of the way, now load the code to the Arduino and start testing!

# Loading the Code

The code for the Bug-bot should be easy to follow. This robot has only digital switches, so you can actually use any sensor on any Arduino pin using the digitalRead() command. I have them plugged into the closest pin to each sensor, but you can make adjustments as you need. Just remember to make the corresponding changes in the code.

To make things easier, the Servo motors are controlled using the Servo.h Arduino library. This library looks for an angular input value between 0 and 179 to command the speed and direction of a continuous rotation Servo, where a value of 89 should command the Servo motor to stop. The Arduino Servo library removes some of the complicated coding when working with Servo motor pulse signals.

To learn more about this library, visit the Arduino reference pages at http://arduino.cc/en/Reference/Servo.

## Creating a Delay

The caveat to using a pulse signal to control the Servo motors is that a pulse is required every 20 milliseconds or so to keep the motor spinning. If no pulse is received, the motors stops until it receives a valid pulse. For instance, to back up for 1 second and then turn right for 500 milliseconds using the delay() function would pause the main loop, and no pulse signals would be sent until the delay() was complete.

To get around the delay() issue, record the value of the main system timer into a variable, and use it as a timestamp to carry out an action for a specific amount of time. The while() function creates a loop that repeats until its condition is no longer true, which can be useful with a timestamp. Simply record the system timer value when the while() loop begins, and then check the system timer over and over again until it reaches the specified time. When the condition is met, the while() loop exits and returns to the main loop(). Listing 7-3 avoids using the delay() function to blink an LED on for 3 seconds and then off for 3 seconds.

***Listing 7-3.*** *Blink LED using the* millis() *Timer Value and* while() *Function*

```
// Code 7-3 - Set time without using delay()
// Blinks LED on pin 13 for time set by variable "delay_time"

int led = 13;
int delay_time = 3000;
long timerVal;

void setup(){
  pinMode(led, OUTPUT);
}

void loop(){

  timerVal = millis();  // record the millis() value
  while (millis() < timerVal + delay_time){
    digitalWrite(led, HIGH); // turn LED On for delay_time
  }
  timerVal = millis();  // record the millis() value
  while (millis() < timerVal + delay_time){
    digitalWrite(led, LOW); // turn LED Off for delay_time
  }
}
```

The example records the millis() main system timer value in milliseconds. The desired "delay" for the action is then referenced from the recorded millis() value, whereas the rest of the while() loop continues. Each time the loop circles, it checks the new millis() value and compares it against the original that was recorded (that is, when the bump switch was tripped). If the new value is below the value that you set (that is, 3000 milliseconds), it continues looping; otherwise, the Arduino knows that it has been 3 seconds since it started the action, and exits the while() function back to the main loop. This method enables the motors to be updated continuously, even while the bot is backing up or turning.

## Variables

When reading the millis() system timer value, use a variable type that can accommodate a large number. Now review a few of the common available types.

The standard *int* variable can accommodate a 2-byte value from -32,768 to 32,767. Although this is fine for most variables, the millis() system timer counts in milliseconds, of which there are 1000 each second. This means that the millis() timer value can run over the 32,767 integer value range (defined in the Arduino reference pages), about 32 seconds after you turn on the Arduino. The *int* variable type does not work for this purpose.

See the Arduino reference page for more information about the int variable at
`http://arduino.cc/en/Reference/Int`.

By changing the *int* to an *unsigned int*, the value can no longer be negative, thus yielding a range from 0 to 65,535. This doubles the capacity of only the *int* variable type, which is about 65 seconds when counting in milliseconds, so you actually need a different type of variable.

See the Arduino reference page for more information about the unsigned int variable at :
`http://arduino.cc/en/Reference/UnsignedInt`.

The *long* variable can hold larger 4-byte numbers ranging from -2,147,483,648 to 2,147,483,647. This variable has an exponentially larger value range that should be adequate for your uses. Because 2,147,483,647 milliseconds calculates to approximately 24 days, this variable type should be adequate for your needs in this project.

See the Arduino reference page for more information about the long variable at
`http://arduino.cc/en/Reference/Long`.

You can double the range of the *long* variable by changing it to an *unsigned long* variable. An unsigned value cannot contain a negative number, so the range begins at 0 and counts up. This means an unsigned long can hold a value ranging from 0 to 4,294,967,295, which is about 48 days worth of milliseconds.

See the Arduino reference page for more information about the *unsigned long* variable at
`http://arduino.cc/en/Reference/UnsignedLong`.

Although the long variable would be sufficient for the Bug-bot (I don't plan on running it for 24 days straight!), I used the unsigned long variable to store the millis() value in this sketch because the millis() value is never negative.

The variable in this sketch that holds the millis() value is declared as the following:

`unsigned long timer_startTick;`

The millis() system timer also resets after approximately 48 days, so if your Bug-bot still runs that long without being reset, don't worry. The system timer will overflow at the same time that the *unsigned long* value runs out of room, and your insanely long-lasting robot should keep going.

# The Code

Ready to upload? Copy the text from Listing 7-4 into your Arduino IDE or download the file from `https://sites.google.com/site/arduinorobotics/home/chapter7_files`.

Each line of code is commented to describe what it does. Several motor movement functions are at the end of the code (after the loop) to keep you from writing so many commands.

*Listing 7-4. The Main Code That Should Be Loaded to the Arduino*

```
      // Bug-bot v1.2
// (2) Servo motors (modified for continuous rotation) with tank-steering setup (pins 9⤸
  and 10).
// (5) bump sensors total - 2 in front (pins 2 and 3) and 3 in rear (pins 14, 15, & 16).
// All sensors are normally HIGH (1) using arduino internal pull-up resistors.
// Sensors are brought LOW (0) by contacting the switch connected to GND.
// Either set of sensors can be used (front or back), by changing Mode Switch on pin 4.
// Pin 4 (HIGH or LOW) changes the bots default direction and sensors.
//
```

```
// include the Servo.h Arduino library

#include <Servo.h>

// create instances for each servo using the Servo.h library
// for more information, see: http://arduino.cc/en/Reference/Servo
Servo servo_L;
Servo servo_R;

///////////////////////////// Variables used for testing (you can change these)↵
/////////////////////

// use to determine direction of bot and which sensors to use.
int mode_pin = 4; // connect the mode switch to digital pin 4

int antennae_L = 3; // connect left antennae sensor to digital pin 3
int antennae_R = 2; // connect right antennae sensor to digital pin 2

int bumper_R = 14; // connect right bump sensor to Analog pin 0, which is pin 14 when used↵
 as a digital pin
int bumper_C = 15; // connect center bump sensor to Analog pin 1 (digital pin 15)
int bumper_L = 16; // connect left bump sensor to Analog pin 2 (digital pin 16)

// Value to change servo stopping point pulse - use Code 7-2 to determine the specific↵
 pulse for each motor
int servo_R_stop = 89;  // set the Neutral position for Right Servo - change as needed
int servo_L_stop = 89;  // set the Neutral position for Left Servo  - change as needed

// integers to use for updating Servo motors
// change these values to change the various motor actions
int stop_time = 1000;  // stop for 1000 milliseconds = 1 second
int backup_time = 700; // backup for 700 milliseconds = .7 seconds
int turn_time = 300;   // turn (either direction) for 300 milliseconds = .3 seconds

///////////////////////// End of variables used for testing /////////////////////////////////

// value names used to hold timing variables.
unsigned long timer_startTick;

// value names used to hold antennae states
int antennae_R_val;
int antennae_L_val;

// value names used to hold bumper states
int bumper_R_val;
int bumper_C_val;
int bumper_L_val;

// Set the forward and reverse speed values for the Right Servo based on the Neutral position
int servo_R_forward = servo_R_stop + 50;
int servo_R_reverse = servo_R_stop - 50;
```

```
// Set the forward and reverse speed values for the Left Servo based on the Neutral position
int servo_L_forward = servo_L_stop - 50;
int servo_L_reverse = servo_L_stop + 50;

// end of variables


// Begin Setup
void setup(){

  Serial.begin(9600); // start Serial connection at 9600 bps

  servo_L.attach(9);  // attach servo_L to pin 9 using the Servo.h library
  servo_R.attach(10); // attach servo_R to pin 10 using the Servo.h library

  pinMode(mode_pin, INPUT);   // declare input
  digitalWrite(mode_pin, HIGH); // enable pull-up resistor

  pinMode(antennae_R, INPUT);   // declare input
  digitalWrite(antennae_R, HIGH); // enable pull-up resistor
  pinMode(antennae_L, INPUT);   // declare input
  digitalWrite(antennae_L, HIGH); // enable pull-up resistor

  pinMode(bumper_R, INPUT);   // declare input
  digitalWrite(bumper_R, HIGH); // enable pull-up resistor
  pinMode(bumper_C, INPUT);   // declare input
  digitalWrite(bumper_C, HIGH); // enable pull-up resistor
  pinMode(bumper_L, INPUT);   // declare input
  digitalWrite(bumper_L, HIGH); // enable pull-up resistor
}
// End Setup


// Begin Loop
void loop(){

  //////////////////////////////////////////////////////////
  // if the switch_pin is LOW, use the Antennae sensors
  //////////////////////////////////////////////////////////
  if (digitalRead(mode_pin) == 0){

    antennae_R_val = digitalRead(antennae_R); // read Right antennae
    antennae_L_val = digitalRead(antennae_L); // read Left antennae

    // Use Antennae sensors
    // check to see if either antennae sensor is equal to GND (it is being touched).
    if (antennae_R_val == 0 || antennae_L_val == 0){

      // now check to see if only the Left antennae was touched
      if (antennae_R_val == 0 && antennae_L_val == 1){
        // if so, print the word "Left"
```

```
        Serial.println("Left");
        // reset timer
        timer_startTick = millis();
        // Stop motors
        stop_motors();
        // back up a bit
        backup_motors();
        // turn Right for a bit
        turn_right();
    }

    // otherwise, if the Right sensor was touched and the Left was not
    else if (antennae_R_val == 1 && antennae_L_val == 0){
        // print the word "Right"
        Serial.println("Right");
        // reset timer
        timer_startTick = millis();
        // Stop motors
        stop_motors();
        // back up a bit
        backup_motors();
        // turn Left for a bit
        turn_left();
    }

    else {
        // otherwise, both antennae sensors were touched
        // print the word "Both"
        Serial.println("Both");
        // reset timer
        timer_startTick = millis();
        // Stop motors
        stop_motors();
        // back up a bit
        backup_motors();
        // turn either direction
        turn_left();
    }
}

else {
    // otherwise no sensors were touched, so go Forward!
    forward_motors();
}

// print the states of each antennae
Serial.print("Right sensor");
Serial.print(antennae_R_val);
Serial.print("    ");
Serial.print("Left sensor");
Serial.print(antennae_L_val);
Serial.println("    ");
```

```
  // End Antennae sensors

}
//////////////////////////////////////////////////////////
// Else, if the switch_pin is HIGH, use the Bumper sensors
//////////////////////////////////////////////////////////
else{

  // read the bumper sensors
  bumper_R_val = digitalRead(bumper_R);
  bumper_C_val = digitalRead(bumper_C);
  bumper_L_val = digitalRead(bumper_L);

  // Use Bumper sensors
  // check to see if the right bumper was touched
  if (bumper_R_val == 0){
    // if so, print the word "Right"
    Serial.println("Right");
    // reset timer
    timer_startTick = millis();
    // Stop motors
    stop_motors();
    // back up a bit
    ahead_motors();
    // turn Left
    turn_left();

  }

  // check to see if the left bumper was touched
  else if (bumper_L_val == 0){
    // if so, print the word "Left"
    Serial.println("Left");
    // reset timer
    timer_startTick = millis();
    // Stop motors
    stop_motors();
    // back up a bit
    ahead_motors();
    // turn Right
    turn_right();
  }

  // check to see if the center bumper was touched
  else if (bumper_C_val == 0){
    // if so, print the word "Center"
    Serial.println("Center");
    // reset timer
    timer_startTick = millis();
    // Stop motors
    stop_motors();
    // back up a bit
```

```
      ahead_motors();
      // turn Left
      turn_left();
   }


   else{
      // otherwise no sensors were touched, so go Forward (which is actually Reverse when↵
the direction is switched)!
      reverse_motors();
   }

   // print the states of each bumper
   Serial.print("Right Bumper: ");
   Serial.print(bumper_R_val);
   Serial.print("    ");
   Serial.print("Left Bumper: ");
   Serial.print(bumper_R_val);
   Serial.print("    ");
   Serial.print("Center Bumper: ");
   Serial.print(bumper_L_val);
   Serial.println("    ");
  }
  // End Bumper sensors
}
///////////////////// End Loop /////////////////////



// Beginning motor control functions

void stop_motors(){
  // stop motors for the amount of time defined in the "stop_time" variable
  while(millis() < timer_startTick + stop_time){
    servo_L.write(servo_L_stop);
    servo_R.write(servo_R_stop);
  }
  timer_startTick = millis();  // reset timer variable
}


void backup_motors(){
  // backup for the amount of time defined in the "backup_time" variable
  while(millis() < timer_startTick + backup_time){
    servo_L.write(servo_L_reverse);
    servo_R.write(servo_R_reverse);
  }
  timer_startTick = millis();  // reset timer variable
}

void ahead_motors(){
```

```
  // go forward for the amount of time defined in the "backup_time" variable
  while(millis() < timer_startTick + backup_time){
    servo_L.write(servo_L_forward);
    servo_R.write(servo_R_forward);
  }
  timer_startTick = millis();  // reset timer variable
}

void turn_right(){
  // turn right for the amount of time defined in the "turn_time" variable
  while(millis() < timer_startTick + turn_time){
    servo_L.write(servo_L_forward);
    servo_R.write(servo_R_reverse);
  }
}

void turn_left(){
  // turn left for the amount of time defined in the "turn_time" variable
  while(millis() < timer_startTick + turn_time){
    servo_L.write(servo_L_reverse);
    servo_R.write(servo_R_forward);
  }
}

void reverse_motors(){
  // go reverse indefinitely
  servo_L.write(servo_L_reverse);
  servo_R.write(servo_R_reverse);
}

void forward_motors(){
  // go forward indefinitely
  servo_L.write(servo_L_forward);
  servo_R.write(servo_R_forward);
}
// End motor control functions

// End Code
```

The main loop() starts out by reading the state of the mode switch to see if it should use the front antennae sensors or the rear bumper sensors. After that is determined, the individual sensors are read to determine their states. As long as no sensor is touched, the Bug-bot can drive forward until it bumps into something.

You can program random or timed changes in direction to surprise children or pets that might be following your Bug-bot with anticipation. The possibilities for movement are entirely up to you, but you have the basic movements and actions for a simple exploring.

When you finish testing and want to make your robot nice to look at, proceed to the next section to make a bug-themed hat for the Bug-bot.

# Making a Top Hat

With the frame assembled and the sensors installed, now put a hat on your little Bug-bot. Cut a piece of plexiglass the same size as the base (8 inches), but this time just cut the circle with no cutouts. The top can be painted or masked, or you can add a mascot to ride along. You can make a design on a computer and paste it to the top of the plexiglass lid with Mod-Podge crafting paste to add some character.

Because there are two bolts in the front of the bot going through the antennae sensors, I used them to mount the lid to the front. You need to add a third bolt in the rear of the bot near the bumper sensors to hold the back end of the lid, mounted from the bottom pointing upward. You can again use two nuts on each bolt to hold the plexiglass lid at the wanted height above the electronics, battery, and wheels (see Figure 7-25).

*Figure 7-25. Cut another 8-inch piece of plexiglass to use for a top piece for the Bug-bot. This can serve as a lid and protect the Arduino from damage.*

After cutting the top piece, mark the three bolt locations with a permanent marker and drill holes at the three marked locations. After drilling, test fit the clear lid onto the bolts to make sure it fits correctly and is centered above and parallel to the lower plexiglass piece. After the top is verified to fit, it is time to style it up a bit.

My wife used the open-source program Inkscape to create an 8-inch template with a neat design, modeled after an insect. We designed a small box directly above the Arduino to leave clear with no design, so you can see the "brains" of the robot through its new skin. The design was printed onto regular white paper using a color printer, placed on top of the plexiglass lid, with the excess paper trimmed off with an Exacto knife. We used Mod-Podge crafting paste to apply a thin layer beneath the design and then another layer on top of it, removing all air bubbles with a small paint brush while applying. Be sure you get the design where you want it the first time; if you try to move it after pasting it down, you will likely tear the moist paper.

**Note** If you get Mod-Podge on the clear window in the center, gently remove it before it dries (within 15 minutes from application) with a few damp cotton swabs to make sure the plexiglass dries perfectly clear.

Make sure you get the orientation correct (top/bottom of lid) so It shows the printed side of the design when installed. In Figure 7-26, you can see the bottom of the lid after pasting the design; the unprinted white paper and the clear window box are all that is visible from the bottom.

*Figure 7-26. The lid with design printed out and pasted on top. Here you can see the bottom view of the design (white paper) and the mounting holes and see-through cutout in the center for viewing the Arduino below.*

After mounting the lid to the frame, you see the finished view of the Bug-bot in Figure 7-27. I painted two washers orange to place on the front bolts because this makes the Bug-bot look like it has eyes. I also spray painted the antennae sensors black (only the ends) to give it a more realistic robotic bug look.

*Figure 7-27. The finished Bug-bot with antennae contact sensors, rear bump sensors, and decorative top hat to give the robot a bug-themed exterior.*

## Summary

In this chapter, you built a simple frame with two continuous rotation Servo motors, five contact sensors, a battery, some wheels, and an Arduino. This simple robot is programmed to autonomously explore a room as an insect would, using antennae "feelers" to notify it of any obstructions.

If the Bug-bot's antennae touch anything, it immediately stops driving and turns (depending on which antennae was touched) to find a new path. The antennae sensors were designed to extend a few inches beyond the front of the robot frame, so when an object is detected, the bot has enough time to stop moving before hitting anything. There are also three bumper types sensors attached to the rear of the robot, used to detect objects going the other direction. Using a mode switch, the direction of travel and sensors used can be changed from the front antennae sensors to the rear bumper sensors for a dual-mode operation.

The Bug-bot can be tuned and tweaked to react differently when it touches an object, or even possibly trained to go through a maze. Bump sensors are used on the popular home cleaning robots from iRoomba and are always useful to keep your robots from accidentally running something over. The next chapter focuses on a larger scale robot capable of driving outside...at night...wirelessly. Did somebody say night-vision camera?

# CHAPTER 8

# Explorer-Bot

The previous robots in this book were intended to be completely autonomous in operation with no user input. This project puts the control in your hands, letting you decide where the robot goes and what it does. It is strong enough to carry a human and can traverse the outdoors with ease. To make this robot even more accessible, it has a wireless camera mounted to the top, so you can operate the bot without seeing it (see Figure 8-1).

*Figure 8-1. The finished Explorer-bot, ready to go.*

Although it is fun to watch a robot wander around, making decisions as to where it travels next, sometimes you need to direct the bot to a specific location that can be achieved only by a human. To do this, you need a control system that responds to your inputs several times per second to ensure that the bot stops when you tell it to. We have briefly discussed Radio Control (R/C) methods in Chapter 2, "Arduino for Robotics," but it is now time to implement this control on a robot.

# How the Explorer-Bot Works

The Explorer-bot is similar to Linus from Chapter 4, "Line-Bot," but much larger and more powerful. A few features make this robot unique from the previous projects in this book; let's discuss them before continuing.

## R/C Control

I use standard Hobby-grade R/C equipment to interface directly to the Arduino. This type of radio system requires a Transmitter (Tx) and a Receiver (Rx) used to link your inputs to the Arduino to control the motors (see Figure 8-2). The control signals are updated approximately 50 times each second, so changes to the inputs appear smooth at the motors.

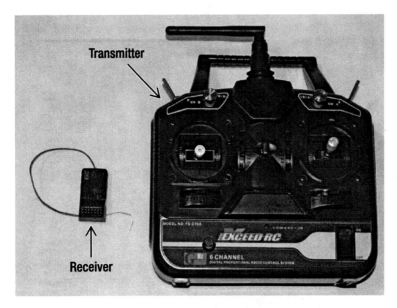

**Figure 8-2.** *A 2.4GHz radio transmitter and receiver*

Use 2.4GHz radio equipment for the R/C link because it is allowed for use on surface operated vehicles and R/C aircraft.

You can purchase a good hobby radio control system online for approximately $40 (www.hobbypartz.com part# *79P-CT6B-R6B*) or at your local hobby shop. Using 2.4GHz radio equipment ensures that there will be no other R/C operators nearby on the same channel that could cause interference. These systems are also easily interfaced to the Arduino using any digital input pin. The R/C receiver requires a +5v power signal, which can be supplied from the Arduino's +5v regulated supply. Remember to also connect the GND supplies together.

■ Note: The R/C receiver needs only one power supply connection; although, there are +5v and GND pins for each R/C channel, and any one channel can supply power to the entire unit.

# Powerful Motors

Although there are many good DC gear motors to choose from, I prefer a set of power wheelchair motors because they have excellent power and appropriate speed for a large robot. They are typically operated anywhere from 6V to 30V DC (rated at 24VDC) and can together carry approximately 400 to 500lbs, making them a versatile choice for medium-to-large robots that weigh between 30 to 300lbs. Depending on the weight of the bot, these motors draw anywhere from 3amps to 30amps continuously but can consume upwards of 50 to 100 amps if stalled.

I used two FRACMO brand power wheelchair motors that are rated at 24v and 9amps. The motors have six holes on each side of a flat gear-box that are used to mount the motors to the power wheelchair. I used these mounting holes to secure two 18-inch pieces of 3/4-inch angle iron to the top of the motor gear boxes, and a third piece of shaped angle iron bolted to the gear boxes, also used to mount the front caster wheel.

# Current Sensing

The motor controller for these massive motors needs to handle approximately 30 amps continuously and have some kind of feedback to determine if the motor controller is over-stressed. To accomplish this, I designed a simple dual H-bridge that incorporates a +/– 30amp current sensor into each H-bridge to tell the Arduino exactly how much power is pulled through the motors each time they are updated. If either motor consumes more current (amps) than the limit set in the Arduino code, the Arduino sends stop commands to both motors for 1 second to keep them from over-heating the motor controller. This ensures that the PCB is protected and the bot cannot be allowed to draw an excess of heat through the board that would result in a burned PCB trace. (Trust me, I have done this several times, and it is not fun to rebuild.)

# Video-Enabled

The bot can be driven in plain view or using the on-board wireless video camera to transmit the video feedback to a base station. The video camera has pan and tilt functions to enable a full 180 degrees of rotation along two axes, which provides an adjustable view of the bot's surroundings. The video comes from a wireless outdoor camera with an automatic night-vision feature enabled using a built-in photo detector. When the light level is too low, the infrared LEDs automatically turn on to provide an excellent view at night.

# Xbee-Enabled

In addition to having R/C control, this bot uses another wireless protocol called Xbee, which is used to create a Serial connection between the Arduino and your PC. This can be used to replace the R/C control completely if you want to control the bot solely from your computer. Because Xbee is a 2.4gHz device, the range is comparable to that of the R/C radio systems. Xbee works using two radios: one connected to your computer and the other connected to the Arduino controlling the robot. Using a two Xbee radios setup is like having your Arduino plugged into the computer, only wirelessly. You can send and receive values using a serial connection from your PC or programmed device (like another Arduino).

In this chapter, the Xbee modems transmit data from the Arduino to a computer for you to view the real-time current sensor and R/C readings on your serial monitor. In Chapter 13, "Alternate Control Bot ,"I enlist the help of a friend to revisit the Explorer-bot and write a serial interface between the Arduino and your computer (through the Xbee link) to control the robot using a PC game pad controller.

Now take a look at what you need to build the Explorer-bot.

# Parts List for the Explorer-Bot

Several parts on this robot can be substituted for similar parts. The motors can be nearly any DC gear motor that fit in your frame. Both the Arduino and motor controller can be built or purchased, depending on how much work you want to put into the project (see Table 8-1).

*Table 8-1. Explorer-Bot Parts List*

| Part | Description | Price |
|---|---|---|
| Two high power DC motors with wheels attached | You can find these power chair motor/wheel combos on eBay or pulled from an old power wheelchair. | $150 per/set |
| 2.4gHz R/C transmitter/receiver | For R/C control you need a standard (min 2 channel) transmitter with receiver. | $35.00 |
| Arduino Clone–from Chapter 6. (Any Arduino works.) | Homemade Arduino clone–uses FTDI cable for programming, has own +5v regulator, and accepts most Arduino shields. | $10–$15 |
| 12 feet of 3/4-inch angle iron | Hardware store comes in 3-foot, 4-foot, and 6-foot sections. I bought two of the 6-foot sections and had a bit left over. | $10.00 |
| Large caster wheel (front) | Hardware store: I chose a padded wheel to keep the rest of the bot from rattling. | $10.00 |
| Two Hobby Servo motors– full size | Hobbypartz.com item #Servo_SG5010.  These should be standard; unmodified servo motors will be used for the camera pan/tilt mechanism. | $5.00 each |
| 2.4gHz or 900mHz wireless camera | Sparkfun part#WRL-09189 The camera is used to control the robot remotely; this is optional but cool. | $55.00 |
| 2-inch wide aluminum flat bar 1/16-inch thick | You need two 7-inch pieces to bend into the camera mounting brackets. I would buy a 24-inch piece. | $2.00 |
| 12-inch x 24-inch pc plexiglass | Your local hardware store should sell sheets of 1/4-inch plexiglass, or you can order it online. | $15.00 |

| Part | Description | Price |
|------|-------------|-------|
| 2-inch wide steel flat bar– 1/8-inch thick–24-inch long. | Again, your hardware store should sell assorted pieces of metal; if not look online. | $4.00 |
| Two SPST power switches | Radio Shack part#275-324. These are standard SPST switches: one for power, and the other to toggle the mode of the robot. These are optional but make things easier. | $2.99 each |
| 5-inch x 7-inch plastic project box | Radio Shack part# 270-1807 7-inch × 5-inch × 3-inch. | $4.99 |
| (2) Xbee radios | Sparkfun part#WRL-08876 I bought the high-power version capable of up to 1 mile signal transmission. I also used the 2.5 series radios. | $40 each |
| Xbee Explorer USB | Sparkfun part#WRL-08687 This unit has a built in 3.3v regulator and can be interfaced directly to a PC using a mini USB cable. | $24.95 |
| Xbee Explorer Regulated | Sparkfun part#WRL-09132 This unit has a built in 3.3v regulator and can be directly interfaced to the Arduino using the DIN and DOUT pins. | $9.95 |

**Motor Controller: The Parts Listed Are to Build Two of These Motor Controllers on the Same PCB**

| Part | Description | Price |
|------|-------------|-------|
| Two ACS714 +/-30amp current-sensor ICs | Digikey part#ACS714ELCTR-30A These current sensors read from –30 amps to +30 amps at the motor output. | $4.66 each |
| Eight P-channel power mosfets - STP80PF55 | Digikey part#STP80PF55 These are cheaper if you buy ten or more. | $2.92 each |
| Eight N-channel power mosfets - STP80NF55-08 | Digikey part#STP80NF55-08 These are cheaper if you buy ten or more. | $2.44 each |
| Four N-channel signal mosfets-2n7000 | Digikey part#2n7000 These are cheaper if you buy ten or more. | $0.40 each |
| Two 12v regulator IC | Digikey part#L78S12CV 12v regulator 2amp – 12 to 30vdc input. | $0.82 each |
| Two TC4427 mosfet driver ICs | Digikey part#TC4427CPA It is also helpful to use 8-pin IC sockets to solder to the board. | $1.37 each |

| Part | Description | Price |
|------|-------------|-------|
| (8) 1N914 signal diodes | Digikey part#1N914<br>These are cheaper if you buy ten or more. Used between the gate pin of N-channel power mosfets to speed turn-off time. | $0.12 each |
| Two five-position terminal block | Digikey part#ED2612<br>These are the input terminals. | $0.52 each |
| Two four-position terminal block | Digikey part#A98361<br>These are the motor output and main power terminals. | $1.31 ea |
| Capacitors | Two 1000uF 50v, two 470uF 25v, four 1uF 50v, and two 1nF 50v. | $5.00 |
| Resistors | Eight 10k ohm (Digikey part# CF14JT10K0).<br><br>Eight to twelve 150ohm (Digikey part# CF14JT150R). | $1.44<br>(for 50) |
| One pc copper clad PCB | Digikey part#PC9-ND 3-inch × 4.5inch blank copper one-sided board. | $4.76 |

In addition to the materials in the parts list, you also need a few tools to make this project go smoothly. To make a sturdy frame, you either need to use steel or aluminum, either of which is tedious to cut with a hand saw. I recommend using a reciprocating saw (or jigsaw) with a fine-tooth metal blade to cut through the various pieces of metal in this project. It can also be helpful to have a grinding wheel, Dremel tool, or angle grinder to clean rough edges on the metal created during the cutting process. You also need a handful of 1/4-inch to 3/8-inch nuts and bolts to hold each frame piece together. Lastly, you need an electric drill (with metal bits) to make holes for bolts to connect each piece of the frame together.

## Building the Frame

The frame of this robot can be as simple as possible, built mostly around the motors and wheels. The frame must connect both of the back motors and wheels to the front caster wheel, hold the batteries, and secure all the electronics. I choose to use a 3/4-inch angle iron for most of the frame, with a plexiglass deck to cover the top. I wanted this bot to go through the average door frame in a house, but also be large enough to drive across rough terrain and large hills without trouble.

### Specs

Before building the frame shown in Figure 8-3, review the specs and materials you need to do so:

- Motor gear-box dimensions = 5.5-inch L • 3-inch W • 3.5-inch H
- Battery dimensions = 6-inch L • 2.5-inch W • 3.5-inch H (each)
- Rear wheels = 12-inch diameter

- Caster wheel = 6inch diameter wheel, 7inch from mount plate to bottom of wheel

- Frame = 17-inch L • 19inch W • 7.5inch H

- Total bot dimensions with wheels and camera = 20inch L • 24inch W × 27inch H

**Figure 8-3.** *Explorer-bot frame*

The basic frame is made using five pieces of metal, sixteen bolts, the drive motor/wheel assemblies, and the front caster wheel. Steel is an excellent choice for a large robot because it is extremely strong and can be welded or bolted together. However, steel used in large quantities becomes heavy. As the bot gets heavier, the amperage draw from the motors goes up, so too much steel can over-stress your motor controller and drain the batteries more quickly, reducing run time. Try to use steel only as a skeleton for the frame, and use a plexiglass (acrylic) sheet for the deck of the robot to reduce weight.

Follow several steps to create the frame using metal stock. First, cut a piece of metal to secure the bottoms of the motors together and provide a base to mount the batteries. Next, cut two more pieces to secure the top, a support bar for the caster wheel, and finally the main frame piece that must be cut and bent to give the frame its shape. It is then only a matter of mounting the motors and caster wheel into the new metal frame to get it rolling. The following sections walk you through the steps required to build the frame.

## Adding Battery Bracket

The first thing I did was cut a 19-inch piece of flat steel bar to hold the bottom of the motor gear boxes together, as well as provide a place to mount the batteries. Because the batteries I use are 6 inches each, my frame needed to have a 12-inch minimum space between the motor gear boxes for the two batteries to sit end to end. My motors have six mounting holes on each side of the gear box to mount the bottom bracket, and I used only the two center mounting holes on each motor (see Figure 8-4). I decided to use two 12v batteries on this bot, so it can be arranged for either 24v 7Ah (series) or 12v 14Ah (parallel) operation.

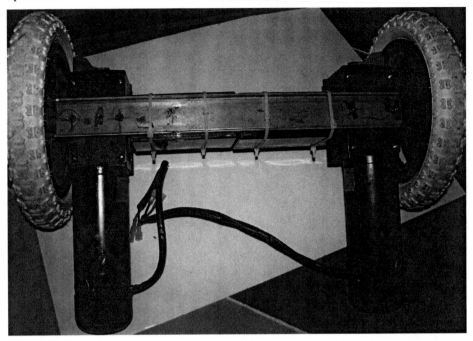

*Figure 8-4. The battery brace attached to the bottom of the motor gear boxes, using two bolts to secure the brace to each motor*

The battery bracket is nothing more than a 19-inch piece of a 2-inch wide flat steel bar (1/8-inch thick). This piece mounts to the center holes in the bottom of the motor gear boxes. I used two bolts in each gear box to hold the bracket in place. When secured, you have a place to mount the two batteries between the motors. My batteries just happened to be the same height as the motor gear boxes, so they fit nicely between the motors (see Figure 8-5).

*Figure 8-5. The two drive motors connected together by the battery brace*

# Cut Top Frame Brackets

The bottom bracket needs to have two holes drilled in each end to mount to the bracket to the motors. Measure the distance between the two mounting holes on each motor. (My motors have a 2.5-inch spacing between mounting holes.) Now mark and drill the two holes (2.5-inches apart) on each end of the bottom bracket. You should then secure this bracket to the bottom of the motor gear boxes. Double-check to make sure both batteries fit in the new space before proceeding to the next step.

# Cut Top Frame Braces

Cut two pieces of the 3/4-inch angle iron to 19-inch using a reciprocating saw if available, or a hacksaw. These two pieces can secure the motors at the top while keeping the wheels parallel to each other. These pieces also require marking and drilling two mounting holes on both ends of each brace. The mounting holes should be the same measurement as in the previous step (2.5-inch for me).

Measure, mark, and then drill holes in the upper frame braces to secure them to the motors (see Figure 8-6).

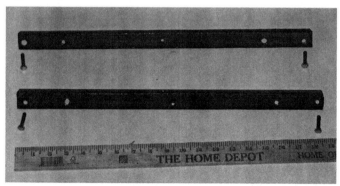

*Figure 8-6. The two upper frame braces, used to hold secure the motors together on the top, which should be the same length as the bottom battery brace.*

Secure only the inside bolts of the top braces for now. You use the outside mounting holes in the next step to also secure the main frame piece to the motors. (see Figure 8-7).

*Figure 8-7. Start by securing the two upper frame braces using four bolts. Do not secure the bolts on the outside of the frame ye, because there will be one more frame piece installed before these bolts are secured to the motors.*

## Cut and Bend Main Frame Piece

The main frame piece gives the robot its shape and enables you to mount a caster wheel to the front of the bot that connects to the rear portion of the frame. I made four cuts with my reciprocating saw and a metal blade, cutting V shapes from one side of the angle iron at premeasured points (see Figure 8-8). When cut, the angle iron is easily bent; you make the shape permanent when you bold the piece to each motor gear box with two bolts per side (four bolts total). You need to measure the distance between the two mounting holes on the motors and drill two holes for each side.

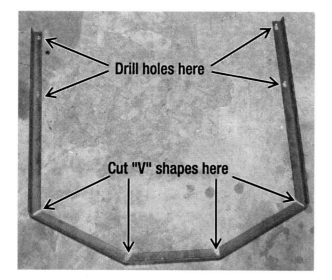

**Figure 8-8.** *Start modifying the main frame piece by cutting V shapes where shown; then drill (measured) holes to mount to each motor as shown.*

To avoid having sharp corners typical to a standard square shape, I decided to go with a semi-octagonal shape that has a flat nose and slanted, less-pointed corners. Bend your newly cut piece into the shape shown in Figure 8-9, making sure the long 14-inch legs are approximately 19 inches apart from each other.

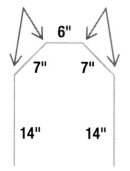

**Figure 8-9.** *This diagram shows the dimensions of each segment of the main frame piece, between each V cut.*

With the main frame piece cut, you still need to add a crossbar to provide support for the front caster wheel.

## Add Crossbar and Mount Caster Wheel

Because you use a thin 3/4-inch wide angle iron, there is only enough room to mount two of the four bolts on the front caster wheel mounting plate. Because this might leave the front wheel a bit wobbly, you need to add a crossbar from the lower bend on each side of the main frame piece, making sure that it travels across the other two mounting holes on the caster wheel mounting plate. If you have a welder, you can tack-weld the crossbar into place (see Figure 8-10). Otherwise you can place a bolt on each end of the crossbar into the main frame piece to hold them securely together.

*Figure 8-10. The main frame piece ready to be mounted to the motors and wheels*

You should now be ready to mount the caster wheel to the main frame piece and crossbar, drilling holes where necessary. A diagram of the top of the frame is shown in Figure 8-11.

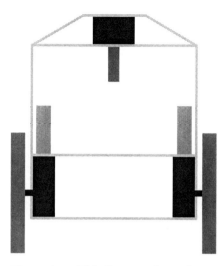

*Figure 8-11. This diagram shows the various pieces of the frame assembled together.*

When selecting a caster wheel, you should measure the height of your rear wheel assemblies to determine the approximate deck height. By matching the height of the caster to the height of the robot's deck, you can avoid having a bend in the frame to compensate for a height difference. The caster wheel mounting plate typically has four holes on a rectangular plate mounted to a swivel bearing. These holes should be used to mount the caster wheel assembly to the front of the bot frame. You should keep in mind when placing objects near the front of the bot that the caster wheel must spin a full 360 degrees without hitting anything.

My caster assembly has a height of 7 inches total, with a wheel diameter of 6 inches. Because the height of the main deck is approximately 7.5 inches as mounted to the motors, the caster wheel I use gives the bot a slight downward angle that is barely noticeable.

With the caster wheel mounted to the front of the frame, you can now mount the rear of the main frame piece into the motors. You can see the main frame piece mounted to the motor gear boxes, through the remaining holes in the two top frame braces, as shown in Figure 8-12.

*Figure 8-12. The main frame piece attached to the rear wheels using four bolts through the remaining mounting holes on each side.*

When the main frame piece is mounted to the rear frame assembly and the caster wheel mounted to the front, the frame is complete. You can now either proceed to building the motor controller or add an optional plexiglass deck to the top of the frame.

## Plexiglass Deck (Optional)

I tend to use sheets of clear acrylic plexiglass in projects that require a top or lid. Because it is clear, the insides of the bot can still be seen when assembled, adding a nice "look, but don't touch" effect. These sheets can also be cut to fit any shape and drilled to mount power switches, electronics, or a project box. Plexiglass is lighter than an equivalently sized piece of plate glass and is far more resistant to cracking or breaking.

I cut the plexiglass to fit the rectangular section on the top part of the frame, 18-inchW × 13-inch L. The plexiglass can then be mounted to the metal frame using 1/4-inch bolts. I later use the plexiglass deck to mount the project-box with all the electronics inside for easy access. The plexiglass sheets usually come with a protective film on each side; leave this film intact until you finish with all cutting. When the film is removed, the clear sheet should be free from scratches.

With the frame finished, you need a motor controller to get this robot moving.

## Building the Motor Controller

If you are not interested in building a motor controller and would like to buy one, please refer to the (Large) motor controller suggestions in Chapter 3, "Let's Get Moving," Chart 3.4 for a few different options.

The motor controller for this project is more complex than the previous controllers because of the size of the motors it powers. Because most motor controllers can handle the dual 9 amp power chair, motors will be in the $100+ range (for two motors). I decided to build a simple mosfet H-bridge that also has a current sensor built in to allow for adjustable current limiting. The current-limiting feature is important because it is the only way you can know if the motors are drawing too much current for the motor controller to handle. The result of drawing too much current through your motor controller is usually a fried PCB copper trace, or a blown up mosfet! By monitoring the current-sensor IC with the Arduino, you can instantly stop either motor if it exceeds the preset level.

## Current Sensing and Limiting

Whether you need current limiting on your robot depends on the power of your motors. If you use a smaller gear motor that has a stall current of 15 amps, you can likely burn up the motor before a motor controller rated for 25 amps continuous current.

These power chair motors however were designed to carry not only a chair the size of a large robot, but also a human being riding in the chair–up hills, through a parking lot, and without burning up. This means that each motor can draw upward of 50 to100amps during a stall (depending on the motor), which is plenty of heat to burn a weak spot on a motor controller.

I used the ACS714 +/-30amp current sensor from Allegro Microsystems to measure the current flowing through one of the two motor outputs on each H-bridge. The AC714 current sensor operates using a +5v power supply, which can be provided by the Arduino. The sensor has three outputs connections: +5v, GND, and the analog output signal. The output voltage of each sensor is actually centered at 2.5v when the motors are not moving (0 amps) and move to 5v as the current flows positively (that is, the motor is spinning forward) or down to 0v as the current flows negatively. (That is, the motor is spinning in reverse.)

The Arduino can read this value from the current-sensor on any Analog Input pin and translate the voltage to a value between 0 and 1023, with the center value of 0 amps being 512 (1023/2). The ACS-714 datasheet lists the voltage sensitivity as 66mV per amp, so you must calculate how many millivolts are in each "step" of the 0–1023 value range of the Arduino's analog inputs to determine how many amps are measured at a given time.

There is only one catch: The current sensor chip is only available as a Surface Mount Device (SMD) chip, which takes a little finesse to solder onto the PCB. I also made an alternative PCB design without the current sensor, for those who do not want to use one.

## H-bridge Design

For this H-bridge, I used standard P-channel and N-channel power mosfets both rated for 80amps and 55vdc. I used the TC4427 low-side mosfet driver as a signal buffer for the Arduino to provide the PWM signal to the N-channel mosfets (similar to the motor controller in Chapter 5, "Bump-Bot"). The TC4427 supplies 1.5 amps to the Mosfet Gate pins during high-speed PWM switching, enabling for use of ultra-sonic (silent) motor operation at 32kHz PWM. The N-channel mosfets also each get a fast-recovery signal diode attached to their Gate pin, to help drain the excess current more quickly between switching cycles.

The P-channel mosfets are switched on using small N-channel signal mosfets, and pulled-up to the supply voltage using a resistor divider to turn them off. The P-channel mosfets (AHI and BHI) are only intended to be turned on or off when changing directions and should not be driven with a PWM signal. The resistor divider enables you to select resistor values based on your desired operating voltage; the resistor values used in this chapter are safe for use with 12v to 24v battery packs.

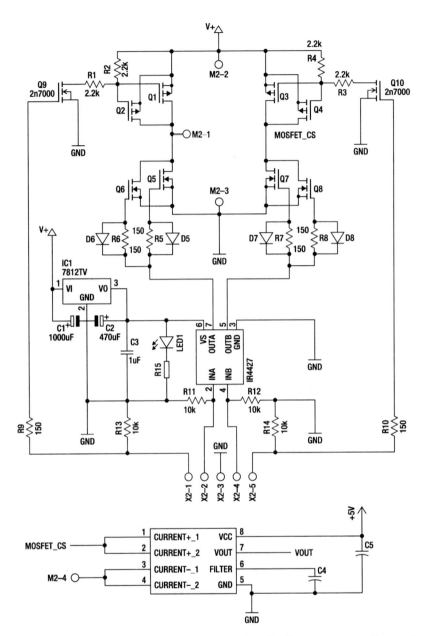

*Figure 8-13. The schematic of the home made H-bridge motor controller used on the Explorer-bot. This schematic depicts one H-bridge circuit; the complete motor controller requires two of these identical circuits.*

In addition to using higher-powered mosfets than the last motor controller, this board gets double mosfets. That is, I placed two mosfets in parallel on each leg of both H-bridges to double the current carrying capacity of the motor controller by halving the resistance. Remember from Chapter 1, "Introduction," lower resistance equals less heat.

It is now time to collect the needed parts and start building the motor controller! If you have not yet tried to etch a PCB, you might need to review Chapter 6. "Making PCBs," to build this circuit. When you are ready, follow these steps to print, transfer, etch, and build the PCB.

1. Download Eagle PCB files from https://sites.google.com/site/arduinorobotics/home/chapter8.

2. Open the .brd file, and select only Bottom, Pads, and Vias from the Layers menu.

3. Click the Ratsnest button to fill in the GND plane.

4. Print onto magazine paper using options Black and Solid.

5. Iron on to copper clad.

6. Etch PCB.

7. Drill PCB.

8. Place components using silkscreen and schematic files; then solder.

9. Test with a 12v power supply and 5v input signals, checking for voltage at the motor terminals.

For instructions on how to etch a PCB, refer to Chapter 6. When assembling each board, make sure to check the silkscreen on the Eagle file, the motor controller schematic, and the component data sheets to verify the proper orientation of each part.

---

■ **Note** To solder the surface mount ACS714 current sensor, it is best to heat the copper pads and apply a small amount of solder before placing the chips. For best results, solder the motor-terminal side of the current sensor first. When you get the first two terminals securely soldered and each pin lined up, carefully solder the remaining pins, heating each pin for as short a time as possible.

---

The Eagle board file in Figure 8-14 shows only one of the two h-bridges needed. You can either print out two separate boards, or use the dual-print board file that has two of these h-bridges side by side and ready to print onto a single board. They both share a common ground plane, so only one GND wire needs to connect from the Arduino.

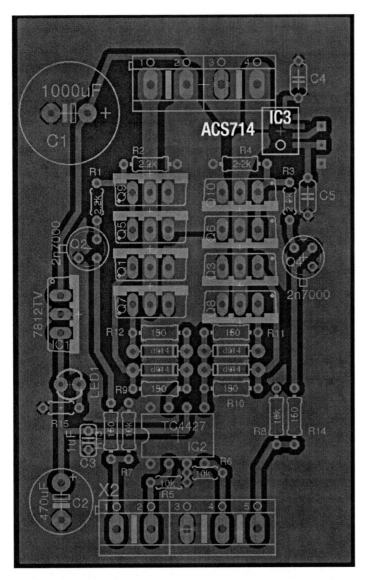

*Figure 8-14. The PCB file used to make the H-bridge schematic shown in Figure 8-13*

Use the silkscreen (component outlines) from the PCB board file shown in Figure 8-14 to place each component before soldering. You should also make sure your finished motor controller looks like the one shown in Figure 8-15.

A few notes about the motor controller layout:

- The striped (cathode) end of the diodes should face the center of each H-bridge.

- The source pins of the power mosfets should face the center of each H-bridge.

- The resistors can be placed in any orientation.

- The indented end of the TC4427 IC should face the left side of the board.

See Figure 8-15 for a picture of the finished dual H-bridge board. Notice the two sets of header pins near the top of the board; these connect to the ACS714 current sensors mounted to the bottom of the board. Also notice that only one of the center GND pins connect to the Arduino at the bottom.

*Figure 8-15. The finished dual motor controller with eight mosfets in each H-bridge.*

This motor controller design enables for individual control of each switch in the H-bridge. Though this bridge is capable of ultra-sonic PWM switching speeds (32kHz), the PWM signals should be used only on the low side inputs that feed into the high-speed mosfet driver IC. The high side inputs that control the P-channel mosfets are not set up for high-speed switching and should be switched on and off only when changing directions or stopping. Now that you have a working motor controller, it is time to set up the Arduino to control it.

## Setting Up the Arduino

You can use a standard Arduino for this project, though I used a home-made breakout board for the Atmega chip that is programmed using an FTDI programming cable. The advantage of using the home-made Arduino (or any Arduino programmed with an FTDI cable) is that the Xbee Explorer Regulated module can plug directly into the FTDI programming port, supplying both power and the required serial connections from the Xbee to the Arduino (see Figure 8-16).

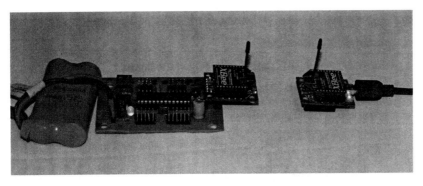

*Figure 8-16. The Xbee breakout board from Sparkfun.com*

Several other Arduino variants also use the FTDI programming port, such as the Arduino Pro and the Pro mini. The purpose of these boards is to create a smaller alternative to the Arduino main board that incorporates the FTDI programming chip into the programming cable, instead of putting one on each Arduino board. This makes each board a bit cheaper and easier to make at home.

Also, because I got to design the Arduino breakout board in Eagle, I added screw terminals to each digital pin and 3-pin male header connectors to each analog pin, supplying +5v and GND signals to the current sensors plugged into these ports. You can also plug servo motors directly onto these pins for easy interfacing.

You can download the Eagle board files to build your own Arduino from https://sites.google.com/site/arduinorobotics/home/chapter8.

If you use a standard Arduino board, you need to use four jumper wires to interface the Sparkfun Xbee Explorer Regulated adapter to the Arduino. The Xbee adapter board has an on-board 3.3v regulator, so it can accept a 5v power supply from the Arduino. You need to connect the GND and +5v to Arduino; then connect the DOUT from Xbee to Arduino DP0 (rx) and DIN from Xbee to Arduino DP1 (tx).

## Connecting the H-Bridges

Each H-bridge provides control of all four switches individually. This basic design works well, but there is no external protection against commanding the bridge into a short-circuit because this is done in the code; you should check all connections twice to ensure proper wiring. The H-bridge connections are labeled as AHI (A High Input), ALI (A Low Input), BLI (B Low Input), and BHI (B High Input). The low inputs connect to the N-channel power mosfets, and the high inputs connect to the P-channel power mosfets. Because only the N-channel power mosfets will be driven with a PWM signal, they connect to four of the six PWM outputs on the Arduino (PWM pins 3, 9, 10, and 11).

I do not use PWM pins 5 and 6 if possible because I plan to change the default PWM frequency and do not want to affect the system timer 0. To use different PWM frequencies requires changing the system timers that the PWM pins use. Because PWM pins 5 and 6 are attached to the main system timer 0, changing that timer changes the outputs of any function depending on Timer 0 (that is `Delay()`, `millis()`, and `micros()`). Because you need only four PWM outputs, but you need to change the default timing of all those outputs, use PWM pins 9 and 10 on timer 1 and PWM pins 3 and 11 on timer 2, changing both to a 32kHz PWM frequency for silent motor operation. Pins 5 and 6 will be used, but only as Digital Output pins; the PWM ability will not be utilized for this project.

Make each connection from the Arduino to the motor controller, Xbee, and R/C receiver according to Table 8-2.

*Table 8-2. Connect Each Wire to the Arduino as Shown Here: Double-Check Each Connection Before Testing*

| Input/Output | Connection to Arduino |
|---|---|
| Xbee DOUT | Arduino digital pin 0 (rx) |
| Xbee DIN | Arduino digital pin 1 (tx) |
| R/C up/down input (ELE) | Arduino digital pin 2 |
| R/C left/right input (AIL) | Arduino digital pin 6 |
| R/C switch input (AUX) | Arduino Analog pin 0 |
| M1 current sensor (on motor controller) | Arduino Analog pin 1 |
| M2 current sensor (on motor controller) | Arduino Analog pin 2 |
| M1 BHI (on motor controller) | Arduino digital pin 7 |
| M1 BLI (on motor controller) | Arduino PWM pin 3 |
| M1 ALI (on motor controller) | Arduino PWM pin 11 |
| M1 AHI (on motor controller) | Arduino digital pin 8 |
| M2 BHI (on motor controller) | Arduino digital pin 5 |
| M2 BLI (on motor controller) | Arduino PWM pin 10 |
| M2 ALI (on motor controller) | Arduino PWM pin 9 |
| M2 AHI (on motor controller) | Arduino digital pin 4 |

I chose to mount all my electronics into the 5-inch x 7-inch project box from Radio Shack. This box provides a place to mount both the motor controller and the Arduino with Xbee. The box can then be moved without disconnecting the Arduino from the motor controller. The project box is optional but makes for a nicer looking installation.

# Setting Up Xbee

You can choose from three different types of Xbee radios: Series 1, Series 2.5, and 900MHz. All these models offer high serial data speeds (115,200 bps+) with both low-power and high-power modules. We focus on the Series 1, low-power modules (Sparkfun part# WRL-08665), which are ready to go out-of-the-box. All you need to do is plug each Xbee radio into the Sparkfun adapter boards to start (see Figure 8-17).

To set up Xbee you need the following:

- Two Xbee radios

- Xbee Explorer Regulated

- Xbee Explorer USB

- XCTU Xbee programming software (Free: download latest version from www.digi.com.)

- Mini USB cable

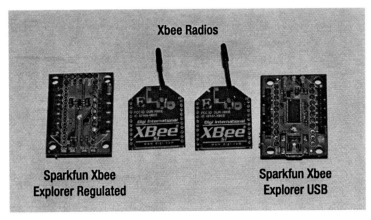

*Figure 8-17. From left to light: Xbee Explorer regulated, two Xbee radios, Xbee Explorer USB*

When using Series 1 modules for simple data transmission, I found that no reprogramming was necessary and that the Xbee modules communicated with each other out-of-the-box at 9600 bps serial data speed. If you would like to use a different serial speed or change the Xbee radios to operate on a private channel, you need to use the programming software XCTU.

Though the Series 2.5 modules are only a few dollars more than the Series 1, they use a different type of networking that requires each Xbee to have a specific role and must be programmed as such; these do not work without being reprogrammed. Although these work just as well as the Series 1 for simple data transmission, there is a bit more setup required to get them going. Unless you have a reason, stick with the Series 1 modules.

Note: The high-power Xbee modules offer a range of up to 1 mile but require more than 200mA of current. The low-power modules have a range of approximately 300 feet and consume only approximately 50mA of current. The Sparkfun Explorer boards can power either type of Xbee. When connected, the Xbee radio link emulates a wireless USB cable; that is, you can connect to the Arduino using the serial monitor to read real-time updates from the current sensors and R/C signals. For this chapter, set up the Xbee modules to communicate between the PC and the robot to send status updates. Chapter 13 uses this link to control the robot from the PC.

# Testing the Xbees

To test the Xbee connection, load the code in Listing 8-1 to the Arduino and open a Serial monitor with the Xbee Explorer USB port to check the connection. With the serial monitor opened, type any character into the space and press send. If everything connects properly, whatever characters you send to the Arduino loop back through the Xbee and appear on the serial monitor.

*Listing 8-1. This Code Can Be Used to Test the Connection of the Xbee Modems from Your PC to the Arduino and Back*

```
// Code 8-1 - Xbee Test code

int incomingByte = 0;    // for incoming serial data

void setup() {
  Serial.begin(9600);    // opens serial port, sets data rate to 9600 bps
  pinMode(13, OUTPUT);

}

void loop() {

  // send data only when you receive data:
  if (Serial.available() > 0) {
    // read the incoming byte:
    incomingByte = Serial.read();

    // say what you got:
    Serial.print("I received: ");
    Serial.println(incomingByte, BYTE);

    digitalWrite(13, HIGH);  // turn on LED pin 13
    delay(1000);  // leave LED on for 1 second

  }

  else {

    digitalWrite(13, LOW); // otherwise, turn off LED pin 13

  }

}
```

When loaded, power the Xbee Explorer Regulated adapter board with +5v and GND, connect the DOUT pin to Arduino DP0 (rx), and the DIN pin to Arduino DP1 (tx). Or if you built the Arduino clone, simply plug the Xbee Explorer onto the FTDI programming port of the Arduino.

Remember that the serial monitor baud rate must be set to 9600bps before you can communicate through the Xbee modems. If a different baud rate is wanted, you need to reprogram both Xbee radios with the wanted speed, and change the speed in the Arduino code.

The last component that to add to the Explorer-bot is a wireless camera used to provide an audio/video link when guiding the robot to a location that cannot be seen by the operator.

## Adding a Camera

To add remote visibility to your robot, you need a wireless camera (see Figure 8-18). Most common wireless video cameras operate at either the 900mHz or 2.4gHz frequency range. If you want to avoid interference with your 2.4gHz R/C radio and the 2.4gHz Xbee, you should probably get the 900mHz video camera if available. Otherwise, you might get slightly more interference from the other devices than ideal, but a 2.4gHz camera can still work.

*Figure 8-18. Any wireless camera can work for this purpose. I used a camera with automatic night vision.*

Because the bot has full speed control and can turn in any direction, you might decide to simply strap a wireless video camera to the top of your bot and go—turning the bot to see what is around. Some video cameras come with a built-in rechargeable battery pack that enables for no wires to connect to the camera. The camera that I bought has an RCA cable coming from the back that powers the camera with a 12v power supply.

The camera receiver has RCA outputs for video and audio. I simply plugged the yellow RCA cable from the video port of the receiver to the video input of my TV, and plugged the 9v AC adapter into the wall, and I was instantly watching video from the wireless camera. You can also use a smaller 7-9-inch LCD screen attached to your R/C transmitter for portable video control; although, you would also need to add a battery pack to your transmitter.

# Pan and Tilt

To allow control of the camera position without moving the robot frame, you need a pan-and-tilt base for the camera. The pan-and-tilt functions are achieved using two standard sized hobby servo motors to create X and Y axes with 180-degrees rotation along either axis. This setup gives a full view of anything in front of the robot and enables much more precise movement than is provided by the robot base and the ability to look up and down.

By connecting the servo motors directly to the R/C receiver, you can control the orientation of the video camera using the R/C transmitter and without the extra overhead of processing the signals through the Arduino. (These servos can alternately be controlled by the Arduino if needed.)

The pan/tilt mechanism requires two standard-size hobby servo motors and two 7-inch long pieces of 2-inch wide aluminum flat bar (see Figure 8-19). The flat bar was cut and bent into two C-shaped pieces that connect together with the video camera mounted on top.

*Figure 8-19. The pan/tilt mechanism is made from a few pieces of aluminum, some nuts and bolts, and two hobby servo motors.*

To make the camera pan/tilt base, complete the following steps.

# Make First Bracket

Cut the first piece of aluminum to 7 inches with a hacksaw or reciprocating saw and a fine-tooth metal blade. Next measure and mark the flat bar into three sections: 2 inches on each end and 3 inches in the center (2-inch left end + 3-inch center + 2 -inch right end = 7-inch total). Use a bench vise to bend this piece of flat bar at these marked points to 90-degree angles, making somewhat of a C shape cut servo mounting hole.

Now use one of the servo motors to mark the outline of the motor casing, centered onto the side of the first aluminum piece. When marked, use a Dremel tool and a metal cutoff wheel to cut out the hole for the servo motor, as shown in Figure 8-20.

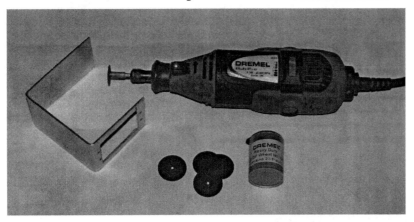

*Figure 8-20. Cut a hole for the servo motor using a Dremel tool and metal cutoff wheel.*

After you test fit the servo motor into the mounting hole, mark the four mounting holes with a permanent marker and drill holes for them. Use four #8 bolts and nuts to secure the servo motor to the bracket, as shown in Figure 8-21.

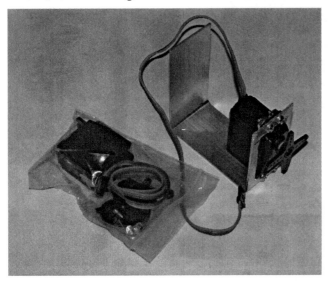

*Figure 8-21. Mount the servo motor into the first aluminum bracket.*

## Make Second Bracket

The second bracket needs only to be bent and have a few holes drilled into it. Measure and mark the bracket at 1.75-inch on each end and 3.5-inch in the center to equal 7 inches total. Bend the bracket at the marked points to make the same shape as the first bracket. This bracket needs to be mounted to the first servo mounting plate on one side (see Figure 8-22), and have a 1/4-inch hinge bolt on the other side that enables the camera to freely pivot. The camera should mount to the top of this bracket.

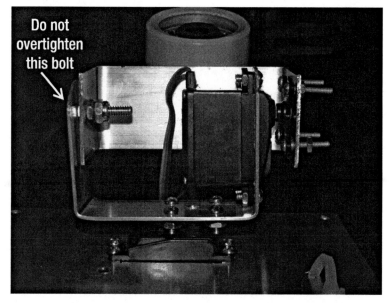

**Figure 8-22.** *Finished servo motor pan/tilt with camera installed*

The second servo motor is the main motor that rotates the entire pan/tilt assembly, as shown at the bottom of Figure 8-22. I mounted this motor into an aluminum plate that is bolted to a 24-inch riser bar, mounted to the back of the robot frame. The riser bar serves to give the camera a better point of view.

To mount the servo into the aluminum plate (obtained as an extra piece from the Radio Shack project box), again mark the outline of the servo motor using a permanent marker, and cut the outline with a Dremel tool and a metal cutoff wheel. You can then mount the pan/tilt assembly to the top of this servo motor. With the servo motors installed, you can control their direction using two open channels on your R/C transmitter.

With the camera pan/tilt assembly completed, all that you need to do is to load the code and start testing.

## Loading the Code

Now it is time to load the code to the Arduino and double-check your connections. When you are comfortable that you have connected everything properly, download Listing 8-2 from the book website, and remember to press the Compile button to check for errors before uploading to the Arduino. Updates

to this code are in the Chapter 8 page of the book website at
https://sites.google.com/site/arduinorobotics/home/chapter8.

*Listing 8-2. This Is the Main Code for the Explorer-Bot. Check All Connections as Per Table 8-2 Before Loading the Code.*

```
// Code 8-2 - Explorer-bot
// Decode 3 R/C signals connected to pins A3, A4, and A5.
// Code is used to drive a tank-steering robot with joystick control (mixed steering)
// AUX channel is used to toggle speed mode fast/slow.
// THIS CODE USES CHANNEL MIXING -- you need to use channel 1 up/down, and channel 2
left/right.

int ppm1 = 17;  // digital input from R/C Elevator channel, marked "ELE" - connect to Arduino
A3
int ppm2 = 18;  // digital input from R/C Aileron channel, marked "AIL" - connect to Arduino
A4
int ppm3 = 19;  // digital input from R/C switch channel, marked "AUX" (if equipped) - connect
to Arduino A5

// variables to read R/C channel 1
unsigned int servo1_val;
int adj_val1;

// variables to read R/C channel 2
unsigned int servo2_val;
int adj_val2;

// variables to read R/C channel 3
unsigned int servo3_val;
int adj_val3;


// Motor-controller connections to Arduino
int motor1_BHI = 7;   // m1_B hi-side (P-channel mosfet) digital output
int motor1_BLI = 3;   // m1_B low-side (N-channel mosfet) PWM output
int motor1_ALI = 11;  // m1_A low-side (N-channel mosfet) PWM output
int motor1_AHI = 8;   // m1_A hi-side (P-channel mosfet) digital output

int motor2_BHI = 5;   // m2_B hi-side (P-channel mosfet) digital output
int motor2_BLI = 10;  // m2_B low-side (N-channel mosfet) PWM output
int motor2_ALI = 9;   // m2_A low-side (N-channel mosfet) PWM output
int motor2_AHI = 4;   // m2_A hi-side (P-channel mosfet) digital output

int ledPin1 = 13;  // used as a neutral indicator
int ledPin2 = 12;  // used as an over-current indicator light that turns On when the
current_limit is exceeded by either motor.

int current_sense_1;  // variable to hold value of left motor current sensor
int current_sense_2;  // variable to hold value of right motor current sensor
```

```
int current_limit = 25;   // sets the amperage limit that when exceeded on either motor, stops
the motors for a "cool_off" time.

int cool_off = 1000; // amount of time (milliseconds) to stop motors if they exceed the
current_limit above (25 amps)


///////////////////////////////////

int deadband = 10; // sets the total deadband - this number is divided by 2 to get the
deadband for each direction. Higher value will yield larger neut
l band.
int deadband_high = deadband / 2; // sets deadband_high to be half of deadband (ie. 10/2 = 5)
int deadband_low = deadband_high * -1; // sets deadband_low to be negative half of deadband
(ie. 5 * -1 = -5)

int x; // variable used for mixing adj_val1
int y; // variable used for mixing adj_val2

int left; // variable to hold mixed value for left motor
int right; // variable to hold mixed value for right motor

int speed_low;  // variable to set lower speed value determined by adj_val3
int speed_high; // variable to set upper speed value determined by adj_val3

int speed_limit = 255; // default the speed limit to 255 (max speed), unless switched.

// variables to hold speed mapping values
int speed_max = 255;
int speed_min = 0;

// end of variables

void setup() {

  TCCR1B = TCCR1B & 0b11111000 | 0x01; // change PWM frequency on pins 9 and 10 to 32kHz
  TCCR2B = TCCR2B & 0b11111000 | 0x01; // change PWM frequency on pins 3 and 11 to 32kHz

  Serial.begin(9600);

  //motor1 pins
  pinMode(motor1_ALI, OUTPUT);
  pinMode(motor1_AHI, OUTPUT);
  pinMode(motor1_BLI, OUTPUT);
  pinMode(motor1_BHI, OUTPUT);

  //motor2 pins
  pinMode(motor2_ALI, OUTPUT);
  pinMode(motor2_AHI, OUTPUT);
  pinMode(motor2_BLI, OUTPUT);
  pinMode(motor2_BHI, OUTPUT);
```

```
  //led's
  pinMode(ledPin1, OUTPUT);
  pinMode(ledPin2, OUTPUT);

  //PPM inputs from RC receiver
  pinMode(ppm1, INPUT);
  pinMode(ppm2, INPUT);
  pinMode(ppm3, INPUT);

  // wait 1 second after power-up to start loop to give R/C time to connect
  delay(1000);

}


void loop() {

  // go to current_sense() function below loop first
  current_sense();
  // then go to pulse() function below loop
  pulse();

  // Now we can check the R/C values to see what direction the robot should go:

  if (x > deadband_high) {  // if the Up/Down R/C input is above the upper threshold, go
FORWARD

    // Going Forward, now check to see if we should go straight ahead,turn left, or turn
right.
    if (y > deadband_high) { // go forward while turning right proportional to the R/C
left/right input
      left = x;
      right = x - y;
      test();
      m1_forward(left);
      m2_forward(right);
      // quadrant 1 - forward and to the right
    }
    else if (y < deadband_low) {   // go forward while turning left proportional to the R/C
left/right input
      left = x - (y * -1);  // remember that in this case, y will be a negative number
      right = x;
      test();
      m1_forward(left);
      m2_forward(right);
      // quadrant 2 - forward and to the left
    }
    else {   // left/right stick is centered, go straight forward
      left = x;
      right = x;
```

```
        test();
        m1_forward(left);
        m2_forward(right);
        // go forward along X axis
    }
}

else if (x < deadband_low) {      // otherwise, if the Up/Down R/C input is below lower
threshold, go BACKWARD

    // remember that x is below deadband_low, it will always be a negative number, we need to
multiply it by -1 to make it positive.
    // now check to see if left/right input from R/C is to the left, to the right, or
centered.
    if (y > deadband_high) {  // go backward while turning right proportional to the R/C
left/right input
        left = (x * -1);
        right = (x * -1) - y;
        test();
        m1_reverse(left);
        m2_reverse(right);
        // quadrant 4 - go backwards and to the right
    }
    else if (y < deadband_low) {    // go backward while turning left proportional to the R/C
left/right input
        left = (x * -1) - (y * -1);
        right = x * -1;
        test();
        m1_reverse(left);
        m2_reverse(right);
        // quadrant 3 - go backwards and to the left
    }
    else {   // left/right stick is centered, go straight backwards
        left = x * -1;
        right = x * -1;
        test();
        m1_reverse(left);
        m2_reverse(right);
        // go straight backwards along x axis
    }
}

else {      // if neither of the above 2 conditions is met, then X (Up/Down) R/C input is
centered (neutral)

    // Stop motors!
    left = 0;
    right = 0;
    m1_stop();
    m2_stop();

}
```

```
// Print the 2 R/C values
  Serial.print(servo1_val);
  Serial.print("    ");
  Serial.print(servo2_val);
  Serial.print("    ");
  // now print the value of the speed limit
  Serial.print(speed_limit);
  Serial.print("    ");
  // lastly, print the values of the current sensors
  Serial.print(current_sense_1);
  Serial.print("    ");
  Serial.print(current_sense_2);
  Serial.println("    ");

}
// End of loop




// Begin current_sense() function
void current_sense(){

  // read current sensors on motor-controller
  current_sense_1 = analogRead(1);
  current_sense_2 = analogRead(2);

  // determine which direction each motor is spinning
  if (current_sense_1 > 512){
    current_sense_1 = current_sense_1 - 512;
  }
  else {
    current_sense_1 = 512 - current_sense_1;
  }
  if (current_sense_2 > 512){
    current_sense_2 = current_sense_2 - 512;
  }
  else {
    current_sense_2 = 512 - current_sense_2;
  }

  // adjust the directional value into Amperes. Divide by 13.5 to get amps
  current_sense_1 = current_sense_1 / 13.5;
  current_sense_2 = current_sense_2 / 13.5;

  // if either Ampere value is above the threshold, stop both motors for 1 second
  if (current_sense_1 > current_limit || current_sense_2 > current_limit){
    m1_stop();
```

```
      m2_stop();
      digitalWrite(ledPin2, HIGH);
      delay(cool_off);
      digitalWrite(ledPin2, LOW);
   }
}
// End current_sense function




// Begin pulse() function
void pulse(){

   // read servo1 pulse from ELE
   servo1_val = pulseIn(ppm1, HIGH, 20000);
   // check to make sure it is valid
   if (servo1_val > 800 && servo1_val < 2200){
      // then adjust it to a -255 to 255 value range for speed and direction
      adj_val1 = map(servo1_val, 1000, 2000, -speed_limit, speed_limit);
      x = constrain(adj_val1, -speed_limit, speed_limit);
   }
   else {
      // if the pulse is not valid, set it equal to 0
      x = 0;
   }

   // read servo1 pulse from ELE
   servo2_val = pulseIn(ppm2, HIGH, 20000);
   // check to make sure it is valid
   if (servo2_val > 800 && servo2_val < 2200){
      // then adjust it to a -255 to 255 value range for speed and direction
      adj_val2= map(servo2_val, 1000, 2000, -speed_limit, speed_limit);
      y = constrain(adj_val2, -speed_limit, speed_limit);
   }
   else {
      // if the pulse is not valid, set it equal to 0
      y = 0;
   }

   servo3_val = pulseIn(ppm3, HIGH, 20000);
   if (servo3_val > 1600){
      speed_limit = 255;
   }
   else{
      speed_limit = 128;
   }
}
// End pulse() function
```

```
// Begin test() function
int test() {

    // make sure we don't try to write any invalid PWM values to the h-bridge, ie. above 255 or
below 0.
    if (left > 254) {
      left = 255;
    }
    if (left < 1) {
      left = 0;
    }
    if (right > 254) {
      right = 255;
    }
    if (right < 1) {
      right = 0;
    }
}
// End test() function


// Create single instances for each motor direction, so we don't accidentally write a shoot-
through condition to the H-bridge.
void m1_forward(int m1_speed){
  digitalWrite(motor1_AHI, LOW);
  digitalWrite(motor1_BLI, LOW);
  digitalWrite(motor1_BHI, HIGH);
  analogWrite(motor1_ALI, m1_speed);
  digitalWrite(ledPin1, LOW);
}

void m1_reverse(int m1_speed){
  digitalWrite(motor1_BHI, LOW);
  digitalWrite(motor1_ALI, LOW);
  digitalWrite(motor1_AHI, HIGH);
  analogWrite(motor1_BLI, m1_speed);
  digitalWrite(ledPin1, LOW);
}

void m2_forward(int m2_speed){
  digitalWrite(motor2_AHI, LOW);
  digitalWrite(motor2_BLI, LOW);
  digitalWrite(motor2_BHI, HIGH);
  analogWrite(motor2_ALI, m2_speed);
  digitalWrite(ledPin1, LOW);
}
```

```
void m2_reverse(int m2_speed){
  digitalWrite(motor2_BHI, LOW);
  digitalWrite(motor2_ALI, LOW);
  digitalWrite(motor2_AHI, HIGH);
  analogWrite(motor2_BLI, m2_speed);
  digitalWrite(ledPin1, LOW);
}

void m1_stop(){
  digitalWrite(motor1_BHI, LOW);
  digitalWrite(motor1_ALI, LOW);
  digitalWrite(motor1_AHI, LOW);
  digitalWrite(motor1_BLI, LOW);
  digitalWrite(ledPin1, HIGH);
}

void m2_stop(){
  digitalWrite(motor2_BHI, LOW);
  digitalWrite(motor2_ALI, LOW);
  digitalWrite(motor2_AHI, LOW);
  digitalWrite(motor2_BLI, LOW);
  digitalWrite(ledPin1, HIGH);
}
// End motor functions
```

This code uses two channels from an R/C receiver to control the direction and speed of the Explorer-bot, using a home made motor controller. Because I used an R/C transmitter with at least four usable control channels, I decided to designate the left transmitter control stick to operate the pan/tilt camera system, and the right transmitter control stick controls the speed and direction of the robot.

Though there are servo motors used in this project, they are not controlled using the Arduino. Instead, they connect directly to the R/C receiver, which alleviates the extra processing power that would be required by the Arduino to process those signals.

I installed two separate power toggle switches, one for the Arduino and the other for the motor controller. This way I can troubleshoot the Arduino without the motors being active. These switches were mounted to the plexiglass deck. When you are comfortable that each input is connected properly, power on the Arduino, waiting to power the motor controller until the R/C receiver LED turns on (verifying a connection). When connected, you can power on the motor controller and give the bot a thorough testing around the yard.

You can use this bot with different code in Chapter 10: Lawn-bot 400, utilizing the 2.4gHz wireless serial connection from the Xbee radios.

## Summary

In this chapter you built a powerful motor controller with built-in current sensing to power a large outdoor robot equipped with an audio/video link, remote radio control, and telemetry for wirelessly monitoring the robot's Arduino. This robot required a steel frame, large (power wheelchair) DC gear motors, and a 2.4GHz radio control system capable of reliable and long distance signal transmission.

The purpose of this robot is still undetermined; although it is extremely fun to play with. You could use the Explorer-bot as a security robot to patrol dark, cold, or otherwise undesirable locations remotely, or just as an excuse to play with a neat robot. I have been known to attach a small chair to the top of this robot (see Figure 8-23 for a view of the potential chair-riding platform), which immediately converts it into a children's (or feline) taxi service.... Just don't let the children drive themselves!

In the next chapter, you head to the open sea with the GPS guided Roboboat. This project focuses on guiding a catamaran style boat around a lake, using a GPS sensor and an Arduino variant designed specifically for integration with hobby R/C products.

*Figure 8-23. The Explorer-Bot ready for action.*

# CHAPTER 9

# RoboBoat

This chapter will focus on the construction of a model catamaran (RoboBoat) that is guided by a GPS autopilot. The RoboBoat will follow a pre-programmed path that is selected by you, and created using Google Earth.

My motivation for this project came from a totally different direction: scuba diving. I have been addicted to this hobby for nearly 30 years now, and during this time I have always tried to combine sports and technical issues. This sometimes led to some weird underwater electronics, like LED lamps, waterproof laser pointers, homebrew diving computers, electronically controlled tank-filling equipment, and so on...

The idea for a robot boat was born on an expedition to a lake in the north Italian Alps that was 7500 ft (2300m) above sea level. The diving site was totally unknown to us, and I assume that we were the first people to carry 100-pound diving equipment on our backs to that altitude and go diving. We had no data about the depth of that lake, and because I am a very curious person, I wanted to know in advance what the dive had in store for us. So I took a sonar with me, mounted it on a body board, and swam crisscross around the lake to see what depths were below the surface. In principle, this method worked fine, but swimming in a lake with a water temperature of 4°C is no fun, even with a 1/4" (7mm) neoprene diving suit.

When I went home, the idea of automating this surveying process continued in my head, and I tried several methods to remotely control a model ship that carried a sonar on it. To make a long story short, none of these methods worked to my satisfaction.

To create a digital depth-map of a lake, you need a platform that is able to follow a straight line for at least some hundred meters. Doing this with an RC-controlled model ship is a real challenge for various reasons:

- To get depth data that can be processed to a 3D map, you need depth values that have been sampled along parallel straight lines.

- Holding a straight line is difficult when the boat is more than 300ft (or about 100m) away, because you are not able to see it anymore.

- Following parallel paths is also difficult if you have no reference path.

Finally, after many trial and error approaches, I ended up with a configuration that worked fine:

- A catamaran with benign, straight-line behavior that gracefully follows a straight line

- A windmill-type assembly with an aircraft-propeller and a brushless DC motor for the propulsion

- A GPS-controlled autopilot hardware/software system, based on an Arduino platform called ArduPilot

# Some Words in Advance

When I was a student at the university (which was quite a long time ago), I was taking a course for control-loop design. One of the tasks was to optimize the control-loop parameters for an assembly that balanced a wooden stick. The stick was mounted on a roller skate, which was fixed on either side to a rope. The rope was connected to a motor that moved the roller skate with the stick on it back and forth. The motor was controlled by an analog PID controller. It worked quite well; the skate oscillated a little bit and held the stick in a perfect upright position. The whole assembly looked very crude, and the wooden stick was indeed a branch from a tree. I asked my professor why they did not make a more perfect assembly with a metal stick instead of a branch, and with a better push-pull assembly. His answer was short:

"If your assembly is mechanically perfect, nobody would believe that the system is balanced by electronics."

With this in mind, I have designed the RoboBoat. The mechanics are very simple and sometimes crude. But, if you see your catamaran on a lake, following a straight line and returning to the launch point like a boomerang, you'll see how right my professor was.

# Parts List for the RoboBoat

Let's first start with the parts list for all the materials that are needed to construct the boat (Table 9-1), the propulsion assembly, and the electronics. I have tried to use materials that are easily available in do-it-yourself stores and model shops.

*Table 9-1. RoboBoat Parts List*

| Part | Description | Price |
| --- | --- | --- |
| *- Propulsion Assembly -* | | |
| PVC tube, 7" (170mm) long | 1" (25mm) outer diameter PVC tubing from Home Depot Store SKU # 193755 | $2.00 |
| PVC rod, 2" (50mm) long | 3/4" (20mm) outer diameter, trimmed on a lathe so that it exactly fits the inner diameter of the tube. If not available, use a 3/4" PVC tubing instead. E.g. Home Depot SKU # 193712 | $2.00 |
| Baseplate | Aluminum or PVC plate 2"L (50mm) × 6"W (160mm), and 1/4" thick (5mm) from Home Depot | $1.00 |
| (2) Rudder horns | Can be found in RC stores or Hobbyking.com, part #OR7-601GRx10 or similar | $1.04 (10-pc set) |

| Part | Description | Price |
|------|-------------|-------|
| (2) Pushrods | Can be found in RC stores, steel wire, 1 or 1.5mm diameter, 4" (100m) length each | $1.00 |
| (2) or (4) Pushrod connectors | Are used to connect the pushrods to the rudder horns; either RC store or from Hobbyking.com, part #GWPHD001 or similar | $2.20 (5-pc set) |
| RC servo | Any "standard" size RC servo will do. e.g. HobbyKing.com, part # BMS-410STD. | $5.00–$12.00 |
| Motor | ROBBE ROXXY3 ROXXY BL-Outrunner 2827-26 part #477926, comes complete with motor mounting kit; or similar BLDC motor, Kv between 800 Rpm/v and 1200 Rpm/v, 100-200W | $30.00 |
| Propeller | APC 10x5" or 11x5" Hobbyking.com, part #APC10x5-E or similar | $2.00 |
| Screw | M5*20mm counter sunk screw, to fix the pivot to the baseplate from Home Depot | $0.10 |

### - Electronics -

| Part | Description | Price |
|------|-------------|-------|
| ArduPilot PCB | ArduPilot board, available from SparkFun: www.sparkfun.com/products/8785. Do not forget to modify as described. | $24.95 |
| Programming adapter | FTDI BASIC Breakout -5V, available from SparkFun: www.sparkfun.com/products/9716 | $14.95 |
| USB cable | You will also need USB type A to Mini-B cable; if you don´t have already in your shack, get this one: http://www.sparkfun.com/products/598cable. | $3.95 |
| (2) Header 3pin | Breakaway headers 0.1" (2.54mm) through-hole, http://www.sparkfun.com/products/116 or similar | $2.50 |
| (2) Header 6pin | Make from foregoing product | -- |
| ESC | Brushless DC motor controller, 20A Type, available in RC shops or from Hobbyking.com, part #TR_P25A | $12.00–$30.00 |
| GPS module | EM406 from SparkFun or DIYDrones.com, http://www.sparkfun.com/products/465 or http://store.diydrones.com/EM_406_GPS_1Hz_p/em-406a.htm, comes ready with cable | $60.00 |

| Part | Description | Price |
|---|---|---|
| Battery pack | Any 3S LiPo pack with at least 3000maH will do, e.g., HobbyKing.com, part #Z50003S15C | $30.00–$40.00 |
| Power connectors | Look in your RC shop for adequate ones; TAMYIA type or similar | $3.00 |

- Boat -

| | | |
|---|---|---|
| EPS or XPS foam board | Base material for the hulls, Home Depot, 40"L (1000mm) × 20"W (500mm) x 4"D (100mm) | $10.00–$20.00 |
| XPS board | Base material for the deck, Home Depot, 24"W (600mm) x 15"D (400mm) x 1"D (25mm) | $5.00–$10.00 |
| Cardboard | Use to make the templates for the hulls, about 1mm thickness | -- |
| Double-sided sticky tape | Used to glue the templates to the Styrofoam block from Home Depot | $4.00 |
| EPS/XPS glue | Contact glue to join the segments together, e.g. from http://www.diysupermarket.com/uhu-por-polystyrene-foam-glue.html | $5.00 |
| (4) Foam anchors | Used to connect the hulls to the deck, Home Depot | $10.00 |
| Fiberglass fabric | Use fine fabric, e.g. Home Depot SKU # 846759 | $10.00 |
| Epoxy resin | Use one with a pot life of about 20 to 30 minutes. From RC stores or marine suppliers. | $20.00–$40.00 |
| Fin | Use PVC foam sheets with 3mm thickness or painted plywood or similar. e.g. from Home Depot | $5.00 |
| (4) M5 bolts with eyes | Used to connect the deck to the hulls, 1.5" (40mm) long from Home Depot | $5.00 |
| Plywood spacers | Make from painted plywood, 1.5" (40mm) × 1.5" (40mm), drill a 5mm hole in the middle from Home Depot | $1.00 |

Additional Tools/Materials (available at Home Depot or other DIY stores)

Disposable rubber or plastic gloves
Hot wire Styrofoam cutter (see below for contruction)
Razor knife (I used one made by Stanley)
Medium grade sandpaper
Disposable paintbrush

Now let's review some of the more important materials and tools you'll need to complete the catamaran structure. The following sections provide more details on each item (later in the chapter, we'll walk through propulsion assembly, electronics, and software).

# Polystyrene Foam

This material is one of the most popular plastics in the world. It is made of polystyrene or PS.

As shown in Figure 9-1, there are two general types available: expanded Polystyrene (EPS) and extruded Polystyrene (XPS).

EPS is more lightweight and less rigid than XPS. Both types can usually be found in DIY ("do it yourself") stores in the form of rigid panels with various thicknesses.

*Figure 9-1. EPS on the left, XPS on the right*

EPS is usually white and has visible pores the size of a few millimeters. When you break this material, you can see some of the pores fly around like small bubbles. This material is very lightweight, soft, and not so easy for sanding.

XPS is usually colored and is usually used for the insulation of basements. It is more expensive, heavier, and harder than the low-density version, but it is easier to treat with sanding paper.

Either of the two materials will work for the construction of the hulls. I personally prefer XPS, because the finish will be better afterward. For the hulls, a material thickness of 4" (100mm) is adequate. If you don't find this thickness in your local store, simply take smaller ones and glue them together until you have the appropriate size. More about the glue later.

Both of these materials share one drawback: they can be easily melted away by most organic solvents. If you want to start any treatment on this material with paint, resin, or putty, please try in advance on a piece of unused material and allow at least one hour to observe what happens. Using the wrong material on polystyrene can ruin your day in seconds!

# Epoxy Resin

We will use this product in combination with fiberglass fabric as a coating for the EPS/XPS to add more strength to the hull. Here is some advice in advance.

Please do not use material for the coating other than this one. There are other two component resins available on the market; most of them can be found in DIY stores as resins or putty. Most of them are based on polyester, and that material is definitely not compatible with polystyrene. Here is one test: if it smells extremely like plastic, you can be sure that you have chosen the wrong product.

Back to epoxy. This is a two-component resin, and it is available in most hobby or modeling shops. Usually it is compatible with most materials, even polystyrene. There are various brand names of that product available. Please ask your local dealer or search the Internet for more information.

After mixing the two components in the right ratio (the resin and the hardener), you will get a honey-like liquid, which can be processed for about 15–30 minutes until it starts to thicken. The total time to cure is about 12 to 24 hours, depending on the product. So it is good practice to start the work in the evening, let it cure overnight, and wake up with a (hopefully) ruggedized hull in your workshop.

There are two methods of mixing you can use: by weight or by volume. Please read the instructions that come with the product; usually both methods are described there. The ratio has to be kept within a certain accuracy (about +-5% is OK). Please be careful about that, otherwise you will end up with a hull that will be sticky for years.

After the mixing of the two components, thoroughly stir it for at least one minute and allow another minute of silence to eliminate the air bubbles.

## Gloves

Please wear disposable rubber or plastic gloves for the whole time you are in contact with the material for these reasons:

1.  The product is not poisonous but may irritate your skin.

2.  You will surely get in contact with that extreme sticky liquid when applying it to the hull, and it is no fun working with sticky fingers.

3.  The material can be easily wiped off from the gloves with paper towels.

## Fiberglass Fabric

Fiberglass fabric is made of very thin glass filaments. These filaments are woven like "ordinary" fabric (Figure 9-2).

There are lots of fiberglass products available. For the coating of the hull, a fine fabric should be used to give a smooth surface and for ease of work.

Thick fiberglass fabric or fiberglass mats are not suitable because these materials are too stiff to handle. Fiberglass is usually categorized on a "weight per surface" basis. Values around 0.3oz per sqft (80 grams per m²) are perfect.

***Figure 9-2.*** *Woven fiberglass fabric with 80g/m²*

Fiberglass fabric can easily be cut in appropriate pieces with a pair of scissors. You will need to buy a pair of scissors especially for your work, because the wear of the blades is much higher compared to cutting tissues or paper, and the scissors may (they surely will) get contaminated by epoxy resin. Hardened epoxy resin on fiberglass can be cut with a sharp razor knife. This is helpful for cutting away excess material prior to sanding.

# Glue

To glue the segments together, you must use Styrofoam glue. This should be available at a hobby shop or most DIY stores. The glue is a contact adhesive, like others, but it has a solvent that is compatible with polystyrene.

With the materials out of the way, let's discuss the tools.

# Styrofoam Cutter and Razor Knife

A hot wire Styrofoam cutter is absolutely mandatory to make a smooth cut of the segments. If you don't want to buy a cutter, you can easily make your own. There are lots of plans on the Internet; please have a look at this site: `www.instructables.com/id/Hot-wire-foam-cutter/`. Or simply Google "Styrofoam cutter" and you will find lots of links for DIY plans to make your own.

You do not need one with a table, because the cardboard template will be your guide. The wire length should at least be 12" (300mm) to have enough room to operate. Please test in advance on some unused Styrofoam pieces.

A sharp razor knife is also useful for trimming and cutting the foam.

# Miscellaneous

Sanding paper is useful for smoothing the surface. After the thermal cutting of the segments, the surface of the Styrofoam is a little bit roughened through the melted material. I would suggest firstly gluing all segments together and then doing a little bit of sanding. Be careful not to use sanding paper that is too coarse and not to apply too much force on the material.

For applying the epoxy resin on the Styrofoam and on the fabric, a disposable paintbrush is perfect. After using it, the paintbrush is useless. I do not know any solvents to wash the resin off. Buy some cheap ones and throw them away after use.

# The RoboBoat Design

Before I arrived at the catamaran solution, I tried lots of mono-hull assemblies, but they all had the same problem: they didn't follow a straight line. This problem can be overcome with a keel that goes deep below the waterline, but I wanted a platform that would only touch the surface, to avoid contacts with water plants (this is also the reason I have an air propeller and not a water propeller).

A catamaran is a very stable construction that can be thought of as a "boat running on rails," and, in addition, there is lot of room between the two keels for any type of payload. Model catamarans of the size I wanted are very rare in RC modeling, so I decided to build one of my own. I first started with a fairly easy construction with a triangular cross-section that did its job very well, but was not optimized for drag, because the wetted surface of a triangular shape is nearly the worst that can be thought of (see Figure 9-3).

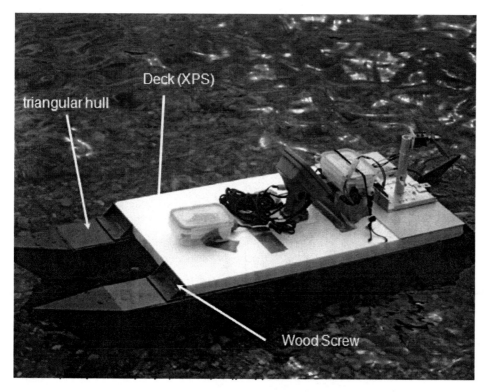

*Figure 9-3. A simple catamaran with triangular hulls*

The final construction I settled on is very easy. As you read this overview, keep in mind that there are many materials that can be used instead of the PVC foam sheets, such as balsa wood, water-resistant plywood, or the like.

I used PVC foam sheets with a thickness of about 1/10" (2.54mm). This material is very lightweight, can be easily cut with a Stanley razor knife and can be glued with hot glue. The side walls are made of rectangular sheets in the size of 40" (1000mm) × 6" (150mm). The front and rear tips are identical and are made of triangular sheets. In the inside of the hull, additional triangular sheets give the hull some stability. The top is also made of a rectangular sheet of the size 40" (1000mm) x 4.5" (110mm). It is helpful to make some templates out of cardboard, especially for the triangular sheets that form the front and rear tips. Glue it all together with hot glue and that's it!

The connection between the two hulls (the deck) is created using a sheet of hard XPS Styrofoam, measuring 15"L x 15"W x 1"D. The foam board is fixed to the hulls by 4"-long (100mm) screws, with the help of 90° angles that are glued on the top of the hulls.

That construction can be easily disassembled, simply by removing the screws.

The overall size of this catamaran is 55" (1400mm) in length, 15" (400mm) in width, and 6" (150mm) in height at a net weight of about 7.7lbs (3500g). The energy consumption to keep up a velocity of about 3.5mph (or 5.5km/h or about 3 knots) is some 110 watts, when the boat has to carry an extra payload of about 4.5lbs (2000g).

This boat design has worked well on many occasions as a proof of concept for the catamaran approach. It also showed that the adjustment of the PID controller parameters (more on that later) is much less critical than on a monohull design. The V-shape of the hulls gives an excellent straight-line stability, and there is no need for additional fins, as on other keel shapes.

If you have enough battery capacity or you only want to make short trips, this design is absolutely sufficient, whereas if you want a more efficient design, a more streamlined keel is mandatory.

After some research on the Internet, I found some interesting designs for model catamaran hulls on a French web site. The one that fit most of my needs was called WR-C 21, and there was also a downloadable .dxf file available. A friend of mine who is specialized on 3D-CAD imported this file into his CAD system and created a three-dimensional model out of the two-dimensional .dxf file. With this model, it was possible to cut the hull in sections 4" (100mm) long.

Now, on to building the boat.

## Assembling the Boat

In this section, I walk you through the process of building the boat hull.

### The Templates

The paper templates with the cross-sections of the hulls can be found as a downloadable .pdf file at http://code.google.com/p/roboboat/downloads/list and Apress.com. Print twice all the segment templates from "Segment 1" to "Segment 14." Each segment template consists of two outlines: the inner and the outer one. This is the reason you shall print it out twice. Glue the printout on cardboard with a thickness of about 0.04" (1mm). Then cut out an inner and an outer template of each segment with a pair of scissors, as I did for Segment 6, shown in Figures 9-4 and 9-5.

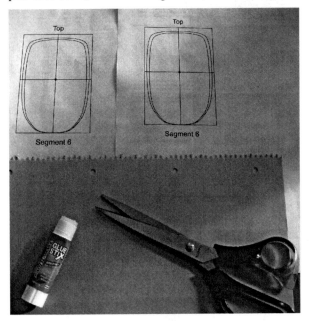

**Figure 9-4.** *The printed templates*

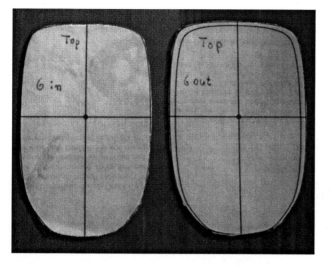

*Figure 9-5. The templates, glued on cardboard and cut*

If there are any burrs, remove them with sanding paper. Apply dual-sided sticky tape on the backs of the templates (Figure 9-6). There is no need to cover the whole template with the tape. A piece 3/4" (20mm) x 3/4" (20mm) should be OK. Do not peel off the protective paper yet.

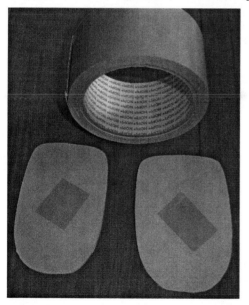

*Figure 9-6. The templates from the back, with sticky tape*

The first and the last segments (1 and 14) are very delicate to handle because the ends are very thin. I have shortened these segments to half of their original length, which was 2" (50mm). This will shorten the overall length of the hull to 50" (1300mm), but this will have no effect on the performance of the boat.

## Gluing the Templates on the EPS/XPS Board

Now, the most critical part of the work begins. You have to adjust the front and back template to each other and then glue it to the Styrofoam board. The boards come pre-cut with very exact edges, and this helps a lot for the adjustment (Figure 9-7). First paint an exact rectangular line on the front side and the adjacent sides of the board.

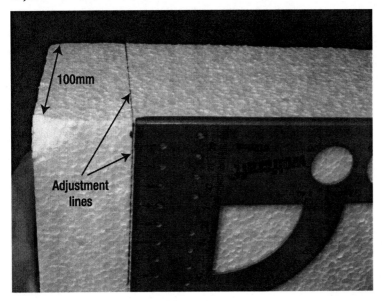

*Figure 9-7. Preparation of the EPS board*

Then take the outer template, peel off the protective paper from the sticky tape, and adjust the line to the vertical crosshair line that is printed on the template. Align this template to the top edge of the board (Figure 9-8).

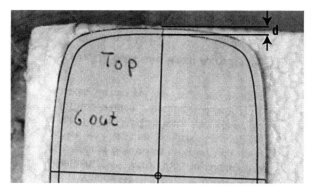

*Figure 9-8. Alignment of the template on the EPS board*

Next, measure the vertical distance (d) between the outer and inner template and adjust the inner template on the back of the board accordingly, e.g., move it (d) down from the top edge. Note that the vertical distances in the middle segments are close to zero.

## Cutting Out the Segments

You have to use a hot-wire foam cutter for this purpose. Figure 9-9 shows a picture of my DIY version.

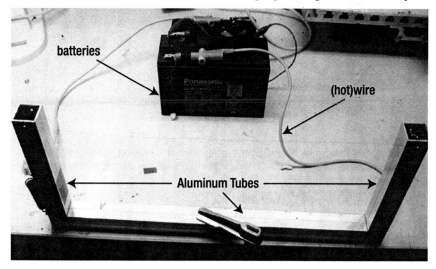

*Figure 9-9. The DIY Styrofoam cutter from the author*

First separate the segment from the panel by making a rough cutout of the segment, allowing about 1/2" of extra Styrofoam around the template, as shown in Figure 9-10. This piece will now be much easier to make perfect with one more pass through the wire cutter.

***Figure 9-10.*** *Coarse cutout of one segment*

Then cut away the excess material by using the cardboard template as a guideline, as shown in Figure 9-11. Adjust the temperature of the wire so that it gives a smooth cut. Temperatures that are too high will melt away the material under the template.

Experiment a little until the results are satisfying.

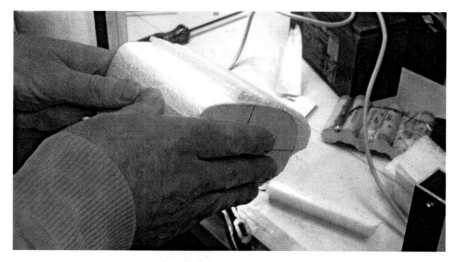

***Figure 9-11.*** *Fine cutting of one segment*

The ready cut segment should now look as shown in Figure 9-12. It is important to label each side of the cut segment with a felt-tip pen after you have peeled off the templates. You will need this labeling afterward, when gluing the segments together.

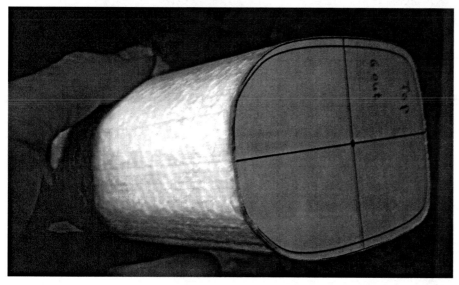

***Figure 9-12.*** *One segment after cutting*

# Gluing the Segments Together

This step is simple. Apply a layer of the glue to one of the surfaces, put the other surface together, press firmly, and then separate the surfaces. With this method, you will have a thin layer of the glue on either side. Allow some minutes to dry until the surface has a rubber-like consistency that is still a little bit sticky. Then put the surfaces together and press firmly. Attention! Adjust the two surfaces exactly, prior to putting them together. There will be no second chance. The glue acts immediately! In Figure 9-13, you can see two segments prior to gluing.

***Figure 9-13.*** *Two adjacent segments with EPS/XPS glue*

After having glued all segments together, the result should look like that shown in Figure 9-14.

***Figure 9-14.*** *All segments glued together*

To smooth out the surface and to remove excess material, use sanding paper. This will take some time. It's best to do the sanding outside and use old clothing because there will be quite a bit of polystyrene dust created during this process.

## Inserting the Foam Anchors

To connect the deck with the hulls, foam anchors are very useful. Normally, these anchors are used to hold screws in walls that have been insulated with foam panels or for use in sheetrock walls. Look in your DIY store for this item. The one I have used looks like that in Figure 9-15.

*Figure 9-15. A foam anchor from the DIY store*

Normally, these anchors are made to hold wood screws. To hold machine screws, I tapped an M5 thread into the anchor (Figure 9-16).

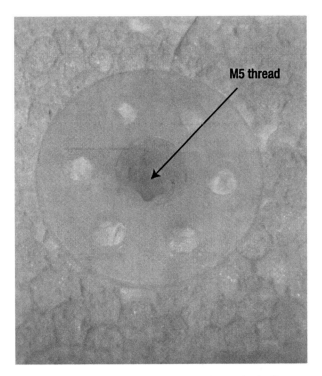

*Figure 9-16. The foam anchor screwed into the hull*

To give more strength, you can apply a little bit of epoxy resin to the anchor prior to inserting it into the foam.

The placement of the anchors is in the middle of segments 7 and 11, as you can see in Figure 9-17.

*Figure 9-17. The placement of the anchors*

# The Coating

This is delicate work, so it is best to be prepared. Put a lot of old newspaper around the area of work before you begin. To hold the hull in place, make a stand from some unused foam, and insert two foam anchors with two M5 threaded bolts, as shown in Figure 9-18.

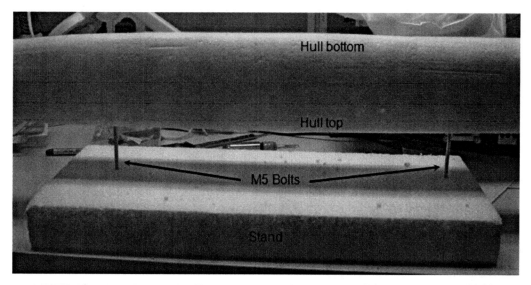

*Figure 9-18. The hull, prior to coating*

This will hold the hull in place for the coating with the fiberglass fabric.

I did the coating in two steps: first the bottom of the hull and then the top. I also made overlapping areas on the top. To secure the fiberglass to the foam, use some pins that can be removed after the hardening of the epoxy.

First cut out a rectangular piece of fiberglass in the size of 53" x 12" (1350mm x 300mm). This will fit the length and will give an overlap to the top of about 0.8" (20mm). Lay it over the hull that sits bottom-up on the stand. Adjust the material. Make a cut in the wrinkles and overlay the material. If the fiberglass is positioned, mix the epoxy according to the instructions of the product you are using. Wear rubber gloves. Then apply the epoxy over the fiberglass by speckling with the paintbrush. The fiberglass will soak up the epoxy and leak through onto the foam. Try to squeeze out air that is trapped between the foam and the fabric.

When you have finished, it should look like Figure 9-19.

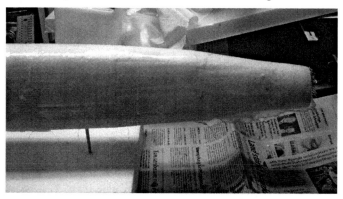

*Figure 9-19. The hull, coated with fiberglass fabric and epoxy resin*

If you don´t have a fiberglass sheet this big, you can also do a "patchwork" with smaller pieces. This will ease the work, especially if you are not familiar with fiberglass work. Simply overlap the patches and speckle them with the paintbrush.

After the epoxy hardens (usually after 12 hours), you can take the hull from its stand and look at your work. Excess material can be cut away with a sharp razor knife cutter. To coat the top side, first put some sticky tape over the holes of the foam anchors to avoid epoxy resin going into it. Then fix the hull (e.g., between two bricks) and apply the fiberglass and the epoxy as described earlier.

## Applying the Finish

After coating both sides of both hulls, there are still some things to do. The tips of the last segments (1 and 14) must also be coated. You can do this by cutting out fiberglass sheets that match the cross-sections and epoxying them to the foam. An alternative way to get the end-points finished is to make a "putty" by mixing epoxy resin and a filler material like cotton flakes or glass bubbles (available in RC model shops). You can then apply this material to the end-points.

After the epoxy hardens, cut away excess material with a razor knife and do some sanding to smooth the surface and the edges.

## The Fins

To give good straight-line stability, you must add small fins to ends of the hulls. The fins are simply triangular sheets that can be made of various materials (Figure 9-20). I used PVC foam sheets with a thickness of about 7/8" (2mm). Any other waterproof material of this thickness will work. You can even use plywood, if painted or treated with urethane. Cut out a triangle the size of 4" (100mm) x 1.5" (40mm), and glue it to the end of the hull. I used hot glue, which works fine if you have roughened the surface with sanding paper prior to applying the glue.

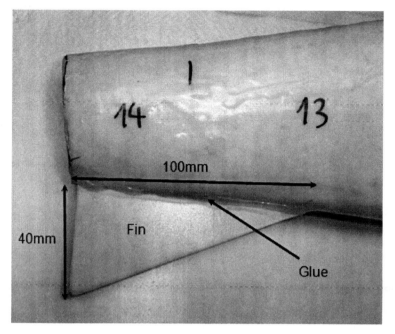

**Figure 9-20.** *The fins*

# Painting

There is no need for painting, but for the sake of visibility, I suggest applying some fluorescent paint onto it. You can use any sort of paint, because the epoxy acts as an isolation layer for the foam. It is good practice to use a white primer layer and then apply the fluorescent layer by either a paintbrush or spray. The white primer layer will increase the visibility of the fluorescent paint.

# The Deck

This is a fairly easy task, compared to the fabrication of the hulls. Simply cut out a 23" (600mm) x 15" (400mm) sheet of an XPS foam panel with a thickness of at least 3/4" (20mm). To add strength, you can coat this board with epoxy, but it is not mandatory, because the XPS is very solid. If you don´t have XPS, use EPS instead and coat it with epoxy. Figure 9-21 shows the dimensions and the position of the four mounting holes for the hulls. The holes are symmetrical, so I put the dimensions of only one for reference. The holes in the middle part of the board are for fixing other superstructures and are not relevant at this point of the assembly.

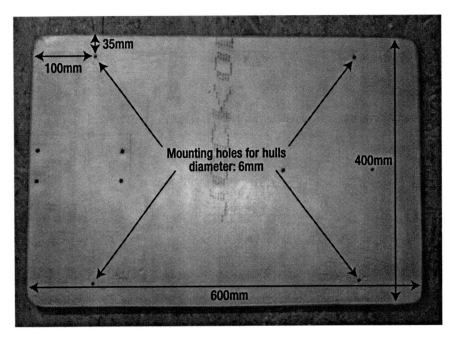

*Figure 9-21. The deck with mounting holes*

## Completing the Assembly

Now, the great moment has come! For the assembly, I have used M5 bolts with "eyes" and some rectangular plywood spacers to hold all pieces together (Figure 9-22). The eyes are useful to tie some of the superstructures to the deck.

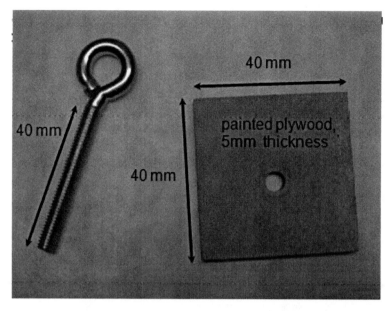

*Figure 9-22. Mounting material for the connection of deck and hulls*

Simply screw the deck panel to the hulls and tighten until the stability is sufficient (Figure 9-23). Do not over-tighten the screws, to avoid damage to the foam.

**Figure 9-23.** *Deck and hull mounted together*

If you have done your work right, you should have something that looks like Figure 9-24.

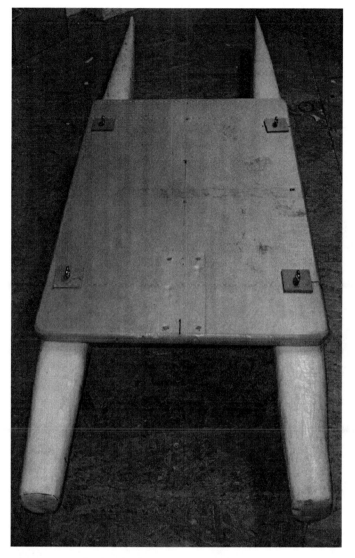

*Figure 9-24.* *The finished catamaran platform*

With the hull assembly completed, we will move on to building the propulsion system. Catamarans are typically propelled by the wind and sails. The RoboBoat has a quite different kind of propulsion: a wind generator that will be described in the next section.

# The Propulsion Assembly

It was a long and troublesome path to arrive at the assembly that I am currently using. I tried several approaches and ended up with something I call the "windmill assembly," shown in Figure 9-25. So, what is it?

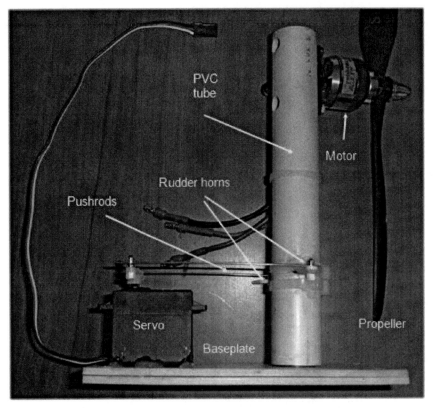

*Figure 9-25. The propulsion assembly*

It is simply a motor with a propeller that is mounted on a tube that sits on a pivot. The tube is turned with an RC servo. That's all.

Compared to the typical water-propelled boat, there are some advantages to an air-powered setup:

- A water propeller is more complicated to install because you have to penetrate the hull, thus introducing the problem of sealing out unwanted water from the hull.

- An air-powered propulsion assembly has no problems with waterplants, which can wrap into the propeller of a water-propelled system.

- R/C airplane motor/propeller kits are very common and widely available.

- The whole assembly is conceived as a "module," which can be easily mounted on different swimming platforms.

- The module is a combination of propulsion and steering and can be changed as a whole.

- The thrust-vector steering that is achieved by turning the propeller is very efficient.

There are lots of ways to build such an assembly. The one I am describing here is not mandatory; give your creativity a chance to find your own solutions. I am in the happy situation of owning a lathe, and so it was fairly easy to make a pivot that exactly fits.

For the construction, I basically have used a PVC tube with an outer diameter of 1" (25mm), which sits on a pivot.

In the next section, we will discuss the propulsion assembly and the steps required to build it.

## The Baseplate

To easily mount and dismount the whole assembly to different hulls, I have put all the components on an intermediate baseplate (Figure 9-26). A 0.15" (4mm)-thick aluminum plate is the best choice, if you want a rock-solid construction. In the pictures in this book, I have used two PVC foam sheets that are glued together. Other materials that are water-resistant and rigid enough will also be suitable (e.g., Plexiglas, painted plywood, etc.). The baseplate is fixed to the deck of the boat with four screws. For that purpose, drill four holes 1/2" away from each edge.

The pivot is screwed to the baseplate with an M5 countersunk screw. Drill a hole of 1/2" (6mm) with a countersink on one side. The baseplate will also hold the servo. The servo has to be adjusted in height to match the rudder horn of the turn assembly.

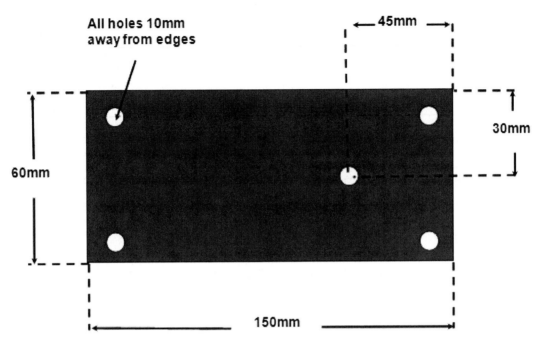

**Figure 9-26.** *Drawing of the baseplate*

## The Pivot

The pivot is made of a PVC rod with a diameter of 3/4" (20mm). On the bottom is an M5 thread, which is used to screw it to the baseplate (Figure 9-27). This is the only component that you may need a lathe to manufacture. The pivot should match closely to the inner diameter of the tube. A PVC fitting that matches the PVC tube (from outside) may also be suitable, but I have never tried.

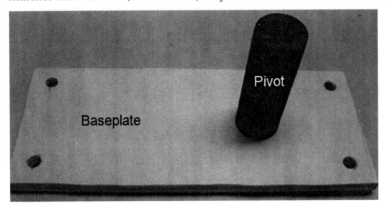

**Figure 9-27.** *The pivot mounted on the baseplate*

# The Tube

The tube shown in Figure 9-28 holds the motor and sits on the pivot. It is made of a 1" (25mm) PVC tube. To use propellers with diameters up to 11", the tube should have a length of 7" (170mm).

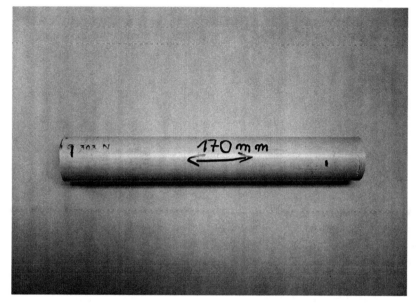

*Figure 9-28. The PVC tube*

To hold the motor, simply drill two holes with a diameter of 1/8" (3mm) in the upper part of the tube, as shown in Figure 9-29. If your motor has a shaft on both sides, drill a hole of about 5/16" (8mm) into the tube to have room for the shaft. For ease of mounting, drill two holes of 5/16" (8mm) on the opposite side of the 1/8" (3mm) holes. Then fix the motor to the tube using M3 screws.

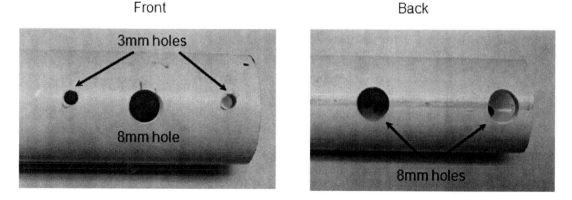

*Figure 9-29. Mounting holes for the motor*

# The Rudder Horns

The rudder horns connect the tube to the servo. There is one on each side of the tube, which will give a push-pull connection to the servo, which is more stable than a single pushrod. I used general-purpose rudder horns for RC models, which are available in hobby stores. The lower part of the tube must be flattened with a file to give space for fixing the rudder horns. The horns can be glued to the tube with contact glue or with two-component epoxy glue (Figure 9-30). Be sure that the holes in the horn are aligned to the center of the PVC tube.

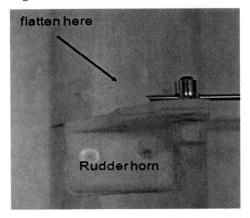

*Figure 9-30. A rudder horn, glued to the tube*

# The Motor

Basically, you can use any motor that can turn a propeller and that produces enough thrust to push the boat forward. I used the brushless DC "outrunner" (BLDC) type shown in Figure 9-31 for several reasons. Brushed motors are also possible, but if you plan long-term trips with the boat, a BLDC is the better choice because there are no brushes that can wear out. BLDC motors that are suited for the boat are widely available, and the price is affordable. I will describe my configuration in depth, but if you want to use other types, here are basic guidelines for the selection:

- Voltage: from 6 to 14V (two or three LiPo batteries in series)

- Kv: between 600 and 1200 rpm/V

- Power: between 100 and 200 watts

With a matched propeller, you should achieve a thrust of at least 1 pound (450 grams). The diameter of the propeller should be in the range of 9" to 11".

Outrunner BLDC motors carry the magnets in a "cage" that runs around the stator coils. The shaft is fixed to the cage. For that reason, most of the "outside" part of the motor is turning. This makes the mounting of the motor different to the mounting of brushed motors. If possible, use one that has a shaft mounting on the cage and that is sold with a mounting kit, which consists of the motor, the propeller, and the propeller driver.

The propulsion-thrust should be in the range of about 1.1 to 1.8 pounds (500 to 800 grams). I have taken several measurements with different types of motors and propellers.

The following combination is the one that I am actually using:

- Motor: ROBBE ROXXY BL-Outrunner 2827-26

- Propeller: APC 11" x 5.5"

The motor is usually sold in a kit with the motor mount and the propeller driver.

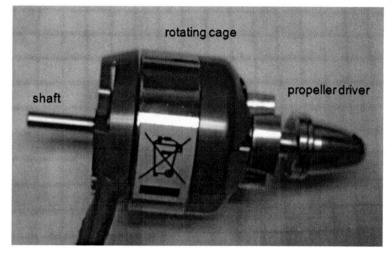

*Figure 9-31. A BLDC outrunner motor*

# The Servo

Use a standard RC servo that can be found in RC model shops. The rudder horn of the servo should have a diameter of 1.75" (45mm). The servo can be either glued or screwed to the baseplate. For better performance, use screws to mount the servo.

# The Pushrods

Steel wires with a diameter of 1–1.5mm are best suited for the connection between the rudder horns of the servo and the tube. If you can find pushrod connectors, the mounting and the adjustment are very easy. If not, you can bend the ends of the wires by 90° and insert them into the holes of the rudder horns.

# Electronics

I must give credit to the ArduPilot (Arduino) community that made it possible to complete this project: the DIYDrones.com home page is a real treasure when you have to deal with unmanned robotics. Special thanks to Chris Anderson and Jordi Muñoz, who are the founders of that great open hardware and open source project. The key element of the electronics I am using here was derived from an Arduino-based autopilot that was originally conceived for model airplanes, called the ArduPilot (AP).

Before we go into depth, let's first look at an overview of the whole system. As you can see from Figure 9-32, the whole electronic system is fairly simple. It consists of the following components:

- The ArduPilot PCB

- A GPS module

- An ESC for brushless DC motors

- A motor

- An RC servo

- A battery pack

**Autopilot Block Diagram**

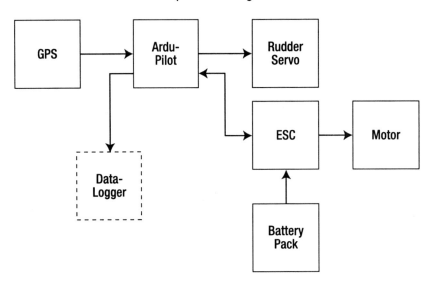

*Figure 9-32. Block diagram of the electronics*

Let's look at these components in more detail, so you can see how they interact with each other.

## The Heart of the System: The ArduPilot PCB

The small printed circuit board shown in Figure 9-33 has all key elements on board that are needed to control a vehicle by GPS. It is based on the same ATmega328 microprocessor used on the Arduino, though the ArduPilot utilizes a very small surface mount version of the chip.

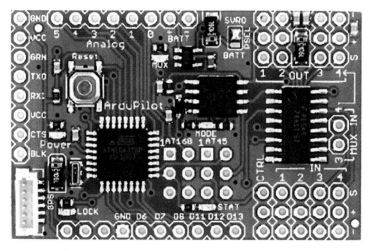

*Figure 9-33. The ArduPilot PCB*

The board is compatible with the Arduino platform, so it is very easy for the user to modify and upload new software to the board. The board consists mainly of the following components:

- An 8-bit AVR microcontroller, the ATmega328

- An ATtiny AVR microcontroller for switching between R/C and autonomous control (not used in this project)

- A GPS interface connector

- Interfaces to control RC servos and electronic speed controllers (ESC)

- A multiplexer that can switch the control between RC control and the microcontroller

- Several other features used for airplane models, which will not be used in this project

## The GPS Module

The GPS module shown in Figure 9-34 is the "sensor" of the autopilot system, similar to what you might find inside a commercial automotive or outdoor GPS unit. It measures the actual position, the velocity, and the heading of the boat. It is connected to the ArduPilot board via a small, SMD-type connector. The cable for the connection between the GPS module and the ArduPilot is usually shipped with the module.

*Figure 9-34. The EM406 GPS module*

The ArduPilot board "talks" to the GPS module over a UART (serial) connection. There is one important thing to consider: the ATmega328 microcontroller has only one UART interface on-chip, which is also used for the programming of the chip. To avoid a conflict, the GPS module *must* be unplugged from the ArduPilot board while programming! More on programming in the section "The Software".

As of my writing this chapter, the EM406 GPS module remains my favorite unit to work with. There are many other GPS modules on the market that may also be suitable, but the EM406 has proved to be very robust and reliable.

## The Electronic Speed Controller (ESC)

The device shown in Figure 9-35 serves two functions: it supplies the ArduPilot Board with a regulated voltage of 5V and it controls the speed of the BLDC motor. The ArduPilot board is powered with 5V that is derived from an ESC with a so-called battery eliminator circuit (BEC). This is simply a linear regulator that sits inside the ESC electronics and provides a regulated 5V supply out of the voltage from the battery pack. The connection to the ESC is done via a standard RC servo connector with three poles. There are lots of ESCs out on the market, and it is impossible to suggest one that is best. It is advisable to buy one that is matched to the motor that you will use.

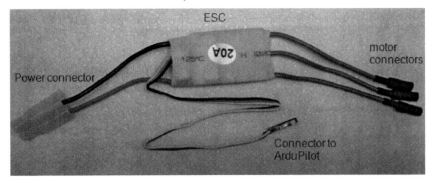

*Figure 9-35. The electronic speed controller (ESC)*

# The Motor

The motor is a so-called "brushless" DC motor (BLDC). It produces the thrust that drives the boat forward.

BLDC motors usually have three cables that are fixed to the motor. The connectors are directly soldered to the cables so that they can be easily connected to the ESC. If your motor turns in the wrong direction, simply swap two cables and the motor turns in the opposite direction. Care has to be taken that the cables do not interfere with the propeller. Use tie-wraps to fix it to the PVC rod, which was already described in the "Propulsion Assembly" section of this chapter.

# The Rudder Servo

The rudder servo turns the "windmill assembly" to steer the boat. Here you can use a "standard" RC servo. Servos of this type are widely available. There are also so-called "high-torque" servos available; they are more powerful, but slower. Any of the two versions are suited to do the job. Please do not use mini or micro servos; they are useful for model airplanes, but for a boat, they may be too small.

# The Battery Pack

The battery pack provides the electrical energy for the whole electronics and—mostly—for the motor.

There are many possible solutions when it comes to selecting a battery pack. Actually, I would prefer to buy a 3S LiPo battery pack with a capacity of about 4000mAh. These types of batteries are now very common in RC modeling, and can be found online for around the same price as older battery types (like NiMH or NiCad). If you want to use other batteries, use the following data as a guideline:

- Voltage: Between 10 and 12 volts

- Capacity: 4000mAh or above

- Sustained current: 6 to 8 amperes (10c discharge rating or better)

Because the weight of a boat is not as critical as on an airplane, you may also find that using lead-acid type batteries will work.

To charge the batteries, use an appropriate charger. Special care has to be taken when using batteries that contain lithium, like LiIon and LiPo types, that they are not over-discharged. The lithium that is in the batteries may start to burn when the battery is overcharged or shorted. A lithium fire cannot be extinguished with water. I strongly recommend charging lithium batteries outdoors, placed on inert materials like stone tiles.

Some words about power connectors—there are some "standard type" connectors available on the market. Usually, the ESC and the battery packs come with connectors. If they are incompatible, you have to cut one side (either the ESC or the battery pack) and solder the appropriate connector to it. I have used TAMYIA-type connectors for all of my projects, because they are widely available and very robust.

# Assembling the Electronics

To get the most out of this section, you should be familiar with the basics of soldering. If you are unsure, ask somebody who has the know-how and who can help you on that topic. I also recommend reading the tutorials at the SparkFun.com web site, where there are lots of articles and "how-to"s that can help newcomers to embedded electronics.

We start the assembly with the ArduPilot board that is usually shipped without connectors for the servos and the programming connector. All connectors that have to be soldered onto the board are breakaway headers with a pitch of 0.1" (2.54mm) that can be found in nearly every DIY electronics shop or at http://www.sparkfun.com/products/116.

They can be easily cut or simply broken to the appropriate size. For the ArduPilot board, we need two 3-way headers and one 6-way header—that's all. Figure 9-36 shows the locations. The servo connectors are called OUT1 and OUT2 in the schematics. The programming connector is named JP2 or USB/SERIAL in the schematics.

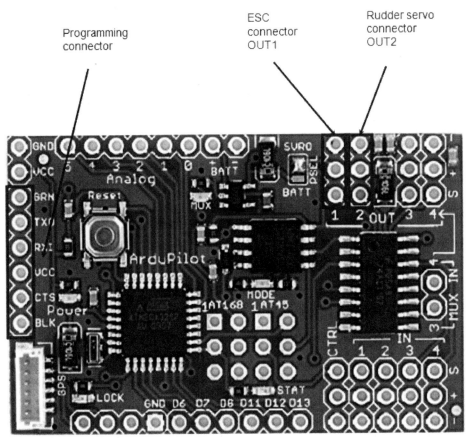

*Figure 9-36. The connectors on the ArduPilot board*

After soldering the connectors, we have to make one modification on the board (Figure 9-37). We need to do this because the board provides an RC override functionality that is indispensable when you use it as an autopilot hardware for flying platforms.

For that, a multiplexer IC is integrated on the board that is used to switch the control of the servos either to the ATmega328 microcontroller or to an RC receiver. The control of the multiplexer is done by the ATtiny microcontroller (located to the right of the ATmega328 chip), which by default switches the control to the RC receiver. For the control of the boat, we do not need this functionality. To make sure that the ATtiny does not switch the multiplexer to the wrong position, we have to give control over the multiplexer to the ATmega328. Actually there is no way to do this function with software, so we have to modify the hardware. This is simply done by lifting pin 6 of the ATtiny microprocessor that controls the multiplexer. You can do this by de-soldering the pin or by cutting it with a sharp knife. If you are familiar with SMD soldering, you may also de-solder the whole chip, because it will not be needed.

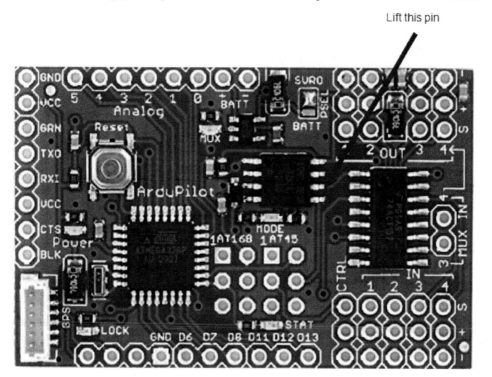

*Figure 9-37. The MUX modification*

## The Programming Adapter

You will need the adapter shown in Figure 9-38 to upload new software/waypoints to the ArduPilot board. It contains a USB to serial converter chip, so that you can connect this adapter to an USB port of your computer that runs the Arduino environment. Prior to using this adapter, you have to install the drivers for this device on your computer. Follow the instructions on the Arduino home page for the setup of the environment. The adapter that I am using comes from SparkFun electronics. You will find the product and all the documentation needed at http://www.sparkfun.com/products/9716.

*Figure 9-38. The programming adapter*

## Software and Mission Planning

As you may expect, software is a major part of any autopilot system. Because the main task of the autopilot is to hold a vehicle on a predefined course, two of its key technologies are the Global Positioning System (GPS) and microcontrollers. So before we delve into the software and mission planning, let's examine more closely one of these key technologies, the GPS.

### GPS Receivers

GPS receivers are widely available now as handheld devices the size of mobile phones or even watches. For our project, we use only the receiver hardware of such devices. They are available as OEM modules that are the size of a dollar coin and smaller. All these modules have a serial interface that transmits a data stream in the form of the National Marine Electronics Association (NMEA) protocol. NMEA has established a communication standard for the connection of marine electronic devices like logs, digital compasses, sonar, and GPS receivers. The NMEA protocol consists of ASCII "sentences" that are output from the device periodically. Each of these sentences contains various navigation information (e.g., current position, speed over ground, heading, UTC time, etc.). For our autopilot system, we need only two pieces of information from the receiver: the actual position of the boat and the direction the boat is heading in.

Some words about the behavior of GPS receivers—a GPS receiver outputs valid heading information only when it is moved with a minimum speed of about 1.5mph (3km/h). When the boat is at a standstill, or moving very slowly, the heading information of the GPS receiver is not reliable and the boat may move in the wrong direction. The behavior of different GPS receiver modules at a standstill is different, and usually the way each module exactly behaves has to be reverse-engineered. The EM406, which I use, performs well at low speeds (above 3km/h) and outputs random heading information when at a standstill. For that purpose, I let the boat go off after launch for some five seconds without any GPS control. After that time, the GPS receiver will output reliable heading data that can be fed into the autopilot software. Another good thing to know is that GPS receivers do not immediately output valid navigation data. There are several modes the receivers perform when powered up. Mainly, two modes are important to know:

- *Cold start*: This normally happens when you switch on your device after long periods without power. In this mode, modern receivers (like the EM406) need some minutes to get their first satellite fix. So don´t worry if the autopilot will not start immediately after power-on.

- *Warm start*: This happens when the receiver is already powered up and had a valid fix some hours ago. In this case, it takes some seconds to some minutes to get a valid fix. The EM406 has a capacitor on board, which holds up the internal clock oscillator and the so-called ephemeris information of the satellites for about one week.

The time for a warm start cannot be predicted, but usually one simple rule applies: the longer the time the module was powered off, the longer it takes to get the first fix.

Consider also that whenever you are testing the receiver, you should have a clear view of the sky. Indoors it will usually not work.

Some receivers have an LED on board that indicates the state of the receiver. On the EM406, the LED is on when the receiver is waiting for a valid fix, and it starts blinking when valid navigation data is available.

Now on to the software part of our autopilot system.

## The Software

The software was developed using the Arduino IDE. You should be familiar with the basics of the C programming language and with Arduino if you want to make your own modifications to the software.

In short, the software on the ArduPilot microprocessor is designed to perform the following tasks:

1. Initialize the hardware; wait until the GPS module has a valid fix, and then start the motor

2. Get the actual position and heading information from the GPS

3. Calculate the distance and bearing to the next waypoint

4. Compare the actual heading with the bearing and feed the difference to the rudder servo (this is a very simplified view of the PID algorithm, but mainly, that is it)

5. When the actual position is close to (within range of) the first waypoint, switch to the next waypoint

6. If/when the last waypoint is reached, stop the motor; if not, proceed with step 2

You can download the software from http://code.google.com/p/roboboat/downloads/list or Apress.com.

There you will find a file called AP_RoboBoat.zip. If you unzip this file, you will get all the source code files for the autopilot that runs the RoboBoat. The software is separated into six modules (Arduino tabs) and two header files. According to Arduino conventions, these files must be placed into a folder that has the same name as the main program. In this case, copy it into a folder called AP_RoboBoat. Double-click the file ending with .pde. The Arduino IDE will open and you can proceed.

In the following sections, I will briefly describe the function of the modules. These modules make up the entire autopilot software system. If you have built your boat and propulsion assembly as described in the previous sections, there should be no further modifications necessary.

## AP_RoboBoat Module

This tab contains the declaration of global variables and the two Arduino functions setup() and loop() (Listing 9-1). The function setup() does all the initialization of the hardware peripherals and waits until a first fix is available from the GPS. The function loop() contains the main program code and does all the navigation.

*Listing 9-1. AP_RoboBoat.pde*

```
/* By Chris Anderson, Jordi Munoz, modified by Harald Molle for use on model boats */
/* Nov/27/2010
/* Version 1.1 */
/* Released under an Apache 2.0 open source license*/
/* Project home page is at DIYdrones.com (and ArduPilot.com)
/* We hope you improve the code and share it with us at DIY Drones!*/


#include "defines.h"
#include "waypoints.h"

// Global variables definition
int waypoints;  // waypoint counter

unsigned int integrator_reset_counter = 0;  // counter variable (in seconds) for the
Integrator holdoff-time after a waypoint switch

byte current_wp = 0; //This variable stores the actual waypoint we are trying to reach.

int wp_bearing = 0; //Bearing to the current waypoint (in degrees)
unsigned int wp_distance = 0; // Distance to the current waypoint (in meters)

//GPS obtained information
float lat = 0; //Current Latitude
float lon = 0; //Current Longitude
unsigned long time; // curent UTC time
float ground_speed = 0;   // Speed over ground
int  course = 0;          // Course over ground
int alt = 0;              //Altitude above sea
```

```
// Flag variables
byte jumplock_wp = 0; // When switching waypoints this lock will allow only one transition.
byte gps_new_data_flag = 0; // A simple flag to know when we've got new gps data.

// rudder setpoint variable, holds the calculated value for the rudder servo
int rudder_setpoint = 0;

byte fix_position = 0; // Flag variable for valid gps position

// Arduino Startup, entry point after power-on
void setup()
{

  init_ardupilot(); // Initialize the hardware specific peripherals

  waypoints = sizeof(wps) / sizeof(LONLAT); // calculate the number of waypoints

  Init_servo(); //Initalize the servos, see "Servo_Control" tab.

  test_rudder(); //Just move the servo to see that there is something living
  bldc_arm_throttle();  // Initialize the BLDC controller

  print_header(); //print the header line on the debug channel

  delay(500);  // wait until UART Tx Buffer is surely purged

  init_startup_parameters();  // Wait for first GPS Fix

  test_rudder();   // Move rudder-servo to see that the launch-time is close

  bldc_start_throttle(); // start the motor

  delay (5000); // go the first five seconds without GPS control to get the direction vector
stabilized

  init_startup_parameters(); // re-synchronize GPS

}

// Program main loop starts here

// Arduino main loop
void loop()
{


  gps_parse_nmea(); // parse incoming NMEA Messages from GPS Module and store relevant data in
global variables

  if((gps_new_data_flag & 0x01) == 0x01)     //Checking new GPS "GPRMC" data flag in position
  {
```

```
    digitalWrite(YELLOW_LED, HIGH); // pulse the yellow LED to indicate a received GPS
sentence
    gps_new_data_flag &= (~0x01); //Clearing new data flag...
    rudder_control(); // Control function for steering the course to next waypoint
    if (integrator_reset_counter++ < WP_TIMEOUT)    // Force I and D part to zero for
WP_TIMEOUT seconds after each waypoint switch
      reset_PIDs();

    send_to_ground();   /*Print values on datalogger, if attached, just for debugging*/
  } // end if gps_new_data...


  // Ensure that the autopilot will jump ONLY ONE waypoint

    if((wp_distance < WP_RADIUS) && (jumplock_wp == 0x00)) //Checking if the waypoint distance
is less than WP_RADIUS m, and check if the lock is open
    {
      current_wp++; //Switch the waypoint
      jumplock_wp = 0x01; //Lock the waypoint switcher.
      integrator_reset_counter = 0;

      if(current_wp >= waypoints)    // Check if we've passed all the waypoints, if yes stop
motor
        finish_mission();
      } // end if wp_distance...

  digitalWrite(YELLOW_LED,LOW);  //Turning off the status LED
} // end loop ()
```

## Debug Module

This tab contains some functions for system test and integration (Listing 9-2). If you have a serial datalogger, you can use it to record the data of the PID control loop that is output every second.

*Listing 9-2. Debug.pde*

```
// PID Debug Variables
float pid_p;
float pid_i;
float pid_d;
float pid_dt;
int dbg_pid_error;

// Debugging output, sends the value of internal variables to the datalogger every second
// Floating point values are multiplied and converted to integers to get it through the
Serial.print function
void send_to_ground(void)
{
```

```
    Serial.print(course);
    Serial.print("\t");

    Serial.print((int)wp_bearing);
    Serial.print("\t");

    Serial.print(dbg_pid_error);
    Serial.print("\t");

    Serial.print(wp_distance);
    Serial.print("\t");

    Serial.print(time);
    Serial.print("\t");

    Serial.print((int)rudder_setpoint);
    Serial.print("\t");

    Serial.print((int)current_wp);
    Serial.print("\t");

    Serial.print((int)pid_p);
    Serial.print("\t");

    Serial.print((int)pid_i);
    Serial.print("\t");

    Serial.print((int)pid_d);
    Serial.print("\t");

    ground_speed *= 18.0; // Scale miles/h to km/h * 10
    Serial.print((int)ground_speed);
    Serial.print("\t");

    Serial.print(alt);

    Serial.println();

}
// Debugging output, sends the value of internal variables to the datalogger once on startup
// Floating point values are multiplied and converted to integers to get it through the
Serial.print function
void  print_header(void)
{
  // Header for the System constants
   Serial.println("KP_HEADING\t\t KI_HEADING\t\t KD_HEADING\t\t INTEGRATOR_MAX\t\t RAM");
   delay(250);
   Serial.print ((int)(KP_HEADING * 100));
   Serial.print("\t\t");
   Serial.print ((int)(KI_HEADING * 100));
   Serial.print("\t\t");
```

```
  Serial.print ((int)(KD_HEADING * 100));
  Serial.print("\t\t");
  Serial.print ((int)(INTEGRATOR_LIMIT));
  Serial.print("\t\t");
  Serial.println( ram_info() );
  delay(250);

  // header for the debugging variables
  Serial.println("Act\t Setp\t err\t Dist\t Time\t Rudd\t WP\t pid_p\t pid_i\t pid_d\t spced\t
alt");
  delay (250);
}

// function to calculate the remaining amount of RAM in Bytes
// Check always, if you have changed the Waypoint array (see the Header of the debug-output)
int ram_info()
{
  uint8_t *heapptr;
  uint8_t *stackptr;

  stackptr = (uint8_t *)malloc(4);    // use stackptr temporarily
  heapptr = stackptr;                 // save value of heap pointer
  free(stackptr);                     // free up the memory again (sets stackptr to 0)
  stackptr =  (uint8_t *)(SP);    // save value of stack pointer

  return ((int) stackptr - (int) heapptr);

}
```

## Init Module

This tab contains all initialization functions for the hardware (Listing 9-3).

*Listing 9-3. Init.pde*

```
void init_ardupilot(void)
{
  gps_init_baudrate();
  Serial.begin(9600);

  //Declaring pins

  pinMode(5,INPUT); // Mode pin (not used)
  pinMode(11,OUTPUT); // Simulator Output pin (not used)
  pinMode(MUX_PIN,OUTPUT);  //MUX pin, applies only to modified Hardware !
  pinMode(BLUE_LED,OUTPUT); // LOCK LED pin in ardupilot board, indicates valid GPS data
  pinMode(YELLOW_LED,OUTPUT);// Status LED, blinks, when valid satellite fix data is received
  pinMode(SERVO1_IN_PIN,INPUT); // Throttle input from RC Rx (only used for RC control)
```

```
    pinMode(SERVO2_IN_PIN,INPUT); // Rudder input from RC Rx  (only used for RC control)

#ifdef RADIO_CONTROL
    init_RC_control();          // Initialize Radio control
#endif

    switch_to_ardupilot();      // default servo control by Ardupilot
}

void init_startup_parameters(void)
{
    //yeah a do-while loop, checks over and over again until we have valid GPS position and lat
is diferent from zero.
    //I re-verify the Lat because sometimes fails and sets home lat as zero. This way never goes
wrong..
    do
    {
      gps_parse_nmea(); //Reading and parsing GPS data
    }
    while(((fix_position < 0x01) || (lat == 0)));

    //Another verification
    gps_new_data_flag=0;

    do
    {
      gps_parse_nmea(); //Reading and parsing GPS data
    }
    while((gps_new_data_flag&0x01 != 0x01) & (gps_new_data_flag&0x02 != 0x02));
    rudder_control(); //I've put this here because i need to calculate the distance to the next
waypoint, otherwise it will start at waypoint 2.
}
```

## Navigation Module

This tab is one of the most important of the autopilot (Listing 9-4). It contains the so called "NMEA-parser," which decodes the data from the GPS module and stores it in global variables. The tab also contains the functions that calculate the bearing angle and the distance to the next waypoint.

*Listing 9-4. Navigation.pde*

```
// Variables used by the NMEA Parser
char buffer[90]; //Serial buffer to catch GPS data
/*GPS Pointers*/
char *token;
char *search = ",";
char *brkb, *pEnd;
```

```
/*************************************************************************
 * This functions parses the NMEA strings...
 * Pretty complex but never fails and works well with all GPS modules and baud speeds.. :-)
 * Just change the Serial.begin() value in the first tab for higher baud speeds
 *************************************************************************/

void gps_parse_nmea(void)
{
  const char head_rmc[]="GPRMC"; //GPS NMEA header to look for
  const char head_gga[]="GPGGA"; //GPS NMEA header to look for

  static byte unlock=1; //some kind of event flag
  static byte checksum=0; //the checksum generated
  static byte checksum_received=0; //Checksum received
  static byte counter=0; //general counter

  //Temporary variables for some tasks, specially used in the GPS parsing part
  unsigned long temp=0;
  unsigned long temp2=0;
  unsigned long temp3=0;


  while(Serial.available() > 0)
  {
    if(unlock==0)
    {
      buffer[0]=Serial.read();//puts a byte in the buffer

      if(buffer[0]=='$')//Verify if is the preamble $
      {
        unlock=1;
      }
    }
    /************************************************/
    else
    {
      buffer[counter]=Serial.read();

      if(buffer[counter]==0x0A)//Looks for \F
      {

        unlock=0;

        if (strncmp (buffer, head_rmc, 5) == 0)    // $GPRMC parsing starts here
        {
          /*Generating and parsing received checksum, */
          for(int x=0; x<100; x++)
          {
            if(buffer[x]=='*')
```

```
            {
              checksum_received=strtol(&buffer[x+1],NULL,16);//Parsing received checksum...
              break;
            }
            else
            {
              checksum ^= buffer[x]; //XOR the received data...
            }
          }

          if(checksum_received == checksum)//Checking checksum
          {
            /* Token will point to the data between comma "'", returns the data in the order
received */
            /*THE GPRMC order is: UTC, UTC status ,Lat, N/S indicator, Lon, E/W indicator,
speed, course, date, mode, checksum*/
            token = strtok_r(buffer, search, &brkb); //Contains the header GPRMC, not used

            token = strtok_r(NULL, search, &brkb); //UTC Time, not used
            time = atol (token);
            token = strtok_r(NULL, search, &brkb); //Valid UTC data? maybe not used...


            //Longitude in degrees, decimal minutes. (ej. 4750.1234 degrees decimal minutes =
47.835390 decimal degrees)
            //Where 47 are degrees and 50 the minutes and .1234 the decimals of the minutes.
            //To convert to decimal degrees, divide the minutes by 60 (including decimals),
            //Example: "50.1234/60=.835390", then add the degrees, ex: "47+.835390=47.835390"
decimal degrees
            token = strtok_r(NULL, search, &brkb); //Contains Latitude in degrees decimal
minutes...

            // Serial.println(token);

            //taking only degrees, and minutes without decimals,
            //strtol stop parsing till reach the decimal point "." result example 4750,
eliminates .1234
            temp = strtol (token, &pEnd, 10);

            //takes only the decimals of the minutes
            //result example 1234.
            temp2 = strtol (pEnd + 1, NULL, 10);

            //joining degrees, minutes, and the decimals of minute, now without the point...
            //Before was 4750.1234, now the result example is 47501234...
            temp3 = (temp * 10000) + (temp2);


            //modulo to leave only the decimal minutes, eliminating only the degrees..
            //Before was 47501234, the result example is 501234.
            temp3 = temp3 % 1000000;
```

```
                //Dividing to obtain only the degrees, before was 4750
                //The result example is 47 (4750/100=47)
                temp /= 100;

                //Joining everything and converting to float variable...
                //First i convert the decimal minutes to degrees decimals stored in "temp3",
example: 501234/600000= .835390
                //Then i add the degrees stored in "temp" and add the result from the first step,
example 47+.835390=47.835390
                //The result is stored in "lat" variable...
                lat=temp + ( (float)temp3 / 600000 );


                token = strtok_r(NULL, search, &brkb); //lat, north or south?
                //If the char is equal to S (south), multiply the result by -1..
                if(*token == 'S')
                {
                  lat = lat * -1;
                }

                //This the same procedure use in lat, but now for Lon....
                token = strtok_r(NULL, search, &brkb);

                // Serial.println(token);

                temp = strtol (token, &pEnd, 10);
                temp2 = strtol (pEnd + 1, NULL, 10);
                temp3 = (temp * 10000) + (temp2);
                temp3 = temp3 % 1000000;
                temp /= 100;
                lon=temp + ((float)temp3 / 600000);

                token = strtok_r(NULL, search, &brkb); //lon, east or west?
                if(*token == 'W')
                {
                  lon=lon * -1;
                }

                token = strtok_r(NULL, search, &brkb); //Speed overground?
                ground_speed = atof(token);

                token = strtok_r(NULL, search, &brkb); //Course?
                course= atoi(token);

                gps_new_data_flag |= 0x01; //Update the flag to indicate the new data has arrived.

                jumplock_wp=0x00;//clearing waypoint lock..

            }
          checksum=0;
        } //End of the GPRMC parsing
```

```
      if (strncmp (buffer,head_gga,5) == 0)   // $GPGGA parsing starts here
      {
        /*Generating and parsing received checksum, */
        for(int x=0; x<100; x++)
        {
          if(buffer[x] == '*')
          {
            checksum_received = strtol(&buffer[x+1], NULL, 16);//Parsing received
checksum...
            break;
          }
          else
          {
            checksum ^= buffer[x]; //XOR the received data...
          }
        }

        if(checksum_received == checksum)//Checking checksum
        {
          token = strtok_r(buffer, search, &brkb);//GPGGA header, not used anymore
          token = strtok_r(NULL, search, &brkb);//UTC, not used!!
          token = strtok_r(NULL, search, &brkb);//lat, not used!!
          token = strtok_r(NULL, search, &brkb);//north/south, nope...
          token = strtok_r(NULL, search, &brkb);//lon, not used!!
          token = strtok_r(NULL, search, &brkb);//wets/east, nope
          token = strtok_r(NULL, search, &brkb);//Position fix, used!!
          fix_position = atoi(token);
          token = strtok_r(NULL, search, &brkb); //sats in use!! Nein...
          token = strtok_r(NULL, search, &brkb);//HDOP, not needed
          token = strtok_r(NULL, search, &brkb);//ALTITUDE, is the only meaning of this
string.. in meters of course.
          alt = atoi(token);
          if(alt < 0)
          {
            alt = 0;
          }

          if(fix_position >= 0x01)
            digitalWrite(BLUE_LED,HIGH); //Status LED...
          else
            digitalWrite(BLUE_LED,LOW);

          gps_new_data_flag |= 0x02; //Update the flag to indicate the new data has arrived.
        }
        checksum=0; //Restarting the checksum
      } // end of $GPGGA parsing

      for(int a=0; a<=counter; a++)//restarting the buffer
      {
        buffer[a]=0;
      }
```

```
        counter=0; //Restarting the counter
      }
      else
      {
        counter++; //Incrementing counter
      }
    }
  }

}
/***********************************************************************
 * //Function to calculate the course between two waypoints
 * //I'm using the real formulas--no lookup table fakes!
 ***********************************************************************/
int get_gps_course(float flat1, float flon1, float flat2, float flon2)
{
  float calc;
  float bear_calc;

  float x = 69.1 * (flat2 - flat1);
  float y = 69.1 * (flon2 - flon1) * cos(flat1/57.3);

  calc=atan2(y,x);

  bear_calc= degrees(calc);

  if(bear_calc<=1){
    bear_calc=360+bear_calc;
  }
  return bear_calc;
}


/***********************************************************************
 * //Function to calculate the distance between two waypoints
 * //I'm using the real formulas
 ***********************************************************************/
unsigned int get_gps_dist(float flat1, float flon1, float flat2, float flon2)
{

    float x = 69.1 * (flat2 - flat1);
    float y = 69.1 * (flon2 - flon1) * cos(flat1/57.3);

    return (float)sqrt((float)(x*x) + (float)(y*y))*1609.344;
}

/***********************************************************************/
//Computes heading the error, and choose the shortest way to reach the desired heading
/***********************************************************************/
int compass_error(int PID_set_Point, int PID_current_Point)
{
    float PID_error=0;//Temporary variable
```

```
    if(fabs(PID_set_Point-PID_current_Point) > 180)
        {
                if(PID_set_Point-PID_current_Point < -180)
                {
                  PID_error=(PID_set_Point+360)-PID_current_Point;
                }
                else
                {
                  PID_error=(PID_set_Point-360)-PID_current_Point;
                }
        }
        else
        {
          PID_error=PID_set_Point-PID_current_Point;
        }

        return PID_error;
}

// This function stops all activity and will never return
// This is the end...
void finish_mission(void)
{
  bldc_stop_throttle();

#ifdef RADIO_CONTROL
    switch_to_radio(); // Give control back to Radio
#endif

  while (1)      // loop forever, if timeout reached (and start to swim and recover the boat)
  {
    digitalWrite(YELLOW_LED,LOW); // Fast flashing Yellow LED to indicate arrival
    delay(100);
    digitalWrite(YELLOW_LED,HIGH);
    delay(100);
  }
}


/***************************************************************************
 * rudder Control, reads gps info, calculates navigation, executes PID and sends values to the
servo..
 ***************************************************************************/
void rudder_control(void)
{

  wp_bearing=get_gps_course(lat, lon, wps[current_wp].lat, wps[current_wp].lon);//Calculating
Bearing, this function is located in the GPS_Navigation tab..

  wp_distance = get_gps_dist(lat, lon, wps[current_wp].lat, wps[current_wp].lon);
//Calculating Distance, this function is located in the GPS_Navigation tab..
```

```
    rudder_setpoint = MIDDLE_RUDDER+PID_heading(compass_error(wp_bearing, course)); //Central
Position + PID(compass_error(desired course, current course)).

    pulse_servo_rudder((long)rudder_setpoint);   //Sending values to servo, 90 degrees is central
position.

}



// This function switches the EM406 into 9600 Baud
// Normally, the EM406 defaults to NMEA and 4800 Baud after long power-OFF times

void gps_init_baudrate(void)
{
    Serial.begin(4800); // Always try in 4800 Baud first.
    delay(100);
    Serial.println("$PSRF100,1,9600,8,1,0*0D"); //  command to switch SIRFIII to NMEA, 9600,
8, N, 1
    delay(100);
    Serial.begin(9600);   // switch finally back to 9600 Baud

}
```

## PID_control Module

This tab contains the function that does the control loop for the straight line navigation (Listing 9-5). This is one of the most important modules, because it uses a PID algorithm that is implemented in a very simple manner. The behavior of the PID loop is controlled by constants that are described in the section "The PID Constants."

*Listing 9-5. PID_Control.pde*

```
//PID loop variables
int heading_previous_error;
float heading_I = 0.0;                   //Stores the result of the integrator

/*******************************************************************************
 * PID= P+I+D This function only works, when GPS with one second update is used.
 ************************************************************/
int PID_heading(int PID_error)
{
  static float heading_D; //Stores the result of the derivator
  static float heading_output; //Stores the result of the PID loop
```

```
    dbg_pid_error = PID_error; // deBug


    heading_I += (float)PID_error;

    heading_I = constrain(heading_I, -INTEGRATOR_LIMIT, INTEGRATOR_LIMIT); //Limit the PID
  integrator...

    //Derivation part
    heading_D = ((float)PID_error - (float)heading_previous_error);

    heading_output = 0.0;//Clearing the variable.

    heading_output = (KP_HEADING * (float)PID_error);  //Proportional part, is just the KP
  constant * error.. and adding to the output
    pid_p = (KP_HEADING * (float)PID_error);

    heading_output += (KI_HEADING * heading_I);  //Adding integrator result...
    pid_i = (KI_HEADING * heading_I);

    heading_output += (KD_HEADING * heading_D);// /Adding derivator result....
    pid_d = (KD_HEADING * heading_D);


    //Adds all the PID results and limit the output...
    heading_output = constrain(heading_output, (float)HEADING_MIN,
  (float)HEADING_MAX);//limiting the output....

    heading_previous_error = PID_error;//Saving the actual error to use it later (in derivating
  part)...

    //Now checking if the user have selected normal or reverse mode (servo)...
    if(REVERSE_RUDDER == 1)
    {
      return (int)(-1 * heading_output);
    }
    else
    {
      return (int)(heading_output);
    }
  }

  /*************************************************************************
   * Reset all the PIDs
   *************************************************************************/
  void reset_PIDs(void)
  {
    heading_previous_error = 0.0;
    heading_I = 0.0;
  }
```

# Servo_control Module

This tab contains the functions that output the pulses to the rudder servo and to the ESC for the motor (Listing 9-6). This module uses the pulse width modulation (PWM) unit of the AVR microcontroller that is used on all Arduino platforms.

*Listing 9-6. Servo_control.pde*

```
/**********************************************************
* Configuring the PWM hadware... If you want to understand this,
*  you must read the Data Sheet of atmega168..
* The following functionsare optimized for speed. The Arduino Servo library
* may not work, because it consumes more processing time than this ones
**********************************************************/

void Init_servo(void)//This part will configure the PWM to control the servo 100% by hardware,
and not waste CPU time..
{
  digitalWrite(RUDDER,LOW);//Defining servo output pins
  pinMode(RUDDER,OUTPUT);
  digitalWrite(THROTTLE,LOW);
  pinMode(THROTTLE,OUTPUT);

  /*Timer 1 settings for fast PWM*/
  //Note: these strange strings that follow, like OCRI1A, are actually predefined Atmega168
registers.
  // We load the registers and the chip does the rest.

    //Remember the registers not declared here remain zero by default...
  TCCR1A =((1<<WGM11)|(1<<COM1B1)|(1<<COM1A1)); //Please read page 131 of DataSheet, we are
changing the registers settings of WGM11,COM1B1,COM1A1 to 1 thats all...
  TCCR1B = (1<<WGM13)|(1<<WGM12)|(1<<CS11); //Prescaler set to 8, that give us a resolution of
2us, read page 134 of data sheet
  OCR1A = 2000; //the period of servo 1, remember 2us resolution, 2000/2 = 1000us the pulse
period of the servo...
  OCR1B = 3000; //the period of servo 2, 3000/2=1500 us, more or less is the central
position...
  ICR1 = 40000; //50hz freq...Datasheet says  (system_freq/prescaler)/target frequency. So
(16000000hz/8)/50hz=40000,
  //must be 50hz because is the servo standard (every 20 ms, and 1hz = 1sec) 1000ms/20ms=50hz,
elementary school stuff...
}

/**********************************************************
 * Function to pulse the throttle servo
 **********************************************************/
void pulse_servo_throttle(long angle)//Will convert the angle to the equivalent servo
position...
{
  //angle=constrain(angle,180,0);
```

```
  OCR1A = ((angle * (MAX16_THROTTLE - MIN16_THROTTLE)) / 180L + MIN16_THROTTLE) * 2L;

}


/*************************************************************
 * Function to pulse the yaw/rudder servo...
 *************************************************************/
void pulse_servo_rudder(long angle) // converts the angle to the equivalent servo position...
{
 OCR1B = ((angle  *(MAX16_RUDDER - MIN16_RUDDER)) / 180L + MIN16_RUDDER) * 2L;
}


void bldc_arm_throttle(void) // "arm" the BLDC controller for the throttle
{
  delay(2000);
  bldc_stop_throttle();  // then switch to approx. zero, Servo controller armed
  delay(4000);
}


void bldc_start_throttle(void)  // brushless Motor (Multiplex controller)
{
  pulse_servo_throttle(MOTOR_SPEED); // set Motor speed
}

// function to stop the Motor    // brushless Motor (Multiplex controller)
void bldc_stop_throttle(void)
{
  pulse_servo_throttle(MOTOR_OFF);  // switch to approx. zero
}

void test_rudder(void)
{
  pulse_servo_rudder(MIDDLE_RUDDER + HEADING_MIN);
  delay(1500);
  pulse_servo_rudder(MIDDLE_RUDDER + HEADING_MAX);
  delay(1500);
  pulse_servo_rudder(MIDDLE_RUDDER);
  delay(1500);
}


// Module to control the ArduPilot via Radio Control (RC)
// You have to use an RC equipment, that supports a failsafe functionality
// e.g. if the Transmitter is switched OFF, on the receiver channel there should be
// "silence" (either HIGH or LOW level)
// I actually have tested this with a 2.4GHZ SPEKTRUM System.
// Analog Systems may always output some pulses due to erroneous received signals
// My cheap 27MHz Radio control did not work
// Please check thoroughly, before you make you first start!
```

```
// Function to Check, if there are pulses on the Rx rudder Input

// I took the rudder channel, because on the SPEKTRUM, the failsafe function
// outputs pulses on the throttle channel (default speed), when the Transmitter is OFF.
// This function checks for "silence" on the rudder channel.
// If there is silence, the Transmitter is switched OFF and the control should be given to
// the ArduPilot



// Return 0 if no pulse available (timeout > 25ms)
int check_radio(void)
{
  return (int) pulseIn(SERVO2_IN_PIN, HIGH, 25000); // Check, if there are pulses on the Rx
rudder Input;
}


// Function to switch the Multiplexer to the ArduPilot
void switch_to_ardupilot (void)
{
  digitalWrite(MUX_PIN,HIGH);  //  servos controlled by Ardupilot
}

// Function to switch the Multiplexer to the RC Receiver
void switch_to_radio (void)
{
  digitalWrite(MUX_PIN,LOW);  //  servos controlled by Radio control

}
```

## Header Files

To adapt the software to your special needs, there are two additional header files that are called defines.h and waypoints.h. The defines.h file contains all constants that can be modified to your needs. I will describe them in depth next. The waypoints.h file contains a predefined constant array that holds the latitude and longitude coordinates of the path that the boat shall follow (this file is further discussed in the section "Mission Planning").

Please refer to http://code.google.com/p/roboboat/downloads/list or Apress.com for the downloadable files.

# Installing the Software

To load the software to the ArduPilot board, you will need the following:

- A PC or Mac computer that runs the Arduino IDE; you can download the most recent version of this development environment from the site www.arduino.cc.

- An FTDI breakout board from SparkFun with the USB cable

- A power supply for the ArduPilot board, a battery pack, and an ESC without a motor

- A folder that contains the autopilot software; remember that the folder must have the same name as the main program.

After you have all the prerequisites ready, you can perform the following procedures:

- Install the Arduino IDE.

- Configure the Arduino IDE.

- Compile and upload the code.

- Customize the code (optional.

## Installing the Arduino IDE

Prior to starting the Arduino IDE, you have to install the drivers for the USB to serial converter and then you have to tell Arduino which serial port it shall use to communicate with the board. The procedure for that is described in depth for the various operating systems on the "getting started" part of the Arduino site: http://arduino.cc/en/Guide/HomePage.

After double-clicking the AP_RoboBoat.pde file, the Arduino IDE should start up and you should see a screen that looks like Figure 9-39.

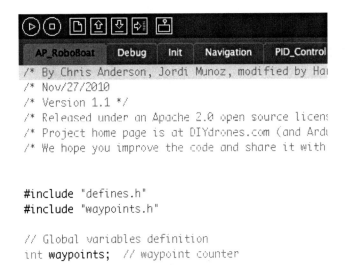

```
/* By Chris Anderson, Jordi Munoz, modified by Ha
/* Nov/27/2010
/* Version 1.1 */
/* Released under an Apache 2.0 open source licen
/* Project home page is at DIYdrones.com (and Ard
/* We hope you improve the code and share it with


#include "defines.h"
#include "waypoints.h"

// Global variables definition
int waypoints;  // waypoint counter
```

**Figure 9-39.** *Screenshot of the Arduino IDE*

## Configuring the Arduino IDE

After having successfully installed the Arduino IDE, you have to tell Arduino which type of board you are using. The ArduPilot uses a ATmega328 microprocessor on it, and the board comes close to the "Arduino Duemillanove Board." Please select Arduino Duemilanove w/ATmega328 in the Arduino IDE Tools menu, as shown in Figure 9-40.

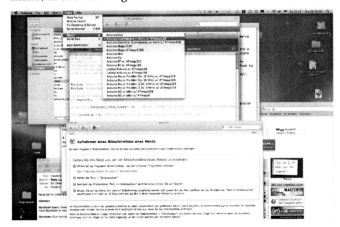

**Figure 9-40.** *Selecting the hardware*

## Compiling and Uploading the Code

Now you should be ready to upload the code to the board. If you have already loaded the AP_RoboBoat into the Arduino IDE, you simply have to press the upload button and the IDE will begin to compile the source code and start the upload automatically (Figure 9-41). You can see this on the fast flashing red and green LEDs on the USB to serial converter (Figure 9-42).

Upload Button

*Figure 9-41. The upload button in the Arduino IDE*

*Figure 9-42. Connecting the ArduPilot with the programming adapter*

If the upload was OK, you are ready to do the first tests with the boat, which are described in the "Integrating the System" section.

## Customizing the Code

Normally, you do not have to make changes in the code itself, if you have done all steps according to the description in this chapter. However, if you want to customize the software to your needs, you have to modify the defines.h header file. I have put all relevant system constants into this file, and I will give a short description of some of the most important settings. In the following six sections, I'll describe all the relevant settings in this file.

## Customizing the Rudder Control

There is one constant that controls the "polarity" of the rudder movements. If you have built the propulsion assembly as described in this book, there is no need to change this directive (the default value is 1):

```
#define REVERSE_RUDDER 1 // normal = 0 and reverse = 1
```
Another constant controls the middle position of the rudder servo:

```
#define MIDDLE_RUDDER 90  // central position of rudder servo in degrees, adjust for trim•
corrections if necessary
```

With this constant, you can fine-adjust the middle position of the servo. If you are using fixed pushrods that cannot be adjusted, you can use this directive to adjust the middle position of your assembly. Keep in mind that this works only for small changes in the range of +- 10°. As a part of the initialization process, the software first moves the rudder to its maximum extents and then re-positions it to the middle position. So you can see where the middle position really is.

## Customizing the PID Constants

The following constants are the most critical and control the stability of the boat:

```
#define KP_HEADING 2.0     // proportional part of PID control
#define KI_HEADING 0.07    // integrator part of PID control
#define KD_HEADING 0.00001 // derivator part of PID control (not used)
```

The software uses a proportional-integrator-derivator (PID) control-loop algorithm for the stabilization of the course. I will not go into depth about control-loop theory, but there are some things you should know: the KP_HEADING controls the "gain" of the difference between the setpoint and the actual course. If you increase this value, the boat will react more directly to changes in direction and is likely to oscillate. If you decrease this value, the curves will get longer and the boat will react more slowly to changes in direction. A value between 1.0 and 2.0 should be OK if you have constructed the boat as described earlier. The KI_HEADING controls the integrator part of the algorithm, and it will add long-term stability, offset correction, and precision to the course. Be very careful when modifying this parameter; values that are too high may result in recovery swimming!

The derivator part is normally used to react to fast changes, but this will not work for the type of boat we are using. What we are using for the boat is only the PI part; therefore the KD_HEADING value is set close to zero.

## Customizing the Motor Speed

The following constant sets the speed for the propulsion motor. It heavily depends on the ESC/motor/propeller/battery combination that you are using. The value is in virtual "degrees" because we are using the same functions that control an RC servo that lies in the range of 0° to +180°. With the combination that I am actually using, the setting of 80 yields a thrust of about 500g.

```
#define MOTOR_SPEED 80  // around 5A with Roxxy Outrunner
```

## Customizing the Waypoint Timeout

The following constant has to do with the optimization of the straight-line behavior of the ship. As mentioned earlier, we are using a PI control loop. This is not the whole truth. The integrator part can drift away when the boat has to perform a turn (usually when switching from one waypoint to another). And so it can take a while for the boat to recover a straight line. To optimize for that, the integrator part of the algorithm is forced to zero for some seconds after a waypoint switch, which in turn makes the control loop a simple proportional type for some seconds. With the actual setting, the integral part of the control loop (which gives the precision) starts about 50m after the waypoint. Note that if you have set your waypoints too close to each other, you will end up with a P-type controller.

```
#define WP_TIMEOUT 15 // Waypoint Timeout counter value in seconds
```

## Customizing the Waypoint Radius

The following constant is necessary, because the measurement accuracy of the GPS and the overall precision of the boat is not absolutely exact. To avoid the boat circling endlessly around a waypoint, a switch to the next waypoint is actuated when the boat is in a perimeter of WP_RADIUS of the actual waypoint. I have used a value in the range of 10 to 20 meters, which will give good results.

```
#define WP_RADIUS 15  // Radius for waypoint-hit in m
```

## Customizing the Rudder Extents

The following two constants define the maximum extend in degrees that the servo can travel around the MIDDLE_RUDDER setting. This setting also defines the minimum radius the boat can achieve on a turn.

```
#define   HEADING_MAX 60  // Servo max position in degrees
#define   HEADING_MIN -60 // Servo min position in degrees
```

---

■ **Note** Normally there is no need to change these constants. You should first be familiar with the code if you want to change the settings for the optimization and customization of your system because any changes may lead to strange behavior of the boat!

---

The next big step is "mission planning," which is the part where you direct your boat where it should go and (hopefully) where it has to come back to.

# Mission Planning

So far so good, but how do we tell the autopilot where to go?

The mission of the boat can be seen as a list of waypoints the boat tries to reach. A waypoint is represented in a WGS84 latitude/longitude format, which is common to most GPS receivers and geographical information systems like Google Earth. The latitude and longitude values are expressed in degrees. The latitude starts at the equator, goes up north to +90° at the north pole, and goes down south to the south pole to -90°. The longitude starts with 0° at Greenwich (which is a small town in the vicinity of London, England, where the royal observatory is placed), goes east with positive values up to +180°, and goes west with negative values to -180°. Usually, for navigation, the coordinates are expressed in degrees, minutes, and seconds. What we will use in the software is a floating point format, where the coordinates are represented in decimal degrees, which makes it easier to calculate with.

The waypoint coordinates are stored in a constant array that can be found in the `waypoints.h` file, which is part of the ArduPilot code. To plan a new mission, you have to simply copy the new waypoint coordinates to that array, recompile the code, and download it to the board.

Here is an example (found in the file `waypoints.h`) with three waypoints that represent a triangular course in a lake in southern Germany.

```
LONLAT wps[] =
{
10.021409,  48.350234,
10.020944,  48.350475,
10.021905,  48.350598  /* Home*/
};
```

In this example, the first value (10.021409) is the longitude of the first waypoint, the second value (48.350234) is the latitude of the first waypoint, the third value (10.020944) is the longitude of the second waypoint, and so on.

The last waypoint should be chosen very close to the shoreline of the lake. After reaching this waypoint, the software of the autopilot switches the motor off, and the boat will (hopefully) glide the last meters to the shoreline without propulsion.

After the startup of the code, the waypoints are copied into the RAM of the microcontroller. The ATmega328 has only 2KB of RAM, so the amount of waypoints that can be stored is limited. The two float values of one waypoint consume 8 bytes of RAM. I suggest not using more than 100 waypoints for a single mission (which is a lot).

## Employing Google Earth for the Coordinates

There are many ways to get the coordinates of the mission. The one that I actually prefer is Google Earth. The use of this program is free; it runs on PC, Mac, and LINUX platforms, and the accuracy of the satellite images is usually in the range of a few meters. The program can be downloaded from `www.google.com/earth`.

To plan a mission with Google Earth, you simply have to create a path. This is done by clicking the path icon on the command bar (Figure 9-43). You can then add waypoints to the path by simply clicking the places you want to go (Figure 9-44).

The „create path" button in Google Earth

*Figure 9-43. Create path button in Google Earth*

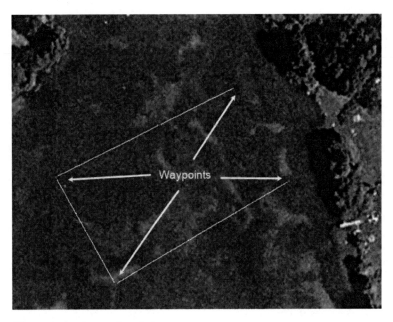

*Figure 9-44. A sample mission*

If you have finished, give the path a name and store it as a .kml file. This is done by right-clicking the name of the created path on the side navigation bar of Google Earth and selecting "save location as". It is important to choose .kml as the file format, because this format is based on the XML language and can be easily edited with a text editor.

Next, you have to open the .kml file with a text editor of your choice. A typical .kml file will look like Figure 9-45.

```
<?xml version="1.0" encoding="UTF-8"?>
<kml xmlns="http://www.opengis.net/kml/2.2" xmlns:gx="http://www.google.com/kml/ext/2.2"
xmlns:kml="http://www.opengis.net/kml/2.2" xmlns:atom="http://www.w3.org/2005/Atom">
<Document>
        <name>Test mit Lineal.kml</name>
        <Style id="sn_ylw-pushpin">
                <LineStyle>
                        <color>ff0000ff</color>
                        <width>2</width>
                </LineStyle>
                <PolyStyle>
                        <fill>0</fill>
                </PolyStyle>
        </Style>
        <Placemark>
                <name>Test mit Lineal</name>                     The coordinates of the waypoints
                <styleUrl>#sn_ylw-pushpin</styleUrl>
                <LineString>
                        <tessellate>1</tessellate>
                        <coordinates>
                                10.02109518987307,48.35076100306986,0
        10.02003617743083,48.35030483570462,0 10.02033731414647,48.34998321856332,0
        10.02158407280307,48.35026252663885,0
                        </coordinates>
                </LineString>
        </Placemark>
</Document>
</kml>
```

*Figure 9-45. Inside a .kml file*

The only thing that we need is the coordinates that are placed between the `<coordinates>` and the `</coordinates>` tags. Copy those coordinates and paste them into a new file. The coordinates are in the format longitude, latitude, altitude. The altitude is usually 0 and that value must be deleted. Format the values so that the lon/lat pairs are each in one line.

If you have finished your editing, the file should look like this:

```
10.02109518987307,48.35076100306986,
10.02003617743083,48.35030483570462,
10.02033731414647,48.34998321856332,
10.02158407280307,48.35026252663885
```

Google Earth creates a lot of positions after the decimal point. Arduino uses only five to six, but this is of no concern, because the compiler will format it to the appropriate floating point representation.

After you have finished the editing, you have to copy and paste it into the array that is defined in the `waypoints.h` tab.

Your result should then look like this:

```
LONLAT wps[] =
{
10.02109518987307,48.35076100306986,
10.02003617743083,48.35030483570462,
10.02033731414647,48.34998321856332,
10.02158407280307,48.35026252663885
};
```

After that step, you must recompile the code and upload it to the board—you only have to press the upload button, as already described earlier.

If all of the foregoing steps have been done, you can start the integration of all components, which will be described in the next chapter.

# Putting It All Together

After having fabricated the hulls, the deck, and the propulsion assembly, and integrated the electronics with the software, the time has come to put all pieces of the whole system together. The professionals call this step the "system integration." Some advice in advance: What we are doing is a hobby project with RC model parts. Some of these parts are not toys and can harm people. Please be extremely careful when following these guidelines.

- The battery pack should be handled with care. Do not shortcut the leads; this can happen when you have to solder the power connector to the cables that come out of the battery pack. LiPo batteries can deliver very high currents when shorted, and this may cause a fire or severe burns. When soldering, always isolate the copper leads with sticky tape. As already mentioned, the charging of the battery pack should always be done outdoors or in a controlled area. The charger must support cell balancing. Please carefully read the instructions that come with the charger.

- The next source of trouble can be the motor. A BLDC motor is very powerful. Before connecting it to the ArduPilot board, be sure that you have secured all screws that hold the motor. If the motor starts vibrating, e.g., when one of the screws gets loose, the other screws will follow in fractions of a second. A drop of glue on the threads will be sufficient to avoid that problem. Also, for your first experience with the motor, make it without a propeller. After you have mounted the propeller, keep away from it! The blades are very sharp and can injure you very quickly.

- When operating the whole propulsion assembly, be sure to have it fixed to something rigid like a table or the boat´s deck.

- The whole assembly will turn arbitrarily when you operate the electronics at a standstill. Keep things away from the turning point of the motor assembly. Secure the cables with a tie-wrap to the PVC tube. If the cables get into the propeller, this may ruin the motor (and the rest of your day).

- When you operate the boat in the water, be sure that no one is in the water. According to Murphy´s law, you can be sure that the boat will hit the one swimmer that is in the water. Believe me—I know what I am talking about! An assembly with around 3kg of weight has a very high impulse when running at 10km/h and crashing into a person. On land, this may only be painful; in the water, it can be lethal!

- Ask the owner of the water whether you can let an unguided boat run there.

- Add a main power switch between the battery back, and make it easily accessible. This may help to switch the whole system off very fast when something unexpected happens (and it surely will).

---

▓ **Note** I did not describe the housing of the electronics. It is up to you to find your own way to encapsulate the electronics and to make it splash-proof. I have used a lunchbox that can be found in most kitchens (be sure to inform the head of your household prior to drilling some holes in one of her (his) beloved Tupperware boxes). The ESC may get hot; put it in a vented place. I have coated mine with silicone rubber to make it waterproof and put it in "free air" outside of the lunchbox.

---

## Integrating the System

Now let's walk through the integration step by step:

1. Connect the hulls to the deck with four M5 screws, as already described in the section "Hull Assembly."

2. Mount the propulsion assembly to the aft of the deck by four M5 screws. Use butterfly nuts for convenience. Do not forget to put the rectangular plywood washers under the butterfly nuts. Secure the cables from the motor so that they cannot interfere with the propeller. I have fixed the cables to the PVC tube with a tie-wrap.

3. Connect the ESC and the servo cable to the ArduPilot board (Figure 9-46). The ground lead is usually black or brown and points to the edge of the PCB.

*Figure 9-46. Connection of the ESC to the ArduPilot board*

4.　Connect the GPS module to the ArduPilot board. Be sure to have the programming adapter disconnected, because the GPS shares the same port and if both are connected, it will not work.

5.　Connect the three motor cables to the ESC. If the motor turns in the wrong direction, simply swap two cables.

6.　Triple-verify all of the connections. If you have put everything together correctly, the wiring should look like Figure 9-47.

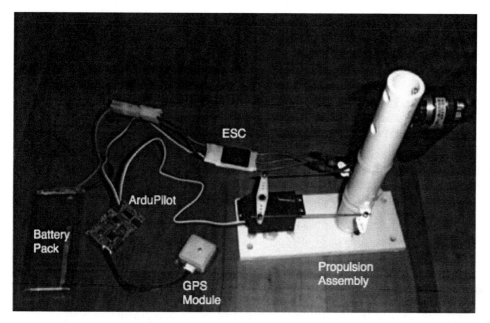

*Figure 9-47. The whole system together*

7. Go outdoors and connect the battery pack. If it is connected correctly, the following should happen:

  • On the ArduPilot board, two red LEDs should be on.

  • The red LED on the GPS module should be on.

  • The servo should turn to the maximum extent and then return to the middle position.

  • After some minutes, the LED on the GPS module should start to blink, and at the same time the blue LED on the ArduPilot board should be on.

  • The motor should start some seconds later.

  • The servo should perform arbitrary movements.

8. If all of the foregoing checks out, the system is now fully operative and you can safely turn off the power.

## Ships Ahoy!

Now, it's time to put the boat into the water. There is always a thrill when doing this for the first time. To avoid unwanted side effects, here are some hints that may be helpful:

- Have your swimsuit ready. If you own a pair of fins, take them with you. If you have a boat (I mean a real one, not an RC model) or you know somebody who owns one, the better. A neoprene suit may be helpful in cold water.
- For the first start, I suggest attaching a fishing line with a length of at least 100m to the aft of the hulls and placing the waypoints some 50m away from the launchpoint. The fishing line may make the boat slower, but you can test if the boat finds its waypoints, and if something unexpected happens, you can pull the boat back without the need to swim. Let the spool of the fishing line flow free, and don´t forget to attach the end of the line to the spool.
- If you have a laptop computer, take it with you; you may need it to adjust the values of the PID controller. If you have planned your mission with Google Earth, be sure to have the region of your mission in the cache. With that, Google Earth also works without a connection to the Internet and you can do a new plan even on very remote sites.

## Troubleshooting

If you have trouble getting it all to work, the following are a couple of basic troubleshooting guidelines. Additionally, there are some helpful hints on this project's web site: http://code.google.com/p/roboboat/.

Please have a look at this site to get updated with the last news and software revisions.

### The Thrust of the Motor/Propeller Is Not Sufficient

This can have more than one reason. First check if the propeller is mounted the right way. If you are using a normal (non-reversed) one, the side with the markings of the propeller should point toward the motor´s body (to the front of the boat). The motor should turn clockwise if viewed from behind, as shown in Figure 9-48.

*Figure 9-48. The turning direction of the propeller*

Maybe the setting for the motorspeed is too low for your ESC/motor combination. Increase the value of the #define MOTOR_SPEED directive in the file defines.h.

## The Motor Does Not Start

Each ESC is different. And each of them has a microcontroller with software on it. Most of them are programmable to adapt them to the needs of the user. Most of them have a failsafe function to avoid an inadvertent start of the motor.

I have added some code on the web site to check what is wrong. Usually, it has to do with the failsafe behavior of your ESC. First read the manual to see how it is implemented. Usually it works this way: put the throttle to a middle value and wait some seconds. Then put the throttle to a minimum value for some seconds—this will "arm" the ESC. You may hear some beeping code coming out of the motor windings. Then put the throttle to the desired value. If you have a remote control with a transmitter and receiver, connect the receiver to the ESC and test the settings with the transmitter. The functions that control the throttle can be found in the Servo_Control.pde tab of the software. Have a look at them and adjust the values to your needs.

Note that on the actual software, the motor starts only after the GPS has a valid fix.

## Summary

I hope that all the information given here is sufficient for you to start your own boating project.

Remember to use this chapter as a guideline for your own ideas. There is no need to follow the descriptions verbatim; there are many roads that lead to Rome. If the materials that I used are not available, feel free to try other ones, make derivations if you like, experiment, and have fun.

For more information on this project, go to http://code.google.com/p/roboboat/.

# CHAPTER 10

# Lawn-Bot 400

Until now, each robot presented has been intended for educational, research, and testing purposes. This robot fuses learning and playing, with actually getting something done.

Simply put, the Lawn-bot 400 (Figure 10-1) is a remotely controlled yard helper.

*Figure 10-1. The completed Lawn-bot400, working in the backyard*

---

▨ Why the Lawn-bot *400*? Well, I didn't like the first 399 prototypes. *Actually*, the 400 was simply added to the end of Lawn-bot as a joke to make it sound more important.

---

I have always enjoyed being outside, but never pushing a lawnmower around the yard. So to avoid the tedious task of having to walk around my backyard for 2 hours every few weeks, getting hit by rocks and sticks, and breathing in a cloud of dust and pollen, I decided to make a robot to push my lawnmower around the yard for me. All that was needed was something strong enough to push the lawnmower deck, which could be controlled wirelessly.

You start by building the frame of the robot and then select and install the electronic components. First see how the Lawn-bot works.

## How the Lawn-bot 400 Works

The Lawn-bot 400 works like a larger version of the Explorer-bot in Chapter 8, "Boat-Bot," using two powerful DC gear motors salvaged from a power wheelchair, a sturdy metal frame, and a 2.4GHz R/C link. This robot is different because it has a gas-powered lawnmower hanging from its frame, a remotely operated dump-truck bucket on top, outdoor pneumatic tires, and a set of high-power headlights to provide light if operating at night.

Because this robot is intended to be a workhorse, it should be outfitted accordingly. With motors easily capable of carrying a person, enough battery power to last several hours, and a motor controller that has built-in over-current protection, the Lawn-bot should handle anything you throw at it.

The Lawn-bot 400 uses two drive motors (left and right) to propel the robot forward or reverse with varying speeds. By changing how much power is applied to each drive wheel, the bot can be turned with great accuracy. The R/C transmitter control sticks determine how fast and in what direction each motor spins (see Figure 10-2).

***Figure 10-2.*** *This image shows the control scheme for the Lawn-bot 400. The left transmitter control stick commands the left motor (forward or reverse) and the right control stick commands the right motor.*

By moving the left control stick upward, the left motor spins forward with proportional speed–moving the same control stick downward spins the left motor in reverse. To make the robot drive forward, you must apply equal power to both motors in the same direction; to turn left or right, decrease the power to the motor whose direction you want to turn. This type of drive enables *zero-turn radius;* if one motor is driven forward and the other in reverse, the robot begins to turn a complete circle in place (without moving forward or reverse).

Following are a few specific features of the Lawn-bot required to help it complete its tasks.

## Lawn Mower Deck

The Lawn-bot can cut grass using a gasoline lawnmower that is hanging from the robot frame. To operate the mower, simply pull the starting cable to crank the engine, then activate the motors using the R/C transmitter to direct the lawnmower anywhere that you want to cut the grass. If you miss a spot, turn it around! You will amazed at how little energy you exert while driving the Lawn-bot. The gas-powered lawnmower does not affect the capability of the Lawn-bot to drive; the drive motors are electric and have no operational dependency on the mower deck.

## High-Capacity Batteries

The Explorer-bot from Chapter 8 used high-power DC gear motors to drive the frame, but it did not weigh nearly as much as the Lawn-bot, so we used small SLA batteries with decent run time. The Lawn-bot is heavy and would drain a small set of SLA batteries in a matter of minutes.

To make sure you have enough battery power to finish an entire yard, you need a set of large, deep-cycle lead acid batteries. This type of battery is usually reserved for use in boats and RVs to power trolling motors, radios, pumps, and lights, and can be discharged/recharged many times. Do not attempt to use a starting type battery because these are not meant to be fully discharged and are likely to fail if drained below a certain point. The batteries that I used were Everlast Marine deep-cycle, rated at 12v and 80AH. This battery pack provides enough power to drive the Lawn-bot continuously for approximately 3 to 6 hours, depending on the terrain.

## Steel Frame

The frame on this robot needs to be made to take a beating. This rolling cage made from 2-inch wide angle-iron can be driven through heavy grass, mud, over rocks, and even through heavily wooded areas without any problems. The rugged steel frame is the backbone of the Lawn-bot, providing the strength it needs to power through most outdoor conditions. You can use bolts to hold each frame piece together, needing only a drill to make holes and a saw to make cuts. A small welding machine can strengthen connections after each piece is verified to fit, but is not necessary.

## Dump-Bucket

After seeing how well the Lawn-bot mowed the grass, I began to think of other uses for it. One of the first seemed to be when my wife asked me to help her carry a few bags of potting soil to the other end of the yard, each one weighing about 50 lbs. As it turns out, the Lawn-bot can carry 150 lbs of potting soil with no problem, which gave me an idea.

To transport dirt, rocks, soil, tools, or anything else that I didn't feel like carrying, I mounted a tilting wheel-barrow bucket to the top of the robot using two gate hinges. And of course, to keep from having to lift the bucket manually I installed a 24v linear actuator (lift motor) to dump the contents of the bucket with the push of a button.

## Pneumatic Tires

This is the first robot to use heavy-duty pneumatic (air) tires. Most push-type lawnmowers come equipped with small plastic wheels that provide little traction and cannot work for the Lawn-bot. Pneumatic tires provide much better traction than solid rubber or plastic wheels, and provide a cushion to absorb shocks and jolts caused by rough terrain. For the front use heavy duty 10-inch caster wheels, and for the rear, use 13-inch heavy-duty utility wheels, each rated for 300-lb load capacity. Each rear wheel must be fitted with a sprocket and a chain that connects it to a smaller sprocket on the motor output shaft.

## Headlights

If you happen to mow grass at night, this robot even has two adjustable headlights that can be activated from the R/C transmitter. By adding two 55W halogen automotive fog lights to the front of the frame and a simple relay interface switch, you can illuminate anything that happens to be in front of the Lawn-bot. These lights are also handy to have around when a project leads you outside at night; just drive the

Lawn-bot near your project and turn on the super bright lights. Using only the headlights, one of the batteries should have enough power to keep them lit for at least 8 hours!

## Failsafe

Now, if you think that an unmanned lawnmower sounds dangerous, you might be right; that's why you also need to include a mandatory remote failsafe switch that can disconnect all power to the motors in case of an emergency or signal loss. The main function of the Arduino in this project is to monitor a third failsafe R/C channel for a valid signal. If the signal is lost at any time, or the operator activates the failsafe switch on the R/C transmitter, the Arduino is programmed to immediately remove all power to the motor controller, thereby disabling the robot. The failsafe is turned off by default, so the only way to activate the robot is to provide the Arduino with a specific R/C signal. By using a separate circuit to control the failsafe, there is little chance that the robot can get out of control.

# Tools and Parts List

You can design your Lawn-bot in several ways, depending on what you intend to do with it. Some lawnmowers have built-in caster wheels on the front and might require replacing only the rear lawnmower wheels with two wheelchair motors. For this reason, I will not say that you *must* have a specific type of frame because it may be easier for you to make minor modifications. But in most cases it will be easier to build a frame around the mower deck to provide a safe mounting place for the batteries and electronics.

## Lawnmower

No matter how you plan to build your Lawn-bot, it needs a lawnmower to cut grass. One of the neat things about this project is that you reuse a standard, old push mower–and nearly any push mower can work. I picked up a used Weed-eater brand 22-inch lawnmower from a small-engine repair shop for about $60 and used it for 2 years before converting it into the Lawn-bot 400. If you don't already own a working push mower, you need to get one before continuing.

If you simply plan to cut grass, you might want to focus on building the smallest frame possible to reduce weight, thereby extending battery run time and reducing the current draw from the motors. I wanted a multipurpose bot that would not only cut my grass, but also carry materials and soil, which requires a sturdy metal frame. There are many possibilities and options when building a Lawn-bot; you should build what works best for you.

## Parts Lists

The parts list for this project is extensive, and because you may not find the exact parts that I used (or you may find something better), minor adjustments may be needed to fit part availability and your unique design.

Because several different sections of the Lawn-bot could be independently replaced and the rest of the bot left alone, I decided to place individual parts lists at the beginning of each corresponding section. There are, however, several tools that can make this project quite a bit easier, which are listed in Table 10-1.

*Table 10-1. Lawn-Bot Tools List*

| Tool | Use | Price |
|---|---|---|
| Drill | Drilling holes in metal. I used an 18v cordless Ryobi drill. | $20 to $75 |
| Drill bits: 1/8-inch, 1/4-inch, 3/8-inch, 1/2-inch, and 5/8-inch | Small bits for pilot holes, other bits need to be the size of the bolts you use. | Assorted pack $10 to $15 |
| Tape measure | You need to measure metal pieces to cut and space holes to drill. | $5.00 |
| Hacksaw or reciprocating saw (with metal cutting blades) | Cutting angle-iron and other metal frame pieces, go for the power saw if you can afford it. Angle-grinders work, too. | $5 for hand saw, $50 for power saw |
| Wrench and/or assorted socket set | Used to tighten nuts and bolts together. | $5 to $20 |
| Welder (optional but handy) | I use a 110v wire-feed welder to weld small joints and permanent pieces on the frame. | $60 to $150 (optional) |
| Dremel rotary tool with metal cutoff discs | Used to cut channels in the frame rails. | $40.00 |
| Zip ties | Holding wires secure. | $3.00 |
| Hammer | Can be helpful. | $3.00 |

Three main parts to the frame are covered separately and in the same order as the frame is built. First, select the wheels, then start cutting and assembling the main frame pieces, and finally install both drive motors and connect the chains to each drive wheel. After the frame is completed, move to installing the electronics.

## The Wheels

The wheels are an important part of the Lawn-bot because they determine how much traction it has and how much weight it can handle. I chose to use pneumatic tires for both the front caster wheels and the rear drive wheels to provide a smoother ride, more traction, and a higher load capacity than solid core wheels.

I have always had good luck finding wheels for robotics projects at Harbor Freight tools stores; the 13-inch drive wheels were around $13 each, and the front caster wheels were around $16 each (see Table 10-2 and Figure 10-3).

*Table 10-2. Parts Needed for the Wheels and Sprockets*

| Part | Description | Price |
|------|-------------|-------|
| Rear wheels: 13-inch diameter x 4-inch width pneumatic tire/wheel (×2) | Harbor Freight Tools part # 67467 | $13.99 each |
| Front wheels: 10-inch x 4-inch width, with 360-degree caster assembly pneumatic caster wheel  (X2) | Harbor Freight Tools part # 38944 | $16.99 each |
| Motor sprockets (×2) | #25, 17 teeth, 1/2-inch slotted bore Goldmine-elec.com part # G13610 | $1.50 each (×2) |
| Wheel sprockets (×2) | #25, 55 tooth PartsForScooters.com part # 127-9 | $17 each (×2) |
| Woodruff key for motor shaft (×2) | Multipack from an automotive store | $5 (variety pack) |

# Front Caster Wheels

The front caster wheels are 10-inch in diameter, with a total mounting height of around 13-inch including the mounting plate (see Figure 10-3, left). Each caster wheel has a caster bracket with 360-degree turn radius, enabling the wheel to move freely in any direction. Make sure that the front wheels are spaced far enough apart that they do not hit each other when turning.

# Rear Drive Wheels

The rear wheels are 13-inch in diameter but mount to an axle instead of a caster bracket (see Figure 10-3, right). So the mounting height for the rear axle is equal to the radius of the wheel, which is 6.5-inch (13 inch / 2 = 6.5 inch). You must use two rear frame riser pieces to bridge the gap between the 6.5-inch rear axle mounting height and the 13-inch front caster wheel mounting height. The bearings used for mounting the wheel to the axle have a 5/8-inch hole, meaning this wheel needs a 5/8-inch threaded rod (axle) to mount to.

***Figure 10-3.*** *The front caster wheel and rear drive wheel from Harbor Freight Tools*

You can use whatever size wheels/tires you can find, though I would recommend using pneumatic tires for outdoor robots because they absorb much of the bumpy ride, which helps protect the electronics. After I was ready to put the finishing touches on the Lawn-bot and start using it full time, I took the rear wheels off, squirted as much packing grease into the center hub of the wheel as would fit, before remounting them to the Lawn-bot, which can keep the rear-wheel bearings from locking up.

---

▪ **Note** Remember when building your frame that the caster wheels swivel in a complete circle. You should take care to ensure that nothing on your frame interferes with the complete rotation of either caster wheel.

---

Now install the sprockets to the main drive wheels and the motor output shafts. These connect together using a chain to transmit the power from the motors to the wheels.

## Installing Sprockets

There are two different types of sprockets used on this bot. The smaller sprockets have 17 teeth and are mounted directly to the motor output shaft. This sprocket has the same size bore (mounting hole) as the motor output shaft, and has a slotted keyway (using a Woodruff key) to keep the motor shaft and sprocket from slipping.

Install the smaller motor sprocket by placing the Woodruff key onto the motor output shaft and sliding the smaller sprocket onto the shaft with the Woodruff key sliding through the slotted bore of the sprocket. When in place, use a small hex wrench (Allen wrench) to tighten the set screw on the sprocket to lock the Woodruff key into place.

The larger sprockets have 55 teeth and are mounted directly to the rear wheels using three bolts (1/4-inch diameter, 4-inch long) to hold each securely. I paid about $2 each for the smaller sprockets and $16 each for the larger ones (see Figure 10-4). Both sets of sprockets are intended for use with #25 chain.

*Figure 10-4. The two different sized sprockets used on each side of the Lawn-bot*

Now secure the large sprockets to the rear-drive wheels. The following three steps guide you through this process.

1. Prepare the rear sprockets. Start by inserting each bolt through the sprocket mounting holes, and use one nut on each bolt to tighten them securely to the sprocket. When tightened, loosely thread one more nut about 1 inch onto each bolt.

2. Mount sprockets. Next, place the new sprocket/bolt assembly onto the center of the wheel, and mark the spot where each bolt touches the wheel. Drill 1/4-inch holes at each mark, making sure the center of the sprocket aligns to the center of the wheel hub. If it is not centered, the wheel cannot spin in a perfect circle, which can cause the chain to break.

---

▪ **Note** Make sure the sprocket is centered on the wheel hub before you secure it down to the wheel.

---

3. Secure sprocket to wheel. Slide the three bolts through the holes in the wheel, flip the wheel over, and thread the last nut onto each bolt, securing tightly. Then, use the second nuts that are loosely threaded between the wheel and

sprocket to serve as a backing nuts, giving the third (and final) nuts something to tighten up against (See Figure 10-5).

**Figure 10-5.** *The rear wheel with sprocket installed*

When you have both of the larger sprockets secured to the rear wheels, you can build the frame. In the next section, assemble the frame pieces needed to mount the wheels.

## The Frame

The frame is mostly composed of steel pieces bolted together to make a metal cage around the mower deck. The interior of the frame must be large enough to accommodate for the lawnmower deck that you use, so each frame measurement should be taken specifically for your lawnmower.

The frame connects the drive wheels, motors, lawnmower, and front caster wheels together to provide a solid platform, so care should be taken to make sure every bolt is tight and each piece fits together securely. Any weak spots in your frame will be apparent when mowing your lawn. It is better to plan ahead than to spend a Saturday fixing your Lawn-bot instead of using it.

Before starting to build the frame, take a brief look at the parts list in Table 10-3.

*Table 10-3.* Parts List for the Frame

| Part | Description | Price |
|------|-------------|-------|
| 2-inch angle-iron | Three 48-inch long pieces, main frame rails (A), one rear cross-bracket (B), and two frame riser bars (E). | $8.00 each |
| 1-inch square steel tubing | One 48-inch long piece, two front cross-brackets used to mount front caster wheels. | $4.00 |
| 1-inch steel flat bar | One 48-inch long piece, support braces. | $3.00 |
| 5/8-inch threaded rod | One 36-inch long piece, used for the rear axle. Also need six 5/8-inch nuts. | $10.00 |
| Twenty-four 3/8-inch nuts, bolts, flat washers, and lock washers | Get twice as many flat washers as everything else; you might need one on each side of the bolts. | $10.00 |
| Two Deep-cycle marine batteries | Automotive store: I used two batteries in series, rated for 12v, 80AH each = to produce 24v, 80AH total. | $62 each |

The complete rolling frame from the Lawn-bot 400 can be assembled using only ten frame pieces. The frame height was decided by the height of the front caster wheels that I chose, which can be different to fit your project.

Figure 10-6 shows the ten main pieces of the frame, which are grouped together by color; pieces that are the same color/letter should be cut the same length.

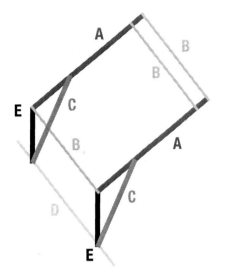

**Figure 10-6.** *The various pieces needed to construct the frame*

Following is a listing of each part of the frame and how each piece should be cut.

- A (•2) – Blue = 2 main frame rails: 2-inch angle-iron, 48-inch long each

- B (•3) – Green = 3 cross-brackets: 2 front are 1-inch square tubing, 1 rear is 2-inch angle-iron, 20" long each.

- C (•2) – Red = 2 support braces: 1-inch flat steel bar, 10-inch long each

- D (•1) – Yellow = rear drive axle: 5/8-inch Threaded rod, 36-inch long

- E (•2) – Black = frame riser bars: 2-inch angle-iron, 8-inch long each

The two main frame rails (A) are the long pieces that span from the rear of the bot to the front. The three cross-brackets (B) are mounted to the two main frame rails (A) on both ends. The front cross-brackets are then mounted to the front caster wheels. The rear frame risers (E) keep the main frame rails level even though the axle (D) is about 12 inches below the top of the frame; these should be measured to fit your frame. The two support braces (C) keep the frame risers securely in place. Figure 10-7 shows a picture of the assembled Lawn-bot, to physically place the parts from the illustration in Figure 10-6.

*Figure 10-7. The axle and frame support bar*

The frame riser bars are not visible because the rear wheels cover them up, but the rest of the pieces can be seen in Figure 10-7. The diagram is for the frame only; it does not include the mower deck that is shown next. These measurements are not rocket science and can be slightly off and still work just fine. The key to building the frame is to get into the mindset to make it work and work around any problems you encounter. If you drill a hole in the wrong place, don't worry about it; just drill a new one in the right place and keep moving. This will be your prototype, so it does not have to be perfect.

If you use a 22-inch lawnmower deck, your basic frame without wheels, batteries, or accessories will be around 46-inch long x 20-inch wide x 13-inch tall (my Lawn-bot dimensions). With the battery rack mounted to the rear, the wheel barrow bucket mounted to the top, and the wheels mounted, my Lawn-bot measures in a bit larger at 52-inch long x 30-inch wide x 26-inch" tall.

The following 11 steps guide you through cutting each piece of metal and assembling the frame:

1. Cut the two main frame rails (A) using a 2-inch angle iron. Depending on the size of your frame, you may not have to cut these; you can buy 36-inch or 48-inch long pieces from the hardware store, which might work nicely. I used 48-inch pieces for these frame rails.

2. Cut the three cross-brackets (B). The rear bracket should be 2-inch angle iron and the two front brackets should be 1-inch square tubing. These three pieces should all be cut the same length to ensure that the bot is square. For my 22-inch lawnmower deck, the width to provide adequate clearance turned out to be 20-inch, which may be slightly different depending on your specific lawnmower design.

3. Bolt the rear cross-bracket (2-inch angle-iron) to the ends of the two main frame rails. You need to drill a hole on each end through both the cross-bracket and the main frame rails to secure them together. Line the cross-bracket flush with the bottom of the main frame rails.

415

4.   Mount the front cross-brackets (1-inch square tubing) with caster wheels to the front of the main frame pieces. Drill one hole on each end of the cross-brackets and through the front of the main frame rails (see Figure 10-8).

*Figure 10-8. The main frame rails connected to the front caster wheel support braces*

5.   Cut the frame riser pieces. Measure the height of your caster wheels; now subtract the radius of the rear wheel and add 1 inch. The extra inch is to provide some room to drill a mounting hole; my frame riser bars were cut to 8-inch each.

6.   Mount the frame riser pieces. I drilled one hole at the top of each frame riser piece to bolt them into the main frame rails. When tightened, you can notice that the frame risers pivot without much force. To keep them in place, you need a support brace on each side of the frame, connecting the bottom portion of each frame riser to the main frame rails at another spot. This creates a triangle that when bolted no longer enables the rear frame riser pieces to pivot. These pieces do not have to be the exact same length because they simply hold the frame risers in place (see Figure 10-9).

*Figure 10-9. The support brace from the frame riser to the main frame rails*

7. Mount the rear drive axle. I used a 5/8-inch diameter threaded rod (36-inches long) to serve as the rear axle. You need four 5/8-inch nuts to mount the axle to the frame and two more nuts to hold the rear wheels onto the axle when installed. To mount the axle, drill a 5/8-inch hole at the bottom of each frame riser piece, centered 1 inch from the bottom of each frame riser.

Slide the threaded rod through the hole on one side; then thread two of the nuts onto the end of the rod. These two nuts should fit securely to the insides of the frame risers. When the two inside nuts are threaded toward the center of the rod, continue sliding the rod through the other axle hole on the other frame riser piece.

Now thread two more nuts on the rod, one on each side. Tighten the two nuts on each side securely to each frame riser piece.

Make sure you have approximately the same amount of excess threaded rod sticking out of each side of the frame; you can cut the excess from this threaded rod with a hacksaw when the wheels are mounted later.

8. Test fit rear wheels and check the top of the frame to make sure it is level. With the 10 frame pieces mounted together and the front caster wheels attached, you can slide the rear wheels onto the rear axle to make sure your measurements are correct and that the top of the frame is level (see Figure 10-10).

*Figure 10-10. The completed frame*

9. Tighten all the bolts. After you decide that the frame is straight, you can go back and tighten each nut/bolt to secure the frame together tightly. I used 3/8-inch diameter bolts (ranging from 1-inch to 2-inch long) for most of the frame, occasionally using 1/4-inch diameter bolts for less important pieces. You should now have a rolling frame capable of carrying several hundred pounds.

10. Attach the mower deck. The mower deck needs only four pieces of metal to hang from the main frame rails of the Lawn-bot. The length of these four mower-deck hanger pieces is determined by the distance from the vertical center of the main frame rails, down to the ground, minus the radius of the old lawnmower wheels.

Example: My frame rails measured 13 inches from center to ground. My old mower wheels had a 4-inch radius, so I made my four mower-deck hangers 9 inches long using 1-inch square tubing (13-inch – 4-inch = 9-inch).

Test fit the mower deck to make sure there is adequate clearance around the frame, specifically the front caster wheels with full swing and the rear tire clearance (see Figure 10-11).

*Figure 10-11. The Lawn-bot with mower deck attached by four metal hanger pieces*

11. Lastly, add a small rack to the rear of the frame to hold the large deep-cycle batteries. This cage can be made from scrap metal or what you have left over from the frame. Just measure the batteries to make sure the rack is large enough to hold them at the base, and use two hangers to tie the rack to the top of the frame. I used a welder to secure these joints (see Figure 10-12).

*Figure 10-12. The battery rack on the rear of the Lawn-bot frame*

With the frame completed, mount the motors and connect the chain and sprockets for the drivetrain.

# The Drive-Train

The drive-train on this bot is slightly more complicated than my other bots, using a chain and sprockets to transmit power from the motors to the wheels. Typically, it is easier to use wheelchair motors that already have the wheels mounted to them (as we did with the Explorer-bot in Chapter 8) because this not only removes an extra building step but is also far more reliable than using chain and sprockets. Nonetheless, we discuss how to set up a chain/sprocket drive-train just in case you cannot find motors with premounted wheels.

The drive-train that I built uses #25 roller chain and #25 sprockets. The sprockets must be the same size (#25) as the chain, or the sprocket teeth will not mate properly to the chain links. Before starting, take a look at the parts list for the drive-train in Table 10-4.

***Table 10-4.*** *Parts List for the Drive-Train*

| Part | Description | Price |
|---|---|---|
| Two DC gear motors | Ebay.com: I used power wheelchair gear motors like the ones used in Chapter 8. | $75 set |
| 2-inch angle-iron | Hardware store: You need 16-inch total, cut in half for the motor mount brackets. | $4.00 |
| Eight 1/4-inch bolts: flat topped, 3/4-inch long with nuts and lock-washers | Hardware store: These are used for securing the motors to the motor mounts. | $2.00 |
| 10 feet #25 roller chain | Allelectronics.com part # CHN-25. | $2.50/foot (×4) |
| Universal chain links (2x) | ElectricScooterParts.com part # CHN-25ML: These enable you to fix or resize a chain. | $1 each |

Start by making a mounting bracket for each motor; mount the sprockets to each wheel and motor output shaft, and cut and install each drive chain. Make some brackets to mount the motors to so that you can adjust the position of each motor, which is how you can adjust the tension of each chain.

## Motor Mount Brackets

When using separate motors and wheels, you must find some way to transfer the power from the motor output shaft to the wheel drive sprockets. I chose to mount a set of sprockets to the motors and wheels and use a chain to connect them. The problem that arises when using a chain to transmit power is finding the proper tension that is not too tight or too loose because either can cause problems when operating. To get proper tension, you need a tensioning mechanism that enables you to adjust each chain until it is correct; this is where the motor mount brackets come in.

To adjust the tension of each chain, I had to make two motor mount brackets. These are nothing more than a piece of 2-inch angle-iron about 8 inches long (each). The motors mount to these brackets using four small bolts (see Figure 10-13), and the brackets bolt into some specially cut holes in the main frame rails. By cutting two "channels" in the top of the frame rails, the motor mount brackets can slide forward or backward when the bolts are loosened.

*Figure 10-13. The motor mounting plate with 1/4-inch bolts*

The following four steps guide you through making each motor mount bracket.

1.  Measure and cut (2) pieces of 2-inch angle-iron, 8-inch long each.

In Figure 10-10, you can see the power wheelchair motor, the 8-inch long motor mount bracket with holes drilled, and the small bolts/washers/nuts to secure the motor to the motor mount bracket. The bolts have perfectly flat heads; this enables the bottom of the motor mount bracket to sit flush on the main frame rails when mounted.

2.  Mount motors to the brackets. To do this, you need to mark and drill six holes in each bracket. The four center holes should be 1/4-inch in diameter and secure the motor to the bracket, whereas the two outer holes will be 3/8-inch and are used to secure the motor mount bracket to the main frame rails.

First, place one of your motors onto the center of each bracket, and mark the mounting holes for each motor onto the motor mount bracket. Next, mark one hole (centered) on each end of the motor mount pieces, about 1-inch from each end of the bracket; these secure the motor mount brackets to the frame.

Lastly, drill the mounting holes into the motor mount piece, and secure the motor to the motor mount using four flat-topped bolts. My motors have four 1/4-inch threaded mounting holes on each gear box.

When finished, the motor mount bracket with DC motor attached should look like Figure 10-14.

*Figure 10-14. The motor secured to the motor mounting plate*

3.  Cut motor mount bracket mounting holes. With the motors secured to the motor mounts, make grooves in the main frame rails for the motor mounts. These grooves enable the bolts holding the motor mount to the frame rails to slide along the frame rails so that you can adjust the tension of the drive chains.

Start by placing the motors mounts (with motors mounted) onto the main frame rails. The 2-inch angle-iron motor mount bracket should sit nicely on top of the 2inch angle-iron main frame rails. Slide the motor mounts as far back as they can go toward the rear of the frame (without protruding from the rear of the frame), and mark the location of both mounting holes (onto the main frame rails) with a permanent marker or pencil. These marks will be the rearmost position of the motor mount bracket. Next, slide the motor mount bracket forward 2 inches, and mark both holes again with a permanent marker or pencil.

Drill 3/8-inch holes at both sets of marks; then draw a line between the tops and the bottoms of each set of holes. Use a Dremel rotary tool with a metal cutoff wheel to cut these two lines, thereby making two channels the size of the drill bit. When you finish cutting out the center of each channel with the Dremel tool, you should slide the 3/8-inch drill bit back and forth through the channel without resistance.

Figure 10-15 shows the two motor mount bracket mounting holes after drilling and cutting out the metal between them with a Dremel tool. You should be left with two grooves: 3/8-inch wide and 2-inch long each.

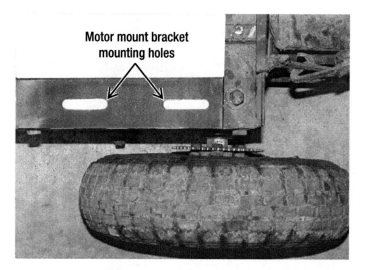

*Figure 10-15. The motor mount bracket holes cut into the main frame rails*

4. Secure motor mount brackets to the main frame rails. You need two 3/8-inch bolts, four regular washers, and two lock washers to mount each motor to the frame.

Place the motor assembly onto the main frame rail, and use the two bolts to secure the motor mount to the main frame. Place one washer on each bolt before placing it through the motor mount bracket mounting hole and then another washer beneath the main frame rail on each bolt. Finally put a lock washer and nut on the end of the bolt and secure only hand-tight because later you need to install the chain and adjust the tension.

To verify that your motor mount bracket works, slide it forward and backward to make sure it moves. The bracket should move forward about 2 inches (the length of the mounting hole channels). Figure 10-16 shows the complete motor mount assembly, mounted to the main frame rails with the two silver bolts holding the motor mount bracket to the frame.

*Figure 10-16. The motor mount secured to the main frame rail using two bolts*

---

▓ **Note** Although I installed my motors "pointing" toward the rear of the bot, this makes no difference in function. I tried mounting the motors both ways and liked the backward look better.

---

With the motors secured to the frame, all that you need to do to complete the drive-train is to cut and install the chain for each motor.

## Installing the Chain

In Figure 10-17, you can see one of the chains used on the Lawn-bot (you need two of these), along with a universal (master) chain link used to adjust the length of the chain if it needs to be resized. I purchased a 10-foot section of this chain for about $25 and the universal chain links are about $1 each; get plenty of these because they are also handy to repair a broken chain.

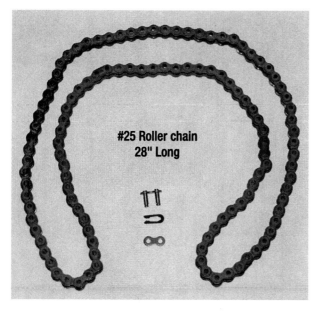

*Figure 10-17. Each drive chain should be approximately 28-inches long and requires a master link to connect each cut end.*

After you place each motor bracket to its center position, you should wrap the chain around both sprockets and use a black permanent marker to mark the link that overlaps at the beginning. Now cut the chain to that length using your Dremel tool. My chains turned out to be 28-inches long each.

After cutting to length, use a universal chain link to connect the two loose ends of the chain together around the wheel sprocket. Now, gently wrap the chain around the motor sprocket, and slide the motor forward until the chain is barely tight. When the chain has about 1/4-inch of play when pressed with your finger, you can tighten down the two motor mount bracket bolts to the main frame rails.

Always double-check the chain tension after securing the bolts down to the frame because they could have caused the chain to tighten or loosen from your previous check. If so, loosen the bolts and make slight adjustments until you get proper tension. When finished, your chain should look like Figure 10-18.

*Figure 10-18. The motor with chain attached to both sprockets*

■ **Note** I always check for proper tension by squeezing both sides of the chain about 3 inches below the motor sprocket with my index finger and thumb. If the chain gives more than 1/4-inch on either side, it is too loose. If it won't give at all, it is too tight.

If you chain is too loose, it can cause unnecessary jerking on the motor sprocket, which can cause breakage of sprocket teeth. If the chain is too tight, it cannot enable any variation or stretching of the frame and will be more likely to break the chain.

After you have the chains attached, your frame should be ready to go. You can test the motor output by connecting a voltage meter to one set of motor terminal and pushing the robot around to see the motor act as a generator, producing voltage on the meter as the bot moves. Now that the building is complete, install the electronics.

# The Motor Controller

For the first version of the Lawn-bot, I decided to design and build my own motor controller, which I called the Triple8. This motor controller worked well for more than a year, until one hot summer day (during heavy use), the power connector melted right off the board. I fixed the Triple8, but this made me think: if it can get hot enough to melt without me knowing, I was eventually going to break it again at some point. I then realized that if the motor controller broke, I would not keep my yard looking nice.

Because this robot is actually used quite a bit and for important household duties, I decided to buy a commercial motor controller unit that would protect itself from over-heating during use.

## Buying a Motor Controller

Most commercially available motor controllers can be controlled using the Arduino, even if it is intended to work with a specific signal type. If you have never built a motor controller before or you are not confident doing repair work with a soldering iron, I recommend buying the Sabertooth 2x25 motor controller (or similar) for the main drive motors.

## Sabertooth 2x25

The Sabertooth 2x25 is a dual DC motor controller made by Dimension Engineering that can handle 25amps continuously with 50-amp peaks (see Figure 10-19). The Sabertooth has a built-in microcontroller (actually the same type of chip as the Arduino, though not reprogrammable) that can accept either R/C signals, analog voltage, or serial commands, depending on the DIP switch settings. This driver also incorporates over-current protection, auto-calibration for R/C mode, and utilizes regenerative braking for more efficient stopping.

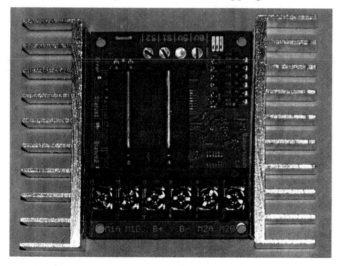

*Figure 10-19. The Sabertooth 2x25 motor controller*

This motor driver automatically shuts down the power to the motors if the current level exceeds 50amps to keep from damaging the PCB and mosfets. This self-preserving limit is evident when the bot appears to have trouble climbing a steep hill or making a fast change in direction. The solution is to go slowly when climbing a hill and distribute the power between both motors evenly to keep from over-stressing either channel of the motor controller.

The Sabertooth has a 6-port DIP switch module on the corner of the PCB near the Input screw terminals. The orientation of these switches can set the Sabertooth to operate in different modes and with different options, including the battery type, input type, and control methods. These DIP switches must be set properly for the Sabertooth to work correctly. Refer to the manufacturers website for a full explanation of these switches at

http://www.dimensionengineering.com/sabertooth2x25.htm.

Use the Sabertooth in R/C mode, connecting inputs S1 and S2 to the two main drive signals from the R/C receiver, THR (left motor), and ELE (right motor). The DIP switches must be set for R/C mode, as shown in Figure 10-20.

*Figure 10-20. Set the Dip switches as shown for R/C control*

Table 10-5 has a few motor controllers suitable to drive the Lawn-bot.

*Table 10-5. Motor Controller Options*

| Motor Controller | Feature | Price |
|---|---|---|
| Sabertooth 2x25 (used in this chapter) www.dimensionengineering.com | Controls both motors, over-current protection, up to 24vdc 25amp, several input methods, built-in heat sink | $125.00 |
| Pololu 24v23 CS (x2) www.pololu.com | Single motor-controller, 24vdc 23amps, current-sensor, must be driven by Arduino or other uC, requires only 1 PWM pin per motor | $63.00 (×2) |
| Basic Micro Robo Claw 2x25 www.basicmicro.com | Similar to Sabertooth in specs, with wheel encoder support | $125.00 |

Even when using a commercial motor controller, you can still add a fan or heat sink to help dissipate more heat. Doing so can increase the maximum amperage limit of the motor controller.

## Cooling Fans

The easiest way to optimize any motor controller is to add a cooling fan to dissipate heat. Because these are relatively cheap ($2 each), it makes sense to plan to install one above any motor controller that will be used continuously for any length of time. I typically use an 80mm PC cooling fan (see Figure 10-21).

The typical case fan spins at 2000 to 3000RPM and only consumes about 150mA at 12vdc. I usually connect these directly to the motor controller's +24v and GND power supply from the main batteries. This causes the fan to run at twice the intended voltage, thereby doubling both the RPM and the current consumption (approximately). The downside is that the fans may not last as long as if they were run at 12v. They do provide much better cooling for the motor controller at 24v, and I have had to replace only one fan in more than a year of use–so it is worth it to me.

*Figure 10-21. A standard 80mm PC cooling fan works perfectly to remove heat from a motor controller.*

## Motor Controller feedback

When using my first few home-made motor controllers, I would periodically drive the Lawn-bot back to me so that I could put my finger on the back of the mosfets to see if they were too hot (despite having a cooling fan mounted directly above them). This was the only way I could get some feedback to see if I needed to park it for a few minutes to let everything cool down.

To look cool while mowing your grass, you probably don't want to stop to check your mosfets every 15 minutes, and you certainly don't want to burn up your motor controller if you forget. The answer is to let the Arduino monitor the motor's current for you, but to do that you need a current sensor. Each of the motor controllers in Table 10-2 has a built-in current sensor to provide over-current protection–if you use a motor controller that does not have a built-in current sensor, fear not! You can use an external current sensor breakout board to monitor your motor controllers using the Arduino.

## Current sensor IC

The ACS714 bidirectional +/− 30amp current sensor (used in Chapter 8) can be used for larger robots like the Lawn-bot to measure the amperage going through the motor controller circuit. Pololu.com sells a breakout board with this chip installed that enables you to simply place it in series with one of the motor terminal wires, between the motor controller and motor (see Figure 10-22). You can then connect each sensor to the Arduino into one of the Analog input pins to read the current level as an Analog voltage.

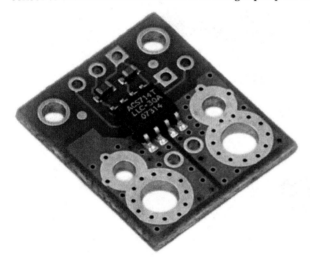

*Figure 10-22. The Pololu ACS-714, +/–30A current sensor IC (item# 1187)*

With a few lines of code, you can tell the Arduino to check this value each time the main loop is run and stop the motors if the desired limit is exceeded. This way the Arduino looks out for the motor controller constantly to make sure it is not over-stressing itself. This feedback method is an effective way to protect your motor controller from overheating and burning a PCB trace or switching component.

Now that you have the motor controller selected, you need to add an Arduino to control everything else on the robot, including the failsafe, headlights, and dump bucket.

## The Arduino

The Arduino in this project can decode several R/C signals to control the Failsafe and any accessories you might have on your bot, such as headlights, a lawnmower kill-switch, or a lift motor for a dump-bucket attachment.

I started with two Arduino boards on my Lawn-bot, using one to decode the R/C signals for the main drive motors, and the other Arduino to decode the remaining channels for the accessories. After switching to the Sabertooth 2x25 as the motor controller for the Lawn-bot, I now use only one Arduino to control the Failsafe and all other accessories, leaving the decoding of the motor control signals to the Sabertooth. You can still use the Arduino to decode the drive signals from the R/C receiver or another control source if you want, and I provide code on this book's website for both options.

With the overhead of decoding the motor drive signals offloaded to the Sabertooth 2x25, the Arduino has less responsibility and can thus decode more R/C channels without worrying about update intervals for the motors. Under these circumstances, you can decode all available R/C channels with the Arduino using pulseIn() and control as many accessories or attachments as you want.

## Securing Connections for a Bumpy Ride

This robot will be driven among some of the bumpiest and hilly terrain that you will encounter with any of your home-made robots. My Lawn-bot typically tramples through tall grass, over wooden tree branches, through brush, into the woods, and anywhere else that I don't feel like going myself. In addition to the bumps, starting the gasoline engine on the lawnmower can ensure that any bolts or wires not secured will promptly be rattled loose. For this reason, it is a good idea to make sure your Arduino has secure connections that won't come out with a few bumps and some constant vibration.

## Building a Breakout Board

Alternatively, you can build your own Arduino board with screw terminals for around $10 to $15 and a little soldering. You can either etch one of the examples in this book, create your own Arduino design in Eagle, or simply use a perforated prototyping board and jumper wires from Radio Shack for an easier approach. I have done both and they work equally well; my current Lawn-bot uses an Arduino clone built on a small piece of perf-board with a screw terminal for each pin.

I prefer to build an Arduino breakout board to use on the Lawn-bot because it gets quite a bit of use and often gets dirty. I would feel bad to see my poor Arduino Duemilanove (that has taught me so much!) getting worked as hard as I work the Lawn-bot. Plus it doesn't hurt as bad if something happens to a $12 breakout board and you have to build another one.

---

**Note** Power the R/C receiver with +5v and GND from the Arduino supply to ensure that it always has power.

---

In Figure 10-23, you can see my bruised and dirty Arduino breakout board on a piece of perf-board, with 0.2-inch spacing screw terminals for each pin, and an LM7805 +5v regulator (all from Radio Shack). I had to order the Atmega328, a reset button, and the 16mHz resonator from Sparkfun.com.

*Figure 10-23. This breakout board is built on perforated prototyping board, using PC board screw terminals for secure connections to each wire.*

The construction of a perf-board Arduino with screw terminals is quite basic; I soldered a 28 DIL IC socket to the center of the board and 20 screw terminals to the left and right sides of the board. Each Arduino output is connected (using jumper wire) to a screw terminal on the edge of the board. There is also a 16mHz resonator for the Atmega328 chip and a +5v regulator to provide a regulated supply voltage for the Atmega chip. I placed two capacitors into the circuit, one tied to the inputs of the LM7805 and another tied to the outputs (+5v).

The screw terminals on the bottom of the board supply power from the unregulated battery supply, whereas the top screw terminal provides access to the +5v regulated supply to power the R/C receiver from the LM7805. You can add the optional reset button shown at the top of the board; although, I have never had to reset this board. (It is easier to toggle the power switch.)

Table 10-6 shows a parts list for the Arduino breakout board.

**Table 10-6.** *Parts List for Arduino Breakout Board*

| Part | Description | Price |
|------|-------------|-------|
| Perforated circuit board | Radio Shack part # 276-150 | $2.00 |
| 28-pin DIP IC socket | Sparkfun part # PRT-07942 | $1.50 |
| 7805 voltage regulator | Sparkfun part # COM-00107 | $1.25 |
| 16MHz Ceramic resonator | Sparkfun part # COM-09420. | $1.00 |
| Nine screw terminals 2-pos | Sparkfun part # PRT-08432. | $0.95 each |
| Two screw terminals 3-pos | Sparkfun part # PRT-08433. | $1.00 each |
| Reset switch | Sparkfun part # COM-00097. | $0.35 |
| LED w/ 330 ohm resistor | Power indicator LED. | $1.00 |
| Two capacitors – 10uf–220uf, 16v–50v | I placed two capacitors on the board for the voltage regulator. | $1.00 |
| Wire | Radio Shack. | $3.00 |

If you want to build your own Arduino breakout board, use the schematic in Figure 10-24 to make proper connections. This schematic is simplistic and does not include an FTDI programming port, so you must use a standard Arduino to program the Atmega chip; then transfer it into the breakout board's IC socket. Because this is not meant to be a test vehicle, but rather a full-time lawn robot, the breakout board likely won't need reprogramming enough to warrant a programming port.

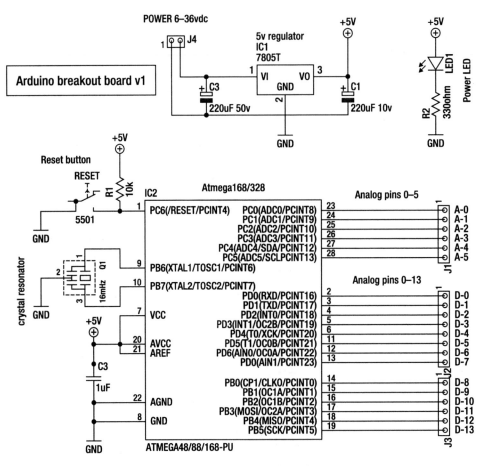

*Figure 10-24. The schematic of the Atmega breakout board*

Because this is not a PCB but rather a prototyping board, you need to make all connections on the board using point-to-point wiring, as shown in the schematic. When you finish, your prototyping board should look similar to the one in Figure 10-25.

*Figure 10-25. Detailed view of the Arduino breakout board with descriptions*

If you would rather build a PCB for the Arduino in this project, Eagle files are available for an Arduino with screw terminals at each digital I/O pin for secure connections. In addition to having screw terminals, each Analog pin is also supplied with a +5v and GND pin for easy integration with your R/C receiver. Using female to female servo plugs, you cannot only provide the Arduino with the signals from each R/C channel, but also provide +5v and GND signals to power the R/C receiver from the regulated Arduino supply.

To download the PCB files for an Arduino clone with screw terminals and other files related to this chapter, visit https://sites.google.com/site/arduinorobotics/home/chapter10.

Now you just need a failsafe to make sure you can shut this robot down if it should get out of range or out of control.

# The Failsafe

This robot is large and dangerous and must have a failsafe switch installed to enable the user to remotely disable the motors. The failsafe consists of an automotive power relay (rated 60amps, 14v), a mosfet or transistor to interface the relay with the Arduino, and an extra channel on the R/C transmitter dedicated to switching the failsafe (see Table 10-7).

*Table 10-7. Failsafe Parts List*

| Part | Description | Price |
|------|-------------|-------|
| 2.4GHz radio system | Spektrum DX5e transmitter and BR6000 receiver | $110.00 |
| Perforated circuit board | Radio Shack part # 276-150: used to build relay interface circuits | $2.00 |
| Logic-level N-channel MOSFET with 10k pull-down resistor Digikey part # FQP50N06L. This (logic-level) N-channel power Mosfet should D switch nearly any relay coil. Rated at 52 amps. | | $1.05 |
| Power Relay SPST | Radio Shack part # 275-001 | $7.00 |

The channel used on the R/C system to control the failsafe should not be a control stick type that returns to center when released (like the drive channels), but instead a toggle switch type that is either on or off.

# R/C Toggle Switch

The Spektrum DX5e radio transmitter and Spektrum BR6000 2.4GHz R/C system utilize a toggle switch available for use on the sixth channel of the receiver (see Figure 10-26). This toggle switch can either output one of two pulses to the R/C receiver: approximately 1000 microseconds if switched LOW and approximately 2000 microseconds if switched HIGH. If you choose to use a different 2.4GHz R/C system and there is not a usable toggle switch already installed on your transmitter, you might have to sacrifice use of another unused channel to add the toggle switch for the failsafe. If using the Spektrum BR6000 receiver, simply connect the AUX channel to the Arduino to access the failsafe signal.

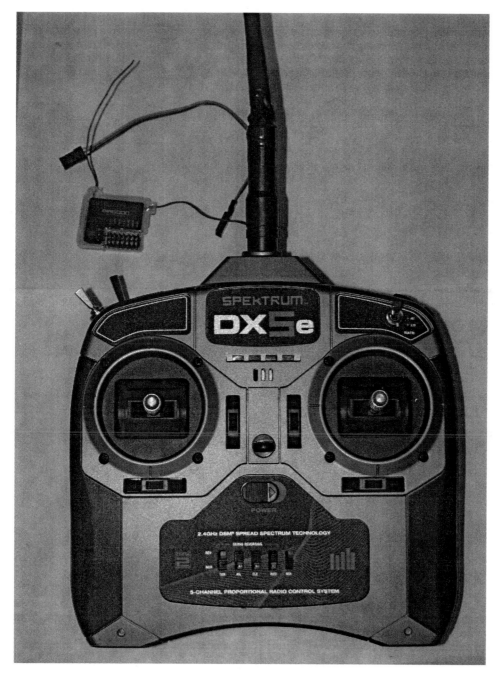

*Figure 10-26.*

The input voltage from the toggle switch on the R/C transmitter can only be either +5v or GND (as there is no potentiometer in the toggle switch), so the Servo pulse value interpreted by the R/C receiver can either be 1000 microseconds or 2000 microseconds (approximately) when read by the Arduino. This is exactly the on/off functionality you need for the failsafe switch, which is simply a wireless kill switch for the +24v supply to the motor controller using a power relay. When decoded, you need to check only the signal for being HIGH or LOW, so to speak–consider Listing 10-1.

*Listing 10-1. Use Single R/C Failsafe Channel to Wirelessly Switch an LED on the Arduino*

```
// Code to read an R/C failsafe channel and turn digital pin On/Off
// Connect R/C receiver to +5v and GND from Arduino supply.
// Also connect AUX channel from R/C receiver to Arduino D2.
// If failsafe is On, LED on D13 will also turn On - otherwise LED is Off.

int ppm = 2;  // read R/C receiver from this pin
int servo_val;  // use "servo_val" to hold the pulse length
int LED_pin = 13;  // control LED on Arduino D13

void setup() {
  Serial.begin(9600); // start serial monitor
  pinMode(LED_pin, OUTPUT); // declare output
  pinMode(ppm, INPUT); // declare input
}

void loop() {

  // use pulseIn() command to read the length of the pulse on D2, with a timeout of 20mS
(20000uS)
  servo_val = pulseIn(ppm, HIGH, 20000);

  // check the pulse length to see if it is above 1600 microseconds (ie. Above neutral)
  if (servo_val > 1600){
    // if so, turn LED On
    digitalWrite(LED_pin, HIGH);
    Serial.println("Failsafe Active!");
  }
  else {
    // otherwise if signal is below 1600 uS, turn LED Off
    digitalWrite(LED_pin, LOW);
    Serial.println("Failsafe turned Off");
  }
}
// end of code
```

This is the exact method that to use to decode each of the digital R/C channels available from the receiver, in the main code for the Lawn-bot. Now that you know how to read the Failsafe channel from the R/C receiver and convert the pulse reading into a HIGH or LOW value on the Arduino, learn how to interface the Arduino to a high-power relay to control the failsafe, lights, lift motor, or anything else you can think of to add on.

# Power Relays

The power relay from Radio Shack that I use is intended for automotive use and rated for 14vdc and 60amps; although I used it to switch 24vdc and approximately 30 to 50amps for more than a year without problems (see Figure 10-27). The coil to activate the relay consumes approximately 200mA at 12v and can be turned on using a single logic-level N-channel mosfet interfaced with the Arduino.

*Figure 10-27. The Failsafe power relay used to switch the main power supply to the motor controller*

The normally open SPST power relay has four terminals: two activate the relay coil by connecting one terminal to the +12v power supply and the other terminal to the Drain pin of the N-channel mosfet, as shown in Figure 10-28. The other two terminals on the relay are the power contacts used to control the +24v power supply going to the motor controller. The relay is "normally open" because you want to make sure that it is disconnected by default, and the only way to activate it (that is, turn on the motor controller) is to bring the Arduino failsafe_relay control pin HIGH.

The power relay can be controlled by any Arduino output pin, using a simple logic-level N-channel mosfet to control the GND supply to the relay coil, as shown in the schematic in Figure 10-28. The mosfet has a built-in protection diode to keep the back-EMF produced by switching the coil, from damaging the mosfet or the Arduino output pin. If you want to use an NPN type BJT transistor to control the relay coil, you should solder an external diode to the two coil terminals of the power relay because most BJT transistors do not have internal diodes built in.

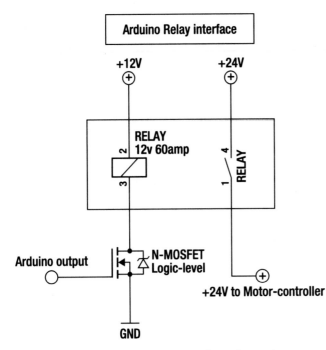

*Figure 10-28. The Failsafe relay interface schematic*

---

▓ **Note** The power relay is a SPST and therefore has four terminals. The two silver terminals marked 85 and 86activate the relay coil, whereas the two copper terminals marked 87 and 30 are the power contacts used to switch the positive voltage supply between the positive battery lead and the Sabertooth 2x25 +VIN terminal.

---

The power terminals of the relay can be reversed without issue, and the relay coil is not polarized (you can reverse the polarity to the coil and it still activates the relay), unless you add the external diode across the coil terminals. If you add the external diode, you have to apply the +12v signal to the striped end of the diode (cathode) and GND (through the N-channel mosfet) to the other end of the diode (anode).

## Avoiding an R/C Failsafe

Most R/C systems have a failsafe pulse that the R/C receiver can revert to if it loses its signal from the transmitter. Most multichannel R/C equipment is made for hobby airplanes, which do not use reverse, so the R/C receiver can typically revert the throttle channel to 0% (or approximately 1000uS pulses) as a failsafe if the receiver loses its connection with the transmitter. This is because you don't want your plane flying off into the sunset at full speed if it is no longer controlled. The rest of the channels hold their last known position when the signal is lost.

This throttle failsafe creates a problem for bidirectional vehicles because the throttle channel is used for both forward and reverse. This means that when the signal is lost and the R/C receiver reverts the throttle signal to a constant 1000uS pulse, it is actually putting the motor connected to the throttle channel in full 100% reverse! You can imagine that this could be potentially dangerous if you have a running lawnmower attached to an uncontrolled bot.

To avoid this, I recommend using the 2.4gHz Spektrum BR6000 Bot receiver, specifically designed for use with robots. This receiver has a programmable failsafe for each channel, which is determined by the position of each channel during the Tx/Rx binding process. If the signal is lost between the Tx and Rx, the receiver reverts each channel to its preset value (centered). This enables you to set each of the motor drive channels to default back to neutral if the signal is lost, and setting the external Failsafe controlled by the Arduino to default off. This means that if the signal is lost or the transmitter turned off, not only are the drive signals reverted to neutral and the motors stopped, but also the failsafe channel reverts to off, which disconnects the power to the motor controller—double failsafe!

All that is left now is to make connections and load the code before showing off your new Lawn-bot to the neighborhood.

# Making Connections

Several connections need to be made to get your Lawn-bot moving. First, connect the Arduino and failsafe; then connect the Sabertooth motor controller to the motors and power supply. Use Table 10-8 to make connections between the Arduino, R/C receiver, and Sabertooth motor controller.

*Table 10-8. Connections to Both the Arduino and Sabertooth 2x25 Motor Controller*

| Connection | Description | Arduino | Sabertooth |
|---|---|---|---|
| THR – R/C receiver | For left drive motor | x | S1 |
| AILE – R/C receiver | For bucket-lift motor | D5 | x |
| ELE – R/C receiver | For right drive motor | x | S2 |
| RUD – R/C receiver | For mower kill switch | D3 | x |
| GER – R/C receiver | For headlights | D4 | x |
| AUX – R/C receiver | For Failsafe relay | D2 | x |
| +12v | Center tap from batteries provide 12v for Arduino and relays | +VIN | x |
| +24v | Positive lead from batteries | x | B+ |

| Connection | Description | Arduino | Sabertooth |
|---|---|---|---|
| GND | Negative lead from batteries | GND | B- |
| Failsafe relay | Interface Arduino output pin with N-channel mosfet that controls failsafe relay | D6 | x |
| Mower kill switch (if used) | Interface Arduino output pin with N-channel mosfet that controls mower kill switch relay | D7 | x |
| Lights (if used) | Interface Arduino output pin with N-channel mosfet that controls lights relay | D8 | x |
| Lift motor up (if used) | Interface Arduino output pin with N-channel mosfet that controls SPDT lift motor up relay | D9 | x |
| Lift motor down (if used) | Interface Arduino output pin with N-channel mosfet that controls SPDT lift motor down relay | D10 | x |
| Left drive motor | Connects both motor terminals to the Sabertooth M1A and M1B | x | M1 |
| Right drive motor | Connects both motor terminals to the Sabertooth M2A and M2B | x | M2 |

Remember to connect the GND and +5v power signals from the Arduino to the R/C receiver.

# The Code

The code for this project reads four servo pulse signals from the R/C receiver and uses those values to control up to four different power relays. One of the power relays should be used as a failsafe switch for the motor controller, but the other three are available for general use. The following sections shows how to utilize these extra three channels, but for now, load the code. To better describe what happens in the code, I commented nearly every line with a brief explanation.

Listing 10-2 shows the code to control the failsafe and accessories. Download the code for this chapter and upload to your Arduino at https://sites.google.com/site/arduinorobotics/home/chapter10.

*Listing 10-2. This Code Reads Four R/C Channel Pulses and Converts Them into Digital Outputs to Control a Set of Power Relays*

```
// Code 10-2 - The Lawn-bot
// Main code used to control the failsafe and accessories.
// Connect Failsafe R/C channel AUX, into Arduino D2.
// Lawnmower kill switch INPUT connects to D3
// Head-lights INPUT connects to D4
// Bucket-lift motor INPUT connects to D5
//
// OUTPUTs are listed by function
// you will need a Relay interface board for each Arduino output
// you will also need a set of SPDT relays to control the lift-motor UP/DOWN functions
// You can change uses for each of these pins to fit your design
// JD Warren 2010

int ppm1 = 2; // R/C input for failsafe channel
int ppm2 = 3; // R/C input for mower kill-switch
int ppm3 = 4; // R/C input for lights
int ppm4 = 5; // R/C input for dump-bucket lift motor - or anything else you like.

int failsafe_switch = 6; // pin used to switch Failsafe relay
int mower_kill = 7;    // pin used to switch lawnmower kill switch relay

int lights_Pin = 8;   // pin used to switch headlights relay or PWM H-bridge for brighness
control.
int bucket_lift_up = 9; // pin used to raise dump-bucket via H-bridge
int bucket_lift_down = 10; // pin used to lower dump-bucket via H-bridge

// LED pin to turn On when Failsafe is active
int ledPin1 = 13;

// variables to hold the raw R/C readings
unsigned int ppm1_val;
unsigned int ppm2_val;
unsigned int ppm3_val;
unsigned int ppm4_val;

// variables to hold the tested R/C values
unsigned int failsafe_val;

unsigned int mower_kill_val;
unsigned int lights_val;
unsigned int bucket_lift_val;

// End Variables

// Begin setup()

void setup() {
```

```
  Serial.begin(9600); // turn on Serial monitor

  // Declare the OUTPUTS
  pinMode(failsafe_switch, OUTPUT);
  pinMode(mower_kill, OUTPUT);

  pinMode(lights_Pin, OUTPUT);
  pinMode(bucket_lift_up, OUTPUT);
  pinMode(bucket_lift_down, OUTPUT);

  //Failsafe LED
  pinMode(ledPin1, OUTPUT);

  //PPM inputs from RC receiver
  pinMode(ppm1, INPUT);
  pinMode(ppm2, INPUT);

  // The failsafe should be OFF by default
  digitalWrite(failsafe_switch, LOW);

  delay(1000); // wait 1 second after power up for the R/C receiver to connect

}

// End Setup

// Begin Loop

void loop() {

  // Use pulseIn() to read each R/C input using the pulse() function created below the loop().
  pulse();


  ////////// Failsafe relay //////////
  // check to see if pulse value is between 1750 and 2000 microseconds
  if (failsafe_val > 1750 && failsafe_val < 2000) {
    // if so, activate motor-controller
    digitalWrite(failsafe_switch, HIGH);
    digitalWrite(ledPin1, HIGH);
  }
  else {
    // otherwise, deactivate motor-controller
    digitalWrite(failsafe_switch, LOW);
    digitalWrite(ledPin1, LOW);
  }

  //////////// Lawnmower kill-switch relay
  // check lawnmower kill-switch relay
  if (mower_kill_val > 1750 && mower_kill_val < 2000) {
```

```
    // if value is high, activate mower kill relay
    digitalWrite(mower_kill, HIGH);
}
else {
    // otherwise, leave motor kill relay Off
    digitalWrite(mower_kill, LOW);
}


////////// Head-lights
// check light switch value
if (lights_val > 1750 && lights_val < 2000) {
    // if value is high, activate lights
    digitalWrite(lights_Pin, HIGH);
}
else {
    // otherwise, turn lights Off
    digitalWrite(lights_Pin, LOW);
}


////////// Lift motor for dump-bucket using (2) SPDT relays - one for each motor terminal.
// Check to see if bucket_lift_val is above 1700uS pulse length
if (bucket_lift_val > 1700) {
    // if so, lift motor Up
    digitalWrite(bucket_lift_down, LOW);
    digitalWrite(bucket_lift_up, HIGH);
}
// if not, check to see if the pulse is below 1300uS
else if (bucket_lift_val < 1300) {
    // if so, lower motor Down
    digitalWrite(bucket_lift_up, LOW);
    digitalWrite(bucket_lift_down, HIGH);
}
// otherwise, the pulse is Neutral so stop the lift motor
else {
    digitalWrite(bucket_lift_up, LOW);
    digitalWrite(bucket_lift_down, LOW);
}


// Now print the values for each R/C channel
Serial.print(" Failsafe:  ");
Serial.print(failsafe_val);
Serial.print("  ");
Serial.print(" Mower kill-switch:  ");
Serial.print(mower_kill_val);
Serial.print("  ");
Serial.print(" Lights:  ");
Serial.print(lights_val);
Serial.print("  ");
Serial.print(" Bucket lift:  ");
```

```
  Serial.print(bucket_lift_val);
  Serial.println("  ");

}
// End of Loop


// Begin pulse() function to check each R/C input pulse

void pulse() {

  // decode and test the value for ppm1
  ppm1_val = pulseIn(ppm1, HIGH, 20000);
  // check each pulse for a valid signal
  if (ppm1 < 600 || ppm1 > 2400) {
    // if the signal is invalid, set to neutral
    failsafe_val = 1500;
  }
  else {
    // otherwise, set the failsafe_value equal to ppm1_val
    failsafe_val = ppm1_val;
  }

  // decode and test the value for ppm2
  ppm2_val = pulseIn(ppm2, HIGH, 20000);
  if (ppm2 < 600 || ppm2 > 2400) {
    mower_kill = 1500;
  }
  else {
    mower_kill = ppm2_val;
  }

  // decode and test the value for ppm3
  ppm3_val = pulseIn(ppm3, HIGH, 20000);
  if (ppm3 < 600 || ppm3 > 2400) {
    lights_val = 1500;
  }
  else {
    lights_val  = ppm3_val;
  }

  // decode and test the value for ppm4
  ppm4_val = pulseIn(ppm4, HIGH, 20000);
  if (ppm4 < 600 || ppm4 > 2400) {
    bucket_lift_val = 1500;
  }
  else {
    bucket_lift_val = ppm4_val;
  }
}
```

```
// End pulse() function

// End Code
```

If you plan to build the motor controllers from Chapter 8, then you should also use the code from that chapter as well to drive them. There are also several other variations of this code used for different Arduino/motor controller configurations that I used for the Lawn-bot, which are available on the book website in the Chapter 10 folder.

With the code loaded, you should test the failsafe relay first and then the Sabertooth 2x25; make sure you are in an open area with no children, pets, rose bushes, or any other valuables nearby when testing this large robot. When you are satisfied with your testing and have proven that your Lawn-bot does indeed work, you can move to the next section where you can add headlights, a dump bucket, and a lawnmower engine kill switch.

## Adding Cosmetics and Accessories

Shortly after you get your Lawn-bot mowing your grass, you can begin to discover more things that it can do with only minor modifications. Because the Arduino has 20 I/O pins available, you have quite a bit of upgrade room to add some accessories to your Lawn-bot.

Be creative: I have 100 suggestions of things I could add to the Lawn-bot to make it better, so I'm sure you can think of a few things. Hopefully, the code and relay interface switches listed in this chapter can help you get your ideas to work.

The following items are just a few of the things that I did.

### Painting

After I got my Lawn-bot working and cut my grass several times without any problems, I decided to paint it to keep it from rusting. I came up with a striped design using 3/4-inch Scotch painters tape and three different colors of spray paint. The entire paint job cost about $15 and about 2 days of intermittent painting and taping.

I removed the electronics and spray painted the frame and mower deck primer gray with Rustoleum spray paint. I then painted the frame flat black and the mower deck bright blue, using Krylon spray paint, both with yellow accents (see Figure 10-29).

***Figure10-29.*** *A can of brightly colored spray paint to make the Lawn-bot look nice while mowing the grass*

## Headlights

The first thing I wanted to add onto my Lawn-bot was a set of headlights, so it can mow in the evening if I needed to. Also I had a few extra R/C channels and thought it would look cool, which it does (see Figure 10-30). This involved building a smaller version of the failsafe relay circuit, using a 10 amp SPST relay to switch the +12v signal to the two headlights.

*Figure 10-30. Lawn-bot 400 fully painted with headlights installed–as clean as it will ever be. Notice the furry inspector that I had to deal with.*

## Dump Bucket

The next thing I added was more for my back than anything else. The wheel-barrow bucket enables me to throw bags of soil, sand, mulch, or chicken food onto the Lawn-bot, and it happily carries whatever I need out to the various parts of my large backyard. Though I looked for one second-hand, I ended up buying a wheel barrow from the hardware store and removed everything but the steel bucket.

After taking some measurements and lining the bucket onto the frame to verify clearance, I welded two Gate hinges to the bottom of the steel bucket and mounted them to a frame riser bar. The frame riser bars are 1/2-inch diameter, 6-inch long steel bolts mounted to a 2-inch angle-iron cross-beams to hold the bucket above the frame. The bucket tilts forward with little effort and is manageable even with a full load of dirt (see Figure 10-31).

*Figure 10-31. The Lawn-bot with dump bucket and linear actuator lift motor installed*

The next idea was of course to remotely control the dump bucket, so I found a 6amp 24vdc linear actuator motor that has a stroke of around 12 inches. The motor is used to lift the rear of the bucket and dump its contents over the front of the bot. To interface this motor to the Arduino, you can use two N-channel mosfets to activate two SPDT relays (one for each motor terminal). See Figure 10-32 for a schematic of the lift motor control circuit.

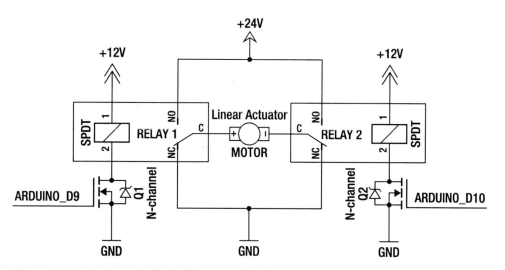

*Figure 10-32. A schematic for the lift-motor circuit using two SPDT relays and two N-channel mosfets to interface the Arduino to the relay coils*

## Lawnmower Kill-Switch

The Lawn-bot has a failsafe kill switch that disconnects the power to the motor controller, but to make the lawnmower engine turn off remotely, you need only another failsafe relay interface. Most lawnmower engines use a wire to short out the spark plug to kill the engine, so you can solder wires to both of the kill-switch contacts on the lawnmower engine and connect them to the power contact of an SPST relay.

This relay should be connected to the Arduino via a Relay interface circuit described earlier in this chapter (see Figure 10-28). I connected the channel to control this relay to the "Trainer" select toggle switch on the R/C transmitter because it is a spring loaded switch that returns to the on position after you have killed the engine. This is a nice addition because it is no fun walking over to the lawnmower and manually killing the engine.

## Summary

In this chapter you built an actual helping robot that does a chore most people despise having to do. Instead of pushing a lawnmower around the yard in the hot sun, breathing in dust, and getting hit with flying debris, you can relax on the back porch under an umbrella, sipping an iced tea while your Lawn-bot does all the hard work for you.

This robot used DC gear motors from a power wheelchair and R/C control as in Chapter 8, but this robot was upgraded with several different useful items, such as high-capacity deep-cycle batteries, rugged pneumatic tires, a sturdy steel frame, a bucket for carrying materials, headlights, and a remote failsafe kill-switch to ensure this big robot can always be disabled.

By using a commercial motor controller (the Sabertooth 2x25), you can drive the bot carefree, knowing that the motor controller has over-current protection built in and can shut down if overworked to avoid damage. The Sabertooth motor controller also has a built-in processor for decoding the two main R/C signals for the drive motors, which frees the Arduino to decode as many other R/C channels as you want to add accessories for.

In the next chapter, you drop down to two wheels to make a balancing, rideable Seg-bot. This balancing scooter uses a gyroscope and accelerometer to correct any tilt from the base, enabling you to control its direction and speed by simply *leaning*. Add a steering potentiometer and a speed knob, and you have a robot that can amaze anyone that sees it.

# CHAPTER 11

# The Seg-Bot

The Seg-bot (Figure 11-1) is the first project in this book intended to carry a human. With this in mind, my primary focus for this project was safety. I should forewarn you that any vehicle that has large motors and weighs 50+ pounds can easily injure a person. You must exercise extreme caution when using or testing this bot, both for yourself and those around you. ***Make sure you understand how the vehicle works before trying to ride it.*** You should also wear protective padding and a helmet while riding. Aside from the safety risk, this is probably the most fun robot in this book to build.

The Seg-bot is a two-wheeled, balancing, rideable robot that is concerned only with one thing: staying level. You control the speed and direction of this robot by leaning front to back; the more you lean, the faster it moves. Steering the Seg-bot is achieved using a potentiometer monitored by the Arduino to determine the direction that you want to travel.

The powerful motors with large rubber tires and a low center of gravity enable the Seg-bot to traverse the outdoors, driving right over rocks, sticks, and bumps, and up steep hills with ease.

This robot does have limitations, so if you try to make it fall, you might succeed–but with some practice, it is surprisingly easy to ride.

*Figure 11-1. The finished Seg-bot*

# How the Seg-Bot Works

To keep this bot balanced, the Arduino needs to know the angle of the frame relative to the ground, so it can command the motors with the appropriate speed and direction needed to keep it from falling over. To accurately measure the angle or tilt of the Seg-bot, you need to detect both the speed of rotation and the gravitational force of its X-axis, using an Inertial Measurement Unit or IMU.

## Inertial Measurement Unit

The IMU is a small PCB that contains a gyroscope and accelerometer, each measuring a different part of the angle.

With the angle measurement from the IMU, the Arduino can determine how fast and in which direction to turn the two motors. The easiest angle approximation (and Arduino coding) is done using a –90 degree to +90 degree scale, where 0 degrees is considered "level" (see Figure 11-2). If the angle measured from the IMU is 0 degrees, the motors stops; above 0 degrees and the motors go proportionally forward; and below 0 degrees and the motors go proportionally reverse. This behavior keeps the Seg-bot level and enables you to control its speed and direction by leaning front to back.

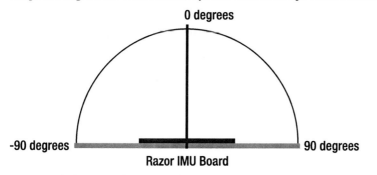

*Figure 11-2. The IMU board measuring 0 degrees (flat on table)*

## Steering and Gain

To steer this vehicle, a potentiometer mounted on the handlebar is turned from left to right while moving. If the dial is centered, the motors receive equal power and drive straight; if turned left or right, the max speeds of each motor is oppositely affected, causing the Seg-bot to turn.

There is also a *gain* potentiometer near the handlebar to adjust the responsiveness or sensitivity of the motors. A higher gain yields faster motor response to angle changes making the Seg-bot much more sensitive (a tighter feel, when riding),whereas a lower gain can result in a slower motor response to angle change (a mushy feel when riding, but more forgiving).

## Engage Switch

Also installed is a button switch that must be pressed to operate the bot. This switch is a large, red button, handily placed where your left thumb sits so that if you fall off the Seg-bot or for any other reason, let go of the handlebar, it immediately stops the motors. There is also an angle limit in the code that kills the motors if tilted too far in either direction. These failsafes keep the Seg-bot rider relatively safe, as long as the rider understands how to operate the bot.

Now that you know the main features of the Seg-bot, take a look at the parts list.

## Parts List for the Seg-Bot

The parts for the Seg-bot are similar to the previous large robots (Chapters 8, "Boat-Bot," and 10, "Lawn-Bot"), using power wheelchair motors, pneumatic tires, and lead-acid batteries. You also use an IMU from Sparkfun.com, and a home-made IMU shield for the Arduino. The Seg-bot also requires a few potentiometers, a button switch, and some square steel tubing for the frame. Take a look at the parts list in Table 11-1.

*Table 11-1. Seg-Bot Parts List*

| Part | Description | Price |
|------|-------------|-------|
| Razor 6 DOF IMU | Sparkfun.com (part# SEN-10010) - Inertial Measurement Unit - +/- 3g accelerometer and gyroscopes. | $59.00 |
| Sabertooth 2x25 motor controller (or similar) | www.dimensionengineering.com - Dual motor controller, 25amp 24vdc. | $125.00 |
| Two DC gear-motors with wheels and tires | eBay - I used two salvaged power wheelchair motors with wheels and outdoor tires; electric brake removed. | $130 total |
| Two 12v, 12AH SLA batteries | BatteriesPlus.com (part# WKA12-12F2) – Werker brand. | $41.00 each |
| Two 5k ohm potentiometers | Radio Shack (part# 271-1714) – used for gain adjustment and steering. | $2.99 each |
| Push-button switch | Radio Shack (part# 275-011) – used as engage switch. | $1.99 |
| 6-foot – 3/4-inch square tubing (metal) | Hardware store – used as frame deck to stand on. | $10.00 |
| 6-foot – 1-inch square tubing | Hardware store – used as main handlebar. | $12.00 |

| Part | Description | Price |
|------|-------------|-------|
| Various bolts | Ten M6 (metric 6mm) bolts for motors, three 1/2" bolts with nuts for frame. All bolts are 2.5" long. | $10.00 |
| Plastic Project Box | Radio Shack (part# 270-1806) – 6"L x 4"W x 2"H, with lid. | $4.99 |
| 120v 20amp Toggle switch | Digikey (part# 360-2087) – any high-power DPST toggle switch should work. | $8.00 |
| 12awg wire, 10 feet | For motors and power to the Sabertooth, should be stranded. | $5.00 |
| Stackable headers 2 x 6-pin and 2 x 8-pin | Sparkfun (part# PRT-09279 and 09280) – Needed for IMU shield, not needed if you buy the Protoshield below | $2 per set |
| Arduino Protoshield (optional) | Sparkfun.com (part# DEV-07914) – used to make adapter board for IMU. | $16.99 (optional) |

The price of the Seg-bot as tested is approximately $500 including the Arduino. You can always substitute similar parts, but you may have to make slight modifications to the steps provided. If you do not want to etch the IMU shield PCB as outlined in this chapter, you can buy an Arduino Protoshield from Sparkfun.com and build an equivalent circuit manually.

Because I was to be riding the Seg-bot (and I value my face), I chose to take no chances and use a commercial motor controller to command the motors. I have been impressed with the Sabertooth 2x25 motor controller as used on the Lawn-bot 400, so I chose to again use the same motor controller for this project but using a different interface method (Simplified Serial).

With the parts list out of the way, following are the sensors used on the Seg-bot.

# Selecting the Right Sensors

After searching around for an accelerometer and gyroscope to use for the Seg-bot, I came across the Razor 6 DOF (Degrees Of Freedom) from Sparkfun.com (Figure 11-3). This sensor board is small, measuring in at 0.75-inch x 1.5-inch and it is extremely thin (hence the name Razor).

*Figure 11-3. The Sparkfun Razor 6DOF IMU*

This IMU is basically a breakout board for the ADXL-335 3-axis (X,Y,Z) accelerometer, the dual-axis (X, Y) LPR530AL gyroscope, and the single-axis (Z) LY530ALH gyroscope. The board includes all needed filtering capacitors and resistors, but there is no voltage regulator on the Razor, so you must provide it with a regulated 3.3v power supply (from Arduino). Each sensor is aligned on the board with respect to each others axes–a 3.3v power supply is all that is needed to start reading from the Analog output pins of the Razor. The Sparkfun Razor 6 DOF IMU specs are listed in Table 11-2.

*Table 11-2. Specifications for the Razor 6 DOF IMU from Sparkfun.com*

| Item | Description |
| --- | --- |
| ADXL-335 | 3-axis Accelerometer (X, Y, Z), +/–3G sensitivity |
| LPR530AL | 2-axis Gyroscope (X,Y),  +/–300 degrees/second sensitivity |
| LY530ALH | 1-axis Gyroscope (Z),  +/–300 degrees/second sensitivity |
| Power input | Requires regulated 3.3v supply from Arduino |
| Signal output | Analog 0v–3.3v |

You can use a different accelerometer and gyroscope if you want; although, you should choose sensors with the same sensitivity range as the Razor 6 DOF if you do not want to alter the code. I chose an IMU with an analog voltage output to create a simple interface with the Arduino. Although the Razor 6 DOF works well for the Seg-bot, you need only accelerometer and gyroscope readings from one the Razor's three measures axes. To save a little money, you might choose a single-axis IMU (X or Y) with the same measurement range as the Razor.

# 3.3v Power

As component parts get smaller, 3.3v devices are becoming more popular. Luckily, the FTDI USB interface chip on the Arduino has a small 3.3v power supply of around 50mA, and the guys who designed the Arduino provided a breakout pin for us to use this 3.3v source. The Razor 6 DOF needs a clean 3.3v power source, but it consumes only a few milliamps of current, so you can power it from the Arduino 3.3v power supply pin. Because the maximum voltage in the chip is 3.3v, you would be right to assume that the analog output voltage for each sensor is also be between 0–3.3v (rather than the usual 0–5v).

The normal range for the Arduinos 10-bit Analog to Digital Converters (pins A0–A5) is 0–1023, where a 0v input yields a value of 0, and a 5v input yields a value of 1023. If you simply plug a 3.3v sensor into an Arduino analog input, the maximum value that the Arduino can read from the sensor is approximately 675 or so (3.3v / 5v * 1023). To get the full range using a 3.3v device, you must connect the desired reference voltage (3.3v) to the Analog reference (Aref) pin on the Arduino and add a line of code to the end of the setup() function to tell the Arduino to use an EXTERNAL analog reference. (That is, use whatever voltage is connected to the Aref pin.) This changes only the reference voltage of the Analog input pins (A0–A5); it does not change any of the other input or output pins, which still produce 5v signals.

To change the analog reference voltage, you need to introduce a new Arduino command;

```
analogReference(EXTERNAL); // add this line to the bottom of the setup() function of your
sketch to use an external analog reference voltage.
```

After you tell the Arduino to look at the Aref pin for the analog voltage reference, don't forget to then connect the 3.3v pin to the Aref pin! For more information about the analogReference() command, visit the following Arduino reference page: http://www.arduino.cc/en/Reference/AnalogReference.

With the board powered and the Arduino reading the proper voltages from the analog inputs, now take a look at the individual sensors that you must interface from the IMU.

# Accelerometer

The accelerometer measures the gravitational force of the IMU relative to the horizon. The accelerometer on the Razor 6DOF can measure the tilt of the IMU to approximately 90 degrees in either direction. To equal 0 degrees (or "level"), the IMU must be parallel to the horizon (see Figure 11-2). If the IMU board is tilted left or right (see Figures 11-4 and 11-5), the angle measurement yields a proportional value in either direction.

Although the accelerometer is capable of measuring tilt of approximately 90 degrees in either direction, you measure up to approximately only 25–30 degrees in either direction for the Seg-bot. Any more tilt than this would result in a hazardous riding condition, so the code is set to shut down the motors in the event that the IMU measures an angle above the limit.

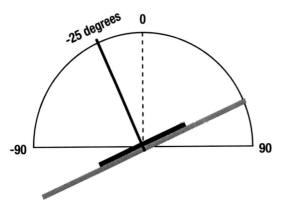

*Figure 11-4. The IMU rotating along its X-axis at –25 degrees (reverse)*

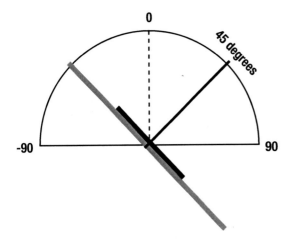

*Figure 11-5. The IMU rotating along its X-axis at 45 degrees (forward)*

Ideally, this sensor can read a steady value proportional to the angle of the board. Using the 10-bit value range of the Analog inputs on the Arduino (0–1023), a "level" IMU can read a center value of 511. If you tilt the IMU board 90-degrees forward (along its X-axis), the value should increase up to 1023, whereas tilting it 90-degrees backward yields a 0 value. The notable feature of the accelerometer is that it can hold its value when tilted; you can test your accelerometer with the code in Listing 11-1.

*Listing 11-1. Use this code to test the readings from an Analog accelerometer.*

```
// Arduino - Analog 3.3v Accelerometer
// Connect accelerometer output into Arduino analog pin 0
// Upload, then open Serial monitor at 9600bps to see accelerometer value
```

```
int angle = 0; // variable used to hold the "rough angle" approximation

void setup(){

  Serial.begin(9600); // start Serial monitor to print values

  analogReference(EXTERNAL); // tell Arduino to use the voltage connected to the Aref pin for
analog reference (3.3v) - remove this command if you are using a 5v sensor.

}

void loop(){

  angle = analogRead(0); // read the accelerometer from Analog pin 0

  Serial.print("Accelerometer: "); // print the word "Accelerometer: " first
  Serial.println(angle); // then print the value of the variable "angle"

  delay(50); // update 20 times per second (1000 mS / 50 mS = 20)

}
```

At first glance, it seems like you could use an accelerometer alone to detect the angle of the IMU board. These sensors are used (by themselves) to detect changes in angular movement for cell phones, laptops, gaming consoles, and many other applications. The reason we cannot use an accelerometer only to detect the angle for the Seg-bot is that it's severely affected by gravity. That is, any sudden change in gravity (even vibrations) can affect the output angle of the accelerometer, even if the angle has not changed.

This is most apparent if you hold the accelerometer at a specific angle and gently vibrate your hand up and down. This can drastically change the output readings, so much so that the signal becomes useless without some sort of filtering to weed out the false readings.

Unfortunately, vibrations and bumps are unavoidable when riding the Seg-bot (or any other moving vehicle) and must be dealt with. This is where the gyroscope sensor comes in handy.

## Gyroscope

The gyroscope measures how fast, or more specifically, how many *degrees per second* the IMU move at a given moment. This value is also represented as a 0–3.3v analog signal from the IMU, so you must convert the 10-bit analog value into an approximate angle. Unfortunately, the gyroscope is not quite as easy to obtain an angular value from because it can measure only the *rate* of angle change.

The gyroscope shows a change in voltage while the sensor is moved along its measured axis. Unlike the accelerometer, when you stop moving the gyroscope, the voltage descends back to its center (zero rate) level. To determine how far the gyroscope has rotated knowing only the rate of change, you must also know the time period of the change. To do this, determine the time of each loop cycle and calculate the distance (in degrees) that the gyroscope has rotated given the speed output.

# Cycle Time

Much like a speedometer in your car, you cannot determine how far you have traveled by looking at the speed alone; you must also know the time of travel at the given speed to calculate the distance. To determine how far the gyroscope has traveled (in degrees/second), you must know the time interval between each loop cycle.

The loop cycle is typically fast (can be several hundred times per second depending on the code) and the gyroscope output is in degrees per second, so you must multiply the gyroscope rate by the time that it occurred during to get the actual rate per second. Because the update time can change slightly from cycle to cycle, I decided to record a timestamp at the end of each loop cycle to determine how long it has been since the last update.

The `millis()` value at the end of each loop is recorded into a variable called `last_cycle` and serves as the previous timestamp for each new loop cycle. With the previous timestamp available at the end of each loop, you can easily calculate how long it has been since the last gyroscope reading by subtracting the most recent `time_stamp` from the current `millis()` timer value. This calculation is done just before the end of the loop where `last_cycle` is updated with the new `millis()` value to set the timestamp for the next cycle.

# Gyro Starting Point

Calculating an angle with the gyroscope is inherently different than with the accelerometer because the gyroscope is measuring only a rotational speed. To obtain a position with the rate of change, you must provide a known *starting point* and a known time interval between readings. Although the starting point will be assumed to = 0 degrees, the cycle time for each loop is calculated and set to 50 milliseconds.

For example:

```
Angle_Rate = analogRead(gyro_Pin) * cycle_time;
```

This snippet of code would calculate the angular rate per second of the gyroscope at a given moment. Although this instantaneous value will be useful to help determine how much the board has moved, it must then be added to previous readings to get an actual current angle. By adding the following line of code after the preceding line, you not only read and calculate the gyro angle change (`Angle_Rate`), but also add that change to the total angle measurement (`Angle`).

```
Angle = Angle + Angle_Rate;
```

You can test your gyro to see how it reads the angle, but notice that without any solid reference to the actual angle (such as the accelerometer), the gyro suffers from a small deviation in accuracy called *drift*.

# Gyroscope Drift

The *drift* of a gyroscope refers to its tendency to deviate from its starting point, even when not moving. This means that the device has a small but steady "error" that adds up each time the loop is cycled. This drift keeps the gyroscope from being 100% correct, even if everything else is tuned perfectly. This error makes it difficult to accurately obtain an angle calculation without an accelerometer to use as a reference point for the angle.

# Gyroscope Versus Accelerometer Summary

From my testing of these devices individually, I learned that while the accelerometer is excellent for referencing an actual angle by itself without any calculations (except mapping), it is highly prone to erroneous readings in an unstable environment (such as the Seg-bot). When I tried to use the accelerometer only, the test bot would quickly fall over due to spikes in the angular readings causing absurd speed values to be written to the motors.

When trying to use the gyroscope by itself, the angle approximation was much more stable from cycle to cycle with no discernible spikes in the angular value. But this "stable" value would drift away from its resting point such that the bot would stay balanced for a few seconds before slowly falling over. This was because the gyro drift was adding up after each cycle and causing the angle reading to deviate from its actual position. (That is, it thinks it is at 0 degrees, level, when it is actually at 5 degrees and counting...TIMBER!)

To keep the angle calculation from experiencing the negative effects from either sensor, you need to combine the best parts of both signals to create a filtered angle, free from both noise and error.

## Filtering the Angle

With both semi-erroneous sensor readings available, you need to combine them to get a stable angle reading. This is commonly done using a Kalman filter, but I found this to be too complicated for my taste–my angle filtering will be done using a type of complementary filter, more commonly referred to as a weighted average. The weighted average is as stable as the gyroscope angle calculation without the drift error and as precise as the accelerometer reading without the spikes from bumps and vibrations.

## Weighted Average

The equation to calculate the total angle of the IMU is determined using a weighted average. The average is split between the gyroscope and the accelerometer, each contributing their perspective as to what the angle should be. We get to decide how much each sensor contributes to the total outcome.

Because the accelerometer is highly susceptible to bumps, vibrations, and other sudden changes in gravity, weight it's contribution to the total angle low (2%). The motor speed commands are issued on a cycle-by-cycle basis in the main loop; if the accelerometer sends an erroneous value, the motors would immediately respond (causing jerky movements). To avoid the spikes found in the accelerometer readings, use it only as a reference, making sure the gyroscope doesn't drift too far from the actual angle.

Weighted average:

Gyroscope = 98%

Accelerometer = 2%

The gyroscope reading is far less susceptible to rough terrain so it is weighted heavily at 98%. The drift error of the gyro is corrected with the filter because the small weighted average from the accelerometer draws the filtered angle back toward the actual angular reading each loop cycle. To implement the weighted average in the code, multiply each sensor's reading by the percentage of weight that it contributes to the total angle; the sum of these two percentages should combine to equal 100%, or 1.0 in this case. The following formula sets the angle variable equal to the sum of each weighted average.

Angle = (0.98 * gyro_angle) + (0.02 * accel_angle);

This formula is simply the angle calculations of both sensors, multiplied by the percentage that each should be weighted toward the total angle. The resulting angle calculation filters out both the gyroscope drift and accelerometer vibrations to yield a stable and usable angle approximation.

Now that you know how to combine the angle values from each sensor, make an adapter board to interface the Razor 6 DOF IMU to the Arduino. Use concepts from Chapter 6, "Making PCBs," to design and build a simple IMU shield to plug into the Arduino and provide a 3.3v power source for the IMU, and route each sensor output to an appropriate Arduino analog input pin.

## Making the IMU Adapter Board

The Razor 6 DOF IMU has two rows of 8 pins (0.1-inch spacing) that are 0.6-inch apart. To make a secure connection with the Arduino, you can either etch a small PCB to use as a shield or buy an Arduino Protoshield.

I used Eagle to design a simple breakout board shield to mate the Razor 6 DOF securely to the Arduino (see Figure 11.6). The shield taps into the 3.3v power supply from the Arduino to power the Razor IMU and connects the X, Y, and Z outputs directly to the six Arduino analog inputs. I had no plans to use the Z-axis of either the accelerometer or gyro, so I cut the traces on the shield (to analog inputs A2 and A3) and used them for the steering and gain potentiometers on the handlebar.

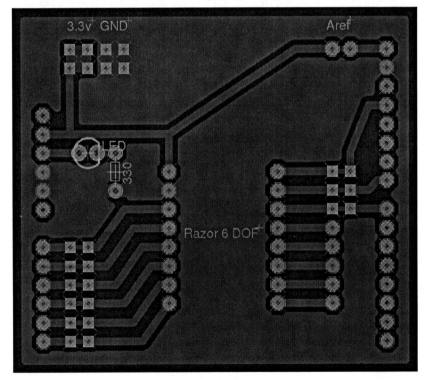

*Figure 11-6. A home-made Arduino shield for the Sparkfun Razor 6 DOF using Eagle*

To make this PCB, you need to download the files from the following website and follow the instructions in Chapter 6 for etching a PCB at https://sites.google.com/site/arduinorobotics/home/chapter11_files.

You might notice that there are different types of headers used to plug the Razor IMU onto the shield (Figure 11.7). The two Female headers are used to supply the +3.3v and GND connections whereas the remaining male pin headers are used to connect the output pins from the IMU to the IMU shield. (You must use opposite pin headers to solder onto the IMU.) I did this to ensure that you cannot plug the IMU onto the shield incorrectly, causing possible damage to the sensors.

*Figure 11-7. The finished IMU shield, with power LED and resistor*

You can alternatively make a shield without etching a PCB, using a Sparkfun Arduino Protoshield. The stackable headers should come with the Protoshield kit, so you should need only 16 female pin headers and 16 male pin headers to complete the board. It does not matter which headers you use on which board; although, I soldered the female headers on the IMU and the male headers on the shield board (except for the power pins which are reversed for polarity protection).

With the IMU shield finished, select some motors to use for the Seg-bot.

# Selecting the Motors

You an choose from several different DC motor types to choose from when building a balancing scooter. Standard DC motors like those found in electric scooters work and can be found for approximately $25 each, whereas DC gear motors like those salvaged from power wheelchairs are slightly more expensive but might be more forgiving on the Seg-bot (see Figure 11-8). Brushless servo motors are the type used in the commercial Segway models and are probably ideal, but their cost is too great for my testing purposes.

*Figure 11-8. The DC gear motors used for the Seg-bot*

I chose to use two 24v DC gear motors from a power wheelchair to drive my Seg-bot. I decided against using nongeared DC motors because they *typically* spin at a much higher RPM (1200–4000 RPM) to get the same torque. The geared motors have a standard high-RPM DC motor spinning into a gear box that reduces the speed while proportionally increasing the torque. The result of using the geared motor is a surprisingly smooth ride with powerful angle correction–far more manageable than I had anticipated. Table 11-3 lists the specifications of the specific motors that I used.

*Table 11-3. The Specifications for Each DC Gear Motor Obtained from ebay.com.*

| Manufacturer | AMT Schmid GmbH |
|---|---|
| Model | Gear-motor SRG 04 |
| Voltage | 24VDC |
| Amperage | 15A |
| Watts | 400W |
| Max speed | 8 mph |
| Price | $130 per pair (used on ebay.com) |

These *used* power-chair motors were purchased from ebay.com and had the original wheels still attached. They are also each equipped with a disengage lever, used to mechanically disconnect the motor gear boxes from the wheels; this is useful for safe transportation and testing purposes.

## Electric Brake Removal

Many power-chair motors are equipped with electric solenoid brakes that clamp to the rear of the motor shaft and keep it from moving when the power chair is turned off. Although this safety feature helps protect the power-chair operator from rolling down a hill in the event of a low battery, it is not necessary for our Seg-bot and should be removed.

You can usually determine if your motors have an electric brake by the number of wires in the harness (see Figure 11.9). If your motor has a wiring harness with four wires, it probably has an electric brake. The two smaller wires are used to control the brake solenoid, which is not released until the terminals are powered, usually by 12vdc.

*Figure 11-9. The wiring harness connector of a motor with an electric solenoid brake installed*

To remove the electric brake, you must first locate it under the dust cap on the rear of the motor housing. Remove the two or three screws that hold the dust cap on to the end of the motor (see Figure 11.10).

**Figure 11-10.** *The dust cap on the end of the motor*

When the brake is visible, you should see 3–5 bolts holding the brake solenoid into the motor housing. These bolts need to be removed, and the wires leading to the solenoid can be snipped (see Figure 11-11). With the brake solenoid removed, the top of the motor assembly should look similar to the top motor in Figure 11-11, whereas the lower motor is pictured with the brake solenoid still installed.

*Figure 11-11. The two motors with dust caps removed–the brake has been removed from the upper motor, while still in place on the lower motor.*

In Figure 11-12, you can again see the difference between the two motors; the brake has been removed from the left motor while still installed on the right motor. After both solenoid brakes are removed, you can reinstall the dust covers onto the end of the motor assemblies. The new (modified) motors should weigh a few pounds less after the mechanical surgery. Now the small center contacts from the harness in Figure 11-9 will no longer be active; you need only the two large outside contacts to operate each motor.

*Figure 11-12. The two motors standing next to each other, the brake has been removed from the left motor, while still in place on the right motor. The dust caps are on the ground next to the motors.*

Alternatively, you *could* leave the solenoid brakes in place, but you would need another relay interface used to supply 12v to the solenoid brakes of each motor when you turn the main power on. This of course, would draw an extra 500mA – 1A continuously from the main battery supply just to keep the motor brakes disengaged while using—so I recommend just removing them.

## Motor Mounting Position

Although it is ideal to have the weight of the motors perfectly balanced, so the bot will balance by itself, it is not necessary. The mounting holes on my motors would have made it extremely difficult to position the motors vertically (which would have provided better balance), so I mounted them pointing toward the front of the bot. Because you need to hold the Engage button to activate the motors, I found no need to make the bot balance without me being on it. When you stand on the bot, it is easy to keep it balanced because your weight is mostly at the rear of the frame. You can still make the Seg-bot balance by itself if you like, by adding a small counterweight to the rear of the frame until it balances by itself without moving forward or backward.

Now that the motors are prepared for use, select a motor controller to supply them power.

## Selecting the Motor Controller

Because the Seg-bot is intended to be a rideable vehicle, I chose to use the Sabertooth 2x25 commercial motor controller (see Figure 11-13). You may recall from Chapter 10, "Lawn-Bot," that the Sabertooth 2x25 can power two brushed DC motors in both directions, at up to 24vdc and 25 amp each, which is plenty for the motors used on this bot.

You can build your own motor controller, but if something goes wrong ,it is your face that will likely suffer. As safety is the primary concern here, I would recommend choosing a tested and reliable motor-controller platform.

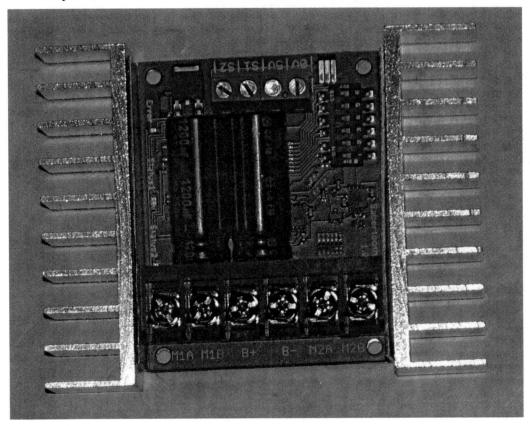

**Figure 11-13.** *The Sabertooth 2x25 motor controller*

> ■ **Note:** Another good option for the Seg-bot would be the open source motor controller, though you would need one for each motor and the code would need to be modified for direct H-bridge control.

In the last chapter, we used the Sabertooth 2x25 to decode the servo signals from the R/C receiver, but here we use the Arduino to command the Sabertooth using the simplified Serial mode. To prepare the Sabertooth to communicate with the Arduino, set the jumpers on the Sabertooth to operate in simplified Serial mode at 9600bps, as shown in Figure 11.14.

*Figure 11-14. Using the Sabertooth DIP switch wizard from:*
*www.dimensionengineering.com/Sabertooth2X25.htm*

To transmit a Serial command from the Arduino to the Sabertooth, you simply connect the Arduino serial Tx pin (D1) to the Sabertooth S1 input, and use the `Serial.print()` command. This however can cause a problem when debugging if you also want to use the `Serial.print()` command to send values back to the Serial monitor on your PC because these values can also be sent to the Sabertooth. To remedy this, send the values to the Sabertooth using a simulated Serial library for Arduino, which is discussed next.

## SoftwareSerial Library

The Arduino SoftwareSerial library enables you to create a separate (virtual) Serial communication line on any Arduino I/O pin. With a max speed of 9600bps, SoftwareSerial is suitable for sending commands from the Arduino to the Sabertooth motor controller. The Sabertooth does not send any information back to the Arduino, so you only need a Serial transmit pin (Tx); although you set up both (Listing 11-2).

*Listing 11-2. Minimal SoftwareSerial setup.*

```
#include <SoftwareSerial.h> // Tell Arduino to use the SoftwareSerial library

// define the transmit and receive pins to use
#define rxPin 2
#define txPin 3

// set up a new serial port to use pins 2 and 3 above
SoftwareSerial mySerial = SoftwareSerial(rxPin, txPin);

void setup() {

  Serial.begin(9600); // start the standard Serial monitor

  // define pin modes for SoftwareSerial tx, rx pins:
  pinMode(rxPin, INPUT);
  pinMode(txPin, OUTPUT);

  // set the data rate for the new SoftwareSerial port
  mySerial.begin(9600);
}

void loop() {

mySerial.print(0, BYTE); // this will print through pin 3 to the Sabertooth
Serial.print("Hello"); // this will print through pin 1 to your computer Serial monitor

delay(100);


}
```

For more information regarding the uses and limitations of the SoftwareSerial library, please visit the Arduino reference page at www.arduino.cc/en/Reference/SoftwareSerial.

Now that you have the Arduino talking to the Sabertooth, consider what it needs to say to the Sabertooth to make the motors move.

## Sabertooth Simplified Serial

The Sabertooth 2x25 motor controller is programmed to accept a simple Serial protocol that enables forward and reverse speed control of both motors. The Sabertooth looks for a Serial value between 0 and 255 in the Byte value range. Two motors are controlled by the Sabertooth and each has to go two directions, so the 255 number range must be broken up into four parts (2 motor x 2 directions = 4). The byte "0" is a full Stop command and can be used to simultaneously command both motors to the stop position.

Bytes 1–127 are used to control Motor1 and bytes 128–255 are used to control Motor2. These two value ranges are each broken up into forward and reverse, with the center positions (64 and 192) being neutral for each motor (see Figure 11-15). There are 64 speed control steps in either direction for either motor, providing adequate resolution and smooth acceleration.

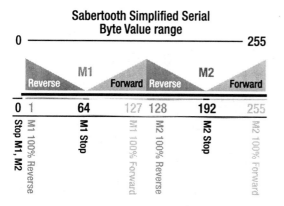

**Figure 11-15.** *I made this graph to better illustrate the Simplified Serial input method of the Sabertooth motor controller.*

The code to control the motors focus on converting the angle value into a speed value centered around the stop points for each motor. To do this, use the Arduino map() command, which takes one value range and stretches it across another.

Now select some batteries that have enough power to drive the Seg-bot to the mailbox and back...or maybe to the coffee shop.

# The Batteries

To get the optimal power from the motors, they should be powered at the recommended operating voltage, which is 24VDC for most power wheelchair gear motors. If you plan to use LiPoly batteries with the Sabertooth 2x25 motor controller, you should limit the battery pack size to 6 cells in series (22.2v) because any higher would surpass the maximum recommended voltage limit. Having built and *rebuilt* several motor controllers, I can attest that the voltage limits of mosfet transistors are sensitive, and the closer you work at their limit, the more likely you are to damage them. Do not exceed a 24vdc battery rating with the Sabertooth 2x25!

The weight of the Seg-bot affects the current draw from the motors, which can in turn affect how long the batteries can supply them power. (Higher current draw = less run time from batteries.) Using lead-acid batteries may be cheaper and provide more Amp-Hour capacity per dollar, but it is much heavier at about 20 pounds per set of batteries. Using LiPo (lithium polymer) batteries would be slightly more expensive, but only weigh about 5 pounds for the same capacity—that's 15 lbs less!

## Sealed Lead-Acid

Lead-acid batteries are the most efficient for the price where weight is not a primary concern. However, if you plan to make a portable or lightweight scooter, you might consider using NiMH or LiPo batteries (at a higher price). Using two 12v, 12AH SLA batteries (see Figure 11-16), the Seg-bot can drive for an hour or more continuously on flat terrain. Remember that driving on hilly terrain draws more current from the batteries, which can drain them quicker.

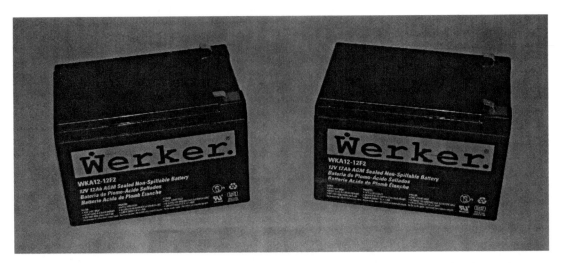

*Figure 11-16. These two 12v 12AH Werker brand batteries provide plenty of run time for the Seg-bot.*

I chose to use two 12v SLA batteries rated at 12AH each, wired in series to produce 24v and 12AH. These batteries are readily available online and in battery stores, measuring 6-inch L x 4-inch W x 3.8-inch H and weighing 10lbs each. You can use a higher capacity battery if you like; my original thought was to use 18AH batteries, but they would not fit in my frame design. As long as the batteries fit on your frame and produce 24v, they should work fine.

## Charging

I charge these batteries with a standard 12v automotive battery charger using the low-power 2-amp charge level. I also disconnect the batteries from their 24v series configuration and use two home-made cables to connect the two batteries in parallel for charging, effectively decreasing the charging rate by doubling the Amp Hour rating from 12AH to 24AH. Charging a 24AH load at 2-amps equals a C/12 charging rate instead of a C/6 rate. I typically charge my batteries at the lowest rate possible to prolong the life of the cells. If you use rapid chargers (that is, high-amperage charge rate) on lead-acid (SLA), NiMH, or NiCad batteries, you notice the total life of the battery decrease significantly.

## 12v Supply

As you may recall, the Arduino boards voltage input is limited to a recommended maximum of 12v (and an absolute limit of 20v), so to avoid damaging the +5v regulator on the Arduino, you need to power it with 12v. In this two-battery series connection, it is easy to get 12v, by simply tapping into the series wire connecting the two batteries (See Figure 11.17).

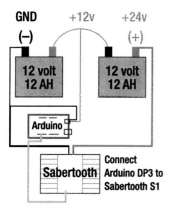

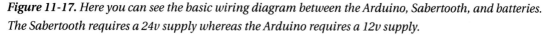

*Figure 11-17. Here you can see the basic wiring diagram between the Arduino, Sabertooth, and batteries. The Sabertooth requires a 24v supply whereas the Arduino requires a 12v supply.*

With the batteries selected, it is time to build the frame. Use the battery dimensions to help determine the required size of the frame base, and after the frame is completed, mount the batteries to the underside of the frame between the motors.

## The Frame

As with most of the larger robots, the frame provide2 the strength needed to hold each piece of the Seg-bot securely together, and provides a canvas to mount buttons, knobs, switches, or any other controls needed to operate the Seg-bot. Although an elaborate frame design might be more visually appealing, use a basic design that is sturdy and provides a comfortable base to ride on.

The Seg-bot frame consists of the following four sections of steel square tubing (and flat bar for the battery rack):

1.  A **base** for the passenger to stand on

2.  A **handlebar** for the passenger to hold on to

3.  A **handlebar riser** to connect the base and handlebar

4.  A **battery rack** to hold the set of SLA batteries beneath the base

I used square tubing instead of angle iron (used in previous chapters) to add strength and provide a flush base to mount onto the motors. I also used two different sizes of square tubing for this project, 1-inch for the handlebar and riser-bar and 3/4-inch for the frame base that both connects the motors together and provides a sturdy platform for the passenger to stand on. You can use 1-inch tubing for the whole project but because it is not necessary, I chose the cheaper and lighter 3/4-inch tubing for the base. Figure 11-18 shows a diagram of the Seg-bot's frame pieces.

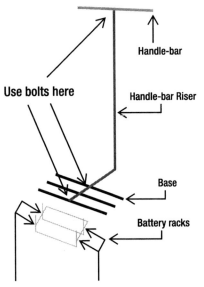

**Use bolts here**

Handle-bar

Handle-bar Riser

Base

Battery racks

**Use bolts or weld here**

*Figure 11-18. This diagram of the entire frame (without motors or wheels attached shows the various pieces of the Seg-bot.*

## Frame Design

The upper frame is a 72-inch piece of 1inch square steel tubing, cut into two pieces. The longer, 52inch piece serves as the main handlebar riser assembly and must be semi-cut and bent into a slightly obtuse L shape (see Figure 11-19).

The shorter 20-inch piece is used as the top part of the T handlebar and houses both steering and gain potentiometers, and the Engage button. It is bolted to the top of the frame riser bar using a large bolt.

The base consists of (three) 18-inch pieces of 3/4-inch steel square tubing, each bolted to the motors and the upper frame piece (see Figure 11-20). To keep the weight centered between the wheels, the batteries are housed under the frame base using a small cage formed from 1/2-inch steel flat bar (see Figure 11.21). Though it could be avoided, I chose to use my wire-feed welder to strengthen a few spots and keep from adding extra support braces and bolts.

The battery cage must be larger enough to house the two SLA batteries which measure 6-inch L x 4-inch W x 3.8-inch H each. I made the battery cage large enough to hold both batteries and contain some of the wiring using (three) 20-inch long pieces of 1/2-inch wide flat steel bar (1/8-inch thick). The flat bars are each bent 90 degrees, 5 inches from each end—it should bend easily using a vise or pliers.

The entire frame assembly connects to each motor gear box using ten 8mm bolts. There are three 1/2-inch bolts used to connect the frame; one connects the upper T handle together, and the other two bolts connect the base frame to the lower part of the handlebar. You may also need four small bolts to hold the battery cage to the frame base if you do not have access to a welder.

With the basic design out of the way, it is time to get out your metal cutting saw, a drill, and a few other standard hand tools to begin building the frame.

# Building the Frame

To build the frame, first cut several pieces from the metal tubing to make the various frame sections. After cutting each piece, drill a few holes where needed and bolt everything together. The following eight steps guide you through the frame building process:

1. Cut a 72-inch piece of 1-inch steel square tube into two sections: 52 inch and 20 inch.

2. Cut a V notch into a 52-inch piece of tube, about 10 inches from the end (see Figure 11.19). Make a V cut into the top and sides of the square tube, but do not cut through the bottom of the piece.

### 1 inch steel square tube – Frame riser

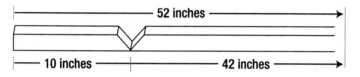

*Figure 11-19. You need to cut a V shape out of the handlebar to bend it.*

3. Bend the 52-inch piece at notch until cut edges touch each other. Either bolt or weld this joint together to keep it from moving after positioned.

4. Cut the three 18-inch frame base pieces of 3/4-inch steel square tubing.

5. Bolt the three frame base pieces to the motor gearbox assemblies, drilling holes where necessary to fit your motors (see Figure 11.20).

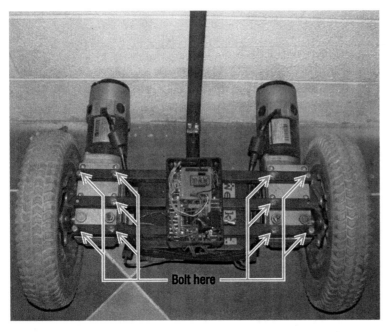

**Bolt here**

*Figure 11-20. The base frame showing the location of needed bolts into the motor gear-boxes*

6. Mount the frame riser bar to the underside of the frame base pieces, centered between the wheels. I used two bolts to secure the base pieces into the 10-inch section (bottom) of the frame riser. (I did not use a bolt on the center base piece.)

7. Mount the T-handle bar piece to the top of the frame riser bar using a 2.5-inch bolt, as shown in Figure 11-23.

8. Make a small cage to hold the batteries beneath the frame base. You either need to bolt or weld this cage together and to the frame base (see Figure 11.21).

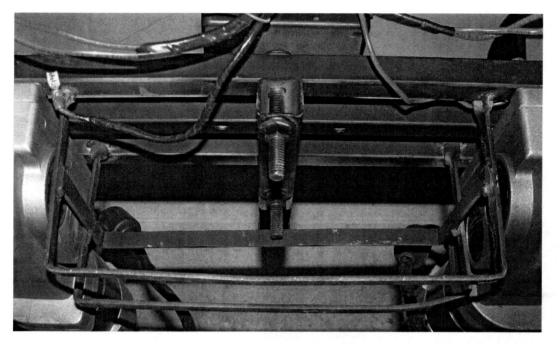

**Figure 11-21.** *The underside of the base frame showing the battery cage*

When assembled, the completed frame should look similar to Figure 11-22. I painted my entire frame black to look nice and protect the metal from rust. Painting is not required, but if you do plan to paint your frame, it is easier to do so before anything is mounted to it.

*Figure 11-22. The finished frame after painting black*

Your frame should be complete and ready for the motors, batteries, and electronics to be mounted. Start by wiring the frame with some input controls near the handlebar to allow steering and sensitivity (gain) inputs, and an Engage button to make sure there is an operator on board before engaging the motors.

# Inputs

The Seg-bot has several user inputs that enable it to manipulate the data received from the IMU before it is sent to the motors. Currently the Arduino reads three inputs : a steering potentiometer, a gain potentiometer, and an engage switch. The steering potentiometer enables the operator to precisely control the direction of the Seg-bot, while leaning to control the speed. To accommodate for different riding preference and styles, a gain potentiometer adjusts the sensitivity of the motor response to angle changes. Lastly, to ensure that there is an operator on the Seg-bot before activating the motors, I placed a simple (large) button switch on the handlebar of the Seg-bot that must be pressed by the operator at all times. This button is backed with a function in the code that when pressed waits until the Seg-bot is completely level before engaging the motors; this keeps the bot from lunging back to the level position if the Engage button is pressed while the Seg-bot is tilted.

## Steering

The Arduino code reads the input from the X-axis on the IMU to determine the forward/reverse speed of *both* motors. Without any further additions, the hardware enables only the Seg-bot to travel either forward or reverse because the two motors are driven at the same speed.

To steer the Seg-bot, the motors need to be sent different speed values. To turn left, the left motor needs a lower speed value than the right motor. For smooth and responsive control, the changes made to each motor should be inversely proportional to each other. That is, as you decrease the left by 1 unit, you also increase the right by 1, causing a total speed difference of 2 units. By creating an imbalance in the values sent to each motor, you can turn the Seg-bot with great precision.

You can implement the steering sensor in several ways, the simplest is with a single 5k potentiometer. The code is set to read the potentiometer value of 0–1023 and convert the value to a range of 10 speed units in either direction. This increases or decreases the normal motor output values by up to a difference of 20 speed units from the left motor to the right, depending on which direction the potentiometer is turned. To drive the Seg-bot straight, the potentiometer must be in the center position.

## Gain

Depending on the battery voltage, charge of the batteries, and gearing of the motors, the maximum speed of the Seg-bot might need to be adjusted for comfortable riding. To make this easy to do without reprogramming, I added another potentiometer to change the maximum speed value. The 0–1023 value from this potentiometer will be converted (mapped) into the maximum speed value for both motors, ranging from 50% to 100%. This enables the user to change the balancing sensitivity of the Seg-bot while in use.

## Engage Switch

The final input for the Seg-bot is the addition of the engage switch, which tells the Seg-bot that you are ready to ride. The engage switch is nothing more than a large Red momentary button-switch mounted to the handlebar and must be pressed for the Seg-bot to move. The Seg-bot stops as soon as the Engage button is released, so you must be sure to keep a good grip on it with your thumb when riding.

## Level-Start

I added a small block of code to not only check the status of the Engage button but also the IMU angle. While the Engage button is open (not pressed), the Seg-bot cannot move; when the Engage button is closed (pressed), the code begins to check the IMU angle to make sure it is at 0 degrees before engaging the motors. When the Seg-bot is leveled to 0 degrees, it smoothly engages the motors and again begins processing the motor speed values. This keeps the Seg-bot from jerking quickly to correct its angle, in case you accidentally push the button while it is not level.... Safety first!

To connect each of these inputs to the Arduino, run some wires from the top of the frame where each input is mounted down to the base of the frame where the Arduino and IMU are mounted. I used a 4-conductor intercom wire from Radio Shack (item# 278-858) and a separate GND signal wire to run the input signals through the square tubing frame riser, thus concealing and protecting each wire. First, mount each input control to the handlebar and frame riser.

## Mounting the Inputs to the Frame

To mount the input controls to the frame, you need a few drill bits and a power drill. Start by taking a look at the finished handlebar in Figure 11-23, showing the Engage button, steering potentiometer, and gain potentiometer mounted into the 1-inch square tube frame.

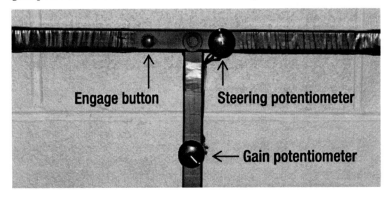

*Figure 11-23. The front view of the handlebar with all three input devices visible.*

The following six steps guide you through installing the input controls:

1.  To mount the gain potentiometer onto the square tubing, you first need to drill a 5/16-inch hole centered on the tube all the way through, about 6-inch below the top of the T-handle. Now use a 5/8-inch drill bit to go through the front hole only; the rear hole should remain 5/16-inch. Now you can slide the potentiometer through from the rear of the square tube; use needle-nose pliers to tighten the nut onto the base through the 5/8-inch hole (see Figure 11.24).

*Figure 11-24. The Gain potentiometer mounted through the steel square tubing. If you look through the 5/8-inch hole, you can see the potentiometer mounting nut tightened down to the backside of the square tubing. Also visible behind the square tubing on the right side is the potentiometer base with three signal leads.*

2. Mount the steering potentiometer in exactly the same way as the gain potentiometer but mount it on the actual T-handle, accessible to your right thumb (when riding the Seg-bot). See Figure 11.25 for a closer look.

*Figure 11-25. The steering potentiometer (without knob) mounted to the handlebar, just to the left of the handlebar grip*

3. Mount the Engage switch (Red button) almost the same as the potentiometers, except reverse the holes; that is, the 5/8-inch hole should be drilled on the back of the square tube, whereas the 5/16-inch hole is to remain on the front side (see figure 11.26).

**Figure 11-26.** *The backside of the Engage button switch, mounted into the square tube frame. There are two wires soldered to the rear terminals of the switch; one connects to GND and the other to Arduino D4.*

4. Now remove the red plastic button top, remove the mounting nut, and slide the button switch through the larger 5/8-inch hole and again through the smaller mounting hole. Lastly, secure the mounting nut to the switch from the front side of the tubing and reinstall the red button top (see Figure 11.27).

5. After installing the input devices, wrap the handlebar with electrical tape to give it some padding for a grip.

*Figure 11-27. The large Red button on the left side of the handlebar is used as the Engage switch.*

6. Run signal wires from T-handle to base. To conceal the wires running from the Arduino to the inputs, I decided to run the wire inside of the square tubing of the frame riser, from the base up to the top of the handlebar. To do this, you drill a 5/8-inch hole or cut a hole with a Dremel tool, near the bottom of the handlebar tube, about 3 inches from the base (see Figure 11.28). I used a spool of 4-conductor wire from Radio Shack. There are however three inputs plus GND and +3.3v, so you actually need five wires to connect each control input to the Arduino, which means an extra single wire must also be used. Remember to use a solid core wire (not stranded) if you plan on plugging it into the Arduino.

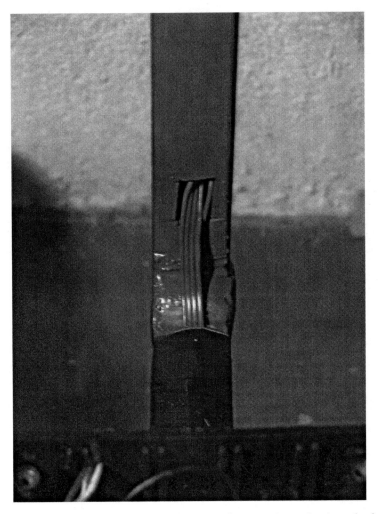

*Figure 11-28. Here you can see the painted Input wires going into the frame riser bar through a hole that I cut. By routing the wires through the steel tubing, they stay protected from being cut or pinched.*

The Seg-bot should now be ready to install the electronics and make the final connections.

## Installing the Electronics

To house the electronics and protect the IMU, I decided to mount everything in a plastic project box (with a lid) from Radio Shack. The 6-inch L x 4-inch W x 2-inch H plastic project enclosure box is the perfect size to house the Arduino, Sabertooth motor controller, and the IMU shield atop the Arduino. Also squeezed into the project box is the high-power Toggle switch used to switch the main power to the Arduino and Sabertooth.

To get the wires through the project box, cut two rectangular pieces out of the plastic box with a Dremel tool and a cutoff wheel. The first piece is cut out to allow easy access to the USB programming port on the Arduino (see Figure 11.29). The second piece is cut to allow the motor and power wires from the Sabertooth to the batteries and motor wiring harnesses (see Figure 11.30).

*Figure 11-29. A rough cut into the project box with the Dremel tool enables easy access to reprogram the Arduino during testing.*

*Figure 11-30. The rear of the box also has a cutout for wires to pass through.*

After test-fitting the Arduino and Sabertooth and cutting access holes in the project box, you need to bolt everything down. You can use #6 bolts and nuts to secure the Sabertooth and the Arduino to the bottom of the plastic project box. To be sure they do not move, you might consider adding a dab of hot glue around the nuts and bolts to keep them from vibrating loose during use.

With the two main boards secured to the box (see Figure 11-31), securing the box to the frame is all that is needed to complete the electronics installation. You can use two #8 bolts to secure the project box to the center base frame bar (one bolt on the left and one on the right). The center bar is then bolted to each motor gear box to keep it securely connected to the frame.

*Figure 11-31. Everything mounted into the project box securely*

You can then mount the power toggle-switch onto the side of the project box I wrapped the toggle-switch contacts in electrical tape before installing it above the Sabertooth (see Figure 11-31) because it was only 1/2 inch from the Sabertooth's metal heat-sink–you don't want any sparks!

## Soldering the Inputs

With the inputs installed, you need to solder the wires to the button and potentiometer terminals. You should run common +3.3v and GND power supply signals to the handlebar, and then share them between the Input devices, as shown in Figure 11.32.

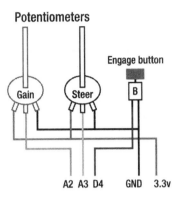

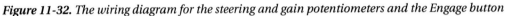

*Figure 11-32. The wiring diagram for the steering and gain potentiometers and the Engage button*

Make sure you connect the outer terminals of each potentiometer with the power signals (+3.3v and GND) and the center terminal of each potentiometer to the Arduino input pin. The Engage button switch has only two terminals and should be connected to the Arduino input and GND.

The Seg-bot should now be ready for wiring.

## Wiring the Connections

The Seg-bot now needs to have each wire connected before you can upload the code and start testing. There is one wire connection between the Arduino and Sabertooth (other than GND), and three input wires from the engage button and potentiometers (and +3.3v and GND) that need to be connected to the Arduino.

Table 11-3 shows how each connection should be made from the inputs to the Arduino, the Arduino to the Sabertooth, and from the Sabertooth to the motors, where an x = no connection to that device.

*Table 11-3. Wiring Connections for Arduino and Sabertooth*

| Wire | Arduino | Sabertooth 2x25 |
|---|---|---|
| SoftwareSerial wire | Digital pin 3 | Input S1 |
| Gain potentiometer input wire (center tab) | Analog Input pin 2 | x |
| Steering potentiometer input wire (center tab) | Analog Input pin 3 | x |
| Engage button wire (either tab) | Digital pin 4 | x |
| +12v wire from battery | VIN pin | x |

| Wire | Arduino | Sabertooth 2x25 |
|---|---|---|
| +24v wire from battery | x | B+ |
| GND wire from battery | GND | B- |
| Left motor wire A | x | M1A |
| Left motor wire B | x | M1B |
| Right motor wire A | x | M2A |
| Right motor wire B | x | M2B |

As always, double-check your connections to make sure everything is wired properly before uploading the code and testing.

# Reviewing the Code

This Seg-bot code can get quite long and difficult to read if it is all placed in one chunk. So to make it easier to read, I created a separate function for each step in the loop. The code contained in each function *could* be inserted into the main loop where the function name is called and the sketch would work the same.

These functions are created in the order that they are called in the loop; see Listing 11-3 for an overview of the main loop (actually this *is* the main loop):

*Listing 11-3. An Overview of the Main Loop, with Descriptions of Each Step*

```
void loop(){

  sample_accel(); // gets the accelerometer angle
  sample_gyro(); // gets the gyro angle
  calculate_angle(); // calculates the filtered angle
  read_pots(); // check for steering and gain pot values
  auto_level(); // check to see if button has been de-pressed
  update_motor_speed(); // update the motor speed
  time_stamp(); // set the loop time equal to 50 mS

}
```

The following sections go through each function in the main loop and describe what each line of code does. Then, at the very end of the chapter, you can find the code in its full form, ready to upload to the Arduino.

The sample_accel() Function

The Accelerometer is the first thing you need to read to get the approximate angle. Listing 11-4 shows the variables used.

*Listing 11-4. Variables Used* for `sample_accel()` *Function*

```
int accel_pin = 5;
int accel_reading;
int accel_raw;
int accel_offset = 511;
float accel_angle;
float accel_scale = 0.01;
```

To determine the `accel_offset`, place the IMU board flat on a table (0 degrees) and read the accelerometer X-axis from an Arduino Analog input pin:

```
accel_reading = analogRead(accel_pin);
```

Whatever value displays on the serial monitor when the IMU board is level will be the `accel_offset` value, which should ideally be 511. his value will be subtracted from each `accel_reading` to yield the `accel_raw` variable. The `accel_raw` variable should read 0 when the IMU board is level:

```
accel_raw = accel_reading - accel_offset;
```

The original plan was to turn the IMU board 90 degrees in both directions and record the lowest/highest values displayed on the Serial monitor. I would then use the Arduino `map()` function to scale this recorded value range to be between –90 and +90.

But after turning the IMU in both directions, the lowest and highest values turned out to be –90 and +90, so there was no need to `map()` them. I did want to make sure that this value did not get out of range, so I added a line of code to set a minimum and maximum allowable value for the variable, using the `constrain()` function. See the Arduino reference pages for more information.

???Okay to use map() as a verb? DD

```
accel_raw = constrain(accel_raw, -90, 90);
```

Finally, it is easier to convert this value into a float variable (decimal number) so it can later be weighted as an average. I set the `accel_scale` variable equal to 0.01, effectively dividing the angle by 100 and setting the angle range to be from –0.90 to 0.90 (90 / 100); because it is a float variable, 0 degrees is actually represented as 0.00 degrees.

```
accel_angle = (float)(accel_raw) * accel_scale;
```

After multiplying the `accel_raw` reading by the `accel_scale` (0.01), the `accel_angle` variable is ready to be weighted into the filtered angle. Next, calculate the gyro angle.

The sample_gyro() Function

The gyroscope reading filters out unwanted spikes from the accelerometer caused by bumps, vibrations, or sudden changes in gravity that have not affected the angle. Because the gyroscope is measuring only how much the angle has changed since the last reading, you must use the previous filtered angle reading as your reference to measure from. Several more variables are required to read the gyroscope, which are shown in Listing 11-5.

*Listing 11-5. Variables Used for the Sample_gyro( ) Function*

```
int gyro_pin = 1;
float angle = 0.00;
int gyro_reading;
int gyro_raw;
int gyro_offset = 391;

float gyro_rate;
float gyro_scale = 0.01;
float gyro_angle;
float loop_time = 0.05;
```

Using the base angle calculation from the accelerometer to reference the gyroscope angle to, you can use the gyroscope reading on a cycle-by-cycle basis, discarding each previous reading. This is how you eliminate the accumulated "drift" error from your filtered angle.

First, read the angular rate value from the gyroscope on one of the Arduino Analog input pins.

```
gyro_reading = analogRead(gyro_pin);
```

As with the accelerometer, calculate the gyro_offset by recording the gyro_reading when the IMU board is at rest. Although this value would instinctively be approximately 511, my IMU reads approximately 391 on the serial monitor for each of the 4x amplified gyro outputs (on a 10-bit scale of 0–1023). I thought this was unusual, but the datasheet for the gyro confirmed that it has a Zero-rate voltage level of 1.23 V, which is less than half of 3.33 V and would yield a value lower than 511 when at rest. If using a Razor 6 DOF IMU, you should leave the gyro_offset = 391.

```
gyro_raw = gyro_reading - gyro_offset;
```

This reading is slightly confusing; because the value is centered at 391, it can go up 632 units to 1023, but it can go down only 391 units to 0. To try and round this value out, I decided to constrain the value to +/–391.

```
gyro_raw = constrain(gyro_raw, -391, 391);
```

Now calculate the gyro_rate variable, which is the gyro_raw input multiplied by the gyro_scale, multiplied by the loop_time (0.05 seconds).

---

▪ **Note:** When I began testing, the gyro reading was reversed from the accelerometer reading and was adding opposite angle changes into the filtered angle, causing it to differ greatly from the accel_angle reading. By adding a negative sign in front of the loop_time variable, the reading was reversed and began adding properly to the filtered angle. You may need to do this.

---

To make sure the angle readings are in unison, open the serial monitor after loading the code and move the Seg-bot back and forth to verify that the angles are measured properly.

# Checking the Angle Readings

With a USB cable connected to the Arduino, serial monitor open, and the main Seg-bot power off, start from 0.00 degrees and tilt the Seg-bot forward a few inches and then stop. You should see both the accel_angle and gyro_angle move in unison on the serial monitor. If not, you may need to adjust the gyro_scale variable.

The gyro_scale is a variable that can be used to tune the sensitivity of the gyro readings. Ideally the angle calculated by the gyro should be close to the accel_angle readings on the serial monitor. By default, the gyro_scale is set to 0.01, just like the accel_scale, but if the gyro_angle is less responsive than the accel_angle after testing, you might try increasing the gyro_scale to 0.02 or so.

```
gyro_rate = (float)(gyro_raw  * gyro_scale) * -loop_time;
```

Now to get an angle value for the gyro, add its current rate to the previous angle value:

```
gyro_angle = angle + gyro_rate;
```

The resulting gyro_angle value should remain close to the accel_angle value, which are both factored into the filtered angle value. With the angle readings from the IMU recorded, you now need to combine them together to determine the filtered value.

The calculate_angle() Function

With the accel_angle and the gyro_angle calculated, you can now come up with a weighted average of the two, by multiplying each angle calculation by a weighted percentage and then adding them together. The variables used to calculate the filtered angle are shown in Listing 11-6. Because the final angle is calculated as a decimal number, these variables need to be declared as *float* types instead of *integers*.

*Listing 11-6. Variables Used for the* calculate_angle() *Function*

```
float angle = 0.00;
float gyro_weight = 0.98;
float accel_weight = 0.02;
float gyro_angle;
float accel_angle;
```

Remember that the accelerometer is greatly affected by vibrations and bumps, so its weight is low in the average, at 2% (0.02). This means that the gyro_angle, which is an updated average loosely based on the previous filtered angle, is weighted heavily at 98% (0.98). This is because the gyro has a much more stable view of the current angle than the accelerometer. The small 2% weight from the accelerometer however is enough to keep the gyro from drifting.

To get the current angle, set the angle variable equal to the sum of the two weighted sensors ((.98)gyro + (.02)accelerometer). You can change the weights of these two variables from 98% gyro and 2% accelerometer to something else; although, going below 95% gyro and 5% accelerometer produced unstable results during my testing.

Following is the formula to calculate the filtered angle:

```
angle = (float)(gyro_weight * gyro_angle) + (accel_weight * accel_angle);
```

With the filtered angle value calculated, the Seg-bot should balance itself. To achieve steering on the Seg-bot, you still need to create an imbalance between the outputs of each motor. To do this, read the steering potentiometer with the Arduino and set each motor's maximum output based on the position of the potentiometer.

## The read_pots() Function

The read_pots() function is called to read both the steering and gain potentiometers. The steering potentiometer does nothing more than spin one motor faster than the other, which makes the bot turn. If the potentiometer is biased to either the left or right, the Arduino causes the Seg-bot to turn in that direction. The gain potentiometer determines how quickly the motors respond to changes in the filtered angle, by changing the maximum motor output speed (for both motors) from between 50% and 100%, depending on the position of the gain potentiometer. The variables used to read the steering and gain potentiometers are shown in Listing 11-7.

*Listing 11-7. Variables Used for the* Read_pots() *Function*

```
int steeringPot = 3;
int steer_reading;
float steer_val;
int steer_range = 7;

int gainPot = 2;
int gain_reading;
int gain_val;
```

The value of the steering potentiometer is read from the steeringPot analog input (pin A3) and stored in the variable steer_reading.

```
steer_reading = analogRead(steeringPot);
```

The steer_reading value is then mapped from 0–1023, to range between –7 and +7. You can change the "steer_range variable if needed–a lower value yields less responsive steering whereas a higher value yields more responsive steering. Values above 15 resulted in far too responsive steering whereas a 0 value would not respond at all.

The steer_range variable needs to be assigned only one number, and the value range will be mapped from -(that number) to +(that number), where zero is straight ahead, (Both motors get equal speed.) If your potentiometer responds opposite as it should, try changing the negative sign of the mapped steer_range variables.

```
steer_val = map(steer_reading, 0, 1023, steer_range, -steer_range);
```

The steer_reading can cause the motors to be turned even if the Seg-bot is not tilted forward or backward, so I added an if statement that checks to see if the Seg-bot is at 0 degrees. If so, the gain_reading will also be set to 0, so the bot will not be affected by the steering potentiometer.

```
if (angle == 0.00){
    gain_reading = 0;
}
```

Now read the value of the GAIN potentiometer to determine the top speed of the Seg-bot. The gain changes the maximum top speed from 50% up to 100%. This is useful to fine-tune the responsiveness of the Seg-bot to fit different riding styles.

```
gain_reading = analogRead(gainPot);
```

After reading the input, map the value to between 32 and 64. This value is your gain_reading and sets the maximum speed in either direction. If the potentiometer is turned down completely, the max speed is between –32 and 32 (or a max of 50% speed). If the potentiometer is turned up completely, the max speed is increased to a range of –64 to 64, allowing up to a 100% max speed.

Why 64? Remember that the Sabertooth serial interface enables 64 speed steps in either direction, where 64 steps above or below neutral can yield full speed in that direction. By allowing the top speed to be 64, it can go 100%. If you allow it to go up to only 32, it can achieve only 50% of its full speed, therefore making the bot less responsive to small angle changes.

```
speed_val = map(gain_reading, 0, 1023, 32, 64);
```

Now that you have processed the input control signals from each potentiometer, check the engage button to see if it is pressed.

## The auto_level() Function

The auto_level() function is used to complement the engage_switch, to make sure the Seg-bot is level before engaging the motors. When the engage_switch is released, the Arduino removes power to the motors until the button is pressed again, notifying the Arduino that there is an operator on board.

At first, I just held the bot approximately level (at 0 degrees) and then pressed the button, but if it were not level, it quickly corrected itself to be level. I began to think this could be slightly dangerous when I had the Seg-bot tilted forward and accidentally pressed the button. The handlebar immediately came flying back toward me and almost hit me in the head!

To fix this bug, I decided to add a small bit of code that checks to see if the engage_switch has been released. If so, it makes sure that when it is pressed again, the angle variable must be close to 0 before it re-engages the motors. The motors now engage smoothly and without any sudden movements, as soon as the Seg-bot is level. The variables used for the auto_level() function are shown in Listing 11-8.

*Listing 11-8. Variables Used for the* auto_level() *Function*

```
float angle = 0.00;
int engage_switch = 4;
int engage_state;
int engage = false;
```

First, read the state of the engage_switch and store it in the engage_state variable:

```
engage_state = digitalRead(engage_switch);
```

Now check to see if the switch is open or closed. To avoid using pull-down resistors on the engage_switch, I used the built-in Arduino pull-up resistors accessible from the code and connected the engage_switch to GND when closed. This means that when the button is not pressed, the switch reads HIGH or 1 and when the button is pressed, the switch will read LOW or 0. I know this is counter-intuitive, but it makes wiring switches much more simple by connecting the Arduino input wire (D4) to one terminal of the button switch and a GND wire to the other.

Use an if statement to see if the engage_state variable is HIGH. (That is the switch is OPEN.) If so, set the engage variable to be false. (That is, disengage the motors.)

```
if (engage_state == 1){
    engage = false;
}
```

Otherwise (else), if the engage_state is LOW (that is, the button is pressed), use another `if` statement to check and see if the engage variable is currently set to false. If the button is pressed, but the engage variable is false, this means the switch was OPEN but someone just CLOSED it.

At this point, the Arduino is ready to start commanding the motors, but it must first make sure the bot is level. To do this, use yet another `if` statement to check the current angle value of the Seg-bot. If the angle is below 0.02 and above -0.02 (that is, it is almost perfectly level), re-engage the motors by setting the engage variable equal to true. Otherwise, if the angle is not close to 0 degrees, keep the motors disengaged until the angle is corrected.

If the engage variable is already true when it enters this `else{}` function, it remains true until the engage_switch is released.

```
else {
  if (engage == false){
    if (angle < 0.02 && angle > -0.02)
      engage = true;
    else {
      engage = false;
    }
  }
  else {
    engage = true;
  }
}
```

Now update the motors with the new speed values. Before you can send the values to the Sabertooth motor controller, you first need to convert the angle value into a corresponding motor speed value and then send that value to the Sabertooth as a serial byte.

## The update_motor_speed() Function

This is by far the longest function in the code, responsible for changing the angle value into a motor speed value, checking that value to make sure it is within range, and then sending it to the Sabertooth motor controller. Listing 11-9 shows the variables used for the update_motor_speed() function.

*Listing 11-9. Variables Used in the update_motor_speed() Function*

```
int engage;
float angle = 0.00;

int motor_out = 0;
int output;
float steer_val;
int gain_val;

int motor_1_out = 0;
int motor_2_out = 0;
int m1_speed = 0;
int m2_speed = 0;
```

Before attempting to write a value to the motors, first check to see if the engage variable is set to equal true (that is, if the engage button is pressed). If so, continue to the next if statement. If engage is set to false, skip down to the else statement that stops both motors by setting their outputs equal to 0 (disengage).

```
if (engage == true){
```

Next, check the angle variable to make sure it is within tilting limits. I recorded the angle of the Seg-bot when tilting it forward until the motors almost touched the ground; this angle was 0.4 (40 degrees) on my Seg-bot, and I have not yet exceeded it. If the angle while riding exceeds the limits set here, the motor_out variable will be set to 0, which stops both motors.

```
if (angle < -0.4 || angle > 0.4){
  motor_out = 0;
}
```

Otherwise, if the angle is within operating limits, set the output variable equal to the angle * 1000. Multiply the angle (which is a decimal number between –0.9 and 0.9) by 1000 to convert it back to a usable integer from a float type variable that you needed to weight the average.

I wanted the full speed to be achieved when the Seg-bot reached a 25-degree deviation from 0 degrees in either direction, so I mapped the motor_out variable from –250 to 250. The number 250 comes from the angle variable where 25 degrees is represented as 0.25. When I multiplied the angle by 1000 to get the output variable, a 25 degree angle now represented as 250.

We are mapping the motor_out variable from –/+250 to –/+ gain_val, which is read from the gainPot potentiometer and can range from –/+32 to –/+64 depending on its position. In any case, when the Seg-bot is at 0 degrees, it yields a motor_out value equal to 0.

```
else {
  output = (angle * -1000);
  motor_out = map(output, -250, 250, -gain_val, gain_val);
}
```

This ends the first else{} statement in the update_motor_speed() function. Now manipulate the motor_out variable into separate variables for each motor called motor_1_out and motor_2_out respectively.

At this point, add the steering bias into the individual motor speeds. To do this, add the mapped variable steer_val (–7 to +7) to motor1 while subtracting it from motor2. This causes the wheels to move at different speeds depending on the position of the steering potentiometer. When the steer_val goes negative, it will actually be subtracting from motor1 and adding to motor2.

```
motor_1_out = motor_out + (steer_val);
motor_2_out = motor_out - (steer_val);
```

With the steer_val added to each motor output value, check motor_1_out and motor_2_out to make sure that neither is above 63 or below –63. If either of these variables were to be higher than 63 (in either direction), it could unintentionally write a command to the wrong motor!

```
if(motor_1_out > 63){
  motor_1_out = 63;
}
if(motor_1_out < -63){
  motor_1_out = -63;
}
```

```
if(motor_2_out > 63){
  motor_2_out = 63;
}
if(motor_2_out < -63){
  motor_2_out = -63;
}
```

Now convert these two values into separate Sabertooth simplified serial commands. Remember from the Sabertooth simplified serial chart (Figure 11-15) the neutral command for Motor1 = 64 and the neutral command for Motor2 = 192. Because the motor_1_out and motor_2_out variables are already mapped between a maximum of –64 to +64, you can simply add them to the neutral points of each motor to get the actual BYTE value needed to send to the Sabertooth. If the byte has a negative value, it subtracts from the neutral points to command the motors to reverse.

```
m1_speed = 64 + motor_1_out;
m2_speed = 192 + motor_2_out;
}
```

This is the end of the first if statement in the motor_speed_update() function [if (engage == true)].

The else statement covers what happens if engage == false when the Engage button is released, which is that the motor speed values are both set to 0, stopping the motors (or disengaging them).

```
else{
  m1_speed = 0;
  m2_speed = 0;
}
```

After all of the if/else statements are completed, use the SoftwareSerial library to write the new BYTE values for each motor to the Sabertooth using Arduino pin 3 (the SoftwareSerial tx pin)—even if the value written is 0 (that is, stop both motors).

```
mySerial.print(m1_speed, BYTE);
mySerial.print(m2_speed, BYTE);
```

After the motor values have been written to the Sabertooth, record the timestamp for this loop() cycle to use when calculating the next gyroscope reading.

## The time_stamp() Function

This function checks the time of each loop cycle, and add a delay() until the time equals 50 milliseconds. You need each loop cycle to equal 50 milliseconds (or some other known time) so that you correctly calculate the gyroscope rate in degrees per second, rather than degrees per loop cycle (which is not useful). I used 50 millisecond update intervals to provide an angle reading that is updated by the Arduino 20 times each second! This provides seamless angle correction from the Seg-bot.

The while() statement continuously runs until the condition is met. By subtracting the last_cycle variable from the current millis() value, you can get the exact time (in milliseconds) since the last update. Furthermore, if the current millis() value minus the last_cycle timestamp is less than 50 (milliseconds), add a 1 millisecond delay over and over again until the last_cycle variable is greater than or equal to 50 mS. This effectively forces each loop cycle time to equal 50 mS, so you know that every cycle is the same length.

```
while((millis() - last_cycle) < 50){
    delay(1);
}
```

When the `last_cycle` variable is equal to 50, the `while()` statement is exited, and the last two variables are recorded. First, the actual recorded `cycle_time` variable is calculated for viewing on the Serial monitor, which should always equal the desired cycle time above (50 in this case):

```
cycle_time = millis() - last_cycle;
```

Next, it is time to write the new timestamp value by recording the current millisecond value from the system timer. The timestamp function is now ready to check itself again with the new time value in the next loop cycle.

```
last_cycle = millis();
```

Finally, print all the important values to the serial monitor for debugging.

## The serial_print_stuff() Function

This is the last function and is used only to print values to the serial monitor. You can edit which variables you want to view on the serial monitor, depending on what part of the system you test.

Be warned, trying to view every variable at once using the `Serial.print()` function causes the loop to take longer than 50 milliseconds, which means that the timing will be off for the gyro calculation, and the angle calculation will be wrong. To avoid this, try to limit the number of variables that you send to the serial monitor to about 3 or 4.

If you are unsure, try viewing the `cycle_time` variable on the serial monitor because it shows you the calculated loop cycle time in milliseconds. If this number is above 50, you might need to stop printing a few variables in this function.

I have the four most important variables printing by default; although, you can change them or add more (Listing 11-10).

*Listing 11-10. The serial_print_stuff() Function*

```
Serial.print("Accel: ");
Serial.print(accel_angle);
Serial.print("   ");

Serial.print("Gyro: ");
Serial.print(gyro_angle);
Serial.print("   ");

Serial.print("Filtered Angle: ");
Serial.print(angle);
Serial.print("   ");

Serial.print(" Time: ");
Serial.print(cycle_time);
Serial.println("    ");
```

```
/*          // from here down are commented out unless testing

Serial.print("o/m: ");
Serial.print(output);
Serial.print("/");
Serial.print(motor_out);
Serial.println("   ");

Serial.print("steer_val: ");
Serial.print(steer_val);
Serial.print("   ");

Serial.print("speed_val: ");
Serial.print(speed_val);
Serial.print("   ");

Serial.print("m1/m2: ");
Serial.print(m1_speed);
Serial.print("/");
Serial.println(m2_speed);
*/
```

These values are used only for debugging purposes and can be changed or omitted.

# The Full Code

Now that you know how the code works, Listing 11-11 presents it in its full form, ready to upload to the Arduino. When uploaded, remember to carefully test the Seg-bot for proper motor direction and correct steering. To safely test the Seg-bot, the base must be propped up so that the wheels do not touch the ground. Do this before you turn on the main power!

*Listing 11-11. The Final Code, Shown in Full Form*

```
// Chapter 11: The Seg-bot
// JD Warren 2010 (special thanks to Josh Adams for help during testing and coding)
// Arduino Duemilanove (tested)
// Sparkfun Razor 6 DOF IMU - only using X axis from accelerometer and gyroscope 4x
// Steering potentiometer used to steer bot
// Gain potentiometer used to set max speed (sensitivity)
// Engage switch (button) used to enable motors
//
// By loading this code, you are taking full responsibility for what you may do it!
// Use at your own risk!!!
// If you are concerned with the safety of this project, it may not be for you.
// Test thoroughly with wheels off the ground before attempting to ride - Wear a helmet!


// use SoftwareSerial library to communicate with the Sabertooth motor controller
#include <SoftwareSerial.h>
// define pins used for SoftwareSerial communication
```

```
#define rxPin 2
#define txPin 3
// set up a new SoftwareSerial port, named "mySerial" or whatever you want to call it.
SoftwareSerial mySerial = SoftwareSerial(rxPin, txPin);


// Name Analog input pins
int gyro_pin = 1;  // connect the gyro X axis (4x output) to Analog input 1
int accel_pin = 5; // connect the accelerometer X axis to Analog input 5
int steeringPot = 3; // connect the steering potentiometer to Analog input 3
int gainPot = 2; // connect the gain potentiometer to Analog input 2

// Name Digital I/O pins
int engage_switch = 4; // connect engage button to digital pin 4
int ledPin = 13;

// value to hold the final angle
float angle = 0.00;
// the following 2 values should add together to equal 1.0
float gyro_weight = 0.98;
float accel_weight = 0.02;

// accelerometer values
int accel_reading;
int accel_raw;
int accel_offset = 511;
float accel_angle;
float accel_scale = 0.01;

// gyroscope values
int gyro_offset = 391;
int gyro_raw;
int gyro_reading;
float gyro_rate;
float gyro_scale = 0.025; // 0.01 by default
float gyro_angle;
float loop_time = 0.05;

// engage button variables
int engage = false;
int engage_state = 1;

// timer variables
int last_update;
int cycle_time;
long last_cycle = 0;

// motor speed variables
int motor_out = 0;
int motor_1_out = 0;
int motor_2_out = 0;
int m1_speed = 0;
```

```
int m2_speed = 0;
int output;

// potentiometer variables
int steer_val;
int steer_range = 7;
int steer_reading;
int gain_reading;
int gain_val;

// end of Variables


void setup(){

  // Start the Serial monitor at 9600bps
  Serial.begin(9600);
  // define pinModes for tx and rx:
  pinMode(rxPin, INPUT);
  pinMode(txPin, OUTPUT);
  // set the data rate for the SoftwareSerial port
  mySerial.begin(9600);

  // set the engage_switch pin as an Input
  pinMode(engage_switch, INPUT);

  // enable the Arduino internal pull-up resistor on the engage_switch pin.
  digitalWrite(engage_switch, HIGH);
  // Tell Arduino to use the Aref pin for the Analog voltage, don't forget to connect 3.3v to
Aref!
  analogReference(EXTERNAL);

}

void loop(){
  // Start the loop by getting a reading from the Accelerometer and converting it to an angle
  sample_accel();
  // now read the gyroscope to estimate the angle change
  sample_gyro();
  // combine the accel and gyro readings to come up with a "filtered" angle reading
  calculate_angle();
  // read the values of each potentiometer
  read_pots();
  // make sure bot is level before activating the motors
  auto_level();
  // update the motors with the new values
  update_motor_speed();
  // check the loop cycle time and add a delay as necessary
  time_stamp();
  // Debug with the Serial monitor
  serial_print_stuff();
```

```
}

void sample_accel(){
// Read and convert accelerometer value

  accel_reading = analogRead(accel_pin);
  accel_raw = accel_reading - accel_offset;
  accel_raw = constrain(accel_raw, -90, 90);
  accel_angle = (float)(accel_raw * accel_scale);
}

void sample_gyro(){
// Read and convert gyro value

  gyro_reading = analogRead(gyro_pin);
  gyro_raw = gyro_reading - gyro_offset;
  gyro_raw = constrain(gyro_raw, -391, 391);
  gyro_rate = (float)(gyro_raw * gyro_scale) * -loop_time;
  gyro_angle = angle + gyro_rate;
}

void calculate_angle(){
  angle = (float)(gyro_weight * gyro_angle) + (accel_weight * accel_angle);
}

void read_pots(){
// Read and convert potentiometer values
// Steering potentiometer
  steer_reading = analogRead(steeringPot); // We want to map this into a range between -1 and
1, and set that to steer_val
  steer_val = map(steer_reading, 0, 1023, steer_range, -steer_range);
  if (angle == 0.00){
    gain_reading = 0;
  }
// Gain potentiometer
  gain_reading = analogRead(gainPot);
  gain_val = map(gain_reading, 0, 1023, 32, 64);
}

void auto_level(){
 // enable auto-level turn On
  engage_state = digitalRead(engage_switch);

  if (engage_state == 1){
    engage = false;
  }
  else {
    if (engage == false){
      if (angle < 0.02 && angle > -0.02)
        engage = true;
      else {
        engage = false;
```

```
      }
    }
    else {
      engage = true;
    }
  }
}

void update_motor_speed(){
// Update the motors

  if (engage == true){
    if (angle < -0.4 || angle > 0.4){
      motor_out = 0;
    }
    else {
      output = (angle * -1000); // convert float angle back to integer format
      motor_out = map(output, -250, 250, -gain_val, gain_val); // map the angle
    }

    // assign steering bias
    motor_1_out = motor_out + (steer_val);
    motor_2_out = motor_out - (steer_val);

    // test for and correct invalid values
    if(motor_1_out > 64){
      motor_1_out = 64;
    }
    if(motor_1_out < -64){
      motor_1_out = -64;
    }
    if(motor_2_out > 64){
      motor_2_out = 64;
    }
    if(motor_2_out < -64){
      motor_2_out = -64;
    }

    // assign final motor output values
    m1_speed = 64 + motor_1_out;
    m2_speed = 192 + motor_2_out;
  }

  else{
    m1_speed = 0;
    m2_speed = 0;
  }

  // write the final output values to the Sabertooth via SoftwareSerial
  mySerial.print(m1_speed, BYTE);
```

```
  mySerial.print(m2_speed, BYTE);
}

void time_stamp(){
  // check to make sure it has been exactly 50 milliseconds since the last recorded time-stamp
  while((millis() - last_cycle) < 50){
    delay(1);
  }
  // once the loop cycle reaches 50 mS, reset timer value and proceed
  cycle_time = millis() - last_cycle;
  last_cycle = millis();

}

void serial_print_stuff(){
  // Debug with the Serial monitor

  Serial.print("Accel: ");
  Serial.print(accel_angle);  // print the accelerometer angle
  Serial.print("  ");

  Serial.print("Gyro: ");
  Serial.print(gyro_angle);  // print the gyro angle
  Serial.print("  ");

  Serial.print("Filtered: ");
  Serial.print(angle);   // print the filtered angle
  Serial.print("  ");

  Serial.print(" time: ");
  Serial.print(cycle_time); // print the loop cycle time
  Serial.println("   ");

  /*  these values are commented out, unless testing
  Serial.print("o/m: ");
  Serial.print(output);
  Serial.print("/");
  Serial.print(motor_out);
  Serial.println("  ");

  Serial.print("steer_val: ");
  Serial.print(steer_val);
  Serial.print("  ");

  Serial.print("steer_reading: ");
  Serial.print(steer_reading);
  Serial.print("  ");

  Serial.print("m1/m2: ");
  Serial.print(m1_speed);
  Serial.print("/");
```

```
Serial.println(m2_speed);
*/
}
```

//End Code

With the code loaded to the Arduino, it is time to begin testing.

# Testing

When testing, place Seg-bot on a crate or box so that the wheels are not touching the ground. This makes testing the bot much safer so there will be no danger of it moving. A few values can be reversed and might need adjusting. I loaded the code to the Arduino and tested the IMU before installing it into the Seg-bot to make sure the Arduino read the angle values properly.

After I powered the Seg-bot for the first time, I immediately noticed that one of the wheels was spinning backward when I tilted the Seg-bot forward, so I had to reverse the wires connected to the Sabertooth for that motor. I then tested the steering potentiometer to make sure the wheels turned appropriately when the steering knob was turned. After verifying some of the basics of how the Seg-bot should work, and making sure the motors didn't spin excessively fast when the bot was tilted, I decided to give it a test drive.

Upon boarding the Seg-bot for the first time (*cautiously*), I felt right at home with the motors responding to my every move, keeping me level. After a few minutes of getting used to the steering control, I was zipping around my basement and garage like I had a new best friend (see Figure 11-33). A quick test drive to the mailbox proved that the Seg-bot would easily climb a steep hill and a curious ride through the backyard surprised me with smooth handling over bumps, holes, and even a few tree limbs!

*Figure 11-33. Me playing on my new Seg-bot...Look Ma, no hands!*

Happy balancing!

# Summary

This chapter used the Arduino to make a balancing Segway-type scooter. Using an accelerometer and a gyroscope to obtain angle measurements, the Arduino can determine what speed and direction to command each motor to stay upright. By adding a few potentiometers and a button switch, you made a small control panel for steering and gain inputs and an Engage button to keep the Seg-bot inactive when not being ridden. Because of the large gear motors and metal frame, this robot can carry several hundred pounds and can traverse both indoor and outdoor terrain. Be careful when riding the Seg-bot, and mind those around you; this is a powerful and dangerous robot and should be handled carefully.

The next chapter builds a high-speed, four-wheel drive robot that bites if you get too close. Keep reading to see why the Battle-bot doesn't play well with others.

# References

You can find several examples online of various DIY balancing scooters and balancing robots. Much of the information is quite technical for the angle calculations; although, a few sources were easy to understand and might better explain some of the complicated concepts in this chapter:

http://web.mit.edu/scolton/www/filter.pdf–This paper was written by an MIT undergraduate and is extremely helpful to better understand how to combine the readings from each sensor of the IMU (gyro and accelerometer). It is full of helpful graphs and illustrations.

http://sites.google.com/site/onewheeledselfbalancing/–This website showcases the projects of Mr. John Dingley and his many self-balancing scooters and skateboards. You an review some insightful angle filtering concepts here as well.

# CHAPTER 12

# The Battle-Bot

You have likely heard of (or watched) the various televised Battle-Bot competitions, in which two or more robots are entered into a ring (actually a bullet-proof cage) and let loose until there is only one robot moving–kind of like ultimate fighting for robots. This chapter focuses on building one of these fighting robots, either to enter into a competition or to act as your personal body guard around the house. When building a Battle-bot (Figure 12-1), the point is to disable and destroy your opponents robot, so let your destructive juices flow and come up with some otherwise really bad ideas!

In this chapter, you build a four-wheel drive robot with a heavy duty steel frame, steel plating on each side, and two types of weapons attached. The primary control method is a 2.4GHz R/C, which provides the Arduino with user commands for both the drive motors and weapon system. Instead of using DC gear motors to drive this bot (as with the other large robot projects in this book), you use ungeared DC scooter motors and reduce the speed of each using a chain and sprocket drive train–even with gear reduction, this robot is fast! I added two types of weapons to my Battle-bot: two dual-tipped steel ramming spears fixed to the front and rear of each side of the frame, and a motor-driven spike hammer attached to a 3-foot swinging arm, both used to impale the opponent.

---

■ **Warning:** The project in this chapter is not suitable for children. This type of robot is intended to be used in a sealed Battle-bot arena and should be tested with extreme caution and the weapons removed!

---

This robot has only what is needed in battle and focuses on speed and agility. The four-wheel drive is composed of four independent DC motors using a separate drive train for each wheel. This way, if one of the drive wheels is damaged, the bot can still move. Unlike previous chapters where SLA batteries are preferred for cost efficiency, I decided to use Lithium Polymer batteries for this robot to reduce weight.

***Figure12-1.*** *The mostly completed Battle-bot, sporting spears and a swinging spike arm*

The Battle-bot in this chapter has some unique features not included on previous robots, which can help its chances in battle:

- **Four-wheel-drive**–Each wheel has its own motor, drive train, and motor controller.

- **All-steel construction**–There is no plexiglass or other easily breakable materials.

- **Lithium Polymer batteries**–Used to reduce weight, while maximizing run time.

- **Multiple weapons**–By using two types of weapons, active and passive, the bot can always defend itself.

- **Symmetrical frame**–Can attack from either direction with a bidirectional spike-hammer weapon and ramming spikes on both sides.

The robots in this book have so far been for "proof of concept" if you will, enabling a beginning robot builder to materialize some popular concepts without breaking the bank. The primary focus in earlier chapters was getting the bot to work using simple and the least-expensive methods. So what do you do after you prove that you can build a robot that does what you programmed it to do? You start strapping weapons to it, and then you look for another robot to get into a fight with—what else did you have in mind?

# Robotic Combat Is Born

I am a person of peace, not wanting to fight anyone or hurt anybody, which is why robotic combat is so much fun to watch. You know that someone is hurting for all the repair work they will have to do on their beloved robot, but no living beings are injured or otherwise harmed in a robotic battle. Safety is the #1 concern at any robotic battle competition—extra precautions are placed on weapon safety, emergency shut-off switches, and radio failsafes to make sure that if humans are nearby, they will not be harmed by one of the robots.

The opposite is true for the robots competing in the match; they are usually subjected to arena hazards meant to distract and damage both bots during the match. If your larger and scarier opponent wasn't enough to deal with, you also have spikes on the walls, saw-blades coming up from the floor, a hammer that smashes you if you get near it, and a pneumatic arm that lifts up a section of the floor if you drive over it—just to name a few of the typical arena hazards.

I'm not exactly sure how the first robot battle came about, but according to http://www.robotcombat.com/history.html (website of the popular Team Nightmare and the Robot Marketplace), robotic combat dates back to at least 1994, when a man named Marc Thorpe decided to organize an event made specifically for battling robots, which was called, Robot Wars. I won't get into the many popular subsequent event names, but it is safe to say that as long as people are building robots, they will want to fight them.

A Battle-bot should not be designed simply to work; it must work through the roughest conditions a robot builder can imagine. In battle, there is no timeout to fix a loose wire, or asking the other guy to avoid ramming your left side because that's where you motor controller is mounted. You have to plan ahead for the worst, and hope you designed a better robot than your opponent. Any hidden weaknesses your bot has will become obvious when it is hammered, rammed, and impaled by its opponent.

## Battle-Bot Rules and Regulations

As with any "sport" there has to be a set of rules or guidelines that each contestant must follow to make the game more interesting and keep things fair. Certain attack methods and weapon types are not allowed to be used because they require little ingenuity and seem a bit insulting to other robot builders. For instance, your weapon cannot shoot water, oil, or other liquids or chemicals onto your opponent or the arena floor; Although this might disable their bot, it is not exactly the "exciting" type of combat that robot battles are designed for.

The most important regulation to many builders is the weight restrictions that separate the contestants into classes. There have been several different weight classes throughout the robotic combat saga; Wikipedia describes them with corresponding class names. These classes range from under 1 lbs to 340 lbs and are not from any one specific league or competition, but rather a collection of different weight classes from various events (see Table 12-1).

*Table 12-1. List of Battle-Bot Weight Classes Obtained from Wikipedia*

| Weight | Class |
|---|---|
| 75 grams (g) | Fleaweight |
| 150 g | Fairyweight |

| Weight | Class |
|---|---|
| 1 pound (454 g) | Antweight |
| 1 kilogram (2.2 lbs) | Kilobot (Canada) |
| 3 pounds (1.36 kg) | Beetleweight |
| 6 pounds (2.72 kg) | Mantisweight |
| 12 pounds (5.44 kg) | Hobbyweight |
| 15 pound (6.80 kg) | BotsIQ Mini class |
| 30 pound (13.6 kg) | Featherweight |
| 60 pound (27 kg) | Lightweight |
| 120 pound (54 kg) | Middleweight/BotsIQ Large class |
| 220 pound (100 kg) | Heavyweight |
| 340 pound (154 kg) | Super Heavyweight |

\* For more information about Battle-bots, visit http://en.wikipedia.org/wiki/Robot_Combat.

## No Price Limit!

Although there are weight and safety restrictions, there are no rules about how much money you can spend on your Battle-bot. This means that you can expect there to be some expensive robots entering the ring. The heavy-weight Battle-bots competing in the televised competitions would routinely cost several thousand dollars to build. Machined aluminum frames, titanium weapons and armor, CAD designed parts, and engineering-grade battling robots are what came from this phenomenon—along with a wave of inspired DIY robot builders each concocting their own version of the ultimate techno-warrior. Although this new "sport" is not productive in nature, it is extremely competitive, which grabbed the attention of many who would normally have no interest in building a robot. I can honestly say that no sport (on TV) has ever kept my undivided attention, but when a Battle-bot competition starts, it's extremely hard to look away until the match finishes.

Price may not be an issue for some builders, but it is for me (and probably you, if you are reading this book)–so it is good to plan to make a Battle-bot that is within your price range. You will have to replace some parts, so try to make sure you don't use parts that are impossible or extremely difficult to replace.

## Is This Going to Be Expensive?

The total cost of the robot depends on your parts supply and how long you have to acquire them. Can you be thrifty, use recycled parts, and be patient? If so, you might find a perfectly good scooter with dead batteries in the dumpster at work (like I did), and use pieces from it as your weapon drive system. If you don't want to pay retail, eBay often has some excellent deals on things such as surplus or discontinued wheels, sprockets, motors, and other harder to find items. I found the brand new scooter wheel assemblies used in this project on eBay for $12.99 each, when the same item at several online scooter-part retailers was selling for $40 or more each. My point is, if you don't have a lot of money, you can still find excellent parts for cheap—just keep looking and be patient.

I have tried to make the projects in this book affordable by limiting the price of any one project to $500. I originally met my budget by using some smaller motor controllers (Sabertooth 2x12), but the extra weight of the weapons made the bot draw a bit too much current to be effective in battle using these controllers. I decided to use larger motor controllers (Sabertooth 2x25) for this project, driving the price higher; this project ended up costing approximately $650 as tested.

Although this sounds like a lot of money, it is a small amount if you want to build a competitive Battle-bot. This bot should classify as a Lightweight or Middleweight, depending on weapons, armor, and batteries used. Also, you can build only the base of this robot and install any type weapon that you want. See what you can come up with on your own.

## Parts List for the Battle-Bot

The parts list for this project is more of a guideline than an exact list of materials. The part numbers for each part that I used on the Battle-bot are listed, but there are many different options that you could substitute for parts that I used.

If you built the Lawn-bot from Chapter 10, you might have some chain and a few universal chain links left over, and some bolts and scrap metal that might come in handy.

I always peruse my parts supply from previous robots and acquired thrift-store finds before buying any parts for a new robot. You might be surprised how many things can be recycled and repurposed. Take a look at the parts list for the Battle-bot in Table 12-2.

*Table 12-2. Battle-Bot Parts List*

| Part | Description | Price |
|------|-------------|-------|
| **Electronics** | | |
| 2.4 GHz R/C transmitter and receiver pair | HobbyPartz.com (part# *79P-CT6B-R6B-RadioSystem*): I have used these 2.4Ghz 6-channel hobby radio pairs on several bots. | $32.00 |

| Part | Description | Price |
|------|-------------|-------|
| Two Sabertooth Dual motor controllers | Dimension Engineering Sabertooth 2x25: These are used for Drive motors. | $125.00 ea (x2) |
| One OSMC motor controller | Used for weapon: Any high-power H bridge works here, assuming it has a voltage rating of +24vdc or better. I provide plans for you to make a smaller OSMC clone for about $40. | $40.00 |
| **Drive Train** | | |
| Four DC motors | Allelectronics.com part# XYD-15B – 24VDC, 135W, 10 Amp: Currie Technologies and electric scooter motors. | $15.00 ea |
| #25 chain – 10 feet | Allelectronics.com part# CHN-25: 10 feet should give you some extra in case of a break. It is sold by the foot for $2.50/ft. | $25.00 |
| Four Master chain links | Allelectronics.com part# ML-25: You need at least 4 of these, maybe 8 to 10 for good measure. | $1.00 ea |
| Four wheel/tire/sprocket set | PartsforScooters.com part# 119-49: These wheel/tire/sprocket assemblies are made for an E300 Razor electric scooter. I purchased these from the PartsforScooters eBay store (same wheels for less money) instead of its website. | $15.00 ea |
| (4) Motor drive sprockets | PartsforScooters.com part# 127-6: These sprockets have an 8mm bore and 11 teeth for #25 chain. They may also need shaft collars to secure. | $6.00 ea |
| **Power** | | |
| two 3-cell LiPoly batteries – 11.1v, 3000mAH | HobbyPartz.com part# *83P-3000mAh-3S1P-111-20C:* You need at least two of these packs to achieve 22.2vdc, but you can alternatively arrange the packs in parallel, operating the bot at 11.1v and 6000AH. | $16.00 ea |

| Part | Description | Price |
|------|-------------|-------|
| **Frame** | | |
| 2-inch wide angle iron 6 feet long | Hardware Store: This composes the perimeter of the square frame, in equal 18-inch sections. | $17.00 |
| 3/4-inch wide angle iron – 36-inch long | Hardware Store: I cut this into two equal pieces and used them as cross braces for the center of the frame, also used to mount the electronics (Battle-box) to. | $6.00 |
| two 5/16-inch (8mm) diameter threaded-rod – 36-inch long | Hardware Store: Use these for the front and rear axles. | $4.00 ea |
| two 3/4-inch square steel tubing – 36-inch long | Hardware Store: Use these to mount the active weapon to the frame. | $8.00 ea |
| two pc. Sheet metal 36-inch x 36-inch | Hardware Store: These sheets are used as armor to coat the top and bottom of the frame to protect the electronics and wiring. | $12.00 ea |
| **Weapon** | | |
| 24v, 350w, 22 Amp - electric scooter motor | Allelectronics.com part# DCM-1352. | $20.00 |
| two 3/4-inch steel square tubing | Used two 36-inch long pieces to make the weapon brackets. | $4.00 ea |
| two 5/8-inch solid steel round-rod | Used for the ramming spears on the front and rear of the frame. | $7.00 ea |
| Scrap-metal for spike-hammer weapon | Angle iron, steel flat bar, or anything you can find. | $0.00 |
| Sprocket assembly | I used the rear-wheel assembly from a Schwinn electric scooter that I found in a dumpster at work. For me this included a motor and all, but I have included the model number in case you are not so fortunate. | $0.00 |

Now consider some provisions for using R/C control in a battle-bot competition, and select a control system to use accordingly.

## Input Control

If using a hobby R/C system in a battle-bot competition, as of July 1, 2009, it must be a 2.4GHz system because legacy radio systems (27 MHz , 49MHz, 72MHz , 75MHz, and so on) are no longer allowed to be used. As earlier discussed, the 2.4GHz spread-spectrum radio transmitters must "bind" to their receivers rendering them nearly impervious to crossing signals.

This rule is in effect because the legacy 75MHz controllers rely on two crystals of the same frequency (one in the tx and one in the rx) to avoid interference. If another transmitter in the same vicinity (possibly a poor loser) uses a crystal of the same frequency as a competing robot–well, this could cost someone a match and an expensive robot. Maybe this is how the first robot battle began?

Other methods of wireless control are sometimes allowed, provided they meet the other general guidelines. This means that you could use an Xbee 2.4GHz Serial link to control your bot using a laptop, home-made controller, or joystick. If you try this you will likely be heavily inspected by the officials for safety, so make sure any custom control systems have the appropriate failsafe features as required by the contest rules. I encourage such actions because they make these events more interesting.

### Fly Sky CT-6: The $32, 5-ch*, 2.4GHz Radio Alternative

When they first became available, 2.4GHz transmitter/receiver pairs were quite expensive and rarely found for under $100. As of 2010, several places online sell quality 6-channel 2.4GHz radio systems for approximately $35. I have used the Fly Sky CT-6 system from HobbyPartz.com on several projects and have been pleased (see Figure 12-2).

Most 2.4GHz R/C transmitters can be paired with various R/C receivers using the bind process described in the transmitter instruction manual. If you already own a 2.4GHz R/C system (as used in Chapter 8, and Chapter 10), you might want to simply buy an additional 2.4GHz R/C receiver and use your existing transmitter. This would help save a bit of money if you plan to build several remotely controlled robots and want to keep from buying multiple R/C systems; you can purchase additional R/C receivers (HobbyPartz.com part# 79P-R6B-Receiver) for under $10 each!

*Figure 12.2.* Fly-sky 2.4GHz R/C system

Normal airplane receivers typically have built-in failsafe functions that upon signal loss, continue sending the previous good value to each channel. Although that may be good for an airplane, it is bad for most robots. The FlySky CT-6 is programmable to be used for either airplane, helicopter, or in our case, a robot. The CT-6 radio system even comes with a free programming cable and programming software that enables you to change the settings of each channel.

Upon losing signal, the receiver in this system is set to output a LOW signal with no previous pulse or other failsafe signal. This is handy when reading the R/C signal with the Arduino, because it is easy to determine when the signal has been lost. The Fly Sky CT-6 (and several other brands using the same software) have computer programmable servo reversing, channel mixing for helicopters, and assignable switch features–all accessible using the free software called T6_config (Figure 12-3), downloadable at http://www.mycoolheli.com/t6config.html.

This transmitter has four channels contained in the two dual-axis joysticks, and another usable channel for robots in the form of an on/off switch or an analog potentiometer knob. I operate this system so that the up/down channels of each joystick control the motors direction, whereas the left/right channel of one of the joysticks controls the weapon, enabling one person to control both the bots direction and weapon simultaneously. You can also use steering-mixing to control the bot's motion with one joystick and its weapon with the other joystick (either axis)–it all boils down to what feels most natural to you when driving. (I prefer independent control of each wheel.)

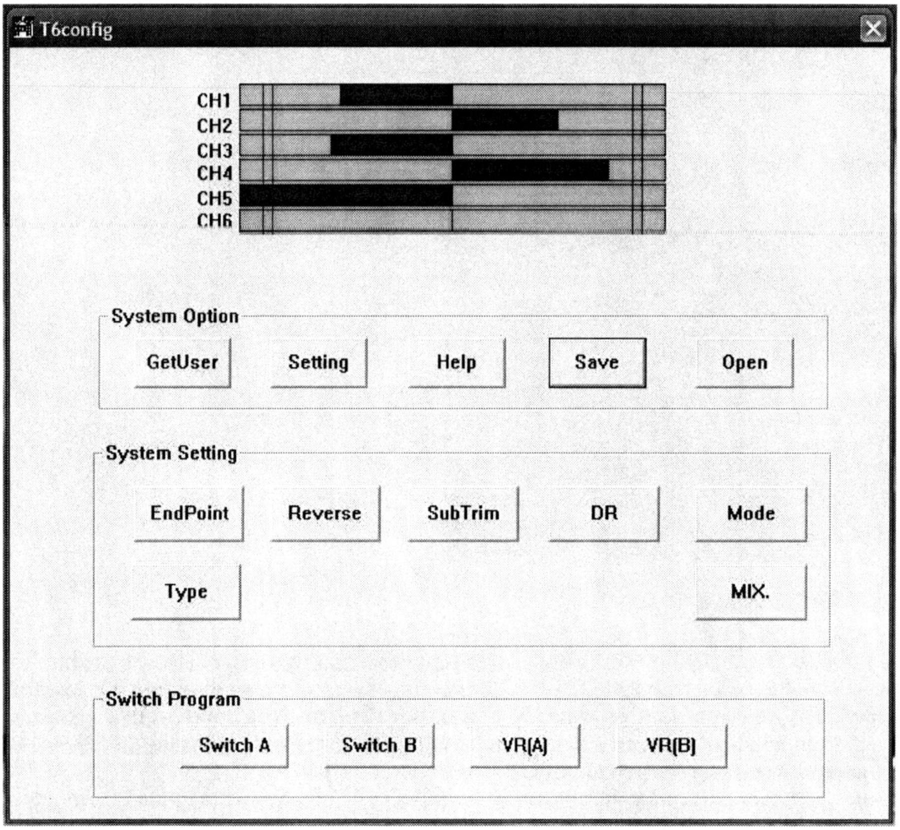

*Figure 12-3. The T6_config tool is used to re-program the Fly-sky R/C transmitter.*

I am including my T6 configuration file for you to download, which makes this transmitter/receiver pair robot-friendly allowing use of all four joystick channels with no mixing and the use of a switch or potentiometer as a fifth channel. Simply upload my file to the configuration program with your transmitter connected via the USB adapter cable (which should come with your R/C system), and you can have the same configuration as the transmitter I used for this project. The one hindering aspect of this system is that there are no servo reversing switches located on the transmitter. You must use the T6 config tool to reverse the servo direction, which was not a problem for me on this project because I was near my computer for most of the build.

Download my T6 configuration file at
https://sites.google.com/site/arduinorobotics/home/chapter12_files.

This configuration enables channels 1 to 4 to be a standard/proportional control with no channel mixing. Channel 5 is a combination of SW.B, which is an on/off toggle switch, and VR(A), which is a variable potentiometer. If you want to use the variable control, turn SW.B on and you can use the potentiometer VR(A) for a variable signal. If you want to use the digital on/off signal (as in this chapter) turn VR(A) all the way to the left, and you have an on/off output.

You can play with the settings of the T6 config tool because you can always download my file to get it back to normal if you need to. I tried for quite some time, playing with the limited configuration settings, and could get only solid use of either Ch5 or Ch6–but not both at the same time. This means that I could get it to work only as a 5-ch system, which is one more channel than I use, so it worked out well.

## Attention Hackers

The sixth channel on this system is only available to use with channel mixing for a 3D helicopter or airplane. However two toggle switches and two potentiometers are available for use, and a USB-programmable microcontroller is obviously telling each channel what to do (because you can reprogram the transmitter with a USB cable). My hope is that someone with better knowledge of these systems can program the use of the sixth channel for robot use...anyone?

---

**Note:** As this writing, the T6_config software works only on Windows systems. As an Ubuntu Linux user, I had to get out the old, dusty laptop that still has Windows installed to reprogram my transmitter.

---

With the CT-6 transmitter programmed for this project, now proceed to building the electronics.

# The Electronics

Most robots that compete in battle competitions use multiple electronic speed-controllers (ESC) to interface the R/C system to the motors and weapon. These are simple to use but are limited to what you can do with your robot. The only reason that I included a Battle-bot as a project in this book is because there are many things that you can potentially do with an Arduino that you cannot do with a standard ESC or other preprogrammed microcontroller. If nothing else, you can simply pass the signals through the Arduino to add a software failsafe in case of signal loss. This enables you to work with a variety of input signal types, while still producing the type of output failsafe conditions required by the rules of the particular event you enter.

By feeding the R/C channels through the Arduino, you can utilize a remote weapon disable switch, internal failsafe in case of lost signal, and power external LED lighting for visual feedback of your bot's condition during battle, and add Telemetry using Xbee, or control your bot using a 2.4GHz wireless Serial link (Xbee) rather than R/C. Using an Arduino, you can control any aspect of the robot using one central microcontroller that you can change as you want. You no longer have to use a separate ESC to read each R/C signal.

## The Arduino

I again chose to use a nonstandard Arduino design (for reliable connections), similar to the ones used in Chapters 8 and 10. This board features built-in LEDs for D12 and D13 to act as both neutral indicator lights for the drive channels, and an acquiring-signal indicator when there is no R/C link. (They blink back and forth until the signal is restored.)

Also installed on the board are a 5v 1.5A voltage regulator, 3-pin servo connectors for each Analog pin, and screw-terminals used for secure connections to each I/O pin–remember, this is going to be used in battle! The Arduino design that I used in this project can be programmed using a standard FTDI programming cable from SparkFun.com, just as the other Arduino designs in this book. Figure 12-4 shows the Eagle PC board layout file of the Arduino used in this chapter.

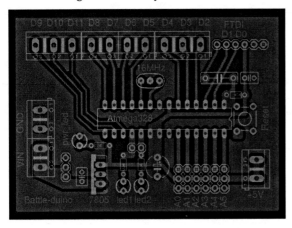

**Figure 12-4.** *The Battle-duino Eagle layout file*

You can download the design files to build your own Arduino and OSMC motor controller from https://sites.google.com/site/arduinorobotics/home/chapter12_files.

To build the Battle-duino clone, simply download the Eagle files and print your own using the instructions from Chapter 6. If you already know how to etch a PCB, then you know what to do.

# The Motor Controllers

Five different motors in this project need bidirectional control. Four of them are drive-motors, and each set (left or right) of those four are controlled by the same signal. The fifth motor controls your weapon of choice: spinning-blade, lifting linear actuator, reversible hammer-spike, or anything else you can come up with. The result will be three inputs (left, right, and weapon), and five outputs (four drive motors and a weapon motor).

You can choose many different options for motor controllers, but I tend to go for what I can afford and what works. What I can afford usually limits my options down to one of the cheapest, commercially available options, or making one myself. As you might have noticed by now, that I am drawn toward using two specific motor controllers other than my own designs: the OSMC H-bridge and the Dimension Engineering Sabertooth line of motor controllers.

I almost always recommend the Sabertooth 2x25 motor controllers for most projects. They are inexpensive (comparatively), easy to use, and have an over-current limit that can keep you from burning them up. The Sabertooth drivers are for the people that don't want to build their own motor controller but want their robot to work without worry. In a Battle-bot competition, there is no time to worry about your electronics, so I recommend trusting the movement of your Battle-bot to a well-tested motor controller platform.

To prepare each Sabertooth to work for this project, set onboard DIP switches 2 and 5 to the on position, while leaving the remaining switches turned off. This enables the Sabertooth controllers to operate using lithium batteries (with low voltage cutoff), R/C pulse signal inputs, no timeout for use with a microcontroller (the Arduino), and independent mode (tank) steering. Or you can use the DIP Switch Wizard on the Sabertooth 2x25 product page to determine a different configuration: http://www.dimensionengineering.com/datasheets/Sabertoothdipwizard/start.htm.

The Open Source Motor controller has no internal current-limiting, but it offers extreme power for those times when you just need to push your bot to the limit. And because the OSMC is an open-source project, you can use the same tested schematic used for the original to design your own OSMC specific to your project's needs. The OSMC design used in this book is also suitable to use for the drive motors; although, you would need four more of them (one for each motor).

I currently use a set of two Sabertooth 2x25 motor controllers for the drive motors and a home-made OSMC motor controller for the weapon. If you plan on building a monster Battle-bot that weighs several hundred pounds, you might consider upgrading to the Sabertooth 2x50HV (dual 50-amp controller).

In Figure 12-5, you can see my single-sided PCB, through-hole component version of the OSMC motor controller, easily capable of powering a drive motor or weapon. Remember that the OSMC is nothing more than a highly efficient H-bridge, so you must have one for each motor and a microcontroller like the Arduino to send the drive signals to control it.

*Figure 12-5. These three pictures show the various stages of the mini-OSMC board used for the weapon: the Eagle board file (left), the etched and drilled board (center), and the finished mini-OSMC board (right).*

To build the mini-OSMC for your weapon motor, download the Eagle files from https://sites.google.com/site/arduinorobotics/home/chapter12_files.

With the Arduino and motor controllers selected and built, you need to build the frame.

# The Frame

The frame is the backbone of any robot and should be extremely sturdy while attempting to remain as lightweight as possible (depending on your intended weight class). I made an 18-inch square frame using the 2-inch wide angle iron. I then mounted the motors to the inside of these pieces and the wheel axles to the outer corners. By adding four more braces across the front, back, and middle of the bot, it is strong enough to hold me jumping on top of it (155lbs) without flexing, which is a good start (see Figure 12-6).

*Figure 12-6. The basic frame with motors, wheels, and batteries test-fitted*

I cannot as of yet, inexpensively create my own aluminum parts for each robot, so I chose to build my frame from materials that are easy to obtain at the local hardware store: angle iron, nuts and bolts, a drill and drill bits, and a saw.

Even if you plan to go in a different direction with your Battle-bot for weapons or attack methods, this frame is a solid base for you to start on. The frame without the wheels attached is slim, at only 3-inch thick. After you install the wheels to the frame, the height is increased to the diameter of the wheels used (in this case, 9 inches).

For a fully concealed design, you might use smaller solid-core wheels (3-inch to 5-inch diameter) and place the wheels and drive motors completely inside of the frame; although you might need to increase the frame dimensions to accommodate. Many of the popular Battle-bots used this design, as it leaves little in harm's way.

## To Buy or Build?

If you are interested in building a Battle-bot but are not excited about building your own frame, RobotMarketplace.com sells Battle-kits made using machined aluminum pieces, a multilink chain drive system that utilizes two motors for complete four-wheel drive with speed reduction, and space for a speed controller and batteries (see Figure 12-7). The base for this type of bot comes with no motor, motor controllers, or batteries, for a mere $699. Although these kits are well made, they might be relatively expensive for someone just getting into the sport, so you can attempt to make your own frame.

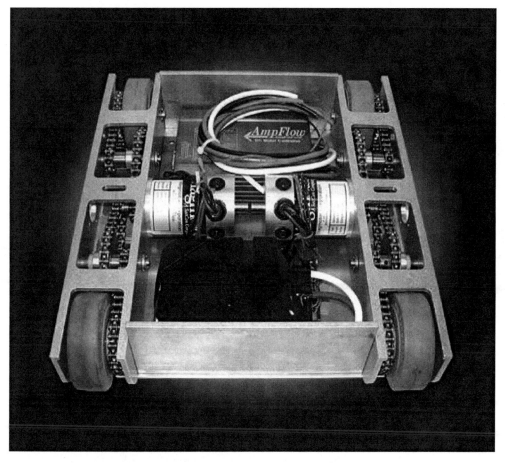

*Figure 12-7. A prebuilt Battle-kit from RobotMarketplace.com*

If you can afford the price tag, more power to you. If I ever have that much money laying around, I would love to have one of these frames! If not, you can follow my guide to building your own. I know that my design is basic, but it can get you moving in the right direction.

## Modifying the Wheels

I found some surplus electric scooter wheels that included the wheel, tire, bearings, and 65-tooth sprocket all for under $16 each including shipping. There is one caveat with this wheel assembly that I did not realize until I received them; they have a free-wheeling hub assembly that enables them to spin freely in one direction. Although that is great for a nonreversing scooter, it is not ideal for a bidirectional Battle-bot. How can you get around this? I had to weld a few spots on each free-wheel mechanism so that it would not freely spin in reverse (see Figure 12-16). This was annoying but well worth the money I saved versus buying the proper wheel and sprockets separately.

The proper wheel and sprocket pair is pictured in Figure 12-8, with a flat-topped tire for more traction and a direct bolt-on sprocket with no free-wheeling mechanism. You also select how many teeth you want for specific gearing of your bot when buying the sprocket separately. If you are willing to pay the extra money, it can make your installation much easier and more reliable.

*Figure 12-8. A wheel-and-sprocket pair, perfect for the Battle-bot*

With the wheels modified and ready to mount, we must now start making the pieces needed for the main frame.

## Building the Frame

To build the frame, you need the metal pieces, nuts and bolts, motors, wheel-assemblies, sprockets, chain, a Dremel tool, and a drill with drill-bits. It also helps to have an angle grinder and a reciprocating saw with a metal blade to quickly cut the metal pieces and smooth any sharp edges. This frame can be easy to measure, in that every metal piece (except the axles) should be exactly 18 inches.

The following five steps guide you through the frame building process:

1. Cut four main frame pieces. Start by cutting the 2-inch angle iron (6 foot) segment into four equal 18-inch pieces. Two of these pieces will be drilled and cut (in step 2) with a Dremel tool to accommodate the wheel axles, motor-mounting, and tension adjustments. The other two pieces simply bolt to the front and rear of the frame, providing added support and a place to adjust the tension of each chain.

2. Cut axle mounting grooves. Now you can cut the axle grooves at each end of the left and right frame pieces. They should be the width of the axle itself (5/16-inch), and the length should span about 2 inches to allow for adequate adjustment room. Start by measuring 1/2 inch away from the end of the angle iron from either side, and drill a 5/16-inch hole centered between the top and

bottom of the 2-inch angle iron. (One inch from either the top or bottom is centered.) With the first pilot hole drilled, you can measure approximately 2 inch from the first pilot hole and drill another centered pilot hole. You can now cut out the space between the tops and bottoms of the two pilot holes with a Dremel to reveal the needed axle-groove to adjust the chain tension. This procedure is similar to what you did on the Lawn-bot in Chapter 10 to allow the motor-mounts to slide forward or backward. Figure 12-9 provides a better idea of how to cut the axle grooves and motor-mounting holes.

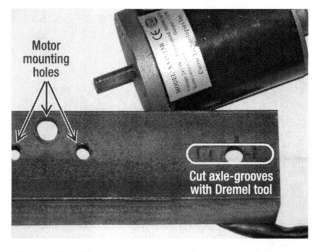

*Figure 12-9. The motor-mounting holes and axle grooves are cut into the left frame piece.*

In Figures 12-9 and 12-10, you can see the needed placement of each mounting hole and axle groove. When cut, the two side pieces should look similar to Figure 12-10; they should also be interchangeable, so you don't have to worry about labeling them. The motor output-shaft hole should be approximately 5 inches from each end of the 2-inch angle iron. The motor-mounting holes should be measured (from your motors) and marked after fitting the output-shaft hole. (The mounting holes on my motor are spaced 1 3/8inch apart.)

*Figure 12-10. The two finished left and right side frame pieces*

3. Cut frame braces. Now cut the two 3/4-inch wide angle-iron center frame supports (also 18-inch)–if you bought a 36-inch section for this piece, simply cut it in half. You should then drill two holes, one on each end of both pieces,

about 1/2 inch from each end. The hole should be the size of the bolts you use to mount each piece I used 3/8-inch diameter bolts, nuts, and washers to assemble my frame. At this point, you should have six metal pieces all 18 inches; two of them are 3/4-inch angle-iron and the other four are 2-inch angle-iron. Each piece of angle iron used in the frame should have a hole drilled on each end to secure it to the adjacent piece with a bolt/nut. Your side frame rails should also have the appropriate holes drilled for the motors and axle grooves (see Figure 12-11).

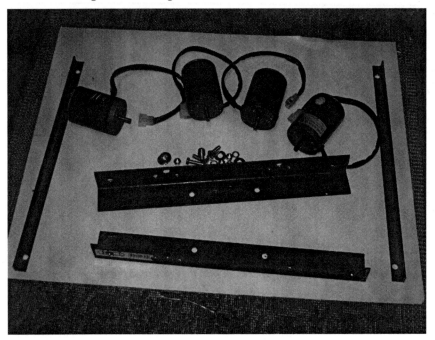

*Figure 12-11.* *The side and center pieces of the sub frame with motors, ready for assembly*

4. Assemble the pieces together. I first mounted the motors using the two lower bolts to secure each motor to the frame and then lined up the two center frame supports as close to the inside of each motor as would fit. I then marked each hole location with a permanent marker and drilled the mounting holes through the base of the side rails and ends of the center supports. After drilling the mounting holes, you can install the center supports using two bolts on each support (one on each end), as shown in Figure 12-12:

*Figure 12-12. The assembled subframe*

5.   With the center supports bolted to the side frame rails, you can now mount the
     front and rear frame rails, using two more bolts on each piece. If you haven't
     already, drill a hole on each end of the front and rear frame rails, line them up
     on top of the left and right frame rails, and drill the remaining holes to bolt the
     front and rear frame pieces to the left and right frame pieces, completing the
     square shape (see Figure 12-13).

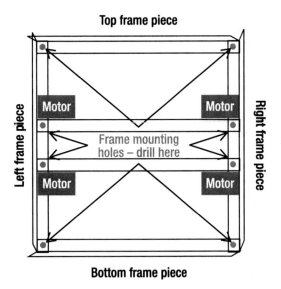

**Top frame piece**

**Left frame piece**

Motor

Motor

Frame mounting
holes – drill here

Motor

Motor

**Right frame piece**

**Bottom frame piece**

*Figure 12-13. A diagram of the pieces used to build the frame*

After you have all six frame pieces bolted together and the motors mounted, the main frame assembly should be completed. You are now ready to add the drive train and get this bot moving.

# The Drive Train

The drive train for this bot has a different purpose than the previous bots in this book, focusing on reliability during "battle." This bot will have four wheels, each wheel being driven by its own motor and H-bridge, such that if one wheel is disabled by the opponent, the bot can still move independently of the disabled wheel. As you can imagine, this means that you need 4x of each of the following:

- Four DC motors

- Four H-bridges

- Four sprockets

- Four wheels

- Four chains

As an inexpensive option, I decided to go with four ungeared electric scooter motors available from Allelectronics.com for $15 each. The motors are Currie Technologies 135watt 24VDC, 10 Amps with a rated speed of 3000RPM. These electric motors are about the size of a soda can with an 8mm diameter output shaft, flattened on one side. They are usually purchased with a 3mm COG pulley sprocket mounted to the output shaft, intended for use with a COG drive belt commonly found on such scooters.

Because of the nature of this bot, I opted to use steel instead of rubber for the drive components. (Use whatever you want.) The COG pulleys can be removed from the motor output shafts, allowing you to replace them with chain-type sprockets.

# Gearing

If you hook wheels directly to the motor output shafts spinning at up to 3000 RPM, the bot would be hard to start but extremely fast once moving. A battle-bot inevitably needs some torque to make sudden direction changes or move another bot in battle, which would be extremely difficult to achieve at 3000RPM with almost no torque. This bot needs to be geared down to provide more torque and less speed.

To reduce the speed of these motors, I used a set of sprockets on each motor/wheel pair to reduce the output speed from the 3000RPM motor speed to an approximate 500RPM wheel speed. This was accomplished using an 11-tooth sprocket on each motor output shaft, and a 65-tooth sprocket on each wheel-hub assembly.

## Calculating Gear Ratio

According to Wikipedia, the smaller sprocket attached to the motor output shaft is called the "pinion or driver" and the larger sprocket attached to the drive wheel is called the "gear or driven." To calculate the gear ratio, you divide the number of teeth on the gear by the number of teeth on the pinion–or assuming you are gearing down, the larger number divided by the smaller number. For example:

65-tooth wheel sprocket / 11-tooth motor-drive sprocket = 5.91:1 gear ratio

This means that the pinion (motor gear) must spin 5.91 times before the (wheel) gear makes one complete rotation. Therefore, you can divide the raw motor-speed output (3000RPM) by the gear ratio (5.91) to find the maximum output speed at the wheel:

3000RPM DC Motor speed / 5.91x gear ratio = 509RPM Max wheel speed.

509 max RPM is a much more reasonable wheel speed than 3000RPM, providing 5.91x more torque to give the Battle-bot more power while still providing a good top speed.

## Modifications

If you want an even slower output speed with higher torque (recommended for heavier bots), you might try using a 9-tooth pinion with a 90-tooth wheel gear: 90 / 9 = 10x gear ratio, which on 3000 rpm motors yields a wheel output speed of approximately 300RPM, about 60% of the speed that I used but with more torque.

For more information on gear ratios, check out: http://en.wikipedia.org/wiki/Gear_ratio. According to my calculations, our Battle-bot (as shown) with 9-inch tire diameter should be capable of a top speed around 14 mph. How so? Ughh, get out your calculator. You need to know the wheel diameter = 9 inches, and the motor output rotation speed = 509rpm. Here's the formula:

- Inches per rotation of wheel = circumference = Pi x Diameter = 3.14 x 9" = 28.26" / rotation

- Inches per minute = Inches per rotation x number of RPM = 28.26" x 509 RPM = 14,384.34" per minute

- Feet per minute = Inches per minute / 12" in one foot = 14,384.34" / 12" = 1198.7' per minute

- Feet per hour = feet per minute x 60 minutes in one hour = 1198.7' x 60 = 71,922' / hour

- Miles per hour = feet per hour / 5,280 feet in one mile = 71,922' / 5280' = 13.62mph

This formula assumes perfect traction and depends on the specifications of the motors, so you may not actually get a full 14mph from your bot, but it should give you a ballpark figure of the speeds possible.

I wanted this bot to be symmetrical, so there are two identical drive-train sections that need to be added to the frame. You can build them in any order because they will be the same. This consists of making the chain-tensioning nut, threading the nuts onto the axle in the correct sequence, measuring and cutting the chain, and then securing everything into place for a test drive.

## Chain Tensioning Nut

Because this bot is chain-driven, each wheel needs to be adjustable to set the proper chain tension after it is fitted on the sprocket. I wanted to keep things simple, so I used one axle to share between the front wheels and one axle to share between the rear wheels. These axles are implemented using a 36-inch, 5/16-inch diameter threaded rod, some specially cut grooves (in the frame rails), and a chain-tensioning nut attached to the axle.

The axle diameter should be the same as the inside diameter of your wheel bearings; in my case that is 5/16-inch (or 8mm). The grooves that should be cut for the each axle should be exactly 5/16-inch wide, and about 2-inch long (or however far you want the axle to travel). Two inches of travel is typically plenty to get the chain easily around both sprockets before tensioning.

There are four tensioning screws, allowing for complete adjustment of all four wheels independently. I made (four) simple nut couplers that allow you to adjust each threaded-rod axle using an adjacent bolt, by welding a 5/16-inch nut (bottom) to a 1/4-inch coupling-nut (top), as shown in Figure 12-14.

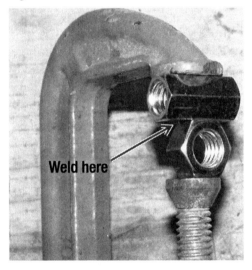

*Figure 12-14. A C clamp holding the two nuts used to build the chain tensioning nut-assembly*

To make the 5/16-inch nut adapters, you need to have a C clamp or pair of vice grips to clamp the two nuts together. When clamped, you can add a small bead of weld to the spot where the two nuts meet. Welding one side should hold the nuts together for your purposes. If you want to be extra sure, also weld the other side of the nut. Make certain that you do not get any welding on the threads of either nut because this can hinder the threading of the bolts. I used a scrap bolt to barely thread into each nut while welding; this kept the stray molten welding bits from getting on the inner threads.When welded, you should be ready to start the threading process. To get everything installed correctly, you need to place the chain-tensioning nut assemblies, wheel nuts, and washers on in a certain sequence.

## Threading Sequence

Start by sliding one of the axles through the axle groove on one side of the frame. Then thread the following parts on to the 5/16-inch threaded-rod axle (from the inside of the frame) in the following order:

1. 5/16-inch flat washer

2. 5/16-inch hex nut

3. One of the chain-tensioning nut assemblies

4. Another of the chain-tensioning nut assemblies

5. Another 5/16-inch hex nut

6. Another 5/16-inch flat washer

For a better illustration of this process, see Figure 12-15.

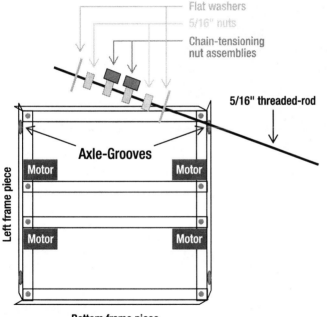

*Figure 12-15. The axle threading process*

After you have the listed pieces onto the axle as shown in Figure 12-15, slide the left end of the threaded-rod into the left axle groove. With the axle through both sides of the frame, you can start making adjustments. Start by threading the two hex nuts (with flat washers in front) all the way to the inside of each axle groove, hand-tight only. Using a 36-inch threaded rod on an 18-inch wide frame yields about 9 inches of excess axle coming out of each side of the frame. You can now add another flat washer to each end of the axle, following a hex nut on each end; hand-tightened to the outside of the frame.

Thread the chain-tension nut assembly to about 2 inches from the axle groove. Now drill a hole in the back (or front) piece of angle iron, lined up with the chain-tension nut assembly. Place the 1/4-inch bolt through this hole and thread it into the 1/4-inch coupling-nut on the nut assembly, as shown in Figure 12-16.

*Figure 12-16. A close-up view of the chain tensioning system*

Now measure and cut each chain; then mount the wheels to complete the drive train.

## Measuring the Chain

Before you can install the wheels, measure and cut the chains. First, mount the small sprockets onto the motor output shafts securing the set screw on each; then place each wheel onto the axle, sliding the axle toward the center of the frame (about 1/2 inches from its forward-most position). Now place the uncut length of chain around the wheel sprocket and the motor sprocket to mark the exact length needed for each wheel.

When measured, I mark the chain with a permanent marker to show where to make a cut with my Dremel tool (cutoff wheel). My chains each measured approximately 19 1/2-inch (or 50mm) in length. This used about 7 feet of chain, so I have a few feet left over to make some spares–trust me, you want a few spares (see Figure 12-17).

**Figure 12-17.** *Measuring and cutting the chains*

Make a mark on the side of a full chain link; then cut one side with a rotary cutoff wheel, and grind down the heads of the two pins. When cut, use a pair of pliers to break each side of the cut segment from the rest of the chain. After the two cut pieces are broken off, the back part of the link will fall out by itself, and you will be left with a clean chain segment, ready to attach to the other end using a Master chain link (see Figure 12-18).

**Figure 12-18.** *A #25 master chain link used to connect two loose chain ends*

Before securing each wheel into place, check each chain to make sure it is parallel to the frame.

## Adding Spacers

Depending on your exact configuration, you may need more than one flat washer (to act as a spacer) between the outside of the frame and the inside of the wheel assembly (for each wheel). You first need to install the chain around both the motor sprocket and the wheel sprocket to determine if it is parallel to the frame.

If the chain is not parallel, you need to add flat washers (one at a time) between the wheel and frame, until the chain travels parallel to the frame. I had to add three flat washers before the chain was parallel, as shown in Figure 12.19.

*Figure 12-19. Drive-train installation*

With your chain parallel, you can adjust the chain-tension adjustment bolt (attached to the axle) until there is proper tension in each chain. I always tighten the chain until it is taut with no slack and then back up one turn to allow a small amount of slack. When using this small #25 chain, more than 1/4inch of slack is probably too much.

When you get one wheel spinning smoothly and without resistance, you must do the same for the other three wheels. This process should be the same on each wheel because the Battle-bot is symmetrical.

After each wheel is installed and all four chains tensioned, it is time to select and install some batteries.

## Batteries

The batteries for this project can be changed depending on what you want to use. I decided to try and keep this bot relatively lightweight by using Lithium Polymer batteries (Figure 12-20), abbreviated LiPo. LiPo batteries are typically 3.7v per cell and lightweight compared to lead acid for their charge capacity. These batteries must be charged with a LiPo-specific charger and must not be discharged beyond 3.0v per cell or risk catching on fire; so only use these batteries if you understand how to handle them.

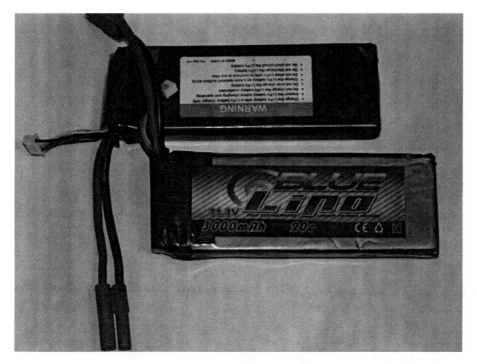

*Figure 12-20. A blue Lipo, hobby grade 3-cell lithium polymer battery pack (11.1v)*

---

■ **Note:** In a Battle-bot competition, you are usually required to mark your robot with a yellow sticker or some other colored marker to identify that you are using Lithium batteries.

---

Many online hobby shops have excellent pricing on LiPo batteries and chargers, making them affordable even on a budget. I found these Blue Lipo 3-cell (3.7v x 3 = 11.1v) 3000mAh (3AH) batteries for only $15 each. They have a 20c discharge rate, meaning that by itself, this battery is capable of discharging approximately 60 Amps continuously (3Ah x 20c = 60 A continuous). If you use two of these packs in parallel, the discharge rate doubles to 120 Amps (6Ah x 20c = 120 A).

To get more power to the motors, I decided to place two packs in series to make 22.2Vdc and 3000mAh. You can buy as many of these as you can afford and place several 22.2V (series packs) in parallel to achieve 6Ah, 9Ah, 12Ah, and so on. The LiPo battery packs weigh only approximately 1 pound per set, whereas a comparable SLA battery weighs approximately 6 pounds. Of course, the LiPo batteries are about twice the price of a comparable SLA battery, but you should buy only as many LiPo batteries as you need Amp Hour capacity to decrease the weight on your robot.

Alternatively, you can use Sealed Lead Acid batteries to get around having to buy a LiPo charger only or worrying about over-discharging. Two standard 12v 7Ah batteries would fit nicely in this frame. As you can see from Figure 12-21, either type of battery has plenty of room in this frame.

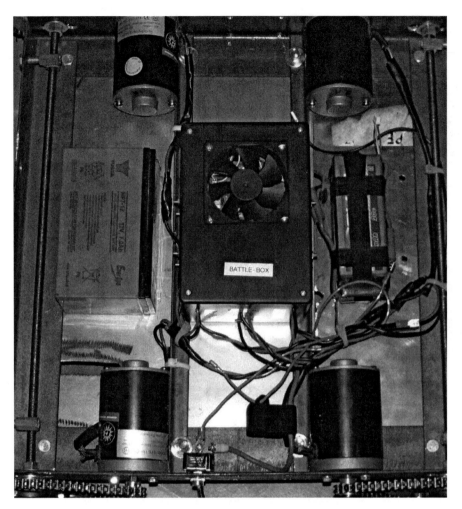

*Figure 12-21. Either SLA (left) or LiPo (right) batteries fit in this frame.*

With the batteries selected, now install the electronics and make connections.

## Securing Electronics

Now you need to secure the Arduino and each motor controller to the Battle-bot frame. I chose to again use a plastic project box enclosure from Radio Shack to house the electronics in a central location. By then protecting the project box with metal armor, the electronics are further protected from outside abuse.

# Protecting Your Brains

To protect all your valuable electronics from damage, you need to house them somewhere away from your opponent's reach. I chose to house the electronics in a plastic Battle-Box that has a cooling fan mounted to its lid to keep the motor controllers from getting too hot. This box is a standard project-enclosure from Radio Shack with all the electronic components mounted to its base, walls, and lid. The idea is to tuck this box safely away into the center of the bot (see Figure 12-22), with some thick metal plating above it to keep it safe from danger.

*Figure 12-22. The electronics housed inside of the Battle-box with a cooling fan in the lid*

If this box is damaged, not only would it immobilize your bot during a match, it would also likely destroy some valuable electronics. It is in your best interest as a competitor to... PROTECT THIS BOX! You wear a helmet in a football-game, right? Well, the Battle-box is the brain of your robot and is subjected to saw blades, hammers, and whatever your opponent has come up with. I recommend securing the Battle-box to your frame using several different methods (for example, bolts, straps, and ties). Imagine the feeling of seeing your robot's brains being scattered all over the floor after a good hit from your opponent–better to be safe than sorry!

# Making Connections

The wiring in this project can be complex because there are three separate motor controllers to supply with a power supply and input signals. The OSMC board requires a minimum of two PWM signals, whereas the Sabertooth motor controllers in R/C mode each use a single digital pin to supply each drive signal (left and right).

The R/C signals must be read by the Arduino in the correct order (ch1 first, then ch2, and so on) to keep from missing any pulses; this is because the pulses are available to the Arduino one after another (in order). Trying to read the last pulse before the others can cause the Arduino to skip the previous pulses each loop. This caused me a bit of confusion when testing. For this reason, it is best to connect the R/C receiver according to channel number, and then assign each pin number accordingly in the Arduino code.

You can either use the Arduino's +5v regulator to power the R/C receiver or you can use the Sabertooth's onboard voltage regulator; although it has a smaller regulator and provides less current than the Arduino. Because these regulators are both linear, you dissipate a good bit of power if feeding either with a 22.2v to 24v input voltage. The OSMC has a switching 12v regulator, but using that pulls power from the OSMC driver chip and still wastes some heat after dropping from 12v to 5v through the linear regulators. When using a series battery connection, I find it easiest to power the Arduino with a 12v tap in the battery set, to avoid connecting the 5v regulators to a 24v input voltage.

Table 12-3 shows the wiring chart used to connect each signal in the Battle-bot.

*Table 12-3. Wiring the Arduino to the Batteries, R/C Receiver, and Motor Controllers*

| Wire | Arduino | Connection |
| --- | --- | --- |
| OSMC – AHI | D8 | Connects the OSMC AHI to Arduino D8. |
| OSMC – ALI | D9 | Connects the OSMC AHI to Arduino D9. |
| OSMC – BLI | D10 | Connects the OSMC AHI to Arduino D10. |
| OSMC – BHI | D11 | Connects the OSMC AHI to Arduino D11. |
| LED 1 – neutral light | D12 | LED1 internally connected on Battle-duino board to D12. |
| LED 2 – neutral light | D13 | LED2 internally connected on Battle-duino board to D13. |
| R/C receiver – channel 1 | D14 = Analog pin A0 | Connects R/C receiver ch1 to Arduino D14. |
| R/C receiver – channel 2 | D15 = A1 | Connects R/C receiver ch2 to Arduino D15. |

| Wire | Arduino | Connection |
|------|---------|------------|
| R/C receiver – channel 3 | D16 = A2 | Connects R/C receiver ch3 to Arduino D16. |
| R/C receiver – channel 5 | D17 = A3 | Connects R/C receiver ch5 to Arduino D17. |
| Sabertooth 2x25 – Left input | D18 = A4 | Connects left Sabertooth S1 and S2 to Arduino D18. |
| Sabertooth 2x25 – Right input | D19 = A5 | Connects right Sabertooth S1 and S2 to Arduino D19. |
| Battery GND | GND | Connects battery GND wire to both Sabertooth motor controllers and the OSMC weapon controller and the Arduino. |
| Battery + (22.2v to 24v) | x | Connects the OSMC and Sabertooth controllers to the B+ positive battery supply, through a 40 to 60amp fuse. |
| Sabertooth +5v | VIN | You can power the Arduino and R/C receiver using the +5v supply from either Sabertooth motor controller. |

You probably need some zip ties to tidy up the wiring after you finish to keep any longer wires from catching on debris and being pulled loose. You may also want to use quick-connect (male/female spade terminals) between the motors and motor controllers to allow you to easily make repairs.

It is also a good idea to install an emergency shut-off toggle switch on the bot to disconnect the power supply quickly if needed. I used a standard On/Off SPST switch mounted to the frame connected to the +24v supply. To protect the motor controllers and Arduino, it is always best to install a fuse in series with the 24v power supply in case of a short circuit. To better visualize the Battle-bot wiring chart in Table 12-3, see Figure 12-23.

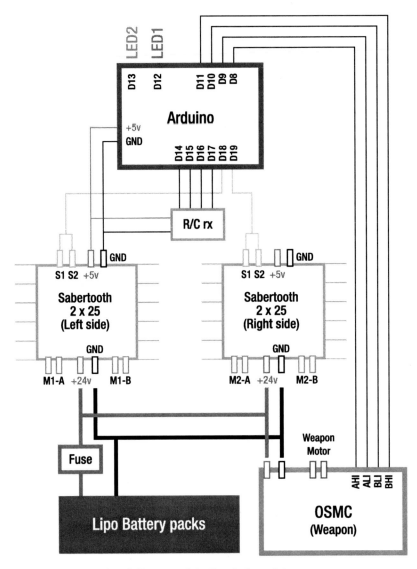

*Figure 12-23. A visual diagram of the Battle-bot wiring*

With the electronics securely installed in the Battle-bot frame and the wiring connected according to Table 12-3 and Figure 12-23, you should be ready to load the code to the Arduino and test the frame before adding the weapons and armor.

# The Code

The code for the Battle-bot reads the R/C pulses from the receiver and decides what to do with each motor and weapon. As a software failsafe, the code checks to make sure both drive channels have a valid pulse before proceeding; if either channel's pulse signal is lost, the Battle-bot goes into acquiring-signal mode and commands the drive motors and weapon to stop. (LED1 and LED2 also flash to indicate a lost signal.) After the Arduino detects a valid signal on both drive channels, the drive motors engage, and the code begins to check the signal value of the weapon disarm toggle switch (connected to R/C channel 5). If the disarm switch is turned on, the weapon disengages and its signal is not processed. After the weapon disarm switch is turned off, the Arduino can begin processing the weapon control signal, and the weapon engages; this provides an extra layer of security to keep from accidentally activating the weapon before you are ready.

Before testing, double-check all connections per Table 12-2 and Figure 12-23. Listing 12-1 shows the final code.

*Listing 12-1. The Final Code for the Battle-Bot*

```
// Chapter 12 – The Battle-bot
// Controls 2 Sabertooth motor controllers using R/C pulse signal
// Controls battle-bot weapon using OSMC (open-source motor=controller)
// Decodes 2 R/C servo signals for the Left and Right drive channels (Sabertooth 2x25 in R/C mode)
// Decodes 1 R/C servo signal for weapon (OSMC)
//
//

// Create names for R/C pulse input pins D14 - D17
int RC_1 = 14;
int RC_2 = 15;
int RC_3 = 16;
int RC_4 = 17;

// Create names for R/C pulse output pins D18 and D19
int Left_OUT = 18;
int Right_OUT = 19;

// Name LEDs and attach to pins D12 and D13
int LED_1 = 12;
int LED_2 = 13;

// Name weapon motor controller output pins and attach to D8 - D11
int OSMC_BHI = 8;
int OSMC_BLI = 11;  // PWM pin
int OSMC_ALI = 10;  // PWM pin
int OSMC_AHI = 9;

// create variables for weapon deadband and arming weapon
int deadband = 10;
int weapon_armed = false;
```

```
// Variables to store R/C values
// values for R/C channel 1
int servo1_val;
int adj_val1;
int servo1_Ready;
// values for R/C channel 2
int servo2_val;
int adj_val2;
int servo2_Ready;
// values for R/C channel 3
int servo3_val;
int adj_val3;
int servo3_Ready;
// values for R/C channel 4
int servo4_val;
int adj_val4;
int servo4_Ready;


// End of Variables

// Begin Setup() function

void setup() {

// changes PWM frequency on pins 9 & 10 to 32kHz for weapon
TCCR1B = TCCR1B & 0b11111000 | 0x01;

//motor pins
pinMode(OSMC_ALI, OUTPUT);
pinMode(OSMC_AHI, OUTPUT);
pinMode(OSMC_BLI, OUTPUT);
pinMode(OSMC_BHI, OUTPUT);

//led's
pinMode(LED_1, OUTPUT);
pinMode(LED_2, OUTPUT);

// R/C signal outputs
pinMode(Left_OUT, OUTPUT);
pinMode(Right_OUT, OUTPUT);

//PPM inputs from RC receiver
pinMode(RC_1, INPUT);
pinMode(RC_2, INPUT);
pinMode(RC_3, INPUT);
pinMode(RC_4, INPUT);

// Set all OSMC pins LOW during Setup
digitalWrite(OSMC_BHI, LOW); // AHI and BHI should be HIGH for electric brake
digitalWrite(OSMC_ALI, LOW);
```

```
digitalWrite(OSMC_AHI, LOW); // AHI and BHI should be HIGH for electric brake
digitalWrite(OSMC_BLI, LOW);

// blink LEDs to verify setup
digitalWrite(LED_1, HIGH);
digitalWrite(LED_2, LOW);
delay(1000);
digitalWrite(LED_2, HIGH);
digitalWrite(LED_1, LOW);
delay(1000);
digitalWrite(LED_2, LOW);

// Write OSMC Hi-side pins HIGH, enabling electric-brake for weapon motor when not being used
digitalWrite(OSMC_AHI, HIGH);
digitalWrite(OSMC_BHI, HIGH);

}

// End of Setup()

// Begin Loop() function


void loop() {

// Read R/C signals from receiver
servo1_val = pulseIn(RC_1, HIGH, 20000); // weapon channel
servo2_val = pulseIn(RC_2, HIGH, 20000); // left drive channel
servo3_val = pulseIn(RC_3, HIGH, 20000); // right drive channel
servo4_val = pulseIn(RC_4, HIGH, 20000); // weapon disable switch


// Failsafe check - Check to see if BOTH drive channels are valid before processing anything else
if (servo2_val > 0 && servo3_val > 0) {

// turn on Neutral LEDs for the drive channels if they are centered (individually).
// LED 1 for left drive channel
if (servo2_val < 1550 && servo2_val > 1450){
 digitalWrite(LED_1, HIGH);
}
else{
 digitalWrite(LED_1, LOW);
}
// LED 2 for right drive channel
if (servo3_val < 1550 && servo3_val > 1450){
 digitalWrite(LED_2, HIGH);
}
else{
 digitalWrite(LED_2, LOW);
}
```

```
// Check to see if Toggle switch is engaged (R/C ch5), before enabling Weapon
if (servo4_val > 1550){
  // arm weapon
  weapon_armed = true;
  // Then, go ahead and process the Weapon value
  if (servo1_val > 800 && servo1_val < 2200){

    // Map bi-directional value from R/C Servo pulse centered at 1500 milliseconds,
    // to a forward/reverse value centered at 0.
    // 255 = full forward, 0 = Neutral, -255 = full reverse
    adj_val1 = map(servo1_val, 1000, 2000, -255, 255);

    // Limit the values to +/- 255
    if (adj_val1 > 255){
      adj_val1 = 255;
    }
    if (adj_val1 < -255){
      adj_val1 = -255;
    }

    // Check signal for direction of motor (positive or negative value)
    if (adj_val1 > deadband){
      // if value is positive, write forward value to motor
      weapon_forward(adj_val1);
    }
    else if (adj_val1 < -deadband){
      // if value is negative, convert to positive (*-1) then write reverse value to motor
      adj_val1 = adj_val1 * -1;
      weapon_reverse(adj_val1);
    }
    else {
      // otherwise, weapon signal is neutral, stop weapon motor.
      weapon_stop();
      adj_val1 = 0;
    }
  }
  else {
    // else, if the weapon toggle switch is disengaged, stop weapon (from above)
    weapon_stop();
  }
}
else{
  // else, if Drive signals are not valid disable weapon - extra failsafe
  weapon_armed = false;
  weapon_stop();
}
}

// If drive signals are not valid, stop using Neutral LEDs and make them blink
// back and forth until the signal is restored - see the acquiring() function.
else {
```

```
  servo2_val = 1500;
  servo3_val = 1500;
  weapon_armed = false;
  acquiring();
 }

 // Lastly, send the R/C pulses to the Sabertooth
 Send_Pulses();

}

// End Loop

// Begin extra functions


void acquiring(){
 // while R/C receiver is searching for a signal, blink LEDs
 digitalWrite(LED_1, HIGH);
 digitalWrite(LED_2, LOW);
 delay(200);
 digitalWrite(LED_2, HIGH);
 digitalWrite(LED_1, LOW);
 delay(200);
 digitalWrite(LED_2, LOW);

}

void Send_Pulses(){
 // send Left R/C pulse to left Sabertooth S1 and S2
 digitalWrite(Left_OUT, HIGH);
 delayMicroseconds(servo2_val);
 digitalWrite(Left_OUT, LOW);

 // send Right R/C pulse to right Sabertooth S1 and S2
 digitalWrite(Right_OUT, HIGH);
 delayMicroseconds(servo3_val);
 digitalWrite(Right_OUT, LOW);
}


// motor forward function for OSMC
void weapon_forward(int speed_val1){
 digitalWrite(OSMC_BLI, LOW);
 analogWrite(OSMC_ALI, speed_val1);
}
// motor reverse function for OSMC
void weapon_reverse(int speed_val2){
 digitalWrite(OSMC_ALI, LOW);
 analogWrite(OSMC_BLI, speed_val2);
}
```

```
// motor stop function for OSMC
void weapon_stop() {
  digitalWrite(OSMC_ALI, LOW);
  digitalWrite(OSMC_BLI, LOW);
}

// End of extra functions
// End of Code
```

After verifying that the code has loaded properly, you can begin testing your Battle-bot frame. Make sure each motor spins in the correct direction and that the motor sides are not reversed (that is, left stick controls left motors, and vice versa). When everything looks good, you should probably give your new robot frame a spin around the back yard to test for any weak joints or loose bolts before installing the armor and weapon.

## Armor

What you choose to clothe your robot in is your business, but I chose a nice pair of sheet-metal knickers and a swinging axe for a top. You can choose from many materials such as steel, titanium, aluminum, carbon fiber, fiberglass, and even weapons that protect the bot like armor. (Look up "Son of Wyachi" on Google.) I chose to use the strongest material for the best price: steel plating in the form of 16 AWG sheet metal (see Figure 12-24). This sheet metal is difficult for me to flex, and when installed and bolted down it is even stronger.

*Figure 12-24. The basic frame fully assembled with armor*

Installation of the armor is much easier if you get pieces the same size as your bot frame. I could not easily find a precut 18-inch x 18-inch piece, but I did find one 12-inch x 18-inch and one 6-inch x 18-inch, which together fit quite nicely without having to cut anything. If you look toward the left side of the bot in the picture, you can see the seam where the two pieces meet. Perhaps a small bead of welding across the seam would make it look more professional, but it is not necessary. Use another piece of sheet metal on the underside of the bot to keep it protected if it happens to get flipped over.

When armored, the Battle-bot should be better suited to take a hit during battle, but until you add some weapons, there isn't much you can do to the opponent.

# Weapons

Although the operator of a Battle-bot must know how to effectively drive the bot, having a few good weapons never hurts. For our Battle-bot, I decided to use two types of weapons: an active swinging-arm weapon used for impaling the opponent, and a passive set of bidirectional spears mounted to the front and rear of the bot used for ramming the opponent at high speeds. The spears act as weapons as long as you have at least 2 motors work, whereas the swinging-arm weapon relies on a separate H-bridge to power its motor.

There are many types of active and passive weapons from wedges, spinning blades, lifting arms, clenching jaws, swinging arms, rams, and over-sized drilling bores–to name a few. Though surprising, sometimes the simplest designs can be the most effective. The ever-popular heavyweight champion BioHazard used a sleek 4-inch tall bot frame with a powerful lifting arm mechanism (much like a forklift) to disable almost anyone in his path.

To build the weapons used on this bot, you need the parts listed for the weapon in Table 12-2. The following eight steps guide you through the weapon building process:

1. Modify the wheel hub for the weapon. I started by looking through my inventory: I stumbled upon a Schwinn S350 electric scooter a few months ago while cleaning up at work. (Someone left it in a dumpster!) I quickly removed it and took it home for a closer inspection; there was a perfectly good 350w, 24vdc, 22Amp electric motor with mounting-bracket, chain, wheels, sprockets, wiring, throttle, and motor controller. I have also found several electric scooters at my local thrift store for under $20, which also included the motor, chain, sprockets, and so on.

I decided that I would sacrifice the rear wheel/motor/sprocket assembly from this scooter to make a spinning axle for an over-head spike hammer that I had in mind. The first thing I did was cut the actual tire/rim from the spokes connecting to the rim, using a reciprocating saw and a steel-cutting blade (see Figure 12-25). I wanted to use this axle assembly because it includes a 90-tooth sprocket, spokes to mount the weapon, and a spinning axle with threaded shaft, and the motor is easily mounted using the scooter motor-mount bracket.

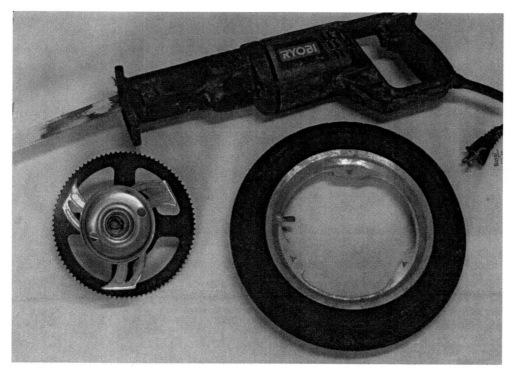

***Figure 12-25.*** *Cutting the wheel hub assembly from a rim to use as the weapon axle*

After cutting the wheel hub from the tire/rim, you can drill one hole toward the end of each spoke. You use only two of these to mount the swinging arm. To build the weapons on this bot, you probably need a welder, so if you don't have a one, you either need to invest about $100 in a small welder or make friends with someone who will loan you one–remember to wear eye protection!

2. Make the weapon mount bracket. You must have something to mount the spinning scooter axle to, so I chose to use two pieces of 3/4-inch square steel tube to hold the axle above the frame. I made two identical parallel braces to mount to the frame and also to the weapon axle assembly.

Start by making two V cuts in the square tube using a reciprocating saw, hacksaw, or angle grinder (see Figure 12-26). I used two 36-inch pieces of steel tubing, cutting 4 inches off of each piece. Measure and mark the V cuts to be 3 inches from one end and 9 inches from the other end. The 9-inch and 3-inch ends should be mounted perpendicular to the frame (at right angles), whereas the 20-inch center section can take the slope between them.

*Figure 12-26. Cutting V notches in the weapon brackets*

You will want to test fit the bracket to make sure it mounts to the front and rear of the frame before securing the V cuts. I used a welder to secure the joints after making sure they fit snugly around the frame. For a better illustration of the weapon brackets, see Figure 12-27).

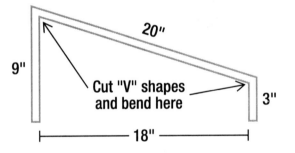

*Figure 12-27. A diagram of the shape for each weapon bracket*

3. Test fit the axle into the weapon brackets. After making both brackets (the same size), drill a hole near the top of the 9-inch piece to mount the weapon axle assembly. You can lay the two weapon brackets flat on top of one another and drill the hole through both at the same spot to make sure they line up for the axle. The weapon axle needs to be mounted as high in the brackets as possible (about 1- inch or 2 inches from the top). Use the two nuts from the axle assembly to mount it to the weapon brackets, making sure the axle spins freely after mounting. Now mount the weapon brackets to the center of the frame by drilling one hole at the bottom of each square tube, and then bolt each weapon bracket to the frame (see Figure 12-28).

*Figure 12-28. The frame with the weapon brackets and axle test-fitted*

4. Mount the DC motor assembly. Using a DC motor assembly from a scooter, mount onto the weapon axle and install into weapon brackets. The square tubes should be parallel to each other when mounted, as shown in Figure 12-29.

*Figure 12.29. The finished frame with weapon axle and motor installed*

5.    Cut a small semicircle in the 2-inch wide steel flat bar.

Cutting a small semi-circle (about 1-inch radius from the edge) near the end of the swinging-arm allows it to contour to the weapon axle shaft. I used an angle-grinder wheel to cut out the area marked with permanent marker (see Figure 12-30).

*Figure 12-30. Modify the swinging arm to fit around the weapon axle (left, and the swinging-arm test fitted onto the weapon axle assembly (right).*

6. Mount a steel flat bar arm to the weapon axle assembly. Place the flat bar onto the axle assembly, and mark the holes that you drilled through two of the wheel spokes (from step 1) onto the flat bar. You need to drill holes on these marks and use two bolts to secure the flat bar swing arm to the wheel spokes on the weapon axle (refer to Figure 12-30).

7. Add whatever kinds of scrap metal you can find to the end of the swinging arm; this is up to you. I used a few pieces of angle iron to fashioned into a spike and mount to the front of the arm to act as a small wedge when the spike is not used. Again, I used a welder to attach these pieces to the end of the arm (see Figures 12-31 and 12-32).

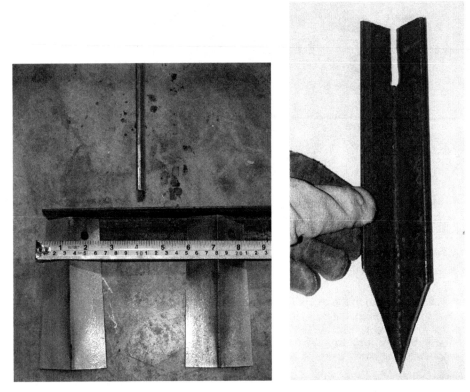

*Figure 12-31. These two pictures show the scrap pieces I used for the weapon spike.*

*Figure 12-32. These two pictures show how I attached weapon (welding).*

8. If you want ramming spikes, get out the 5/8-inch solid steel round rod and start sharpening with an angle grinder. I spent an hour grinding and cutting on the ends of the steel rod until it had some mean looking points. Get ready for a spark shower though and wear a dust mask; these particles are not good to get in your lungs (see Figure 12-33).

*Figure 12-33. Grinding the spikes to make sharp points*

By drilling a set of 5/8-inch holes through the frame on both ends, you can slide these ramming spears through the frame to mount them. You can either weld them into place for a permanent fix, or drill a hole through the rod just inside the frame on each end placing a bolt through each hole. The rod cannot slide past the frame, and you can remove the spears easily for transporting/safety.

***Figure 12-34.*** *The spikes protruding from the frame, ready to impale an opponent*

With the weapons installed, you should be almost ready for battle. Time to check all your wiring connections, chain tension, tire air pressure, battery levels, and a place to make sure nobody gets hurt while you test out your creature of doom.

Now it is time to start signing up for a Battle-bot competition! Check the following "Additional Information" section to find out where to look for battles in your area.

## Additional Information

For additional information regarding Battle-bot rules, regulations, building advice, and upcoming events, you can check the Battle-bots website at http://www.battlebots.com.

For other events go to http://www.robogames.net/.

One of the most complete and detailed guides to building a Battle-bot comes from team RioBotz, which produced a 367-page PDF file jam-packed full of design comparisons, weapon types, building tips, frame construction, and so on. If you are serious about building a competition Battle-bot, you MUST read this, available at http://www.riobotz.com.br/riobotz_combot_tutorial.pdf.

For building information, first check out Team Nightmare and the Robot Marketplace. The Robot Marketplace has nearly any part you can imagine for a Battle-bot and is also an excellent source for most general robotics projects. Go to http://www.robotcombat.com/.

A former Battle-bot judge gives his tips for winning at http://www.robotics-society.org/jds-rules.shtml.

Team Davinci has some excellent tips on building at http://www.teamdavinci.com/.

# Summary

This chapter discussed several aspects of building a competitive fighting robot. The concepts were merely suggestions to get you started if you are interested in this growing sport. Because there is no "right" way to build a Battle-bot, I encourage you to use your creativity and try something new!

I designed my Battle-bot to have four independently powered drive wheels, a fifth motor to control the active swinging spike-hammer weapon, and two ramming spikes protruding from the front and rear of the metal frame. Using LiPo batteries helped reduce the weight of the Battle-bot by up to 10 pounds (versus SLA) while maintaining the same charge capacity. For added protection, the electronics were placed in a plastic project box mounted to the frame and covered by a layer of metal armor on each side.

The next chapter revisits a previous robot (the Explorer-bot from Chapter 8) to provide a new method of control. Using a pair of Xbee radios and a custom interface, you create a wireless Serial link between the Explorer-bot and your computer to control the robot using a PC game pad.

# CHAPTER 13

# Alternate Control

Although hobby-type R/C radios are easily found, relatively cheap, and have excellent range (at up to a mile or so in clear view), they might not always provide the *type* of control that you want on your robot. Many modern robots are controlled by computers, which typically use a Serial connection to send multiple commands at once. Some can afford to be connected to a computer using a wire, whereas others will require a wireless link with reasonable speed and range.

Recall from Chapter 8 that we set up an Xbee wireless link to transmit data from the bot, back to the Serial monitor on our computer screen. Although it is neat to read the values from the bot without using any wires, this chapter focuses on controlling the bot using that Serial data link by sending values from the computer, through the Xbee radios, to the Arduino. Once received, the Arduino can decode the data and command the left and right motors with the correct speed and direction values received from the computer.

You might wonder how you can control the bot using your computer. For those more hobby-minded people that are not as familiar with computer programming, we provide a simple and easy to setup method of controlling the Explorer-Bot (from Chapter 8) using a USB PC video-game controller. The PC controller joystick values are decoded by the computer and sent out via the Xbee radio, also connected to the computer via USB. The general workflow (and the layout of the chapter) is as follows:

1. Send signals to the computer by moving the gamepad's analog control sticks.

2. Decode those signals in Processing (Listing 13-1), and send them over a serial link (the Xbees provide this) to the Arduino on the Explorer-Bot.

3. Receive these commands on the Arduino (Listing 13-2) over the serial link, apply some error correction, and decode them into values for the motors on the Explorer-Bot.

4. Profit!

Let's get started.

## Using Processing to Decode the Signals

To decode the signals, we use the popular open-source computer programming tool, "Processing," designed to create images, animations, and interactions. You can think of Processing as your tool with which to easily communicate from Computer to Arduino. The Processing IDE is nearly identical to the Arduino IDE and the commands are similar in nature, though not interchangeable. After you feel comfortable using the Arduino IDE, Processing will become second-nature to you. If you don't already have Processing, download it now from the following website:

http://processing.org

Check out the Reference pages for both Processing and Arduino to see a list of each command and examples of how to use them:

**Processing**—http://www.processing.org/reference/

**Arduino**—http://www.arduino.cc/en/Reference/HomePage

To prove how at home an Arduino programmer should feel with the Processing IDE, check them out side by side in Figure 13-1.

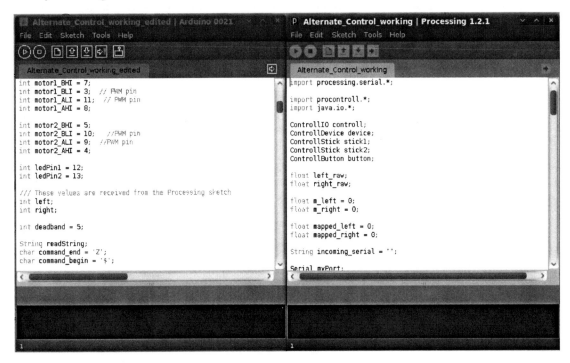

*Figure 13-1. Comparing Processing's IDE (right) to Arduino's (left)*

## Parts List for Alternate Control

The only parts you need for this project are an existing robot, existing Xbee radios, and a USB game controller (Table 13-1). The control scheme we discuss is adaptable to a wide range of robots, but for our project we use a basic driving robot.

*Table 13-1. Alternate Control Parts List*

| Part | Description | Price |
|------|-------------|-------|
| A Robot | I used the Explorer-bot from Chapter 8, but you can use any robot you have, changing the motor-control code if needed. | $$$ |
| Saitek PC controller | Saitek P2600 (Figure 13-2)—Though any Saitek or similar USB PC game controller should work. | $5–$20 |
| (2) Xbee radios | Sparkfun (part #WRL-08665)—Avoid using the Xbee Pro models because they have power issues with the Sparkfun regulated Xbee explorer boards. | $23.00 ea |
| Sparkfun Xbee Explorer <u>USB</u> Regulated | Sparkfun (part #WRL-08687)—You also need the USB cable that goes with this product. | $25.00 |
| Sparkfun Xbee Explorer Regulated | Sparkfun (part #WRL-09132)—I used female pin headers to solder onto this board. | $10.00 |

# Selecting the Input

There are actually endless ways that you might control a robot using your computer and Processing: your keyboard, mouse, Wii controller, or almost any other input device that you can connect to a computer. PC game controllers are usually found cheap either online or at a thrift-store. I chose to use the UP/DOWN values from each joystick on the USB controller to gather values for the left and right motors. This method uses basic tank-steering inputs. If you want to control the pan/tilt camera as well, you might want to mix the channels of each joystick to provide one joystick for robot control and the other for camera control.

*Figure 13-2. Saitek P2600 PC game controller USB*

## Processing Prerequisites

The best way to get input from a USB controller into processing is using the proCONTROLL library available at http://creativecomputing.cc/p5libs/procontroll/. This library is based on JInput and is extremely easy to use. It provides a simple way to use attached devices (such as USB controllers) by simply picking a serial port that represents the controller and picking which buttons/sticks in which you want to interact.

To install this library, download procontrol.zip from the website, and then extract the archive into your Processing Sketchbook—into a folder named "libraries" (if the folder is not there, create it). Now open Processing and the library should work.

## Following Protocol

The idea with this project is that the Processing code is entirely responsible for determining the values to send to the robot, and the Arduino code somewhat blindly takes the values sent to it via the Xbee and sends them to the appropriate motor controllers. Consequently, we needed a control protocol. What we decided on was a simple protocol in which a given command had a single alpha character to represent which command was called, plus a numeric component representing the argument to send to the actuator.

For example, in this case there is an L command and an R command, each of which can take values from –255 to 255 to determine speed and direction. –255 is full reverse, 255 is full forward, and 0 is neutral.

---

■ **Note** In our final sketch, we went only from −128 to 128 (half speed either way, basically). Our robot was almost uncontrollably fast at full speed for indoor purposes.

---

The Arduino sketch sits and listens on the serial port for a string. Each string it gets is sent to a command-handling routine, which determines what to do with the command it was sent. In practice, this caused some problems because the serial buffer filled up and we ended up having the Arduino receive values like "R20202," which is greater than the 255 max value the R command should receive. Consequently, we introduced "command begin" and "command end" characters that had to bookend any legitimate command. For these we chose "$" and "Z," somewhat arbitrarily. So any legitimate command ends up looking like "$R100Z" and anything else is ignored.

With that explanation, let's review the two sketches, starting with the Processing sketch.

# Examining the Processing Sketch

This Processing sketch shown in Listing 13-1 takes the USB controller input in and processes it into right and left motor components, which it then sends on to the Arduino.

*Listing 13-1. Processing Sketch*

```
// Alternate Control - Processing Sketch
// This code is copied into the Processing IDE screen
// The Arduino code must be loaded and Xbee radios powered before pressing play.
// Uses left (up/down) and right (up/down) joysticks to control left/right motors
respectively.
// Code - Josh Adams and JD Warren 2010


import processing.serial.*; // to use Serial communication in Processing, you must include the
serial library


import procontroll.*;  // Import the procontroll library for assistance using the USB game pad
import java.io.*;

// NOTE: The procontroll library comes with examples that are
// excellent for learning how to use it.  They're located in the
// examples directory of the library's zipfile.

// This is the variable in which we'll store the main instance of the procontroll library.
ControllIO controll;

// This variable will be used to hold a single connected controller device.
ControllDevice device;

// These variables are used to address each of the joysticks we're using in this sketch.
ControllStick stick1;
ControllStick stick2;
```

```
// We use these variables to store the raw values given to us by procontroll

// for each stick.
float left_raw;
float right_raw;

// These variables will be used to store the stick values, mapped to the range
// we'd like to send over the serial connection.
float m_left = 0;
float m_right = 0;

String incoming_serial = "";

Serial myPort;

void setup() {

  println(Serial.list());  // will show all Com ports, select the correct USB port listed

  myPort = new Serial(this, Serial.list()[0], 19200);

  size(20,20);

  // Prepare the procontroll library for use
  controll = ControllIO.getInstance(this);

  // Get the USB controller device.
  device = controll.getDevice(0);
  device.printSticks();

  // Grab the left stick in the stick1 variable.
  stick1 = device.getStick(1);
  stick1.setTolerance(0.05f);

  // Grab the right stick in the stick2 variable.
  stick2 = device.getStick(0);
  stick2.setTolerance(0.05f);

  // Just some processing boilerplate, not important.
  fill(0);
  rectMode(CENTER);
}


void draw() {
  background(255);

  // Get the raw stick values
  get_values();

  // Map the stick values to the range we want to use for the motor values we
  // send over serial.
```

```
    map_motor_values();

    // Read any incoming serial data.  We use this on the arduino side to send
    // debugging information across the xbees.
    while(myPort.available() > 0){
      incoming_serial = myPort.readString();
    }
    debug(); // Print some useful debugging info to the console.

    // Write our basic control protocol commands to the serial port.
    myPort.write("$L" + (int)m_left + "Z");
    delay(50);
    myPort.write("$R" + (int)m_right + "Z");
    delay(50);

}

void get_values() {
  left_raw = stick2.getX() * 100.0;
  right_raw = stick1.getY() * 100.0;
}

void map_motor_values() {
  // First, set m_left and m_right both to the mapping
  // from -255 to 255 of their respective sticks.
  // mapping to a MAX +/-255 will yield 100% speed control
  // to the Arduino PWM pins (0-255 value).
  m_left  = map(left_raw, 100, -100, 255, -255);
  m_right = map(right_raw, 100, -100, 255, -255);
}

void debug() {
  // show what m_left and m_right do

  print("m_left: ");
  print(m_left);
  print("   ");
  print("m_right: ");
  print(m_right);
  print("   ");

  // You can uncomment this line to print any debugging info sent across
  // the xbee from the arduino sketch.
  /*
  if(incoming_serial != null){
    println((String)incoming_serial);
  }
  */
}

// End of Processing Sketch
```

# Explanation

The code is not long, and most of it is just boilerplate. Here's the rundown.

First, we import the libraries we need for this processing sketch:

```
import processing.serial.*; // to use Serial communication in Processing, you must include the
serial library
```

```
import procontroll.*;  // Import the procontroll library for assistance using the USB game pad
import java.io.*;
```

Next, we set up all of the variables we'll use in the sketch. This consists of an instance of ProControll; a variable for the gamepad; variables for each of the analog control sticks we're watching, along with their raw and mapped values; and some variables to interact with the serial port:

```
// This is the variable in which we'll store the main instance of the procontroll library.
ControlIO controll;

// This variable will be used to hold a single connected controller device.
ControllDevice device;

// These variables are used to address each of the joysticks we're using in this sketch.
ControllStick stick1;
ControllStick stick2;

// We use these variables to store the raw values given to us by procontroll
// for each stick.
float left_raw;
float right_raw;

// These variables will be used to store the stick values, mapped to the range
// we'd like to send over the serial connection.
float m_left = 0;
float m_right = 0;

String incoming_serial = "";

Serial myPort;
```

Next, we run the setup function. This consists of some Processing boilerplate, picking the USB device that corresponds to the gamepad, and storing the analog sticks in their respective variables:

```
println(Serial.list());  // will show all Com ports, select the correct USB port listed

myPort = new Serial(this, Serial.list()[0], 19200);
```

```
size(20,20);

// Prepare the procontroll library for use
controll = ControllIO.getInstance(this);

// Get the USB controller device.
device = controll.getDevice(0);
device.printSticks();

// Grab the left stick in the stick1 variable.
stick1 = device.getStick(1);
stick1.setTolerance(0.05f);

// Grab the right stick in the stick2 variable.
stick2 = device.getStick(0);
stick2.setTolerance(0.05f);

// Just some processing boilerplate, not important.
fill(0);
rectMode(CENTER);
```

Next, we come to the draw() function. This is like the loop in an Arduino sketch. It's run each cycle. In this, we again do minor Processing boilerplate, and then we sample the values from the sticks, convert them to the range we want, and send the serial commands to the Arduino:

```
background(255);

// Get the raw stick values
get_values();

// Map the stick values to the range we want to use for the motor values we
// send over serial.
map_motor_values();

// Read any incoming serial data.  We use this on the Arduino side to send
// debugging information across the xbees.
while(myPort.available() > 0){
  incoming_serial = myPort.readString();
}
debug(); // Print some useful debugging info to the console.

// Write our basic control protocol commands to the serial port.
myPort.write("$L" + (int)m_left + "Z");
delay(50);
myPort.write("$R" + (int)m_right + "Z");
delay(50);
```

That should explain all of the interesting bits of the code. Let's put the code into Processing and see it work!

## Testing Processing

Plug in your USB controller, paste that sketch into Processing, and click play. In the console at the beginning, you see it print the available serial ports. Make sure to modify the code to address the proper port. For us, this was the first port in the list (port 0), but it will be different on different computers. If everything works correctly, the debug() command should print the values of the two sticks on your controller to the processing console. Make sure it's printing values between –255 and 255.

Figure 13-3 shows what the Processing sketch looks like as it is starting up. First you see a list of the available Serial ports in the Terminal area, as called by the Serial.list() command. Then despite the several "Failed to open device..." lines, Processing finds the Saitek P2600 remote and lists its available control sticks, "0: y x" and "1: rz slider". We use both of these joysticks to control the bot, referring to them in the sketch as 0 and 1 respectively. Finally, at the bottom of the screen, you can see the beginning values of the Left and Right joysticks—which read 0.0 when not moved up or down.

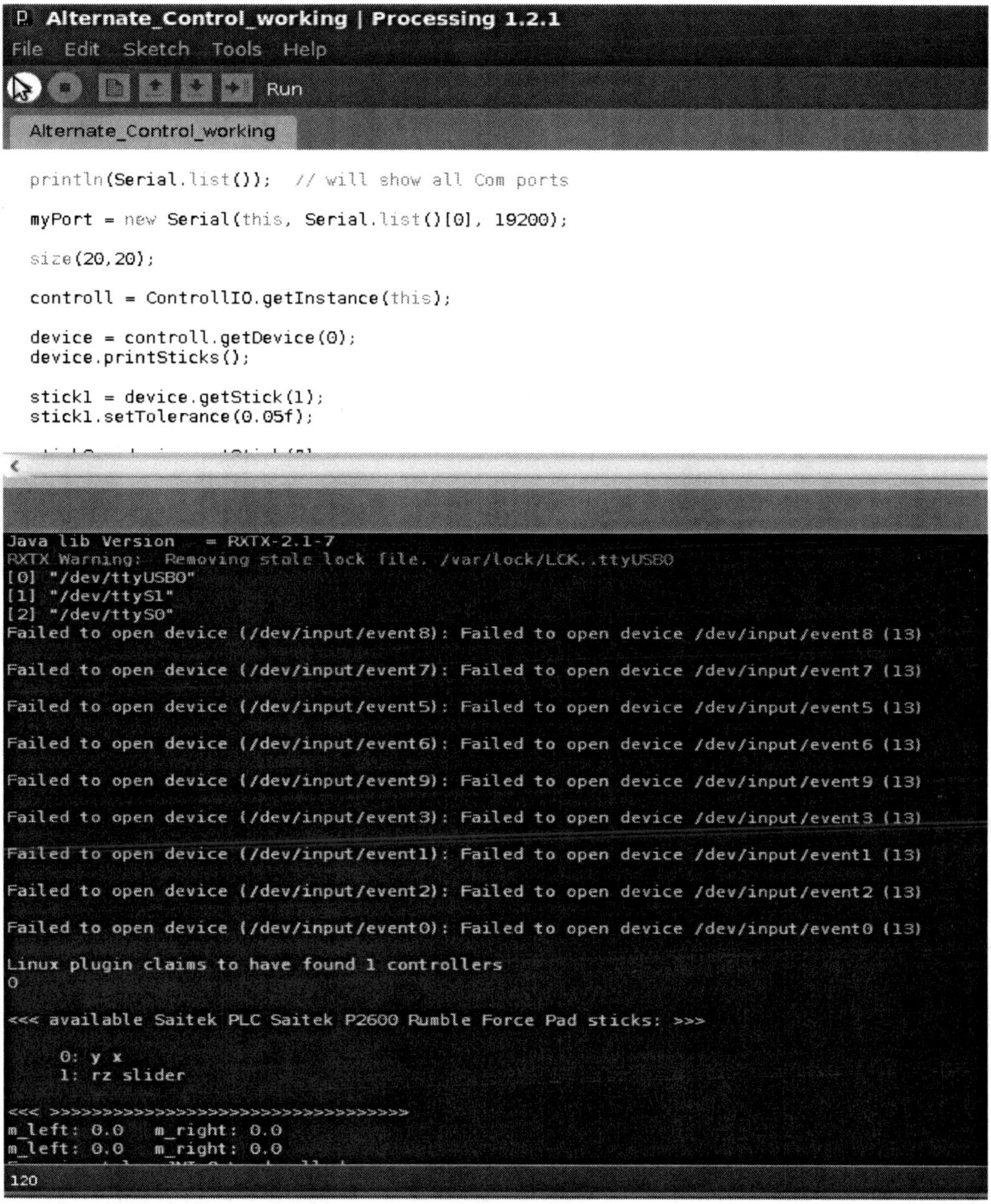

*Figure 13-3. Processing sketch when it is first run*

With that, we send the appropriate values across the serial. If we have an Arduino sketch on the other side that knows how to send values to a left and a right motor, then we should have successful tank steering.

Let's see what the corresponding Arduino sketch looks like.

# Examining the Arduino Sketch

This sketch is basic, even if it's long. It just listens to input from a serial port. When it gets data, it reads in bytes from the serial buffer one by one. It executes the appropriate control code for each valid command it receives. We specify begin and end points for the commands as a mild form of error handling—we do not want to send erroneous commands to the motors as a result of spotty serial communications.

This is basically the same sketch used on the ExplorerBot chapter, but we added a bit to read the incoming serial bits to drive the motors. For clarity's sake, the most relevant code has been set in a bold font.

Please note, it was written and tested on Arduino 0021.

*Listing 13-2. Arduino Sketch*

```
// Alternate Control - Arduino Sketch
// Use XBee radios to communicate with a computer.
// Read Serial string from Processing over Xbee.
// Commands dual motor-controller for Left and Right motors.
// Code - Josh Adams and JD Warren 2010

// leave pins 0 and 1 open for serial communication


// These values are used to control the H-bridge of the Explorer-Bot in Chapter 8

int motor1_BHI = 7;
int motor1_BLI = 3;   // PWM pin
int motor1_ALI = 11;  // PWM pin
int motor1_AHI = 8;

int motor2_BHI = 5;
int motor2_BLI = 10;    //PWM pin
int motor2_ALI = 9;  //PWM pin
int motor2_AHI = 4;

int ledPin1 = 12;
int ledPin2 = 13;

/// These values are received from the Processing sketch
int left;
int right;

// this value sets the neutral range, ie. Deadband.
int deadband = 5;
```

```
// Set up the variables used in our simple protocol handler.

String readString;
char command_end = 'Z';
char command_begin = '$';

char current_char;


void setup() {
  TCCR1B = TCCR1B & 0b11111000 | 0x01;
  TCCR2B = TCCR2B & 0b11111000 | 0x01;

  Serial.begin(19200);

  //motor1 pins
  pinMode(motor1_ALI, OUTPUT);
  pinMode(motor1_AHI, OUTPUT);
  pinMode(motor1_BLI, OUTPUT);
  pinMode(motor1_BHI, OUTPUT);

  //motor2 pins
  pinMode(motor2_ALI, OUTPUT);
  pinMode(motor2_AHI, OUTPUT);
  pinMode(motor2_BLI, OUTPUT);
  pinMode(motor2_BHI, OUTPUT);

  //led's
  pinMode(ledPin1, OUTPUT);
  pinMode(ledPin2, OUTPUT);

  // turn motors OFF at startup
  m1_stop();
  m2_stop();

  delay(1000);

  readString = "";

}


void loop() {

  ////////// use Serial
  while (Serial.available()) {

    // So, how this protocol works:  We'll read in bytes from the serial buffer one
    // character at a time.  This will allow us to easily figure out if we're inside of
    // a legitimate command.

    // -  We don't start into the main block until we get our first begin character.
```

```
// - Once we get that character, we'll continue reading until we get to the end
// character.
// - When we've received the end character, we pass the string we received on
// to our handle_command() function.  If it's a command we understand, we act
// on it.  Otherwise, we just ignore it.

current_char = Serial.read();  // gets one byte from serial buffer

if(current_char == command_begin){ // when we get a begin character, start reading
  readString = "";
  while(current_char != command_end){ // stop reading when we get the end character
    current_char = Serial.read();  // gets one byte from serial buffer
    if(current_char != command_end){
      //Serial.println(current_char);
      readString += current_char;
    }
  }
  if(current_char == command_end){ // since we have the end character, send the whole
command to the command handler and reset readString.
    handle_command(readString);
    readString = "";
  }
}
}

// Test values to make sure they are not above 255 or below -255, as these values will be
sent as an analogWrite() command (0-255)

if(left > 255){
  left = 255;
}
if(left < -255){
  left = -255;
}
if(right > 255){
  right = 255;
}
if(right < -255){
  right = -255;
}

// Here we decide whether the motors should go forward or reverse.
// if the value is positive, go forward - if the value is negative, go reverse
// We use a deadband to allow for some "Neutral" space around the center - I set deadband =
5, you can change this, though I wouldn't really go any lower.
// If no deadband is used, a sporadic signal could cause movement of the bot even with no
user input.

// first determine direction for the left motor
if(left > deadband){
  m1_forward(left);
}
```

```
      else if(left < -deadband){
        m1_reverse(left * -1);
      }
      else {
        m1_stop();
      }

      // then determine direction for the  right motor
      if(right > deadband){
        m2_forward(right);
      }
      else if(right < -deadband){
        m2_reverse(right * -1);
      }
      else {
        m2_stop();
      }

      // add a small Delay to give the Xbee some time between readings
      delay(25);

      // end of loop

}

// In this function we set the left value, if we get the "L" command.
// - If the string sent begins with an "L" we'll move on and try to read
// in an integer from the remaining characters.  Otherwise, we ignore
// the call to this function entirely.
void set_left_value(String the_string){
  if(the_string.substring(0,1) == "L"){
    char temp[20];

    // read in anything past the L to the temp character array.
    the_string.substring(1).toCharArray(temp, 19);

    int l_val = atoi(temp); // turn this value from a string into an integer.
    left = l_val;
  }
}

// This function works identically to the set_left_value function.
void set_right_value(String the_string){
  if(the_string.substring(0,1) == "R"){
    char temp[20];
    the_string.substring(1).toCharArray(temp, 19);
    int r_val = atoi(temp);
    right = r_val;
  }
}
```

```
void handle_command(String readString){

  // We actually just pass the string we read in from serial to every possible
  // command handler.  Those that it doesn't apply to will ignore it.
  set_left_value(readString);
  set_right_value(readString);


  // Here you can send the values back to your Computer and
  // read them on the Processing terminal.
  // Sending these values over Xbee can take slow the sketch down,
  // so I comment them out after testing.  They're useful for making sure
  // that the arduino is getting the values from the string protocol properly.
  /*
  Serial.print("left: ");
   Serial.print(left);
   Serial.print("      ");
   Serial.print("right: ");
   Serial.print(right);
   Serial.println("      ");
   */

}


// From here down are motor-controller functions only.

void m1_forward(int val){
  digitalWrite(motor1_AHI, LOW);
  digitalWrite(motor1_BLI, LOW);
  digitalWrite(motor1_BHI, HIGH);
  analogWrite(motor1_ALI, val);
  digitalWrite(ledPin1, LOW);
}

void m1_reverse(int val){
  digitalWrite(motor1_BHI, LOW);
  digitalWrite(motor1_ALI, LOW);
  digitalWrite(motor1_AHI, HIGH);
  analogWrite(motor1_BLI, val);
  digitalWrite(ledPin1, LOW);
}

void m2_forward(int val){
  digitalWrite(motor2_AHI, LOW);
  digitalWrite(motor2_BLI, LOW);
  digitalWrite(motor2_BHI, HIGH);
  analogWrite(motor2_ALI, val);
  digitalWrite(ledPin2, LOW);
}

void m2_reverse(int val){
```

```
    digitalWrite(motor2_BHI, LOW);
    digitalWrite(motor2_ALI, LOW);
    digitalWrite(motor2_AHI, HIGH);
    analogWrite(motor2_BLI, val);
    digitalWrite(ledPin2, LOW);
}

void m1_stop(){
    digitalWrite(motor1_BHI, LOW);
    digitalWrite(motor1_ALI, LOW);
    digitalWrite(motor1_AHI, LOW);
    digitalWrite(motor1_BLI, LOW);
    digitalWrite(ledPin1, HIGH);
}

void m2_stop(){
    digitalWrite(motor2_BHI, LOW);
    digitalWrite(motor2_ALI, LOW);
    digitalWrite(motor2_AHI, LOW);
    digitalWrite(motor2_BLI, LOW);
    digitalWrite(ledPin2, HIGH);
}

// end of sketch
```

The essential part of the control scheme is that we read characters from the serial buffer one by one. Each time we find an valid command, we send it to the handle_command function. If we read a value that does not match the protocol, we throw out the data we have and start over. This way, even in a noisy environment where the serial connection is not 100% reliable, the control protocol still works.

Next, we need to make sure that the Xbee radios are communicating properly. To do this, you can uncomment the "Serial.print..." blocks inside the Arduino sketch's handle_command function, as well as the "println((String) incoming_serial)" block in the processing sketch. If the arduino sketch sends back the left and right motor values you're expecting, it should be safe to send them on to your robot's motors and hey, you're driving it around the room!

If you're having any problems with the control at this point, you should be able to send debugging information across the Xbee serial link and read it in the processing console. Otherwise, after you got it working like you want, you can comment back out the two blocks you uncommented previously.

# Summary

The great thing about the way we handled this control scheme is how flexible it is. Even without any significant changes, you can handle 25 or so different independently addressable functions on your robot—and that's without using lowercase letters. It's an unbelievably simple protocol—just assign any given function a letter, and you're done. Is it the absolutely best protocol to use of all time? No, of course not. But it's absurdly simple to understand and extremely flexible.

A fun thing about this protocol is that it's in no way dependent on having a typical remote control. Because it's just a series of strings sent over serial to the Arduino via the Xbee, you can use anything you can get into processing to send those commands. The following are additional ideas:

- Add in code to control the pan/tilt camera with the gamepad.

- Allow a user to control the robot via a website and send video back to the browser.

- Attach a Wiimote to the host computer via any Bluetooth library and control the robot with the signals from the accelerometers.

- Use a keyboard command.

- Build an AI for your bot that runs on the PC.

# Index

## ■ F

## ■ N

## ▓ X, Y

## Z

HILLSBORO PUBLIC LIBRARIES
Hillsboro, OR
Member of Washington County
COOPERATIVE LIBRARY SERVICES

CPSIA information can be obtained at www.ICGtesting.com
Printed in the USA
238369LV00003B/118/P